Chapter 25

VIRAL INFECTIONS

1. 18 year old develops high grade fever with petechial rash on her legs. Her laboratory reports for thrombocytopenia. You suspect her to have Dengue fever. Which of the following investigations is most specific for diagnosis in the acute phase of Dengue virus?

A. NS1 antigen
B. Dengue IgM antibodies
C. Dengue IgG antibodies
D. RT-PCR
E. Viral culture

Key: D

2. 36 year old gentleman is diagnosed with Dengue fever and presents to emergency with high grade fever, lethargy, abdominal pain and difficulty in breathing. On cutaneous examination, he has a petechial rash involving lower legs up to his knees. Torniquet test is positive. Which of the following investigations is most appropriate as an early warning sign for this patient developing Dengue shock syndrome?

A. USG Abdomen for ascites
B. CXR for pleural effusion
C. Blood complete picture for increased hematocrit
D. Peripheral smear for thrombocytopenia
E. USG Abdomen for hepatomegaly

Key: C
Ref: Rooks (25.74)

3. 40 year old gentleman develops acute fever with severe joint pains followed a generalized maculopapular rash primarily involving the trunk and to a lesser degree his limbs. His Dengue NS1 antigen, Measles IgM and Rubella IgG comes back to be negative. Considering the current epidemic, you want to rule out Chikungunya virus. Which of the following is the fastest test for diagnosis?

A. Chikungunya IgM
B. Chikungunya IgG
C. PCR of viral DNA
D. PCR of viral RNA
E. PCR of envelope protein

Key: D
Ref: Rooks (25.79)

4. A 61-year-old man with a past medical history of a kidney transplant in 2015 for polycystic kidneys presented to the dermatology clinic with complaints of multiple asymptomatic skin-colored papules on the face and ears, and some slightly pruritic pink papules on the trunk and extremities. These lesions appeared 1 year after transplant and were progressing for the past 2 years.His immunosuppressive regimen included tacrolimus, mycophenolate mofetil (MMF), and prednisone.

On clinical examination, there were multiple millimetric folliculocentric hyperkeratotic skin-colored to pink papules on the face, ears, trunk and extremities.

What is the causative organism?

A. papilloma virus
B. Cytomegalovirus
C. Epstein Barr virus
D. human polyoma virus

E. Human herpesvirus

Key: D
Ref: Rooks 25.42

5. It is caused by human polyomavirus 8. What is the 1st line treatment in the above scenario?
   A. Topical acylovir
   B. Topical cidofovir
   C. Oral acyclovir
   D. Topical valgancicloviria

Key: B
Ref: Rooks (25.43)

6. A 22 years old made presents with plantar warts. All of the following causes plantar warts EXCEPT:
   A. HPV 1
   B. HPV 2
   C. HPV 3
   D. HPV 4
   E. HPV 27

Key: C
Ref: Rooks (25.47)

7. Malignant change is present in which type of warts
   A. Mosaic warts
   B. Pigmented warts
   C. Periungal warts
   D. Filiform warts
   E. Digitate warts

Key: C
Ref: Rooks (25.51)

8. A 20 years old boy presents with plane warts
All of the following are first line treatment EXCEPT:
   A. Salicylic acid
   B. Occlusion
   C. Vitamin D analogues
   D. Zinc
   E. Formalin

Key: D
Ref: Rooks (25.54)

9. The most common vector for Chikungunya virus is:
   A. Monkey
   B. Rodent
   C. Mosquito
   D. Cattle
   E. Airborne transmission

Key: C
Ref: Rooks (25.79)

10. 11 years old boy known case of hepatitis B presented with profuse eruption of dull red, flat topped papules over thighs and buttocks that involved extensor aspects of arms and face over a spanb of 3 days.

There is also axillary and inguinal lymphadenopathy. Considering the diagnosis all of the following can cause this except

A. streptococcal infection
B. Staphylococcal infection
C. Bartonella
D. Borrelia
E. influenza vaccine

Key: B
Ref: Rooks 25.88

11. treatment of above scenario is

A. acylovir orally
B. IV acylovir
C. Gancylovir
D. oral antibiotics
E. Emollients and topical steroids

Key: E

12. 14 years old female was vaccinated against influenza presented with dull red papules asymmetrically distributed over both thighs and legs. This eruption likely to fade with desqumation in...

A. 10 to 12 weeks
B. 12 to 14 weeks
C. 2 to 8 weeks
D. 8 to 10 weeks

Key: C
Ref: Rooks (25.88)

13. A 13 year old child presented to emergency dept. with a 1 week history of fever and cough and pruritic skin rashes for the last 4 days. On cutaneous examination you noticed macules and some papules coalescing in irregular concentric pattern. On oral examination you noticed bluish white spots with bright red areolae. Which appropriate routine investigation can help you reaching the diagnosis?

A. Specific IgM antibodies
B. Skin biopsy
C. Viral culture
D. Molecular diagnosis and pylogenetic analysis
E. Throat swab

Key: A
Ref: Rooks' 9th edition pg. 25.85 (Pdf pg. 655)

14. A 13 year old child presented to emergency dept. with a 1 week history of fever and cough and pruritic skin rashes for the last 4 days. On cutaneous examination you noticed macules and some papules coalescing in irregular concentric pattern. On oral examination you noticed bluish white spots with bright red areolae. What is the most appropriate management of this case?

A. Antiviral with systemic steroids
B. Antiviral only
C. Bed rest and symptomatic treatment only
D. Antibiotics
E. Antiviral & IVIG

Key: C
Ref: Rooks 9th edition pg. 25.86 (Pdf pg. 656)

15. A 6 year old child presented to you with complaints of fever of sudden onset and dysphagia. On oral examination there were several tiny vesicles of 1–2 mm in diameter, with a vivid red areola mainly on the pharynx, tonsils, uvula and soft palate. Within few days the vesicles eroded into shallow ulcers. Keeping the diagnosis in mind, what is the pathogen commonly involved in this case?

A. Echovirus
B. Coxsackie A virus
C. Cytomegalovirus (CMV)
D. Enterovirus 71
E. Herpes virus

Key: B
Ref: Rooks 9th edition pg. 25.82 (Pdf pg. 652)

16. An 8 year old child presented to you with complaints of fever of sudden onset and dysphagia. On oral examination there were several tiny vesicles of 1–2 mm in diameter, with a vivid red areola mainly on the pharynx, tonsils, uvula and soft palate. Within few days the vesicles eroded into shallow ulcers. What is the common association of this case?

A. Measles
B. EBV infection
C. Rubella
D. Hand, foot and mouth disease (HFMD)
E. All of the above

Key: D
Ref: Rooks 9th edition pg. 25.82 (Pdf pg. 652)

17. A 6 year old child presented to you with a 3 day history of fever and dysphagia. On oral examination there were several tiny vesicles of 1–2 mm in diameter, with a vivid red areola mainly on the pharynx, tonsils, uvula and soft palate. Within few days the vesicles eroded into shallow ulcers. Regarding prognosis complete recovery is expected within?

A. 7 days
B. 2 weeks
C. 0ne month
D. 4 months
E. 6 months

Key: A
Ref: Rooks 9th edition pg. 25.83 (pdf pg. 653)

18. A 31-year-old male presented in Dermatology OPD with erythematous papules on the cheeks coalescing to form congested and swollen erythema giving a 'slapped-cheek' appearance. Few days later he developed macules & papules on his upper arms and thighs and trunk. Further examination revealed red macules on buccal mucosa as well.
Which of the following is the likely causative organism?

A. Cytomegalovirus
B. Bocaparvovirus 1
C. Bocaparvovirus 2
D. EbsteinBar Virus
E. Parvovirus B-19

Key: E
Ref: Rooks (25.66)

19. A 31-year-old male presented in Dermatology OPD with erythematous papules on the cheeks coalescing to form congested and swollen erythema giving a 'slapped-cheek' appearance. Few days later he developed

macules & papules on his upper arms and thighs and trunk. Further examination revealed red macules on buccal mucosa as well.
Keeping diagnosis in mind, which of the following explains the prognosis of the this condition?

A. Skin lesions fade away within a month
B. Skin lesions fade away within 8-10 days
C. Skin lesions fade away within 8-10 weeks D- Skin lesions persist for upto a year
D. Skin lesions persist for uptil 2 years

Key: A
Ref: Rooks (25.66)

20. A 23-year-old male presented in Dermatology OPD with rose-red papules on his cheeks bilaterally for 3 days. There were maculopapules on his proximal extremities as well. After detailed history and examination, a clinical suspicion of Parvovirus B-19 infection was made.
Which of the following investigation would help confirm the diagnosis of acute parvovirus infection?

A. IgM antibodies against capsid proteins VP 1 &2
B. IgM antibodies against capsid VP1 & 3
C. IgM antibodies against VP 2 & 3
D. IgG antibodies against capsid proteins VP 1 & 2
E. IgG antibodies against capsid proteins VP 1 & 3

Key: A
Ref: Rooks (25.67)

21. 13 years old girls after being treated for measles developed intensely pruritic macular and papular erythema at hands,wrists, feet and ankles associated with mild oedema.following are the main associations of this disease except...

A. EBV
B. Hepatitis B
C. Parvovirus B 19
D. borellia
E. mycoplasma

Key: D
Ref: Rooks (25.87)

22. A 22-year-old male presented with intense pruritis of hands and feet for 1 week. Cutaneous examination showed erythematous macules and papules on the hands and feet bilaterally along with few purpuric lesions as well. The lesions had a sharp cut-off at wrists and ankles. His oral mucosa had a few vesiclular and pustular lesions. He was febrile with temperature of of 100*F and Lymph node examination revealed palpable lymphadenopathy of anterior and posterior cervical chain.
Which of the following is the most common infection associated with this skin condition?

A. CMV
B. EBV
C. HHV-6
D. HHV-7
E. Parvovirus B 19

Key: E
Ref: Rooks (25.87)

23. A 25yr old pregnant lady in her first trimester presented with papular and urticarial lesions which soon developed a ring of fine scale.what is the prognosis of her condition?

A. outcome of pregnancy is unaffected
B. risk of premature abortion
C. premature delivery of an infant with hypotonia and hyporeactivity

D. intrauterine death
E. B and C

Key: E
Ref: Rooks (25.92)

24. A 20 yr old boy presented with discrete oval dull pink lesion covered by fine silvery grey scales on the thighs and upper arm. Histopath showed spongiosis, patchy parakeratosis and apoptotic keratinocytes. What is the likely diagnosis?
A. psoriais
B. drug reactions
C. Pityriasis rosea
D. pityriasis versicolor
E. PRP

Key: C
Ref: Rooks (25.90)

25. A 42-year-old homosexual man, was diagnosed with HIV infection and neurosyphilis. His CD4+ count was <120 cells/μl and his HIV viral load was 35,000 copies/ml. On examination patient was having wasted look, temp: 103F, his cervical and inguinal lymph nodes were enlarged, pedal oedema + , there were multiple non-tender red to purplish macules and papules involving his upper chest back and right post auricular area, similar lesions were also visible in his mouth. He states that he developed these lesions over the span of 1week. His lab showed hb: 7gm/dl, plt: 50,000. His lymphnode biopsy was inconclusive.
Which of the following can be the likely cause of his presentation?
A. KHSV-inflammatory cytokine syndrome
B. kaposi sarcoma
C. multicentric Castleman disease
D. primary effusion lymphomas
E. non-hodgkin lymphoma

Key: A
Ref: Rooks (25.37)

26. An 86-year-old white man, who presented with a 2.5×2.0×1.2 cm solitary, red nodule on the right thigh which was non-tender, and according to him is increasing in size rapidly.
Considering the diagnosis which of the following is predisposing factor?
A. atopy
B. EBV infection
C. epidermodysplasia verruciformis (EV)
D. ultraviolet radiation
E. laser therapy

Key: C
Ref: Rooks (25.41)

27. A 30-year-old male patient with end stage kidney disease received a cadaveric kidney transplant and discharged with a maintenance immunosuppressive therapy. In the fourth month after transplantation the patient admitted to hospital because of development of several round bluish skin lesions started as flat patches now evolving into plaques and nodules. There is also lymphedema on the left leg and recent occurrence of bilateral inguinal lymphadenopathy. Biopsy of the lesion showed many small vessels.
Considering the diagnosis what is the best treatment option for this patient?
A. Stopping immunosuppressive drug
B. topical 5% immiquimod
C. rapamycin

D. radiotherapy
E. famciclovir

Key: C
Ref: Rooks (25.38)

28. Treatment of KS in immunosuppression.
which of the following is not associated with HHV8 infection?
A. POEM syndrome
B. Castleman syndrome
C. Primary effusion lymphoma
D. Pityriasis rosea
E. Kikuchi's histiocytic necrotizing lymphadenitis

Key: E
Ref: Rooks (25.37)

29. 42-year-old homosexual man, was diagnosed with HIV infection and neurosyphilis. His CD4+ count was <120 cells/μl and his HIV viral load was 35,000 copies/ml. On examination patient was having wasted look, temp: 103F, his cervical and inguinal lymph nodes were enlarged, pedal oedema + , there were multiple non-tender red to purplish macules and papules involving his upper chest back and right post auricular area, similar lesions were also visible in his mouth. He states that he developed these lesions over the span of 1week. His lab showed hb: 7gm/dl, plt: 50,000. His lymphnode biopsy was inconclusive.
Considering the diagnosis which of the following is most suitable treatment option?
A. radiotherapy
B. intralesional chemotherapy
C. HAART
D. valaciclovir
E. sirolimus

Key: C
Ref: Rooks (25.38)

30. 7 years old child after atending a summer camp presented with c/o low grade fever malaise painful stomatitis for 2 days her motger also noted small vesicles on palm and sole,o/e there was flaccid grry 2-3 mm small oval vesicles on both palm and a few around margin of heel on both feets you suspect hand foot mouth disease, For investigation sample can be collection form
A. swab from vesicle fluid soft palate urine
B. swab from vesicle /tgroat/rectum and skin/ blood
C. swab from vesicl and throat
D. swab from blood and nose

Key: B
Ref: Rooks (25.82)

31. A young female presented with a large red plaque over the thigh which soon disappeared and small discrete pink lesions having fine scales appeared. Most likely etiology is
A. HHV6
B. HHV7
C. HHV8
D. H1N1
E. HSV

Key: B
Ref: Rooks (25.90)

32. A 19yr old patient presented with intensely pruritic papular erythema on hands and feet with distinct cut off at wrist and ankles most likely diagnosis is papular pruritic gloves and socks syndrome,in adults most common associated infection is,

A. EBV
B. CMV
C. HHV6
D. Parvo virus B19
E. Hepatitis B

Key: D
Ref: Rooks (25.87)

33. 35 years old farm house worker who is dealing with live stock on daily basis came via opd with c/o fever malaise and burning sensation felt on oral mucosa lips and tongue followed in 24 hour by formation of painful vesicle in mouth
what tst is use to help diagnosis

A. detection of antigen in vesicle
B. detection of antibody in vesicle fluid
C. detection of bacterial protein in vesicle fluid
D. none of the above

Key: A
Ref: Rooks (25.80)

34. a young male presented with oval erythematosus pink lesions which were present on the upper chest and back. The lesions line of cleavage was parallel to the ribs and were covered by scales. What is the characteristic of the scale?

A. collarette of scales attached peripherally and free edge internally
B. collarette of scale attached peripherally and free edge externally
C. collarette of scales attached centrally and free edge internally
D. collarette of scales attached centrally and free at externally
E. none of these options

Key: A
Ref: Rooks (25.91)

35. a newborn baby presented with pallor, pinpoint red lesions all over the body, few vesicles and a small ulcer in the oral mucosa. which of the following organism is most likely to be involved

A. toxoplasma
B. cmv
C. rubella
D. hsv
E. HIV

Key: D
Ref: Rooks (25.87)

36. A 25 yr old male presents with acute acral dermatosus after a viral infection followed by fever, malaise and lymphadenopathy,oral cavity is involved with petechiae, vesicopustules and ulcerations most likely diagnosis is

A. HSV 1
B. Pemphigus vulgaris
C. Hand foot and mouth disease
D. Herpangina
E. Papular pruritic gloves and socks syndrome

Key: E
Ref: Rooks (25.87)

37. who has announce a rubella outbreak and you a part of vaccination team, you decided to visit school, who u will vaccinate
    A. All school teacher should b vaccinated irrespective of age
    B. All male teacher and non-pregnant female trachr should be vaccinated
    C. ALL male teacher and pregnant female teacher shoild be vaccinated
    D. There is no need to vaccination

Key: B
Ref: Rooks (25.79)

38. A 3 yr old male presents with eruption of red,flat topped papules on thighs, buttocks and face with asymmetrical distribution,itchng is not predominat ,lymph nodes are enlarged,there is h/0 polio vaccination most probable diagnosis is
    A. cutaneous warts
    B. EM
    C. Scabies
    D. Gianotti crostti syndrome
    E. drug reaction

Key: D
Ref: Rooks (25.88)

39. Which of the following immunization is not associated with Gianotti Crostto syndrome
    A. MMR
    B. Hep A
    C. Hep
    D. BCG
    E. Influenza

Key: D
Ref: Rooks table (25.18)

40. young age male patient came with c/o fever sore throat suffusion of conjectiva for 2 days now he has sone greety sensation in both eyes associated with appearance of pink macular rashes that coalescence to form diffuse erythema on face that extending to involve the trunk and limb his labs show HB 14 TLC 3000 and smear shold unexpectedly inc level of plasma cells what is the possible diagnosis
    A. Infections mononucleosis
    B. Varicells
    C. Cerebella
    D. Measles

Key: C
Ref: Rooks (25.78)

41. An immunocompromised child came with filiform, keratotic papules protruding from the follicles over the nose for few months. Biopsy showed dilated follicles with enlarged keratinocytes having cytoplasmic inclusion bodies and trichohyaline granules. What is the most likely diagnosis?
    A. Keratosis Pilaris
    B. Follicular Mucinosis
    C. Trichodysplasia Spinulosa
    D. Lichen Nitidus
    E. Lichen Spinulosus

Key: C
Ref: Rooks (25.42)

42. A poultry farm worker presented with multiple, firm, skin colored papules having a rough horny surface on both hands. Which type most frequently associated with this condition?
   A. HPV type 7
   B. HPV type 2
   C. HPV type 42
   D. HPV type 3
   E. HPV type 43

Key: B
Ref: Rooks (25.50)

43. A 45 years male known case of lymphoma, on immunosuppressants developed widespread flat hyper and hypopigmented macules and patches and few erythematous non-warty plaques over whole body for 6 months. No family history of similar lesions. What is the most likely diagnosis?
   A. Pityriasis versicolor
   B. Acquired EDV
   C. Multiple plane warts
   D. Congenital EDV
   E. Disseminated Superficial Actinic Porokeratosis

Key: B
Ref: Rooks (25.62)

44. A 7 years female child presented with low grade fever for 5 days, sore throat and oral blisters. After 2 days she developed flaccid greyish 2-5mm vesicles over palms and soles. Which of the following is responsible for this condition?
   A. HSV 1
   B. CV A2
   C. CV A4
   D. CV A5
   E. CV A16

Key: E
Ref: Rooks (25.82)

45. A young female patient presented with high grade fever, severe arthralgia and body aches for 2 days associated with maculopapular rash over trunk and mild facial flushing. What is the most likely diagnosis?
   A. Dengue fever
   B. Malaria
   C. Chickungunya fever
   D. Lassa fever
   E. Yellow fever

Key: C
Ref: Rooks (25.76)

46. What associated mucosal changes are seen in patient infected with rubella infection
   A. Koplick spot
   B. Forschheimer sign
   C. C.aphthus ulcer
   D. Grey thck membrane seen in throat region

Key: B
Ref: Rooks (25.78)

47. What investigation should be perform for diagnosis of past rubella infection
    A. IgG antibodies 2 3 weeks latter
    B. igM 2-3 weeks later
    C. IgG 1-2 weeks later
    D. igA 3-4 week later

Key: A

48. A renal transplant patient on long term immunosuppressant developed Hpv-warts. Which of the following strain is frequently found?
    A. HPV 6 and 11
    B. HPV 2 and 4
    C. HPV 16 and 18
    D. HPV 5 and 8
    E. HPV 14 and 17

Key: B
Ref: Rook (25.63)

48. 3years old girl with history of mildly pruritic dermatitis most marked on scalp, around ears , nose and neck. On examination small erosion and crusting was present around nose , also conjunctivitis lymphadenopathy was found. Serology showed positive result for HTLV1. She is at high risk of developing following in adolescence:
    A. ATL-lymphoma
    B. Tropical spastic paraplegia
    C. uveitis
    D. myositis
    E. arthritis

Key: B
Ref: Rook (25.68)

48. Major route of transmission of HTLV-1 via:
    A. Breast milk
    B. Sexual transmission
    C. Blood leukocyte transfer
    D. Transplacental
    E. Droplets

Key: A
Ref: Rook (25.68)

49. Which of the following immunodeficiency syndrome is not associated with HPV:
    A. Ataxia-telengiectasia
    B. Fanconi anemia
    C. Wiskot aldrich syndrome
    D. GATA-2 deficiency
    E. X-linked agammaglobulinemia

Key: E
Ref: Rook (25.61)

49. 35 year old man from New York USA who works as sewage cleaner presents with 5 days history of fever, myalgias, vomiting and abdominal pain. This is quickly followed by cough and acute respiratory distress. The patient is put on mechanical ventilation for 2 days after which he quickly recovers. Considering the most likely viral infection this patient has, what is the most common reservoir of this virus?

A. Arthropods
B. Rodents
C. Cats
D. Cattle
E. Seafood

Key: B
Ref: Rooks (25.72)

50. 18 year old develops high grade fever with petechial rash on her legs. Her laboratory reports for thrombocytopenia. You suspect her to have Dengue fever. Which of the following investigations is most specific for diagnosis in the acute phase of Dengue virus?
A. NS1 antigen
B. Dengue IgM antibodies
C. Dengue IgG antibodies
D. RT-PCR
E. Viral culture

Key: D
Ref: Rook (25.74)

51. 40 year old gentleman develops acute fever with severe joint pains followed a generalized maculopapular rash primarily involving the trunk and to a lesser degree his limbs. His Dengue NS1 antigen, Measles IgM and Rubella IgG comes back to be negative. Considering the current epidemic, you want to rule out Chikungunya virus. Which of the following is the fastest test for diagnosis?
A. Chikungunya IgM
B. Chikungunya IgG
C. PCR of viral DNA
D. PCR of viral RNA
E. PCR of envelope protein

Key: D
Ref: Rooks (25.79)

52. A 61-year-old man with a past medical history of a kidney transplant in 2015 for polycystic kidneys presented to the dermatology clinic with complaints of multiple asymptomatic skin-colored papules on the face and ears, and some slightly pruritic pink papules on the trunk and extremities. These lesions appeared 1 year after transplant and were progressing for the past 2 years. His immunosuppressive regimen included tacrolimus, mycophenolate mofetil (MMF), and prednisone.
On clinical examination, there were multiple millimetric folliculocentric hyperkeratotic skin-colored to pink papules on the face, ears, trunk and extremities.
What is the causative organism?
A. papilloma virus
B. Cytomegalovirus
C. Epstein Barr virus
D. human polyoma virus
E. Human herpesvirus

Key: D
Ref: Rook (25.42)

53. What is the 1st line treatment in the above scenario?
A. Topical acylovir
B. Topical cidofovir
C. Oral acyclovir

D. Topical valganciclovir

Key: B
Ref: Rook (25.43)

\

54. A 22 years old made presents with plantar warts.
All of the following causes plantar warts EXCEPT:
A. HPV 1
B. HPV 2
C. HPV 3
D. HPV 4
E. HPV 27

Key: C
Ref: Rook (25.47)

55. Malignant change is present in which type of warts
A. Mosaic warts
B. Pigmented warts
C. Periungal warts
D. Filiform warts
E. Digitate warts

Key: C
Ref: Rook (25.51)

56. A 20 years old boy presents with plane warts
All of the following are first line treatment EXCEPT:
A. Salicylic acid
B. Occlusion
C. Vitamin D analogues
D. Zinc
E. Formalin

Key: D
Ref: Rook (25.54)

57. A 20 years old boy presents with plane warts
All of the following are first line treatment EXCEPT:
A. Salicylic acid
B. Occlusion
C. Vitamin D analogues
D. Zinc
E. Formalin

Key: D
Ref: Rook (25.54)

58. 11 years old boy known case of hepatitis B presented with profuse eruption of dull red, flat topped papules over thighs and buttocks that involved extensor aspects of arms and face over a spanb of 3 days. There is also axillary and inguinal lymphadenopathy. Considering the diagnosis all of the following can cause this except
A. streptococcal infection
B. Staphylococcal infection
C. Bartonella

D. Borrelia
E. influenza vaccine

Key: B
Ref: Rooks (25.88)

59. treatment of above scenario is
A. acylovir orally
B. IV acylovir
C. Gancylovir
D. oral antibiotics
E. Emollients and topical steroids

Key: E
Ref: Rooks (25.89)

60.14 years old female was vaccinated against influenza presented with dull red papules asymmetrically distributed over both thighs and legs. This eruption likely to fade with desqumation in.
A. 10 to 12 weeks
B. 12 to 14 weeks
C. 2 to 8 weeks
D. 8 to 10 weeks

Key: C
Ref: Rooks (25.88)

61. 14 years old female was vaccinated against influenza presented with dull red papules asymmeotrically distributed over both thighs and legs.This eruption likely to fade with desqumation in...
A. 10 to 12 weeks
B. 12 to 14 weeks
C. 2 to 8 weeks
D. 8 to 10 weeks

Key: C
Ref: Rooks 25.88

62. Treatment of the above scenario is mainly
A. symptomatic
B. antivirals
C. antibiotics
D. systemic corticosteroids

Key: A.
Ref: Rooks 25.87

63. A 13 year old child presented to emergency dept. with a 1 week history of fever and cough and pruritic skin rashes for the last 4 days. On cutaneous examination you noticed macules and some papules coalescing in irregular concentric pattern. On oral examination you noticed bluish white spots with bright red areolae. Which appropriate routine investigation can help you reaching the diagnosis?
A. Specific IgM antibodies
B. Skin biopsy
C. Viral culture
D. Molecular diagnosis and pylogenetic analysis
E. Throat swab

Key: A
Ref: Rook 9th edition pg. 25.85 (pdf pg. 655)

64. A 13 year old child presented to emergency dept. with a 1 week history of fever and cough and pruritic skin rashes for the last 4 days. On cutaneous examination you noticed macules and some papules coalescing in irregular concentric pattern. On oral examination you noticed bluish white spots with bright red areolae. What is the most appropriate management of this case?

A. Antiviral with systemic steroids
B. Antiviral only
C. Bed rest and symptomatic treatment only
D. Antibiotics
E. Antiviral & IVIG

Key: C
Ref: Rook pg. 25.86 (pdf pg. 656)

65. A 6 year old child presented to you with complaints of fever of sudden onset and dysphagia. On oral examination there were several tiny vesicles of 1–2 mm in diameter, with a vivid red areola mainly on the pharynx, tonsils, uvula and soft palate. Within few days the vesicles eroded into shallow ulcers. Keeping the diagnosis in mind, what is the pathogen commonly involved in this case?

A. Echovirus
B. Coxsackie A virus
C. Cytomegalovirus (CMV)
D. Enterovirus 71
E. Herpes virus

Key: B
Ref: Rook pg. 25.82 (pdf pg. 652)

66. A 6 year old child presented to you with a 3 day history of fever and dysphagia. On oral examination there were several tiny vesicles of 1–2 mm in diameter, with a vivid red areola mainly on the pharynx, tonsils, uvula and soft palate. Within few days the vesicles eroded into shallow ulcers. Regarding prognosis complete recovery is expected within?

A. 7 days
B. 2 weeks
C. One month
D. 4 months
E. 6 months

Key: A
Ref: Rook pg. 25.83 (pdf pg. 653)

67. A 31-year-old male presented in Dermatology OPD with erythematous papules on the cheeks coalescing to form congested and swollen erythema giving a 'slapped-cheek' appearance. Few days later he developed macules & papules on his upper arms and thighs and trunk. Further examination revealed red macules on buccal mucosa as well.
Which of the following is the likely causative organism?

A. Cytomegalovirus
B. Bocaparvovirus 1
C. Bocaparvovirus 2
D. EbsteinBar Virus
E. Parvovirus B-19

Key: E
Ref: Rooks (25.66)

68. A 31-year-old male presented in Dermatology OPD with erythematous papules on the cheeks coalescing to form congested and swollen erythema giving a 'slapped-cheek' appearance. Few days later he developed

macules & papules on his upper arms and thighs and trunk. Further examination revealed red macules on buccal mucosa as well.
Keeping diagnosis in mind, which of the following explains the prognosis of this condition?

A. Skin lesions fade away within a month
B. Skin lesions fade away within 8-10 days
C. Skin lesions fade away within 8-10 weeks
D. Skin lesions persist for upto a year
E. Skin lesions persist for uptil 2 years

Key: B
Ref: Rooks (25.67)

69. A 19-year-old male presented with erythematous papules on his cheeks bilaterally along with maculopapules on his proximal extremities. After detailed history and examination, a clinical suspicion of Parvovirus B-19 infection was made.
Which of the following are the cutaneous conditions associated with this virus infection?

A. Bechet disease
B. Erythema Nodosum
C. Erythema Multiforme
D. Lichen Planus
E. Seborrheic Dermatitis

Key: A
Ref: Rooks (25.66)

70. A 23-year-old male presented in Dermatology OPD with rose-red papules on his cheeks bilaterally for 3 days. There were maculopapules on his proximal extremities as well. After detailed history and examination, a clinical suspicion of Parvovirus B-19 infection was made.
Which of the following investigation would help confirm the diagnosis of acute parvovirus infection?

A. IgM antibodies against capsid proteins VP 1 &2
B. IgM antibodies against capsid VP1 & 3
C. IgM antibodies against VP 2 & 3
D. IgG antibodies against capsid proteins VP 1 & 2
E. IgG antibodies against capsid proteins VP 1 & 3

Key: A
Ref: Rooks (25.67)

71. A 22-year-old male presented with intense pruritis of hands and feet for 1 week. Cutaneous examination showed erythematous macules and papules on the hands and feet bilaterally along with few purpuric lesions as well. The lesions had a sharp cut-off at wrists and ankles. His oral mucosa had a few vesiclular and pustular lesions. He was febrile with temperature of 100*F and Lymph node examination revealed palpable lymphadenopathy of anterior and posterior cervical chain.
Which of the following is the most common infection associated with this skin condition?

A. CMV
B. EBV
C. HHV-6
D. HHV-7
E. Parvovirus B 19

Key: E
Ref: Rooks (25.87)

72. 13 years old girls after being treated for measles developed intensely pruritic macular and papular erythema at hands, wrists, feet and ankles associated with mild oedema. following are the main associations of this disease except...

A. EBV
B. Hepatitis B
C. Parvovirus B 19
D. Borellia
E. mycoplasma

Key: D
Ref: Rook (25.87)

Chapter 26

BACTERIAL INFECTIONS

1. A 26 year old fisherman presents with acute febrile illness, muscle pains and intense conjunctival infection. Headache and respiratory symptoms are present. On examination there is blotchy erythema most constant on the legs. There is polymorph nuclear leucocytosis of peripheral blood. What is the likely diagnosis?
   A. Canicola fever
   B. Relapsing fever
   C. Infectious mononucleosis
   D. Pinta

Key: A
Ref: Rooks: (26.71)

2. Reviewing a diagnosed pt. of botryomycosis. Most case are caused by?
   A. Rhizopus
   B. Antinomies Israeli
   C. Mycobacterial tuberculosis
   D. Staphylococcus aureus
   E. Streptococcus pyogenic

Key: D
Ref: Rooks: (26.72)

3. A 45 yrs. old poorly controlled diabetic present with large erythematous tender swollen plaque on left thigh. Bullae appeared on plaque and broke to produce necrotic ulcer. There is as deviated fever n prostration. The most imp step in management is.
   A. A third generation antibiotic
   B. Meticulous correction of blood glucose
   C. Surgical exploration of affected area
   D. Swabs for aerobic n anaerobic culture
   E. Use of plasma expanders

Key: C
Ref: Rooks: (26.74)

4. In necrotizing subcutaneous infection. Focus of disease lies in soft tissue of deep dermis, adipose tissue n subcutaneous fascia. Hallmark of infection is extensive necrosis accompanying cellulitis. Which includes
   A. Clostridial cellulitis
   B. Necrotizing fasciitis
   C. Progressive bacterial synergistic gangrene
   D. Gangrenous cellulitis due to other pathogens like pseudomonas
   E. All of the above

Key: E
Ref: Rooks: (26.73)

5. A 45 yr. old diabetic male presented in emergency department in shock. There was a large necrotizing wound over his left leg, about which his son gave the history that his father had a minor injury at same site a week ago. His urine output was less than 20ml/ hr in the ER. He was semiconscious with rapid heart rate. What should be expected on direct microscopic examination of the smear from wound?
   A. pleomorphic and fusiform and spiral bacteria

B. Spirochetes stained with Warthin-starry stain
C. Granules containing masses of bacteria stained with methenamine silver stain.
D. Gram negative curved bacilli
E. Gram positive, acid fast narrow branching hyphae

Key: D
Ref: Rooks: (26.64)

6. A 12 year old child presented in opd with complaint of development of small bumps around his mouth and nares. These lesion were appearing in crops and some were ulcerated and scales over them. On detailed cutaneous examination there was an atopic scar over his left hand which was there for quite a few months. Keeping the probable diagnosis in mind, what's the best treatment which can be offered to this patient?
A. Inj. Benzedrine penicillin 1.2M U
B. Azithromycin 250mg once daily
C. Injbenzathine penicillin 0.6MU
D. Doxycycline 100mg once daily
E. Dispone 50mg once daily

Key: C
Ref: Rooks: (26.68)

7. Regarding Lyme's disease, all are the complications except,
A. Neuroborreliosis
B. Acrodermatitis chronical atrophicans
C. Lymphadenitis benign cutis
D. Morphed
E. Lichen planus

Key: E
Ref: Rooks: (26.70)

8. For Borrelia burgdorferi causing Lyme disease which one of the following test has rapid diagnostic value
A. Western blot
B. Indirect immunofluorescence
C. PCR on serum or tissue
D. ELISA
E. Skin biopsy H/P.

Key: C
Ref: Rooks: (26.70)

9. Regarding prognosis of Vibrio vulnificus infection
A. It is mild and self-limiting
B. Can be successfully treated with penicillin
C. Surgical debridement is curative
D. Third generation cephalosporin's with surgical debridement
E. Mortality is 70%

Key: D
Ref: Rooks: (26.60)

10. 68-year-old white male with insulin-dependent diabetes was admitted one day before his death. The chief complaints were the occurrence of chills and fever since passing a kidney stone two days earlier. In the last day, the right leg had become swollen. The most striking physical findings were redness of the right posterior calf and repentance in both legs. The patient's white blood cell count was found to be 34,000

cells/cmm and the packed red blood cell volume (pcv) was 18%. Within hours, the right calf became tense and the crepitance spread up to the nipple line. The patient vomited, aspirated the vomitus, and died 10 hour. What is the likely diagnosis?

A. Myocardial infarction
B. Pulmonary embolism
C. Gas gangrene
D. Aspiration pneumonia
E. Urosepsis

Key: C
Ref: Rooks: (26.47 and 26.48)

11. 50 years old male patient came in casualty department with the history of road traffic accident 2 days ago with c/o-multiple open wounds and swelling, pain. And heaviness of right leg since 2 days, fever and lightheadness since 1 day. on examination-7-8 multiple open wounds on right leg, varying in size and shape, oozing out serosanguinous discharge, few were ulcerated with bronze discoloration of surrounding skin. Few wounds involving muscles tissues which were necrosis, oedematous swelling over right leg. On palpation, warmth ++, tenderness ++, crepitus +++ .on systemic examination:-cvs-nad, respond, cns-nad.following are treatment options except:

A. I/v penicillin's
B. Ciprofloxacin
C. Immediate surgical debridement
D. Metronidazole
E. Clindamycin

Key: B
Ref: Rooks: (26.48)

12. A young lady developed grouped papules which became vesicular and undergo crusting. She has cat as pet in her house. Biopsy showed sarcoid type granulomas. All of them are true about the disease except:

A. There may be systemic involvement rarely
B. In uncomplicated case there may be polymorph nuclear leucocytosis
C. Benign and self-limiting
D. Granulomatous infection of liver and spleen can occur
E. Fatal if lung involvement occur.

Key: E
Ref: Rooks: (26.61)

13. Bartonella causes all diseases except:

A. Relapsing fever
B. Cat scratch disease
C. Oraya fever
D. Verruga perianal
E. Bacillary angiomatosis

Key: A
Ref: Rooks: (26.59)

14. A 18 yrs. old boy presented with 2 weeks history of fever with chills with subsequent malaise, weakness, myalgia's, headache, nausea, vomiting, and arthralgias.on examination, the petechial rash and purpura located on the trunk and legs .what is the drug of choice for this disease?

A. Penicillin v
B. Amphotericin
C. Methicillin

D. Penicillin g
E. Fluoroquinolones

Key: D
Ref: Rooks: (26.49)

15. A 34yrs old HIV patient presented with h/o multiple friable papules and nodules on arms and face. On skin biopsy, there is lobular proliferation of small blood vessels. What is the complication of this disease?
A. Encephalitis
B. Thrombocytopenia
C. Bacillary pelisses
D. Purpura
E. Leukocytoclastic vasculitis

Key: C
Ref: Rooks: (26.62)

16. A 34yrs old HIV patient presented with h/o multiple friable papules and nodules on arms and face. On skin biopsy, there is lobular proliferation of small blood vessels. What stain will you use to diagnose this disease?
A. Acid fast stain
B. Crystal violet stain
C. Warthin starry stain
D. Z-N staining
E. Giemsa stain

Key: C
Ref: Rooks: (26.62)

17. True regarding the treatment verruca Parana
A. Chloramphenicol is the treatment of choice
B. Ciprofloxacin
C. Response to antibiotics is unsatisfactory
D. Streptomycin
E. Doxycycline

Key: C
Ref: Rooks: (26.63)

18. Among the serogroups of Neisseria meningitides given, which of these are the most important associated with meningococcal infection?
A. A, B, C, Y AND W135
B. A, B, C, X, Y, AND W135
C. A, B, C, X, Y, AND W125
D. A, B, C, X AND W135
E. A, B, C, Y AND W125

Key: B
Ref: Rooks: (26.49)

19. A middle aged obese lady who is a known case of diabetes mellitus presented with irregularly shaped and sharply marginated reddish-brown patches involving both axillae for past three months. The lesions were asymptomatic. Gram staining of the scraping from the affected skin showed fine filament. The likely organism involved is
A. Candida albicans
B. Corny bacterium minutissimum

C. Melanesia globose
D. Melanesia furfur
E. Corny bacterium tenuis

Key: B
Ref: Rooks: (26.40)

20. A 50 year old diabetic female presented where asymptomatic toe cleft lesion that showed fissuring scaling. Wood light examination showed Coral red fluorescence. Patient did not respond to topical clotrimazole. What is the most effective oral treatment available in this case?
A. Erythromycin
B. Itraconazole
C. Rifampicin
D. Terbinafine
E. Doxycycline

Key: A
Ref: Rooks: (26. 40)

21. A young woman who is into fifth day of her menstrual bleeding presented in emergency with complain of fever, vomiting and diarrhoea. Patient was admitted in high dependency unit and hemodynamic resuscitation was started. What is the mortality rate of the disease even with appropriate management?
A. 2%
B. 5%
C. 7%
D. 20%
E. Full recovery

Key: C
Ref: Rooks: (26.31)

22. A 22-year-old young male presented with pruritic erythematous papules on both lower extremities and Buttocks for 2 days .On examination there were multiple erythematous follicular papules, thin walled pustules situated just at the orifice of hair follicle about 1-6mm in diameter with a yellow crust. There was no surrounding erythema and no scarring.
Which of the following is the most appropriate diagnosis?
A. Pustular Acne
B. Chromatic folliculitis
C. Buckhorn impetigo
D. Frunculosis
E. Pseudo folliculitis

Key B.
Ref: Rooks: (26. 26)

23. 30 year old female who had her normal vaginal delivery two weeks back presented with history of fever associated with vomiting and diarrhoea for past one week. On examination there was widespread papulopustular eruption with areas of desquamation. There was retiform purpura involving dorsum of the hand. Conjunctivae were hyperaemic. What is the first line treatment in this case?
A. IV clindamycin
B. IV immunoglobulin
C. IV ciprofloxacillin
D. IV vancomycin
E. IV amikacin

Key: A

Ref: Rooks: (26. 31)

24. The above mentioned scenario is complicated by multiorgan failure. How many systems need to be involved to fulfil the diagnostic criteria?
    A. 1
    B. 2
    C. 3
    D. 4
    E. 5

Key: C
Ref: Rooks: (26.31)

25. A 33- year- old male presented in dermatology OPD with painful red lump on right buttock for one week. Initially it was small in size and now increasing with purulent discharge. On examination it was hot, tender about 3x2 cm in diameter with sloughing base. Patient was also febrile.
What is the prognosis of this condition?
    A. Lesion usually heals without scarring.
    B. Lesion usually heals with scarring.
    C. Lesion heals spontaneously after incison and drainage
    D. Non carriers mostly heal without scarring
    E. Both B and D

Key: B
Ref: Rooks: (26.26)

26. A 38 years old alcoholic previously healthy male presented in emergency with nausea, vomiting, and respiratory distress. On admission HR is 130/min, BP 80/60.his blood tests indicate sepsis sec to pleural involvement and endocarditis, there is h/0 hot violaceous tender erythema on left hand 2 weeks back with sharp gyrate border which extended centrifugally, what could be the causative organism
    A. Listeria monocytogenes
    B. Bacillus anthraces
    C. Pseudomonas
    D. Corynebacterium
    E. Eryseipelothrix rusiopathiae

Key: E
Ref: Rooks: (26.46)

27. 55-years old female known case of chronic kidney disease presented in dermatology for recurrent painful boils on lower extremities, abdomen and buttocks. She has been treated with multiple courses of oral and topical antibiotics but not recovered fully. On examination there were multiple tender boils few of them were necrotic with pussy discharge and perifollicular erythema. Medical history revealed that she has been visiting hospitals 3 times a week for haemodialysis.
Which of the following is the most appropriate step regarding suppression of recurrence?
    A. Clindamycin 300mg bd for 14 days
    B. Flucloxacillin 500mg tds for 7 days
    C. Intranasal mupirocin daily for 5 days only
    D. Oral rifampicin 600mg daily for 10 days
    E. Topical antibiotics only

Key: D
Ref: Rooks: (26.8)

28. A one-year-old previously healthy child admitted in emergency department with altered level of consciousness seizures, fever and necrotic ulcers on umblicus.On examination temp was 102f, o2 saturation

96%, and heart rate 120b/min and bilateral crept on auscultation. Cutaneous examination revealed ill-defined necrotic ulcer, surrounded by black eschar studded with pustules. Bluish green discharge was also oozing from umbilicus.
Which of the following organism is responsible

A. Gram negative diplococci
B. Gram positive anaerobes
C. Gram negative aerobes
D. Gram positive, rod shaped
E. Gram negative anaerobes

Key: C
Ref: Rooks: (26.51)

29. A 75yrs having a known history of depression, admitted to the intensive care unit for management of hypotension following a multiple medications overdose subsequently deteriorated rapidly with sepsis. A cannula site was noted to be bruised, swollen and erythematous and the X-ray demonstrated gas sitting within the tissues surrounding the metacarpal bones. The patient was referred to the orthopaedic surgeons and quickly taken for debridement of the affected area and fasciotomies of the forearm. Considering the diagnosis, which one of the below options is correct:

A. It is due to Clostridium botulinum infection
B. Clostridia species are gram negative spore forming anaerobe
C. The clinical features are due to release of protein endotoxin
D. Gas is invariably present in the muscle compartments
E. The toxin produced by causative organism is copper containing molecule

KEY: D
Ref: Rooks: (26.47 and 26.48)

30. A 58 years tribal man presented with H/0 single painless bulla on erythematous base which has ruptured to form haemorrhagic crust surrounded by enema for last 10 dash/0 fever asset with rigors and chills for 3 days, there is h/0 slaughtering og goat with bare hands 2 week back most probable diagnosis would be

A. Anthrax
B. Erysipeloid
C. Listeriotic
D. EBA
E. Bullous impetigo

Key: A
Ref: Rooks: (26.43)

31. A 12-year old boy presented in dermatology with complains of macular popular rash on upper and lower extremities for 7 days. He noted this rash after swimming in stagnant pool. On examination numerous pustules was seen along with foul smelling discharge. Cultured report revealed gram negative rods with pyocyanin pigmentation.
Which of the following is most effective treatment?

A. Oral tetracycline
B. Oral acyclovir
C. Kmno4 soaks frequently
D. IV penicillin
E. Oral 3rd generation cephalosporin

Key: E
Ref: Rooks: (26.52)

32. 60 year's old female diabetic admitted in hospital for management of acute pancreatitis. On 5th day of admission she developed 2*3 cm tender indurated crusted plaque on erythematous base Crust removed with difficulty revealing purulent irregular ulcer present on right thigh on enquiry the lesion started as small pustule.
Microbiological swab taken revealed streptococcus pyogenic.
What is the prognosis of this condition?
   A. Recurrences are usual
   B. Healing occurs after few weeks with scarring
   C. Heal without scarring
   D. Resistant to antibiotics treatment
   E. Healing takes years to complete

Key: B
Ref: Rooks: (26.17)

33. 45 years old diabetic female admitted to hospital after 3 days of redness swelling and pain in her right leg. U r suspecting cellulitis. U have aspirated fluid from oedematous swelling .what protein concentration in fluid favours cellulitis as compared to deep vein thrombosis?
   A. Less than 5g/l
   B. Less than 10 g/l
   C. More than 10 g/l
   D. More than 5g/l
   E. Value less than 2 g/l

Key: C
Ref: Rooks: (26.21)

34. 60 years old diabetic female allergic to penicillin presented with complain of redness swelling and pain in her left leg .ultrasound Doppler ruled out dvt. She has history of similar episodes for past 2 years on and off which settles with some oral antibiotics.
To prevent such episodes in future .what prophylaxis u will advise?
   A. Fulucloxacillin
   B. Penicillin v
   C. Erythromycin
   D. Clindamycin
   E. Amikacin

Key: C
Ref: Rooks: (26.21)

35. 5 year old child hx of atopic eczema presented with history of vesicular eruption on erythematous base 1 week back these vesicles ruptured in a day and exuded serum which dried and form yellowish brown crusts present on face around nose and mouth considering the diagnosis which of the following complication is not associated with this condition?
   A. Scarlet fever
   B. Urticarial
   C. Erythema multiform
   D. Rheumatic fever
   E. Acute glomerulonephritis

Key: D
Ref: Rooks: (26.13)

36. 5 year old child presented with golden yellow crusted plaques around the nose for 1 week. hx of similar lesions in a sibling. Patient is otherwise well no constitutional symptoms no lymphadenopathy.how will u manage?

A. Wash skin remove crust use disinfectants and apply mupirocin for 1 week
B. Wash skin remove crust use disinfectants and apply fluidic acid for 4 weeks
C. Wash skin remove crust use disinfectant plus oral flucloxaciliin
D. Topical mupirocin for 2 weeks
E. Wash skin remove crusts use disinfectants oral erythromycin for 7 days

Key: A
Ref: Rooks: (26.16)

37. A 50 year old male presented worth black eschar on his left forearm along with hyperaemia and edema, it started as a painless papule, no h/0 trauma patient was associated with livestock management, and antibiotics were started by local practitioner, now anthrax is suspected, blood and tissue cultures were sent, and next step would be

A. Treatment should be continued until bacteriological confirmation is obtained
B. Discontinue antibiotic
C. Wait for labs then strt treatment
D. No treatment is needed

Key: A
Ref: Rooks: (26.43)

38. Middle aged male develop painless indurated ill-defined crusted plaque on top of nose. History of change in voice character n decrease sense of smell n taste. Occasional episode of epistaxis for 2 yrs. On h/p dense plasma cell infiltrate in dermis with large vacuolated histiocytic n colloid bodies. Diagnosis?

A. A, rhinoscleroma
B. Leishmaniosis
C. Paracoccidiomycosis
D. Nasal tb
E. Leprosy

Key: A

39. Prognosis of above scenario is

A. Progressive pharyngeal scarring
B. Nasal scarring
C. Disfiguring
D. Seldom fatal
E. All of the above

Key: E

40. 1st line treatment for above scenario is

A. Ciprofloxacin
B. Tetracycline
C. Cephalexin
D. Co2 laser
E. All of the above

41. Young boy with red painful ulcerated nodule at site of tick bite. Associated with breakdown of regional lymph nodes n systemic symptoms present. Causative organism

A. Francisella tularensis
B. Bartonella
C. Klebsiella pneumonia

D. Pneumonias
E. Acinobacter

Key: A

42. Disease course in above scenario
A. Untreated prolonged course
B. Mortality 5 to 30 percent
C. Pulmonary form more fulminating
D. All of the above

Key: E

43. 14 years old child presented with exfoliative dermatosis in which classically most of the body surface becomes tender and erythematous and the superficial epidermis strips off. What is the first line treatment for this condition?
A. First generation cephalosporin's
B. Tobramycin
C. Vancomycin
D. Parenteral penicillin's-resistant antibiotics such as flucloxacillin.

Key: D
Ref: Rooks: (26.29)

44. 5 years child develops fever, irritability and skin tenderness. A widespread erythematous eruption follows which is usually accentuated in the flexures and progresses rapidly to superficial blister formation (Nikolsby positive). The tender skin becomes gathered into folds and, as it shrinks, leaves raw areas which are extremely painful. The condition usually heals within 7–14 days. It is associated with all of the following except?
A. Renal failure
B. Malignancy
C. Immunosuppression
D. Liver failure

Key: D
Ref: Rooks: (26.27)

45. Sass is characterized by following?
A. Localized form of the disease is more severe than generalized form
B. Histologically, there is splitting of the epidermis between the gran ular and spinous layers which does not usually contain inflame amatory cells.
C. Swabs and cultures of blister fluids usually grow the staphylococci
D. Healing of the generalized form of the disease classically leaves wrinkled desquamating skin with hyperpigmentation

Key: B
Ref: Rooks: (26.28)

46. Sycosis is a subacute or chronic pyogenic infection involving the whole depth of the follicle and usually refers to disease in the beard area, sycosis barbae. If the follicles are destroyed with clinically evident scarring then it's termed as?
A. Pseudo folliculitis
B. Folliculitis decal vans
C. Lipoid sycosis
D. Carbuncle

Key: C

Ref: Rooks: (26.26)

47. All of the following are characteristics of sycosis except?
   A. Its relapsing and remitting condition
   B. Staphylococcal aureus is the causative organism
   C. It occurs in adolescence
   D. It occurs in childhood
   E. Swabs are taken from affected skin and from the anterior nares for microbiology.

Key: D
Ref: Rooks: (26.26)

48. A 25 yr. old female presented with complain of red concretions on hair shaft and red coloured staining from axillary sweat from 3 months. On examination hair were brittle. What treatment would you prescribe?
   A. Aluminium chloride
   B. Ketoconazole
   C. Shave hair
   D. Terbinafine
   E. Amoxicillin

Key: A
Ref: Rooks: (26.41)

49. A 40 yr. old lady presents with discrete, shallow circular lesions with punched out appearance on both soles. Most likely organism involved is
   A. Kytococcus sedentarius
   B. Trichomycosis axillaris
   C. Microspore canines
   D. Trichophytes rubrum
   E. Candidiasis

Key: A
Ref: Rooks: 26.42

50. A new-born baby presented with purpuric lesions over body along with discrete bluish papules on legs. There was also complain of profuse diarrhoea along with respiratory difficulty. The drug of choice will be
   A. Ampicillin
   B. Tetracyclines
   C. Amphotericin
   D. Ciprofloxacin
   E. Doxycycline

Key: A
Ref: Rooks: 26.42

51. 45 yr. old male presented with punched out circular lesions on both soles along with hyperhidrosis. All of the following help in treatment except
   A. Aluminium chloride
   B. Fusain ointment
   C. Clotrimazole
   D. Iitraconazole
   E. Botulinum toxin

Key: D
Ref: Rooks: 26.42

52. A 30 yr. old male presented with yellow black nodular concretions on hair shaft. On examination hair are brittle. Which of the following is first line investigation

A. Gram staining and culture
B. Woods lamp
C. Demoscopy
D. Biopsy
E. Serology

Key: A
Ref: Rooks: 26.41

53. A 60 years old male, HIV +ve, presented with clusters of papules and some nodules on his trunk and in oral mucosa.
Skin biopsy shows lobular proliferation of small blood vessels and endothelial swelling.
There were granular structures in the lesion which revealed clumps of bacteria with Warthin starry stain.
Cultures were unremarkable.
What do you think is the most probable diagnosis?

A. Rickettsia
B. leptospira
C. Bacillary angiomatosis
D. Cat scratch disease
E. Oroya fever

Key: C

54. A patient presented with a scar on his neck. There is history of bite from a cat in winters.
On examination there was a pulsatile discharging swelling in in his neck, which was biopsied to make the diagnosis.
What types of granuloma will you think will be present on microscopy?

A. Tuberculoid
B. Rheumatoid
C. Sarcoid
D. Epithelioid
E. Histiocytic

Key: C

55. A 14 year old boy presented to skin opd with history of fever for 1 week and a painful swelling in right axilla.
On examination, there is a popular and vesicular lesion with some crusting on his right hand. He has a cat as pet at home.
Keeping in mind the diagnosis, what is the other name for this disease?

A. Carrion disease
B. Teeny disease
C. Oasis
D. Cysticerosis
E. Wails disease

Key: B

56. Which is not a complication of Cat scratch disease?

A. Myelitis
B. Radiculitis
C. Pericarditis
D. Arthritis

E. Cerebral arteritis

Key: C

57. A 55 years old male presented with fever and enlarged lymph nodes.
On physical examination, jaundice and anaemia are +ve and tenderness in right upper quadrant of abdomen.
Patient is severely immunocompromised.
CT scan of abdomen showed cyst like inflammatory structures in the liver.
Biopsy of these cystic lesions showed lining of endothelial cells and large numbers of organisms.
What is the most appropriate treatment?
1st generation cephalosporins

A. Rifampicin
B. Ivermectin
C. Doxycycline
D. Oral steroids

Key: D

Chapter 27

MYCOBACTERIAL INFECTIONS

1. 30 year old patient having low socioeconomic status having asymptomatic skin color papules few were lichened mainly of trunk and thighs since 2 month! On systemic examination patient had hepatosp lenomegaly rest unremarkable what is your probable diagnosis?

A. Lichen nitidus
B. Keratosis spinolosa
C. Follicular Lp
D. Lichen scrofulosorum
E. Prosea

Key: D

2. Which of following does not have haematogenous method of inoculation?

A. Lupus vulgaris
B. Tubercular
C. Scrofuloderma
D. Tuberculous gumma

Key: C
Ref: Rooks (27.13)

3. HIV positive patient started HAART therapy develop crops of symmetrical hard dusky red papules some are ulcerated on legs and arms. Which of the following is correct?

A. Humoral immunity plays a role in pathogenesis
B. Rise in Interleukin 1 &6
C. Rise in CD4 leading to cell mediated immune complex
D. Interferon gamma plays a role in pathogenesis

Key: C

4. A 48 year old women comes to your OPD with complaint of chronic brownish-red plaques on her lower limbs. The lesions have an Apple-Jelly colour on diascopy. The most likely mechanism of disease in this patient is:

A. Spread from a distant site
B. Exogenous reinfection
C. Reinoculation
D. Id reaction
E. None of the above

Key: C
Ref: Rooks (27.21)

5. 25-year-old female presents to the OPD with a complaint of ulcerated nodule with sinus formation in the sub mandibular area of the left cheek with a seropurulent exudate and a malar facial rash is also noted. She also complains of worsening shortness of breath that has not responded to bronchodilators, a nonproductive cough, and a three-week history of low-grade fevers. On review of her labs, it is noted that she has chronic kidney disease and has received some drug multiple times in the past for the treatment of a chronic medical condition. You note the patient's BMI to be greater than the 30th percentile. You obtain cultures of the seropurulent exudate and after 3 weeks the presence of non-motile, non-spring, gram positive acid-fast organisms is noted. What are the predisposing factors in this disease?

A. Hairy cell leukemia

B. HIV infection
C. Corticosteroid therapy
D. Connective tissue disease
E. C and D

Key: E
Ref: Rooks (27.39)

6. A 38-year-old male immigrant from the Philippines presents to the Dermatology OPD with nodular skin lesions in a sporotrichoid pattern on his distal lower extremities of approximately four weeks duration. He also has a history of intermittent fevers, bilateral knee pains, intermittent productive cough, and unintentional weight loss. He had recurrent community-acquired pneumonia growing up as a teenager. He does not smoke and he has no significant family history. On examination, the patient has cervical lymphadenopathy, mild bilateral knee joint effusions and auscultation reveals bronchial breath sounds in the right anterior chest. The rest of the physical exam is unremarkable.
What is the causative organism of his disease?
A. Mycobacterium avium
B. Mycobacterium intracellular
C. Mycobacterium Kanssasii
D. Mycobacterium Marinum
E. Mycobacterium srofulaceum

Key: C
Ref: Rooks (27.36)

7. Which of the following skin manifestations of Mycobacterium Tuberculosis infection is a Tubercular?
A. Military TB
B. Lupus Vulgaris
C. Scrofuloderma
D. Lichen Scrofulosorum
E. Warty TB

Key: D
Ref: Rooks (27.25)

8. A 43-year-old man with no known medical conditions presents to the hospital with a red popular rash on his tattoo, which he got 2 weeks ago. Biopsy specimens obtained from the lesion show sparse lymphohistiocytic infiltrates in the upper dermis, granulomas, and acid-fast organisms. Mycobacterial culture grows the organism in 1 week. What is the best initial therapy for the patient's condition?
A. Amikacin
B. Clarithromycin
C. Doxycycline
D. Levofloxacin
E. Suiphonamides

Key: B
Ref: Rooks (27.43)

9. A 52-year-old HIV positive male who has been non-compliant with his treatment regimen comes for evaluation of papules and pustules often forming veracious plaques confined to the distal extremities. He also complains of cough which is progressively getting worse since last four months. He complains of low-grade fevers. He also complaints of blood in his sputum occasionally. Examination shows hepatosp lenomegaly and axillary lymphadenopathy. Chest x-ray shows right upper lobe cavitary lesion and pulmonary infiltrates bilaterally. Sputum from acid-fast bacillus stain is positive. Cultures are obtained from the exudates which showed growth of gram-positive, non-motile and non-spore-forming organism.

Colony morphology ranges from flat to raised and smooth to rough, colonies are at first non-pigmented but turn yellow after exposure to light .His CD4 count is 34.
What is the most appropriate treatment regimen for this patient?
A. Rifampin, ethambutol, and isoniazid
B. Rifampin, ethambutol, and streptomycin
C. Rifampin, trimethoprim-sulfamethoxazole, and isoniazid
D. Rifampin, linezolid, and clarithromycin
E. Rifampicin, isoniazid and Doxycycline

Key: A
Ref: Rooks (27.36)

10. Most common complication of Lupus Vulgaris includes:
A. Melanoma
B. BCC
C. SCC
D. Lymphoma
E. Satcomas

Key: C
Ref: Rooks (27.24)

11. A positive Tuberculin skin test after 48hours will read:
A. 0.5mm
B. 2mm
C. 5mm
D. 10mm
E. 1mm

Key: D
Ref: Rooks (27.4)

12. Which of the following types of Cutaneous Tuberculosis has the highest host immunity?
A. Orofacial TB
B. Surofuloderma
C. Tuberculous Chancre
D. Lupus Vulgaris
E. None of the above

Key: D
Ref: Rooks (27.21)

13. Clinical form of Cutaneous Tuberculosis usually associated with measles is:
A. Plaque form
B. Ulcerative form
C. Vegetating form
D. Papular and nodular forms
E. Tumor like forms

Key: D
Ref: Rooks (27.23)

14. 34 yrs. old laborer presented to skin opd with complaint of swelling of lips and painful lesions in oral cavity. He also complaints of fever, cough and night sweats since few weeks. O/E there were multiple ulcers with undermined bluish edges mostly on tip and lateral margins of tongue as well as on gingiva. He

was febrile with temp of 100F. NW keeping the diagnosis in mind which of the following is not a predisposing factor.

A. Systemic Tuberculosis.
B. Immunosuppression.
C. Malnutrition.
D. Cigarette smoking.
E. HIV.

Key: D
Ref: Rooks (27.16)

15. Which of the following is NOT a part of the Diagnostic Criteria of Tubercles?

A. Tuberculoid histology on skin biopsy
B. Strongly positive Mantoux test
C. The presence of M.Tuberculosis in the smear and culture
D. Resolution of skin lesions with ATT
E. None of the above

Key: C
Ref: Rooks (27.25)

16. Rapid & specific tool in diagnosis of cutaneous Tuberculosis

A. Tuberculin skin test
B. INF-gamma release assay
C. PCR
D. Histopathology
E. All of the above

Key: C
Ref: Rooks (27.8)

17. True regarding DNA PCR in diagnosis of cutaneous Tuberculosis

A. 100% sensitive and specific in paucibacillary Tuberculosis
B. 95%sensitive & 100% specific in paucibacillary Tuberculosis
C. 100% sensitive & specific in multi Bacillary Tuberculosis
D. 95% sensitive & 100% specific in multi Bacillary Tuberculosis
E. 73% sensitive & 100 %specific in multi Bacillary Tuberculosis

Key: C
Ref: Rooks (27.9)

18. Multi drug resistant Tuberculosis is defined as

A. Resistant to Rifampicin & pyrazinamide with or without resistance to other anti-Tuberculous drugs
B. Resistant to Rifampicin & isoniazid with or without resistance to any other anti-Tuberculous drugs
C. Resistant to Rifampicin & Ethambutol with or without resistance to any other anti-Tuberculous drugs
D. Resistant to isoniazid & Ethambutol with or without resistance to any other anti-Tuberculous drugs
E. Resistant to isoniazid & pyrazinamide with or without resistance to any other anti-Tuberculous drugs

Key: B
Ref: Rooks (27.10)

19. Clinical response to anti-tuberculous drugs in cutaneous Tuberculosis usually occurs within

A. 2---3 weeks

B. 2---4 weeks
C. 6---8 weeks
D. 4---6 weeks
E. 8---10 weeks

Key: D
Ref: Rooks (27.10)

20. Therapeutic use of BCG vaccination is
A. Renal cell carcinoma
B. Hepatocellular carcinoma
C. Used as immunotherapy in superficial & in situ transitional cell carcinoma of the bladder
D. Used as immunotherapy for melanoma
E. Both c & d

Key: E
Ref: Rooks (27.12)

Chapter 28

LEPROSY

1. A soldier 29 year returned from UN mission presents to OPD with hundreds of confluent lesions over trunk and dorsal lower limbs, having vague edges and distributed in symmetrical pattern. The lesion may elicit:

A. Early onset autonomic loss
B. Paucibacillary lesions
C. Mucosal and systemic involvement in type 2 reaction
D. Marked early nerve involvement in few nerves
E. Type 1 reaction is common

Key: C
Ref: Rook (table 28.1, page 28.7)

2. A 25 year old male presented with fever and ulcerated nodules on limbs and trunk, further examination reveals large brown polygonal scales on the limbs and pedal edema was also positive. This type of reaction occurs in:

A. Borderline tuberculoid
B. histoid leprosy
C. Lepromatous Leprosy
D. mid borderline leprosy
E. tuberculoid leprosy

Key: C
Ref: Rook (28.12)

3. A 30 year old male who took MDT for 06 months for borderline lepromatous leprosy, now presented with fever and painful nodules on face and limbs. What is the treatment of choice in this patient?

A. Clofazimine
B. High dose steroids
C. Hydroxychloroquine
D. NSAIDS
E. Thalidomide

Key: E
Ref: Rook (28.16)

4. Incubation period of lepromatous leprosy is:

A. 2 to 5 years
B. 5 to 7 years
C. 8 to 12 years
D. 20 to 30 years
E. 2 to 5 months

Key: C
Ref: Rook (28.7)

5. The most suitable nerve for biopsy in a leprosy patient is:

A. Any nerve distal to the lesion
B. Thickened peripheral nerve
C. Nerves in the colder reigion of affected individual
D. Superficial Cutaneous nerve

E. Any nerve proximal to the lesion

Key: B
Ref: Rook (28.14)

6. 56 year old male presents with an erythematous copper coloured, purple raised plaque with clear cut edges slopping towards a flat hypopigmented centre on the arm. Running a finger around the plaque a thick nerve was palpated .What is the finding on H/p

A. Cutaneous nerves contain epitheloid cell granulomas surrounded by zone of lymphocytes.
B. Thinning of epidermis and flattening of rete ridges. foamy macrophages in derp dermis
C. no AFB detected
D. both A and C
E. Large number of AFB in dermis in clumps

Key: D
Ref: Rook (28.7)

7. A 9-year-old boy was referred to a hospital with a fever, cough and sore throat for 5 days. On the first day of illness, he had been taken to a rural clinic and diagnosed with pharyngitis. The patient was prescribed an unknown oral antibiotic and acetaminophen. By the third day of illness his fever had gradually declined however, he subsequently became worse and experienced neck swelling, dyspnoea and dysphagia. On examination of throat there were ulcers with tough grey adherent membrane over tonsils and phayrnx edge was rolled and raised. upon dislodging the membrane bleeding started.
What is the definite treatment for this patient?

A. systemic steroids
B. clindamycin oral 300mg twice daily
C. C)iv clindamycin plus benzyl pencillin
D. D)specific antitoxin 20000-50000 units im along with erythromycin
E. E) erythromycin or penicillin

Key: D
Ref: Rook (26.38)

8. 12 year old boy from Afghanistan presented with epistaxis and leg odema. on examination multiple confluent faint hypopigmented macules sparing midline on his back. On oral exam there was a nodule on the palate. What is the feature of this disease?

A. Lagophthalmos
B. nail dystrophy due to dermatophyte
C. C)both A and B
D. severe nerve damage
E. spared mucosa

Key: C
Ref: Rook (28.10)

9. A 50 year old afebrile lady presented with erythemayous nodules and odematous plaques on the face with scaling. Some had ulcerated. Hx of many small new lesions appearing on the face. Patient complained of foot drop. Diagnosis.

A. Borderline Tuberculoid
B. Lepromatous leprosy
C. Tuberculoid leprosy
D. Both A and B
E. Intermediate leprosy

Key: A
Ref: Rook (28.12)

10. 32 year old male previously disgnosed with lepromatous leprosy presented to the the opd with painful red nodules on face limb extensors. Some were ulcerated with induration. Hx of fever and malaise. On fundoscopy features confirming to b/l uveitis and cataract in left eye. What is the complications?

A. Type 1 ENL
B. Type 2 ENL
C. Type 3 ENL
D. Type 1 earlier followed by Type 2
E. Onchocerciasis

Key: B
Ref: Rook (28.12)

11. A 60 year old man from afghanistan presents with raised erythematous purple plaques with a flat hypopigmented centre on his face. The man complains of a dry skin and loss of hair on his body .He reports numbness and tingling in on the left side of his face as well .Features of this disease include.

A. No detectable M leprae
B. Numerous M.leprae
C. The lesion distribution is symmetrical
D. A and C
E. Axilla groins are spared.

Key: A
Ref: Rook (28.7)

12. A 30 year old diagnosed case of lepromatous leprosy presents with severely ulcerated plaques, bullae, desquammation, and widespread erythema. The offending organism most likely is

A. M.Canus
B. M. Tuberculosis
C. M.Lepromatosis
D. M.bovis
E. M.kansai

Key: C
Ref: Rook (28.12)

13. A patient presented with fever, malaise and arthralgia. On examination, he has tender nodules on fave and extensors of limbs, and lymphadenopathy.
He is on a regular medicine for some infection.
Which of the following is his primary disease for which he is taking medication?

A. Tuberculoid leprosy
B. borderline
C. BT
D. BL
E. lepromatous leprosy

Key: E

14. All of the following are true regarding clofazimne except??

A. It is weakly bactericidal
B. It has anti-inflammatory properties
C. It is also used for treatment of ENL
D. One of its side effects is irreversible skin pigmentation
E. GIT side effects occur because of clofazimne crystal deposition in wall of small bowel.

Key: D

15. A 25 yr old female patient presented in opd. she complaints that she has a few reddish patches on her face and body which she noticed just because change of colour... otherwise there is no pain or itching.
On exam...you feel 2 erythematous well defined dry plaques on her face with mild scaling. One same plaque was seen on abdomen. Sensory impairment was difficult to comment on facial plaques, but obvious on abdominal plaque.
What would be the most probable treatment according to diagnosis??

A. Rifampicin 600mg per month and Dapsone 50mg once daily for 6 months.
B. Rifampicin 600 mg per month and dapsone 100 mg OD. for 6 months
C. Rifampicin 600 mg per month and dapsone 100 mg plus clofazimne 50mg OD. for 6 months
D. Rifampicin 600mg per month and dapsone 100 mg OD. for 1 year
E. Rifampicin 600mg per month plus clofazimne 300mg per month and dapsone 50mg. for 6 months.
F.

Key: B

16. A 50 yr old patient presented to you in ER with c/o fever, vomiting and generalized body rash on examination there is lymphadenopathy, and labs show leukocytosis, eosinophilia and deranged LFTs.
Which statement is not true?

A. Dapsone is stopped and systemic corticosteroids started
B. Dapsone can be introduced again with caution,once condition stabilises.
C. Occurs usually in first month of start of medicine.
D. It is an idiosyncratic side effect of dapsone.
E. Fatality rate is 50 percent

Key: E

17. Which of the following statement is true regarding leprosy treatment?

A. New guidelines recommend a 3-drug regimen of Rifampicin + clofazimne + dapsone for all leprosy pts. given for 6mon in PB and 112 months in MB leprosy.
B. Monthly dose is taken at the start of treatment and then every 30 days.
C. If treatment is stopped or missed,it must b completed within 9 months for PB leprosy
D. In case of MB, if treatment is stopped or missed, it must b completed within 18.
E. Thalidomide is used for treatment of ENL,that decrease TNF alpha levels

Key: B

18. A 35 years old female came with complain of skin lesions at trunk and back since 2 years. On ex there were multiple large erythematus annulare punched out plaques at back and trunk with no sensation over it, surrounding nerve was also enlarged. Fungal scraping was negative. No surounding lymphadenopathy.
Keeping diagnosis in mind what are histopathological findings in this case.

A. Multiple foci of globi surrounding neurovascular bundle with no AFB
B. Thin epidermis, grenz zone, diffuse leproma with foamy macrophages
C. Histocytic and lymphocytic infiltration surrounding appendages
D. Multiple epitheloid granuloma, foreign body giant cell, clear papillary zone with moderate AFB
E. Palisading of histiocytes around a focus of necrobiosis and increased mucin deposition. The intervening dermis appears normal. Multinucleated giant cells are frequently seen.

Key: D

19. What is the significance of PGL 1 antibody serology in diagnosis of leprosy?

A. Can be comparable with bacterial load in skin biopsy
B. Can be comparable with thickness of nerve
C. Can be comparable with bacterial load of skin split smear
D. Correlate with anesthesia of skin lesions

E. Correlate with number of globi in nerve biopsy

Key: C
Ref: Rook (28.14)

20. A 35 years old female came with complain of skin lesions at trunk and back since 2 years. On ex there were multiple large erythematus annulare plaques at back and trunk with no sensation over it, surrounding nerve was also enlarged. Fungal scraping was negative. No suurounding lymphadenopathy.
Keeping diagnosis in mind how many cardinal signs should be present to diagnose it clinically

A. 3/4
B. 4/4
C. 2/3
D. 1/3
E. 3/3

Key: C
Ref: Rook (28.14)

21. A 50 years old male came with complain of discharge from nose and skin lesion since 5 years. On ex there were diffuse thickning of ear lobes with multiple skin colored nodules at both arms and buttock. He started some medicine after 1 month he got developed fever, malaise, swollen joints with some erythmatous and ulcerated nodules. Keeping diagnosis in mind what are characteristic histopathological findings

A. multiple foci of globi surrounding neurovascular bundle with no AFB
B. multiple epitheloid granuloma, foreign body giant cells, clear papillary zone with moderate AFB
C. Histocytic and lymphocytic infiltration surrounding appendages
D. thin epidermis, grenz zone, multiple diffuse epitheloid granuloma with polymorphs infiltration, vasculitis, degenerated macrophages and foam cells
E. Palisading of histiocytes around a focus of necrobiosis and imucin deposition.The Multinucleated giant cells in dermis

Key: D
Ref: Rook (28.5)

22. A 45 years diabetic male came with complain of difficulty in walking since 1 year. He had history of difficulty in doing his daily routine work by right hand due to pain at elbow. On examination no skin lesions were found except signs of healing ulcers at left forefoot. His right ulnar nerve and left common peroneal nerve was thickened and tender. Keeping diagnosis in mind what will be investigation of choice in this case.

A. skin biopsy from healing margin
B. slit skin smear
C. PGL serology
D. Nerve biopsy
E. clinical diagnosis with HbA1C

Key: D
Ref: Rook (28.11)

Chapter 29 SYPHILIS AND CONGENITAL SYPHILIS

1. A 35–year–old black male known to have asymptomatic HIV seropositivity for 2 years without any specific treatment, complained of 3 months of moderate occipital headache. He presented with worsened headache, blurry vision, visual scotomas and mild left hemiparesis. On examination he was afebrile and had a generalized lymphadenopathy, oral thrush and perianal warts suggestive of condyloma. His neck was stiff. On eye examination there was evidence of posterior uveitis in the right eye, and the left eye was normal. Neurological examination revealed normal mental status, and lower extremity motor, reflex and sensory function. He had a left facial palsy and right upper extremity weakness .complete blood count and urinalysis is normal. VDRL test was reactive.
Examination of the CSF revealed 120WBC/mm3 with 90% of lymphomononuclear cells), an elevated protein level. Keeping in mind the diagnosis, what is the best management for this patient?

A. Procaine penicillin 2g IM daily plus probenecid 500 mg orally four times daily for 17 days
B. Ceftiaxone 500 mg IV daily for 10 days
C. Procaine penicillin 1g IV daily plus probenecid 500 mg orally 5 days for 17 days .
D. Amoxicillin 1 g orally twice a day for 15 days.

Key: A
Ref: Rooks (29.25)

2. A 42 year old man presented with headache, nausea, and arthralgias. The patient had exclusively had sex with men and had been in a monogamous relationship during the past 6 months. Physical examination revealed grey, round or oval mucous patches on the palate and coppery red round oval spots over glans penis and nonpruritic hyperkeratotic maculopapular palmar rash and bilateral submandibular lymphadenopathy.
No alopecia, gummas, neurologic deficits or ocular or cardiovascular abnormalities were noted. Given the clinical presentation and laboratory findings results, secondary syphilis was considered the most probable diagnosis. Best treatment given to this patient is

A. Benzyl penicillin 20 units daily every 6 hour for 20 days
B. benzathine penicillin G 2.4 mega units IM single dose or x 2 (day 1 and 8)
C. benzathine penicillin G 4 mega units IM single dose or x 2 (day 1 and 15)
D. None of the above.

Key: B
Ref: Rooks (29.25)

3. A 28 year-old, (HIV)-negative male , presented with painless ulcer on the glans penis from last few days. reported 3 sex partners in the past 2 months. On examination, there is hard and button like painlesa ulcer with regular edge and base and narrow red border. Right side inguinal lymph nodes are enlarged. They are discrete, rubbery and mobile. He was treated with benzathine penicillin G 2.4 mega units IM single dose. Follow up for clinical and serological assessment should be done at?

A. 4 and 6 months
B. B. 2 , 4 and 12 months
C. 3 , 6 and 12 months
D. After 12 months

Key: C
Ref: Rooks (29.26)

4. A 50 year old man presented with reduced concentration and attention, memory loss, and behavior changes such as apathy, anxiety, and agitation within the last 2 years.
Impaired auditory acuity was found, more pronounced in the left ear. The patient also reported bilateral paraesthesia in the distal parts of the extremities. Laboratory workups including a complete blood count and differential, serum electrolytes and glucose, liver and renal function tests, thyroid function tests, serum B12 and folate levels, and an ECG were normal.The serum and CSF test for human immunodeficiency virus (HIV) was negative. The diagnosis of neurosyphilis was made on the basis of csf examination and vdrl. He was treated with penicillin G and probenecid. Regarding follow up which one is correct?

A. repeat csf examination every 12 months until cell count become normal
B. b. repeat csf examination every 6 months until cell count become normal
C. repeat csf examination every 2 months
D. None of the above.

Key: B
Ref: Rooks (29.27)

5. A 45 year old man presented with headache, nausea, and arthralgias. The patient had exclusively had sex with men and had been in a monogamous relationship during the past 6 months. Physical examination revealed grey, round or oval mucous patches on the palate and coppery red round oval spots over glans penis and nonpruritic hyperkeratotic maculopapular palmar rash and bilateral submandibular lymphadenopathy.
No alopecia, gummas, neurologic deficits or ocular or cardiovascular abnormalities were noted. Given the clinical presentation and laboratory findings results, secondary syphilis was considered the most probable diagnosis. Regarding management of sexual contacts, which statement is true?

A. contacts occurring within 2 months plus duration of symptoms for sec. Syphilis
B. contacts occurring within 1 month plus duration of symptoms for sec. Syphilis
C. No need of treatment
D. contacts occurring within 6 months plus duration of symptoms for sec. Syphilis

Key: D
Ref: Rooks (29.27)

6. 30 years old pregnant female was diagnosed with secondary syphilis 3 years back. She didn't get any treatment because her lesions were resolved.. Which of the following statement is true in the above circumstances

A. The patient is infectious to sexual partners
B. Syphilis infection can pass from pregnant woman to her fetus
C. The patient has no chance of getting tertiary syphilis
D. Patient is in early latent phase of Syphilis
E. All of the above

Key: B
Ref: Rooks (29.13)

7. A 60 years old diabetic female complains of parasthesias of both legs with progressive ataxia and bowel and bladder dysfunction. On examination she had charcot joints of knees and hips. A single perforating ulcer was present on right foot. What is the most common form of Neurosyphilis present in the pre antibiotic era

A. Asymptomatic Neurosyphilis
B. Meningeal Neurosyphilis
C. Meningeavascular Neurosyphilis
D. Tabetic Neurosyphilis
E. Gummatous Neurosyphilis

Key: D

Ref: Rooks (29.19)

8. In older infants and children the recommended regimen is
   A. Aqueous penicillin G 0.2 -0.3 mega /units/Kg
   B. Aqueous penicillin G 0.8 -0 10 mega /units/Kg
   C. Aqueous penicillin G 0.5 -0.6 mega/units/Kg
   D. Procaine penicillin G 50,000units/Kg
   E. Procaine penicillin G 10,000units/Kg

Key: A
Ref: Rooks (29.34)

9. Transmission of Treponema Pallidium from mother to fetus can occur during any stage but the risk is higher in women with
   A. Primary stage
   B. Secondary Stage
   C. Both a and b are correct
   D. Tertiary stage
   E. All if above

Key: C
Ref: Rooks (29.27)

10. A 50 years old man presented with well defined solitary painless plaque with central necrosis and ulceratin. Peripheral healing and tissue paper scarring is also seen. On examination of oral cavity there is loss of uvula and scarring perforation of hard palate. Saddle nose deformity is also seen. What is the most likely diagnosis
   A. Primary Syphilis
   B. Secondary Syphilis
   C. Early Latent syphilis
   D. Late Latent Syphilis
   E. Tertiary Syphilis

Key: E
Ref: Rooks (29.16)

11. Congenital syphilitic facies with saddle nose deformity and frontal bossing of late congenital syphilis results from early nasopharyngeal and impaired development of
   A. Maxilla
   B. mandible
   C. zygomatic arch
   D. Temporal bone
   E. ALL are incorrect

Key A
Ref: Rooks (29.29)

12. Wimberger's sign is present in congenital syphilis, it is characterized by:
   A. Thickening of medical part of clavicle
   B. Short maxilla and protubersnt mandible
   C. paresis and paralysis
   D. Scaphoid scapula
   E. Destruction of proximal metaphasis of tibia

Key: E

13. An infant has abnormal physical examination that is consistent with congenital syphilis, fourfold increase in serological tests and positive dark field test, should be treated with

A. Aqueous crystalline penicillin G and procaine penicillin
B. Ceftriaxone
C. CSF should be examined
D. Both A and B are correct
E. All above are correct.

Key: A
Ref: Rooks (29.34)

14. 45-year-old man is screened for syphilis and has a positive Treponema pallidum-specific enzyme-linked immunoassay (EIA). The laboratory performs a reflexive Rapid Plasmin Reagin (RPR) test that is nonreactive. Tests for HIV, Neisseria gonorrhoeae, and Chlamydia trachomatis are negative. He has no medical problems, takes no medications, and does not use illicit drugs. He has been sexually active with the same female partner for the past 3 years. He has no prior history of any sexually transmitted infections, and has never been tested or treated for syphilis. He is asymptomatic and the physical examination is normal. What is most appropriate next step in the management of this man?

A. Repeat both the EIA and the RPR
B. Send an alternative nontreponemal test
C. Send an alternative treponemal test
D. No further work-up at this time

Key: B

15. 25-year-old man presents for evaluation of new nontender penile lesion (Figure 1). He has no other symptoms. He has no medical problems, denies medications or illicit drugs and has no antibiotic allergies. He reports insertive-only anal intercourse with multiple male partners and rare condom use. Physical examination reveals a 1 cm, nontender ulcer on the dorsal surface of his penis and no other significant findings. Further testing reveals a positive syphilis enzyme immunoassay (EIA) and a positive Rapid Plasma Reagin (RPR) at a titer of 1:32. He has never been diagnosed with or treated for syphilis in the past. An HIV test returns negative.
What is the appropriate therapy for this man?

A. Amoxicillin 500 mg orally three times a day for 7 days
B. Azithromycin 2 grams orally once
C. Benzathine penicillin G 2.4 million units intramuscular in a single dose
D. Benzathine penicillin G 7.2 million units total, administered as 3 doses of 2.4 million units intramuscular each at 1-week intervals

Key: C

16. 31-year-old male presents to his primary care medical provider for evaluation of a rash. He denies taking any new medications, but reports three new male sexual partners in the last 8 weeks. The rash began several days prior as an erythematous, maculopapular rash on the chest and back (Figure 1) and now it also involves the palms (Figure 2) and soles. He does not have any ocular or neurologic symptoms. Serologic testing for syphilis is ordered.
What is the most appropriate treatment of this patient with presumed secondary syphilis?

A. Azithromycin 2 grams orally once
B. Doxycycline 100 mg orally twice daily x 28 days
C. Benzathine penicillin G 2.4 million units intramuscular in a single dose
D. Benzathine penicillin G 7.2 million units total, administered as 3 doses of 2.4 million units given at 1-week intervals

Key: C

17. Which of the following tests is a specific test for infection with Treponema pallidum?
    A. RPR
    B. VDRL
    C. FTA-ABS
    D. CBC
    E. Darkfield microscopy

Key: C

18. Confirmatory test in primary syphilis is Dark field.
Most specific test in primary and secondary is FTA -ABS
Most specific INITIAL test in secondary ELISA
Which test is the first to become reactive in syphilis?
    A. RPR
    B. FTA-ABS
    C. VDRL
    D. ELISA
    E. Lumbar puncture

Ans: D

Chapter 30 OTHER SEXUALLY TRANSMITTED BACTERIAL DISEASES

1. 35 year old male, presents with genital ulceration. He has multiple Hypertrophic penile ulcers, they are painless but bleed on touching. There is no lymphadenopathy. All the following are its complications except

   A. SCC
   B. Spinal cord compression
   C. Dissemination to abdominal viscera
   D. Peri nephric abscess
   E. Hepatic abscess

Key: E
Ref: Rook (30.25)

2. For the above scenario, the treatment of choice is

   A. Azithromycin 1gm orally on first day followed by 500mg daily for minimum 6 wks or until lesions heal
   B. Doxycycline 100 mg orally on first day followed by 100 mg twice daily till it heals
   C. Co-trimoxazole 960 mg daily till lesion heals
   D. Ciprofloxacin 500 mg twice daily for 6 wks.
   E. Azithromycin 1 GM single dose

Key: A

3. 56 years old male patient, presents with 2 months history of eruption of pruritic erythematous papules and pustules on face and trunk. They were perifollicular.
Swabs were negative and lesions were sterile. Labs showed peripheral eosinophilia and raised Ig E levels.
He also has significant weight loss in the last 6 months.
What is the diagnosis?

   A. Pruritic popular eruption of HIV
   B. Eosinophilic folliculitis in HIV
   C. Seborrheic dermatitis's in HIV
   D. Atopic dermatitis in HIV
   E. Folliculitis in HIV

Key: B

4. A 40 yr. old male, known case of Psoriasis, on 10 mg MTX per wk. He now complains of significant weight loss, generalized itching, diarrhea. Regarding the development of his new illness which statement is false?

   A. Methotrexate can cause severe complications
   B. Cyclosporine can cause severe complications
   C. Acitretin can be used successfully
   D. Phototherapy can be used successfully
   E. Cyclosporine in combination with other drugs gives good disease control

Key: E

5. A 47 yr. old male, truck driver by profession, presents with history of fatigue and weight loss for 6 months. He also has off and on fever, generalized pruritus, dry skin & diarrhea. All the following are true regarding course and prognosis of his disease except

A. The median time from seroconversion to full blown syndrome is approximately 10 years in absence of treatment
B. CD 4 count less than 200 x 10*6 /l is diagnosis of AIDS
C. CD 4 count decreases by 100 x 10*6 /l annually
D. 20 to 100 x 10*6 /l is the CD 4 count for AIDS defining illness
E. Time from HIV seroconversion to AIDS is 7 years in transfusion recipients, 10 years for IV drug users and 10 to 12 years for homosexual men

Key: C

6. A sexually active male presented with history of painful papule at the sight of inoculation which progress to form pustule and then non indurated ulcer. On examination there were multiple kissing ulcers on opposing skin and lymph nodes were enlarged. What is diagnosis?
A. Granuloma inguinal
B. Lymphogranuloma venereal
C. Cancroid
D. Chlamydia
E. Gonorrhea

Key: C
Ref: Rook (30.21)

7. A young female presented with painful ulcer on vulva it started as papule and underwent central necrosis to evolve into an ulcer with undermined edges on microscopic examination there was shoal of fish pattern.. What is the first line treatment option for this patient?
A. Ciprofloxacin
B. Erythromycin
C. Ceftriaxone
D. Azithromycin
E. Both C and D

Key: E
Ref: Rook (30.23)

8. A young sexually active male presented with history of painful defecation bloody discharge and tenesmus for last one month. On examination there was an ulcer on penile sulcus and bilateral lymph nodes were enlarged. What is the treatment option?
A. Erythromycin
B. Clindamycin
C. Azithromycin
D. Doxycycline
E. Co- trimoxazole

Key: D
Ref: Rook (30.20)

Chapter 31 HIV AND THE SKIN

1. A known case of HIV/AIDS patient presented with multiple flesh coloured papules on face and neck with central umbilication. What is the Diagnosis?

   A. Molluscum contagiosum
   B. Sebaceous hyperplasia
   C. Syringoma
   D. Cryptococcosis
   E. Histoplasmosis

Key: A
Ref: Rooks (31.25)

2. A young man with history of fever, weight loss and chronic diarrhoea presents to skin opd with generalized herpes zoster.O/E no evidence of malignancy. What is the most likely diagnosis?

   A. CMV Diarrhoe
   B. Cryptosporodiosis
   C. HIV Seroconversion
   D. Histoplasmosis
   E. Lymphoma.

Key: C
Ref: Rooks (31.23)

3. A HIV positive patient presented with rapidly growing purple papules on face and trunk of 5 days duration. Papules are large in number, rounded in configuration and bleed easily on minor trauma. The best diagnosis would be?

   A. Pyogenic granuloma
   B. Bacillary angiomatosis
   C. molluscum contagiosum
   D. Sebaceous hyperplasia
   E. Cambell de morgan spot

Key: B
Ref: Rooks (31.21)

4. A patient with AIDS developed umblicated papules consistent with molluscum contagiosum. What anatomical sites are favoured for molluscum papules in HIV?

   A. Head
   B. Abdomen and back
   C. Face and neck
   D. Upper and lower extremities
   E. Chest and Shoulder

Key: C
Ref: Rooks (31.25)

5. A 34 year old homosexual male presented with wide spread papulonodular necrotising skin lesions with central umblication. On examination he also exhibited signs of meningism. Direct microscopy of CSF with India ink stain was positive with large budding cells. The most probable diagnosis is

   A. Cryptococcosis
   B. Histoplasmosis

C. Penicilliosis
D. Molluscum contagiosum
E. Systemic canidiosis

Key: A
Ref: Rooks (31.27)

6. A 38 year old HIV positive male presented with progressively increasing plaques and nodules on his lower legs and feet. A biopsy of one of the lesion showed vascular expansions lined with single layered plump endothelial cells. Which virus is associated with this presentation?
A. Cytomegalovirus
B. Human herpes virus 8
C. Human herpes virus 6
D. Epstein Barr virus
E. HPV virus

Key: B
Ref: Rooks (31.29 and 139.1)

7. A 40 year old HIV positive male developed an asymptomatic whitish patch along the lateral margin of his tongue. On examination it appeared rough looking. He had been using anti-fungal medication for last one month with no improvement. Biopsy of the lesion was done which revealed hyperkeratosis, ballooning of prickle cells and presence of EBV DNA. What percentage of these patients will progress to AIDS in next 2 to 3 years?
A. 20%
B. 5%
C. 75%
D. 50%
E. 90%

Key: C
Ref: Rooks (31.33)

8. A 45 year old HIV Positive Male presented with an irregular scaly plaque on his trunk. On examination the central zone was atrophic and scaly and bounded peripherally by slightly raised thread like margin. It had not improved with topical steroid application of last few weeks which was prescribed by his GP. Biopsy of lesion was done which showed pallisading basal cells and foci of atypical basaloid cells. A diagnosis of basal cell carcinoma was made. The most common type of BCC in HIV patients is
A. Nodular BCC
B. Infiltrative BCC
C. Superficial BCC
D. Morpheic BCC
E. Ulcerated BCC

Key: C
Ref: Rooks (31.30)

9. A 35 year old female was stated on combination antiretroviral therapy after being diagnosed with AIDS. On one of her follow up visits her physician noticed that her eyelashes and thickened and increased in length considerably and was causing discomfort to the patient. Which drug is most probably the cause of her eyelash trichomegaly?
A. Zidovudine
B. Indinavir
C. Didanosine
D. Saquinavir

E. Lamivudine

Key: A
Ref: Rooks (31.33)

10. A patient with AIDS developed umblicated papules consistent with molluscum contagiosum. What anatomical sites are favoured for molluscum papules in HIV?

A. Head
B. Abdomen and back
C. Face and neck
D. Upper and lower extremities
E. Chest and Shoulder

Key: C

Chapter 32

FUNGAL INFECTIONS

1. A farmer developed warty papule on left foot few months ago which slowly increases in size to become a thick hyperkeratotic non-indurated plaque of size 5×3 cm. No history of contact with T.B and travel. Histopathology showed pseudoepitheliomatous hyperplasia with granulomatous infiltrate and muriform bodies. What is the most likely diagnosis?
   A. Cutaneous Leishmaniasis
   B. Blastomycosis
   C. Chromoblastomycosis
   D. Verrucous Syphilis
   E. Mycetoma

KEY C
Ref: Rook (32.76)

2. For a biopsy proven diagnosed case of localized Cutaneous Sporotrichosis. What will be the most appropriate second line treatment option for it?
   A. Potassium Iodide
   B. Amphotericin B
   C. Itraconazole
   D. Terbinafine
   E. All of the above

KEY A
Ref: Rook (32.73)

3. On the basis of etiological agents of mycetoma species. Select the correct one
   A. Madurella grisea dark grain
   B. Fusarium red grain
   C. Actinomadura pale grain
   D. Both A and C
   E. All of the above

KEY A
Ref: Rook (32.74)

4. An AIDS patient presented with multiple papules over whole body with central depression associated with mild neck stiffness and headache for 2 days. On further evaluation there are few tender erythematous nodules on shins bilaterally. Pathology report revealed budding cells stained with mucicarmine. Which organism is responsible for this condition?
   A. Talaromyces marneffei
   B. Coccidioides immitis
   C. Histoplasmosis capsulatum
   D. Cryptococcosis neoformans
   E. Blastomyces dermatitidis

KEY D
Ref: Rook (32.92)

5. A 17 years male patient came in outpatient department having non-scaly patches on both palms for 10 days. No associated itching, lymphadenopathy and sexual history. What is the most likely diagnosis?
   A. Syphilis

B. Tinea nigra
C. P.versicolor
D. Atypical P.rosea
E. Arsenic poisoning

KEY B
Ref: Rook (32.15)

6. A 34 year old female patient a case of pemphigus vulgaris presented with patch of creamy crumbly membrane in her oral cavity which when removed left an erythematous base. likely diagnosis is

A. Denture stomatitis
B. Candidal stomatitis
C. Chronic pseudomembranous Candidosis
D. Candidal leukoplakia
E. Chronic plaque like candidosis

Key: B
Ref: Rook (32.62)

7. 30 year old male presented with transient tiny papules and pustules on the glans which ruptured to leave a peeling edge, few hours after intercourse. He complained of mild soreness and irritation likely diagnosis is

A. Hsv infection
B. Candida balanitis
C. Plasma cell balanitis
D. Syphilis
E. Erythroplasia

Key: B
Ref: Rook (32.65)

8. an infant presented with few nodules some as large as 2 cm on the buttocks. The nodules are brownish in colour and some have scaling over the lesions. what is the likely diagnosis?

A. Genital candidosis
B. Furunculosis
C. Granuloma gluteale infantum
D. Granulomas
E. Perineal candidosis of infancy

Key: C
Ref: Rook (32.65)

9. 30 years old unmarried male was presented to a pulmonologist for SOB chronic cough his HRCT shows ground glass accentuation cavitation and fibrosis, on further evaluation he complains of painful mouth ulcer and was now unable to eat because of gradual loss of teeth, you were asked to evaluate the patient on oral examination you notice multiple mouth ulcer swollen gums with overlying mucose ulceratrd giving appearance of mulberry like erosions hoe will you preceed fr diagnosis

A. Examining sample for KOH
B. Examining of sample by flourescenc antibody
C. Take nutritional hx as ulcers will be due to b12 deficiency
D. Examining sample of skin for microfilaria

Key: A
Ref: Rook (32.90)

10. A female obese lady presented with fringed irregular edge and subcorneal pustules in her groins. The pustules ruptured to leave tiny erosions. What is the likely diagnosis?

A. Subcorneal pustular dermatosis
B. Hailey hailey disease
C. Candidal intertrigo
D. Seborrhoeic dermatosis
E. Bacterial intertrigo

Key: C
Ref: Rook (32.64)

11. 32 years old male presented to opd with complain of multiple itchy lesion on the back and shoulder, according to him these lesion appear after attending a beach party last Saturday/e you found multiple papules and a few pustules scattered on shoulder and upper back, on examination of face he has comedonl acne, you treat him on line of bacterial folliculitis, after 5 days pt returns with no benefit, what could be the possible diagnosis

A. Acne vulgaris
B. Steroid induce acne
C. Malassezia folliculitus
D. Non-malassezia folliculitus
E. Pt is non compliebt to treatment

KEY C
Ref: Rook (32.13)

12. 20 years old met an accident and was in urgent requirement of blood transfusion, his friend has same blood group he was asked for blood screening for infectious disease before transfusion, his lab results was positive for HIV, before starting of HAART therapy he was asked to take opinion about his ulcer and multiple nodules on left leg, according to patient these nodules and ulcer are present fr 6 months and didn't get heal by treatment, o/e you find multiple erythema nodosum like swelling firm in consistency, and a ulcer about 2*2cm with oozing of purulent discharge, you take swab pus for culture ,culture shows cream to pale brown mucoid colony, microscopy shows yeast with no filaments what is not true about culture of suspected organism

A. incubation at 30degrer for 4 weeks
B. B. stain with indian ink
C. nigrosin mount can be used
D. should be inoculated on media with cycloheximide

key: D
Ref: Rook (32.93)

13. jack known case of AIDS on HAART landed in emergency with complain of ALIC since morning according to his siblings he develops fever headache for last 2 days then suddenly in night family notice GTC with urinary incontinence, o/e sign of meningeal irritation was positive, and there was acneiform papules and pustules on trunk and limbs esp around nose and mouth, CT Scan brain shows cerebral oedema you started pt on line of bacterial meningitis until csf dr awaits, on next morning csf report shows protein was raised glucose was low wbc 450cells per microliter on direct microscopy it shows budding cells.
what alteration should be done in treatment

A. amphotrcn B for 4 to 6 weeks, followed by fluconazole 400 mg od fr 4 weeks and continue HAART
B. Amphotrcn B for 4 to 6 weeks, followed by fluconazole 400 mg od fr 3weeks
C. immediatly discontinue HAART and add amphotrcn B for 4 to 6 weeks
D. no further changes are required

Key: A

Ref: Rook (32.93)

14. What common malignancy is associated with cryptococus neoformis
    - A. non hodgkin lymphoma
    - B. hodgkin lypmoma
    - C. ca lung
    - D. sarcoidosis

KEY B
Ref: Rook (32.92)

15. A 40-year-old male presented in Dermatology OPD with a lesion on right arm. Examination revealed a nontender plaque surrounded by keloidal scar tissue on his right upper arm. It was located at the site of a scar from a previous injury.
Skin biopsy with H&E stain showed lymphocyte, macrophages and giant cells that contain fungal cells. Fungal stains showed chains of 3-8 cells connected by short tubular structures.
Which of the following explains the above mentioned clinical condition?
    - A. Blastomycosis
    - B. Keloidal Blastomycosis
    - C. Keloidal Histoplasmosis
    - D. Rhinosporidosis
    - E. Phaeohyphomycosis

KEY: B
Ref: Rook Dermatology 32.79

15. A 4-year-old boy presented with a painless swelling on his left thigh for 1 year which was gradually increasing in size. Examination showed an indurated subcutaneous swelling on the left thigh. It was non-tender, hard in consistency with smooth and rounded edges and was freely mobile over the underlying structures. The swelling did not pit when pressure was applied. The overlying skin was hyperpigmented. Skin biopsy showed inflammatory infiltrate with fragments of aseptate hyphae.
Fungal stain showed few, broad, thin walled, and aseptate fungal hyphae.
Which of the following is the causative organism of the clinical condition?
    - A. Basidobolus Ranarum
    - B. Conidiobolus Coronatum
    - C. Cladophilalophora Bantiana
    - D. Histoplasmosis capsulatum
    - E. Phialophora Verrucosa

KEY: A
Ref: Rook Dermatology 32.80

16. A 45-year-old male presented with ulcerated polyps in the oral & nasal cavity for 1 year. They were gradually increasing in size and recently patient has been experiencing difficulty in breathing. Examination revealed pink-red coloured lobulated masses in the right nasal cavity and around the soft palate with cauli flower like appearance with few white specks on the surface.
Histopathology with methenamine silver stain showed the presence of endospores.
Which of the following is the causative organism for this clinical condition?
    - A. Conidiobolus Coronatus
    - B. Exophiala Dermatitidis
    - C. Fonsecaea Pedrosoi
    - D. Lacazia Loboi
    - E. Rhinosporidium Seeberi

KEY: E

Ref: Rook Dermatology 32.80

17. 36 year old male presented in Dermatology OPD with a slowly growing lesion on left arm. Examination revealed dusky-red, plaque measuring 2 cm surrounded by keloidal scar tissue on his left upper arm. It was non tender and was located at the site of a previous scar.
Skin biopsy with H&E stain revealed diffuse infiltrate containing fungal cells. Fungal stains showed short chains of 3-8 cells aligned by short tubular structures.
Which of the following is a complication of the disease if become chronic?
   A. Basal cell carcinoma
   B. Lymphatic stasis
   C. Squamous cell carcinoma
   D. Sepsis
   E. Underlying bone destruction

KEY: C
Ref: Rook Dermatology 32.79

18. A 40- year-old male presented with right sided nasal obstruction and a growth inside right nasal cavity for last 1 year. Since last 2 months he's been having recurrent episodes of epistaxis. Examination revealed a pink coloured pedunculated mass protruding from the right nasal cavity with lobulated surface. Closer examination showed small white spots on the surface. Examination of the left nasal cavity and oral cavity was unremarkable.
Keeping diagnosis in mind, which of the following statements is true?
   A. It is a contagious disease
   B. The disease resolves spontaneously
   C. The disease can be confirmed by culture growth
   D. Treatment of choice is Systemic antifungal
   E. Treatment of choice is surgical removal

Key: E
Ref: Rook 32.80

19. 16 year old girl has a repeated history of developing hyperpigmented confluent, mildly scaly lesions in seborrheic areas every summer. Wood's lamp examination shows yellow florescence and skin scraping microscopy shows characteristic spaghetti and meatballs appearance. Which of the following is the most appropriate treatment for her?
   A. Topical azoles twice weekly for 2–3 weeks
   B. Ketoconazole shampoo twice monthly for 2–3 weeks
   C. Itraconazole 200 mg daily for 5 days
   D. 2.5% selenium shampoo alternative days for 2–3 weeks
   E. Fluconazole 150mg once every week for 4 weeks

Key: C

20. 18 year old boy presents with sharply demarcated confluent macules, hyperpigmented to slightly erythematous characterized essentially by fine scaling primarily in the seborrheic area. In few of the lesion's scaling is not too obvious. Which of the following signs can be used to demonstrate the scaling?
   A. Samitz sign
   B. Besnier sign
   C. Thumb sign
   D. Rope sign
   E. Wimbergers sign

Key: B.

21. 25 year old pregnant lady living in Texas US sharp localized pain in chest with shortness of breath, cough and fever. She also had generalized aches, malaise and lassitude and a severe headache. During admission generalized, macular erythematous rash could also be appreciated. After many investigations and treatment, the clinicians are unable to formulate a diagnosis and are considering the possibility of an endemic fungal infection. What is the treatment of the most likely diagnosis?

A. Fluconazole 800 mg daily for 6–8 weeks
B. Intravenous amphotericin B (0.5–1 mg/kg daily)
C. Oral itraconazole (200–400 mg daily)
D. Voriconazole
E. Posiconazole

Key: C

22. 45 year old African gentleman presents with multiple rapidly spreading umbilicated papules on his legs and abdomen with few ulcers, he also has generalized lymphadenopathy. Recently his partner was reported to be HIV positive and he has been concerned about his exposure. Considering the most likely disease, which other organ system must be screened to rule out the focus of infection?

A. Lung
B. Bones
C. Abdomen
D. CNS
E. Paranasal Sinuses

Key: B

23. 35 year old is a nature enthusiasts and often likes to explore caves during vacations in USA. He develops cough with shortness of breath and sharp localized pain in lower left chest. Chest X-ray shows bilateral hilar lymphadenopathy with infiltration of right lower lobe. Few days later, he also develops tender erythematous nodules on bilateral shins. Considering the most likely diagnosis, what is the most appropriate specimen to confirm the diagnosis histopathologically?

A. Skin
B. Lymph node
C. Sputum
D. Spleen
E. Liver

Key: C

24. A 46 years old heroin abuser presented with complaints of fever associated with diffuse muscle tenderness and facial rash. The lesions started as macules which later become papular and nodular. You suspected systemic candidal infection. Which of the following provides rapid diagnosis?

A. Biopsy of skin lesion
B. KOH mount
C. Culture of the lesion
D. Blood culture
E. None of above

Key: A
Ref: Rook 32.94

25. Two weeks after a road traffic accident a 28 years old female known diabetic patient complained of a swollen tender right cheek The PAS biopsy demonstrated ring forms and distorted wide hyphae with few septations and right-angle branching. What is risk factor for this disease?

A. Diabetes
B. Neutropenia

C. Immunosuppresents
D. Trauma
E. All of the above

Key: E.

26. A 68 year old diabetic male patient who was recently diagnosed with pemphigus vulgaris and kept on prednisolone and azathioprine. With this treatment his erosions started to heal and no fresh lesions appeared but he presented two weeks later with a necrotic plaque on the right shoulder about 4×5 cm in size. Biopsy report showed broad aseptate hyphae. What is the causative organism for the above-mentioned case?

A. Rhizomucor
B. Lichtheimia
C. Cunninghamella
D. Saksenaea vasiformis
E. All of above

Key: E
Ref: Rook 32.94

27. A 61 years old man with a recent kidney transplant due to CRF and is currently on tacrolimus and prednisone was admitted with shortness of breath and purpuric plaques involving the face and trunk. A punch biopsy specimen was obtained, and the Histopathology showed broad aseptate hyphae and mixed cellular infiltrate. A diagnosis of mucormycosis was confirmed on tissue culture. What treatment should be initiated in this patient?

A. Echinocandin
B. Fluconazole
C. Liposomal amphotericin
D. Terbinafine
E. Voriconazole

Key: C
Ref: Rook 32.94

28. A 59 years old female a known case of pemphigus who was on prednisolone 80 mg daily. One week prior to her presentation she developed painful black eschar like lesion on right side of neck which was of 16 cm in diameter. Blood glucose test revealed a sugar level of 350 mg/ml. Biopsy from the eschar revealed hyphae. What is the diagnosis?

A. Cutaneous Anthrax
B. Necrotizing fasciitis
C. Mucormycosis
D. Echthyma gangrenosum
E. Atypical mycobacterial infection

Key: C
Ref: Rook 32.94

29. A young man presented with itchy which started from his feet and spread to involve whole body in 1month. On examination annular lesion with raised margin predominantly on in his trunk and Extremities were appreciated. He had been prescribed betamethasone cream but showed no improvement. His skin biopsy revealed fungal hyphae and cultures grew white downy cottony colonies. He was given antifungal targeted topical therapy and showed partial improvement. What second line treatment you can offer for his condition:

A. Oral terbinafine 250mg / day for 2 weeks
B. Itraconazole 100mg/day for 2 weeks
C. Oral fluconazole 150mg/day for 4 week

D. Griseofulvin 1g /dayfor 4 weeks
E. Topical azoles for 2 weeks

Key: D
Ref: Rook (32.37)

30. A young girl presented with itchy rash on face for 20 days. Her complaint of burning itching and exacerbation on sun exposure. On examination erythematous scaly indurated annular lesion was present on left cheek. She gave history of a pet mouse exposure. Considering the diagnosis skin scraping for cultures were sent and grew intensely granular surface colonies with creamy centre and spiky edges with reverse showing tan to brown color. What is likely organism?

A. T. Rubrum
B. T. Concentricum
C. T. Mentagrophytes
D. T. Tonsurans
E. M. Canis

Key: C
Ref: Rook (32.42)

31. 10 years old girl presented to dermatology opd with pruritic scaly plaque on left foot for 4 months which started as maceration between toe clefts. On examination she was healthy, with average height and weight of 18 kgs, there was large erythematous plaque with vesicles and pustules on left foot. She told that pustules rupture leaving collaretes of scaling with intervening normal skin. Now since last 15 days patient developed a vesicular itchy lesion on her hands. Skin scraping from her foot lesion showed fungal hyphae while they were negative for the hand lesion. Patient is concerned regarding for the lesion on hand. What treatment you will offer:

A. Emolients + topical steroids
B. Topical steroids alone
C. Oral terbinafine 125mg /day for 2 weeks
D. Oral terbinafine 250mg /day for 2 weeks
E. Griseofulvin 10mg /kg for 2 weeks

Key: C
Ref: Rook (32.45)

32. A 30years old female presented with scarring alopecia almost involving entire scalp and multiple yellow crusted lesions with depressed centres and raised edges over the vertex and occipital region. She revealed that these yellow crusting started 5 years back and led to hairless. Her nails and mucus membranes examination was normal. Skin biopsy of crusted lesion revealed numerous fungal hyphae. What first line treatment would you like to offer?

A. Itraconazole 2-4 mg/kg/d for 2 weeks
B. Terbinafine 250mg daily for 4 weeks
C. Griesofulvin 10mg /kg for 2 weeks
D. Ketoconazole for 2weeks
E. Itraconazole 5mg/kg in weekly pulses for 2 rounds

Key: B
Ref: Rook (32.40)

33. 55 years old man with history of HIV presented with patchy baldness. He complained that his hairs were fragile and broke off easily. On examination fragile hair with formation of black dots in affected area were appreciated. Also his nails examination revealed discoloured nails with subungal debris. Woods lamp examination of scalp showed no florescence. Hair microscopy revealed interpilary hyphae contained within the hair shaft. Considering the diagnosis most likely organism is:

A. T.Schoenleinii
B. B. M. Audouinii
C. M. Canis

D. T. Tonsurans
E. M. Fulvus

Key: D
Ref: Rook (32.39)

34. A 36-year-old male presented in our skin outdoor for the evaluation of asymptomatic palpable nodules along the beard and moustache since 3 months. On clinical examination, beard and moustache hairs were normal looking without evidence of sparseness. However, individual hair showed barely visible but well-palpable soft, whitish to cream-colored, easily detachable nodules of size 1–1.5 mm present over the shaft of almost all the hairs, distributed at irregular intervals and easily detachable.
For confirming the diagnosis incubation should be kept at which temperature?
A. 37°C
B. 28–30°C
C. -1 °C
D. >40 °C
E. None of the above

Key: B
Ref: Rook (32.17)

35. A 36-year-old male presented with a nine-year history of slowly enlarging asymptomatic hyperpigmented macules on both palms and soles. Examination revealed multiple blackish, small, oval macules on palms and soles, which were non-scaly located almost symmetrically. Examination of scrapings by 10% potassium hydroxide (KOH) mount showed dematicious, short, septate, and branched hyphae with scattered budding cells. The scales were inoculated on Sabouraudís dextrose agar medium in duplicate. On 20th day of culture, moist, yeast-like colonies were seen which were initially grey but with age, the colonies produced abundant aerial hyphae and turned olive to greenish black in color. Microscopically, there were brown septate mycelia with annello-conidia.
These features are characteristics of which of the following organism?
A. M. globosa
B. Candida albicans
C. Fusarium spp
D. Hortaea werneckii
E. Epidermophyton floccosum

Key: D
Ref: Rook (32.15)

36. A three years old child, presented with black nodules attached to the hair of her scalp for fifteen days. The mother stated that they did not cause itching and were easily seen when the hair was wet. The patient had been previously treated for lice at another medical service, but without any improvement of her condition. Clinical examination revealed woolly hair of medium length with signs of good hygiene, with firmly adherent, black, gritty, hard nodules surrounding the hair sheath.
How will you treat this patient?
A. Shaving or cutting the hair
B. Topical permethrin 1%
C. Topical permethrin 5 %
D. Ivermectin 200 ug/kg
E. Benzoic acid ointment

Key: A
Ref: Rook (32.16)

37. A 62-year-old male patient presented with a two-year history of slowly enlarging, otherwise asymptomatic, superficial black spots on the palms of both hands, light brown with sharp borders, near the wrist of the right hand and a more intense black spot on the centre of the palm of the left hand. The patient also reported excessive hand sweating. There was no family history of a similar condition.
Considering the diagnosis what should be the first line treatment?

A. Benzoic acid compound ointment
B. Topical butenafine
C. Oral fluconazole
D. Topical econazole
E. Topical terbinafine

Key: D
Ref: Rook (32.15)

38. A 36-year-old male presented in our skin outdoor for the evaluation of asymptomatic palpable nodules along the beard and moustache since 3 months. On clinical examination, beard and moustache hairs were normal looking without evidence of sparseness. However, individual hair showed barely visible but well-palpable soft, whitish to cream-colored, easily detachable nodules of size 1–1.5 mm present over the shaft of almost all the hairs, distributed at irregular intervals and easily detachable.
Considering the diagnosis what you will find on culture?

A. Rapidly growing colonies which are soft, creamy and wrinkled, and sometimes mucoid
B. Slow growing colonies which are compact, domed and black
C. Slow growing which initially yield a dirty white to grey, moist, yeast-like colony over the course of several days becomes more filamentous and velvetier.
D. Rapidly growing colony which initially has a white or cream surface, which becomes black as the conidia are produced
E. Colony will grow fast if we use cycloheximide in culture

Key: A
Ref: Rook (32.17)

39. A 47-year-old Timberman presented with a 9-week history of a progressive ulcer with associated nodules of his right shin. He had been systemically well with no fevers.
On examination, there was a lesion of the right shin with central ulceration. Several satellite lesions were near the area of ulceration but there was no sporotrichoid spread. Empirical antibiotic treatment was given for 2 weeks with some improvement. Result of the culture showed slow growing leathery white colony and on microscopy there were septate hyphae with perpendicular conidiophores. Growth on brain heart infusion agar incubated at 37 °C yielded cigar shaped bodies. What will be the best treatment option in this case?

A. Continue antibiotic treatment
B. Itraconazole 100-200mg/day until clinical recovery
C. Cotrimoxazole plus streptomycin until clinical recovery
D. Terbinafine 250mg /day for at least 3 weeks

Key: B
Ref: Rook (32.73)

40. Regarding treatment of chromoblastomycosis all of the following are true except:

A. Itraconazole or terbinafine is the first line treatment
B. Flucytosine alone is less effective than the combination with amphotericin B
C. Surgery is only indicated for large exophytic lesions
D. Surgery when indicated should be combined with chemotherapy

Key: C
Ref: Rook (32.78)

41. A 37 year old farmer presented with large hypertrophic plaque on left leg with warty surface and central scarring slowly increasing in size over the last 2 years and was painless. Biopsy report of the lesion showed Pseudoepitheliomatous hyperplasia in epidermis and granulomatous reaction in dermis. Within the giant cells brown colored thick walled cells with transverse septa were seen. Which of the following is not a complication of this disease?

A. Secondary infection
B. Elephantiasis
C. BCC
D. SCC

Key: C
Ref: Rook (32.77)

42. A 37 year old farmer presented with large hypertrophic plaque on left leg with warty surface and central scarring slowly increasing in size over the last 2 years and was painless. Biopsy report of the lesion showed Pseudoepitheliomatous hyperplasia in epidermis and granulomatous reaction in dermis. Within the giant cells brown-colored thick-walled cells with transverse septa were seen. What is the diagnosis?

A. Blastomycosis
B. Leishmaniasis
C. Tuberculosis verricosa cutis
D. Chromoblastomycosis

Key: D
Ref: Rook (32.76)

Chapter 33

PARASITIC DISEASES

1. A 32 year old male presented with deeply invading ulcer on the buttocks as sloughing coalescing ulcer since 1 month. The ulcers are painful, he had a history of bloody diarrhoea since 2 weeks. What is the prognosis of this disease?
   A. It is easily resolved in next 2 weeks
   B. No need for further treatment at this stage
   C. Early treatment is diagnostic and important as it's a serious diseases if neglected
   D. Will resolve with ordinary treatment in 1 week time
   E. Continue treatment as it's transmitted via contact

Key. C
Ref: Rook (33.35)

2. A patient presented with multiple subcutaneous nodules in the skin, muscle and eye lids' ray shows multiple calcificed cysts in the thighs and pelvis. What would the treatment of choice be if cerebral disease is suspected?
   A. praziquantel 50mg/kg for 10 days aftwr steroids
   B. albendazole 15mg/kg/day for 7 days
   C. metronidazole 500mg bd for 7 days
   D. tinidazole 2g single dose
   E. diethylcarbamazine 4mg/kg/day for 21 days

.Key is A
Ref: Rook (33.31)

3. What is true regarding treatment of enterobiasis?
   A. Albendazole is effective in all stages
   B. pyrantal pamoate is the drug of choice
   C. mebendazole is effective only in larval stage
   D. Second dose of albendazole has a cure rate of 70%Key A. 33.13al

4. A 5 year old female patient presented with anal and perineal itching at night, child is unable to sleep because of intense pruritus. On examination there are excoriated and urticated lesions on perianal and perineal region with some mucoid vaginal discharge. Other family members were also affected. What is the causative organism?
   A. Enterobius vermicularis
   B. Candida albicans
   C. Sarcoptes scabeii
   D. Ancylostoma dudenale
   E. Strongyloides stercoralis

Key A
Ref: Rook (33.13)

5. A 60 yr. old woman with myelodysplastic disease presented with 2 weeks history of painful nodules on buttocks and abdomen. On examination there are erythematous, tender, ulcer one critic nodules of 1-2cm in size/P of the lesion revealed protozoal organism 15-40micrometer in diameter, fungal and bacterial cultures are negative.
   What is your dx?
   A. Syphilis

B. Histoplasmosis
C. Leprosy
D. Ameobiasis
E. Papulonecrotic tuberculids

Key D
Ref: Rook (33.34)

6. Skin atrophy is a sequel of
A. Acute papular onchodermatitis
B. Lichenified onchodermatitis
C. Normal infected skin
D. All of the above
E. None of the above

Key: D
Ref: Rook (33.4)

7. A 40 year old male known case of HIV presented with popular, maculopapular and somewhere urticarial rash all over the body since 2-3weeks.He had a temperature of 101 F, unable to follow commands off and on, CSF confirms a tiny sporozoon. The organism tends to invade which system of the body most commonly,
A. Cadivascular system
B. Skin
C. Reticuloendothelial system
D. Respiratory system
E. immunological system

Key: C
Ref: Rook (33)

8. A 34 year old PT known case of CLL developed acute febrile illness with maculopapular, popular rash followed by scarlantiform desquamation and lymphadenopathy. The PT becomes restless and unconscious. His CSF and lymph mode biopsy examination reveals some protozoal infection.
What is the drug if choice for this pt.?
A. Pyrimethamine alone
B. Folinic acid
C. Trimethoprim plus sulfamethaxozole
D. Albendazole
E. Amphotericin B

Key. C
Ref: Rook (33.52)

9. A 30 year sea water scuba diver presented with a itchy fine macular erythema with tingling sensation followed by multiple papules with erythema and oedema on the left leg. On examination the papules resembled that of popular urticarial. He is most likely suffering from
A. Allergic contact dermatitis
B. Sting bite
C. Cercarial dermatitis
D. Irritant contact dermatitis
E. Aquagenic urticaria

Key: C
Ref: Rook (33.27)

10. A patient presented with multiple subcutaneous nodules in the skin, muscle and eye lids. X ray shows multiple calcified cysts in the thighs and pelvis. What would the treatment of choice be if cerebral disease is suspected?

A. Praziquantel 50mg/kg for 10 days aftwr steroids
B. Albendazole 15mg/kg/day for 7 days
C. Metronidazole 500mg bd for 7 days
D. Tinidazole 2g single dose
E. Diethylcarbamazine 4mg/kg/day for 21 days

Key: A
Ref: Rook (33.31)

11. A 32 year old male presented with deeply invading ulcer on the buttocks as sloughing coalescing ulcer since 1 month. The ulcers are painful, he had a history of bloody diarrhoea since 2 weeks.
What is the prognosis of this disease?

A. It is easily resolved in next 2 weeks
B. No need for further treatment at this stage
C. Early treatment is diagnostic and important as it's a serious diseases if neglected
D. Will resolve with ordinary treatment in 1 week time
E. Continue treatment as it's transmitted via contact

Key: C
(Ref: Rook (33.35)

12. A 25 year old boy presented to your opd with fever, malaise, and arthralgia and urticarial generalized on the body after a swimming session in a fresh water lake. What is the likely diagnosis?

A. Tryptonosomiasis
B. Schistosomiasis
C. Strongyloides
D. Sparganosis
E. Echinococcus

Key: B
Ref: Rook (33.25)

13. A 25 year old boy presented to your opd with fever, malaise, arthralgia and urticaria generalized on the body after a swimming session in a fresh water lake. What is the likely diagnosis?

A. Tryptonosomiasis
B. Schistosomiasis
C. Strongyloides
D. Sparganosis
E. Echinococcus

Key: B
Ref: Rook (33.25)

14. Biopsy from the ulcer of an old world cutaneous leishmaniosis patient shows normal epidermis and no lymphocytic infiltrate. There are masses of parasitized macrophages which are vacuolated too. The biopsy gives the impression of which of the following?

A. Early ulcer
B. Chronic ulcer
C. Espundia
D. Loss of cell mediated immunity
E. None of the above

Key: D
Ref: Rook (33.42)

15. A 28 year old student from some African country presented with a swelling around eyes. There was a large nodule on forehead with many satellite papules. Some of his family members back at home have same problem. What will you prescribe?
   A. Pentavalent antimony 20mg/kg/day for 3 weeks
   B. Pentamidine 4mg/kg/wk for 8 weeks
   C. Pentamidine 2 mg/kg/wk for 8 weeks
   D. Miltefosine 2.5mg/kg OD for 1 month
   E. Amphotericin 1 mg/kg on Alternate days for 2 months

Key: B
Ref: Rook (33.44)

16. A patient presented with an ulcer on his leg. It started as a small brown nodule which expanded and a shallow ulcer appeared in the center. Sporotrichoid spread was present. Your colleague wants to give intravenous pentavalent antimonial to this patient. Which of the following ia not a side effect?
   A. Hepatic toxicity
   B. Pancreatic toxicity
   C. Renal toxicity
   D. Cardiac toxicity
   E. Musculoskeletal toxicity

Key: C
Ref: Rook (33.48)

17. A young female from a village presented with a large crusted plaque on dorsum of right hand. On removal of crust, there was an underlying ulcer with a raised red margin. Multiple small nodules were found around the regional lymphatics. In order to find the species of the organism responsible, which of the following tests cannot help?
   A. DNA analysis
   B. Monoclonal antibodies
   C. Isoenzyme pattern
   D. Giemsa stained smear
   E. None of above

Key: D
Ref: Rook (33.41)

18. A young adult from Afghanistan presented with a scar. His main concern was some lesion developing in the scar. On examination a plaque was seen. According to him it ulcerates in summer. Which of the following is not a form of this disease?
   A. Keloidal
   B. Verrucous
   C. Psoriasiform
   D. Espundia
   E. All of the above

Key: D
Ref: Rook (33.46)

19. A young female from a village presented with a large crusted plaque on dorsum of right hand. On removal of crust, there was an underlying ulcer with a raised red margin. Multiple small nodules were found around the regional lymphatics. In order to find the species of the organism responsible, which of the following tests cannot help?
   A. DNA analysis
   B. Monoclonal antibodies

C. Isoenzyme pattern
D. Giemsa stained smear
E. None of above

Key: D
Ref: Rook (33.41)

20. A patient presented with an ulcer on his leg. It started as a small brown nodule which expanded and a shallow ulcer appeared in the centre. Sporotrichoid spread was present. Your colleague wants to give intravenous pentavalent antimonial to this patient. Which of the following ia not a side effect?

A. Hepatic toxicity
B. Pancreatic toxicity
C. Renal toxicity
D. Cardiac toxicity
E. Musculoskeletal toxicity

Key: C
Ref: Rook (33.48)

21. A 28 year old student from some African country presented with a swelling around eyes. There was a large nodule on forehead with many satellite papules. Some of his family members back at home have same problem. What will you prescribe?

A. Pentavalent antimony 20mg/kg/day for 3 weeks
B. Pentamidine 4mg/kg/wk for 8 weeks
C. Pentamidine 2 mg/kg/wk for 8 weeks
D. Miltefosine 2.5mg/kg OD for 1 month
E. Amphotericin 1 mg/kg on Alternate days for 2 months

Key: B
Ref: Rook (33.44)

22. Biopsy from the ulcer of an old world cutaneous leishmaniasis patient shows normal epidermis and no lymphocytic infiltrate. There are masses of parasitized macrophages which are vacuolated too. The biopsy gives the impression of which of the following?

A. Early ulcer
B. Chronic ulcer
C. Espundia
D. Loss of cell mediated immunity
E. None of the above

Key: D
Ref: Rook (33.42)

23. A 26 yrs old obese female with gestatiotional diabetes haf c- section. After two wks complaint she complaint of tender erythematous dusky swelling on abdomen near wound. Two days Later bullae formed turned into necrotic lesion in a day.. Pt is already taking oral antibiotic Pt is febrile n toxic. She was referred for emergency surgical exploration. She is most probably suffering from.

A. Gas gangrene
B. Ecthyma gangrenosum
C. Necrotizing fascitis
D. Pyoderma gangrenosum
E. Cellulitis

Key: C

24. A 32 years farmer working in cultivated field present with itchy papulovesicular eruption on feet and then developed generalized urticaria, after few days he had cough, SOB, wheeze along with 2 episodes of malena. What is the causative organism

A. Strongyloides stercoralis
B. Ancyclostoma duodenale
C. Ancyclostoma brasiliense
D. Unicararia stenocephala
E. Bubostumum phlebotomum

Key: B

25. Treatment of choice for strongyloidiasis is

A. Ivermectin
B. Albendazole
C. Mebendazole
D. pyrantal pamoate
E. Diethylcarbamazine

Key: A

26. In cutaneous larva migrans, at what rate larval track progress

A. 5cm/ hr
B. 1cm/hr
C. 0.2cm/ min
D. 15cm/ hr
E. 10cm/ min

Key: B

27. An immigrant from sub-Saharan Africa presented e swelling of lf leg with erythema and tenderness along with scrotal swelling. Lymphangiogram showed dilated lymphatics. What is diagnosis?

A. Onchocerciasis
B. Lymphatic filariasis
C. Loiasis
D. Druncunculiosis
E. Trichinosis

Key: B
Ref: Rook (33.8)

28. A 25 year old boy presented to your opd with fever, malaise, arthralgia and urticaria generalized on the body after a swimming session in a fresh water lake. What is the likely diagnosis?

A. Tryptonosomiasis
B. Schistosomiasis
C. Strongyloides
D. Sparganosis
E. Echinococcus

Key: B
Ref: Rook (33.25)

29 A 32 year old male presented with deeply invading ulcer on the buttocks as sloughing coalescing ulcer since 1 month. The ulcers are painful, he had a history of bloody diarrhoea since 2 weeks.
What is the prognosis of this disease?

A. It is easily resolved in next 2 weeks
B. No need for further treatment at this stage

C. Early treatment is diagnostic and important as it's a serious diseases if neglected
D. Will resolve with ordinary treatment in 1 week time
E. Continue treatment as it's transmitted via contact

Key: C
Ref: Rook (33.35)

30. A patient presented with multiple subcutaneous nodules in the skin, muscle and eye lids X ray shows multiple calcified cysts in the thighs and pelvis. What would the treatment of choice be if cerebral disease is suspected?
A. Praziquantel 50mg/kg for 10 days aftwr steroids
B. Albendazole 15mg/kg/day for 7 days
C. Metronidazole 500mg bd for 7 days
D. Tinidazole 2g single dose
E. Diethylcarbamazine 4mg/kg/day for 21 days

Key: A
Ref: Rook (33.31)

31. A 30 year sea water scuba diver presented with a itchy fine macular erythema with tingling sensation followed by multiple papules with erythema and oedema on the left leg. On examination the papules resembled that of papular urticaria .He is most likely suffering from
A. Allergic contact dermatitis
B. Sting bite
C. Cercarial dermatitis
D. Irritant contact dermatitis
E. Aquagenic urticaria

Key: C.
Ref: Rook (33.27)

32. A 34 year old PT known case of CLL developed acute febrile illness with maculopapular, popular rash followed by scarlantiform desquamation and lymphadenopathy. The PT becomes restless and unconscious. His CSF and lymph mode biopsy examination reveals some protozoal infection.
What is the drug if choice for this pt?
A. Pyrimethamine alone
B. Folinic acid
C. Trimethoprim plus sulfamethaxozole
D. Albendazole
E. Amphotericin B

Key: C
Ref: Rook (33.52)

33. A 40 year old male known case of HIV presented with popular, maculopapular and somewhere urticarial rash all over the body since 2-3weeks.He had a temperature of 101 F, unable to follow commands off and on, CSF confirms a tiny sporozoon. The organism tends to invade which system of the body most commonly,
A. Cadivascular system
B. Skin
C. Reticuloendothelial system
D. Respiratory system
E. immunological system

Key: C
Ref: Rook (33.51)

34. Skin atrophy is a squeal of
    A. Acute papular onchodermatitis
    B. Lichenified onchodermatitis
    C. Normal infected skin
    D. All of the above
    E. None of the above

Key: D
Ref: Rook (33.4)

Chapter 35

PSORIASIS AND RELATED DISORDERS

1. Regarding Psoriatic arthritis, the CASPAR criteria includes all except:
   A. Current psoriasis
   B. Current or history of dactylitis
   C. Typical psoriatic nail involvement
   D. A negative test for ANA
   E. Negative test for rheumatoid factor

KEY: D
Ref: Rooks pg.no 35.42

2. 32-year-old Caucasian woman who presents to her primary care provider complaining of intermittent body aches and difficulty picking up her child and cleaning her home. Her past medical history is significant. Her first 5-year history of scalp psoriasis that she has controlled with over-the-counter products. On physical examination, she has tenderness over both elbows, her metacarpalpophalangeal [MCP] and proximal interphalangeal [PIP] joints on both hands. She also has the PIP joints of the right hand and the right knee. Swollen joints are noted in the right knee and the proximal and distal joints of the right hand. Considering the diagnosis, which of the following is not commonly associated ocular disease:
   A. keratoconjunctivitis sicca
   B. Uveitis
   C. Scleritis
   D. Iridocyclitis
   E. Cataracts

KEY: C
Ref: Rooks pg no.35.43

3. A 45-year-old man was seen to outpatient clinic because of back pain and polyarthritis. He had been suffering from back pain occasionally since his 20's. Before visiting outpatient clinic, he had experienced pain in the PIP joints, neck, and back. On admission, he suffered from arthritis in both knees and the left hip, arthritis in PIP, and MCP in the right hand. There were some eruptions on his hands, knees and ankles. Considering the diagnosis, following are correct regarding pathophysiology of disease except:
   A. Immune activation in the synovium and enthesis of affected joints
   B. There is activation of both innate and adaptive immune cells
   C. Overproduction of cytokines including TNF-α, IL-17and IL-23
   D. IL-17, Th17 cells and IL-23 production appear to be more prominent in psoriatic synovitis compared to the skin
   E. IL-17, Th17 cells and IL-23 production appear to be less prominent in psoriatic synovitis compared to the skin

KEY: D
Ref: ROOKS Pg NO.35.44

4. A 28 year old male patient of psoriasis was admitted in a tertiary hospital with the complaints of peeling of skin from the palm and sole for 18 years, ridging and destruction of nails for 16years, progressive joint deformity of small joints of hands and feet with gradual resorption of terminal phalanges resulting in shortening of fingers for 12 years. He developed visual disturbances in the form of redness, irritation and watering from both eyes especially in bright light for 3 years. He had a family history of psoriasis. Her mother and two younger sisters are suffering from psoriasis. On examination the patient was anxious

looking with congested eyes & corneal haziness. Hand examination revealed, flexor deformity and tenderness of both DIP & PIP joints, resorption of the terminal phalanges resulting in shortening of fingers, swelling of the MCP joints of both hands Following are first line treatment for above disease except:

A. NSAIDs
B. Sulphasalazine
C. Etanercept
D. Methotreexate
E. Leflunommide

Key: C
Ref: Rooks (35.46)

5. year's old female has past 2 years hx of on and off episodes of being overly talkative and hyperactive at time with decrease need of sleep .she sometimes become aggressive both verbally and physically .she is on follow up of some psychiatrist and was on some medicine. Now she presented in dermatology opd with complains of erythematous scaly plaques of variable size and shape present on bilateral knees and extensor aspects of forearms? What is the causative medicine for this rash you are suspecting?

A. Bromazepam
B. Beta blockers
C. Lithium
D. Nsaids
E. Valproic acid

Key: C
Ref: Rooks (35.4)

6. 40 years old male patient smoker presented in skin opd with hx of shedding of scale from his scalp for last 4 years for which he takes some topical treatment and it gets resolved temporarily now for last 1 month he is experiencing a asymptomatic rash on his elbows and knees which on examination is characterized by well demarcated red scaly plaques which are encircled by clear peripheral zone. you have done his skin biopsy and sent for histopathology. Which of the following finding you are not expecting on his biopsy report?

A. Hypergranulosis
B. Munros microabsseces in stratum corneum
C. Vasodilatation
D. Papillary edema
E. Spongiform pustule of kogoj

Key: A
Ref: Rooks (35.6)

7. 50 year's old male patient smoker and alcoholic presented with asymptomatic well defined inflamed erythematous patches covered by thin white scales localized to scale back and knees for last 1 year.no mucosal involvement. On nails examination coarse pitting was appreciated in 3 of finger nails. Regarding the pathogenesis of his disease which of the following statement is false?

A. Pathological abnormalities include hyperproliferation of epidermis increased angiogenesis within dermis
B. Macrophages, neutrophils, mast cells, denditic cells present in large numbers in skin lesions
C. Cell cytokines like INf¥,TNF@,IL6,IL22 cause keratinocyte proliferation
D. T lymphocytes appears in skin lesions after epidermal changes has occured
E. It is a the mediated disease

Key: D
Ref: Rooks (35.6)

7. Regarding genetics of psoriasis which of the following statement is true?
   A. Type 1 psoriasis is sporadic
   B. Type 2 is HLA associated
   C. Type 1 is severe
   D. Type 2 is early onset
   E. Type 1 is HLA unrelated

Key: C
Ref: Rooks (35.2)

9. Regarding cigarette smoking implicated in immunological effects of psoriasis .which of the following type of psoriasis has strong association with cigarette smoking?
   A. Sebopsoriasis
   B. Ostraaceous psoriasis
   C. Palmoplantar pustulosis
   D. Acute generalized pustular psoriasis
   E. Plaque psoriasis

Key: C
Reference rooks 35.4

10. A 24 year old male presented with recent onset well demarcated, erythematous scaly plaques predominantly involving the extensors. Histopathology reveal epidermal hyperplasia with suprapapillary thinning, intraepidermal spongiform pustules and predominantly dilated torturous papillary capillaries associated with mixed mononuclear and neutrophilic infiltrate. You start him on Tab Methotrexate 15mg/week.
What will you counsel patient about the results of treatment?
   A. You will start seeing improvement within a week
   B. You will see improvement from 2 months but may take up to 6 months to achieve maximum efficacy
   C. You will see improvement after 6 months
   D. You will see improvement in 2 weeks
   E. You will see improvement in 3 weeks

Key: B
Ref: Rooks (35.27)

11. 45 year old female who was recently diagnosed with severe plaque Psoriasis come to you to discuss her concerns about the disease. She asks about the prognosis of disease. What is the effect on life expectancy in case of severe plaque psoriasis?
   A. No effect
   B. Decrease by 2-4 years
   C. Decrease by 4-6 years
   D. Decrease by 6-8 years
   E. Decrease by 10 years

Key: C
Ref: Rooks (35.22)

12. A 44 year old male patient who is suffering from lymphoma presented to dermatology OPD with erythematous plaques with silvery white scales that involve 10% of the body surface area. Ehat is the safest oral treatment option in this case?
   A. Acitretin
   B. Ciclosporin
   C. Methotrexate
   D. Infliximab
   E. Ustekinumab

Key: A
Ref: Rooks (35.28)

13. A 10 year old boy presented with well demarcated erythematous plaques with silvery white scale involving 20% of the body surface. Various topical and oral treatments have failed to produce result. Now you plan to start biological agent. Which of the following biological agent is approved by FDA for paediatric population?
    A. Infliximab
    B. Etanercept
    C. Adalimumab
    D. Ustekinumab
    E. Secukinumab

Key: B
Ref: Rooks (35.30)

14. 38 year old female known case of Psoriasis had a disease well-controlled on tablet Methotrexate. She presented with complain of fatigue, dizziness, shortness of breath and tachycardia. Urgent labs revealed pancytopenia, normochromic normocytic anaemia with low retic count. Now you plan to switch her to a Biological agent. Which of the following is fully human monoclonal antibody?
    A. Infliximab
    B. Adalimumab
    C. Rituximab
    D. Etanercept
    E. Cetuximab

Key: B
Ref: Rooks (35.30)

15. The metabolic syndrome (truncal obesity, hyperlipidemia, hyper-tension and insulin resistance) is increasing in prevalence in the general population. The strongest of these associations is with which of the following?
    A. Hypertension
    B. Hyperlipidaemia
    C. Insulin resistance
    D. Obesity

Key: D

16. Young man presented with well demarcated erythematous scaly plaques, following is the 1st line topical treatment for him
    A. Local NBB-UVB
    B. Excimer laser
    C. PUVA
    D. Coal tar

Key: D

17. 35 years male diagnosed case of plaque psoriasis, his disease was moderately severe, he was under phototherapy twice weekly for his disease. It binds to DNA and when activated by UVA cause permanent DNA damage with resulting cell death. Characteristic of the therapy is following?
    A. Erythema, maximal at 72–96 h, and blistering that is usually dose and skin phototype dependent.
    B. Erythema, maximal at 48–72h, and blistering that is usually dose and comorbidities dependent.
    C. Should be avoided in patients who are taking ciclosporin due to concerns regarding accelerated cutaneous carcinogenesis.
    D. The relative risk of cutaneous SCCstarts to increase after 300 treatments in a lifetime.

Key is A

18. A 48 years old male presented with sterile pustules with erythematous plaques on acral areas, palmoplantar pustulosis is confirmed correct statememt is
    A. More than 90 % of the patients are current or previous smokers
    B. Smoking has no association with disease
    C. Upto 50 % patients are smokers
    D. Current smoking has association with disease

Key: A
Ref: Rooks (35.38)

19. A 15 years old male presents with sterile pustular eruption at the tip of index finger and thumb, nails of both digits are dystrophic ,proximal edge of lesion is bordered, saddened and irregular most likely diagnosis is
    A. Herpetic whitlow
    B. Staphylococcal infection
    C. Contact dermatitis
    D. Acrodermatitis continua of hallopeau
    E. Scleroderma

Key: D
Ref: Rooks (35.40)

20. A 26 yr. old pregnant lady in her 3rd trimester presented with high grade fever, diarrhea and vomiting. O/E there were minute pustules arising on acutely inflamed area. On histopathology there was lymphocytic infilterate along with subcorneal pustule. Most likely diagnosis is
    A. Subcorneal pustular dermatosis
    B. Impetigo herpetiformis
    C. Acute generalised exanthematous dermatosis
    D. Pemphigoid gestationis

Key: B
Ref: Rooks (35.35)

21 Diagnostic criteria for acute generalised pustular psoriasis of von zumbusch includes following
    A. Leucocytosis
    B. Raised esr
    C. Raised crp
    D. Fever
    E. All of above

Key: E
Ref: Rooks (35.34)

22. Following are the diseases associated with pustular psoriasis except
    A. Metabolic syndrome
    B. Hypertension
    C. Dyslipidemia
    D. Diabetes
    E. Crohns disease

Key: E

23 A 40 yr. old pt of chronic plaque psoriasis stable on treatment developed acute erythema and pustulation on flexures. First line treatment option in this patient will be
    A. Methotrexate
    B. Ciclosporin
    C. Acitretin
    D. Azathiopurine

Key: C

Ref Rooks (35.37)

Chapter 37 LICHEN PLANUS AND LICHENOID DISORDERS

1. Five year old boy presents to dermatology opd with eruption of lichenoid papules in a typical linear distribution. The lesions are located on right lower extremity. He had history of viral infection one week back. What is the likely diagnosis?

A. Darier disease
B. Linear psoriasis
C. Linear porokeratosis
D. Lichen striatus

Key: D
Ref: Rook (37.18)

2. Which of the following is true regarding histopathology of Lichen striatus?

A. Dyskeratotic keratinocytes, like the 'corps ronds' of Darier disease, are seen in about 50% of cases.
B. Dyskeratotic keratinocytes, like the 'corps ronds' of Darier disease, are seen in about 20% of cases.
C. Dyskeratotic keratinocytes, like the 'corps ronds' of Darier disease, are seen in about 35% of cases.
D. Dyskeratotic keratinocytes, like the 'corps ronds' of Darier disease, are seen in about 2% of cases.

Key: A
Ref: Rook (37.18)

3. A 12 year old boy represents with history of skin trauma and eruption of lichenoid papules in a typical linear distribution. The lesion extended over a period of few weeks and coalesces to form erythematous scaly linear band. Keeping in view the diagnosis what is the course of disease?

A. Lesions generally resolve over 6-12 months
B. Lesions never resolve
C. Lesions resolve in 5 years
D. None of above

Key: A
Ref: Rook (37.19)

4. Lichen stratus has strongest association with which of the following conditions?

A. Atopy
B. Viral infections
C. Vaccinations
D. Skin trauma

Key: A
Ref: Rook (37.18)

5. In a patient with acute graft versus host disease which of the following histological changes show grade 3 histological severity?

A. Regional epidermal cell necrosis with bullae
B. Basal cell vacillation with or without mononuclear cell infiltration
C. Complete dermal and epidermal separation

D. Solitary epidermal cell necrosis, surrounded by mononuclear cells

Key:
Ref: Rook (38.3)

6. A 60 years old lady presented with multiple painful oral ulcers for the last 3 months. She also complained about some pain and burning in genital area. On examination there are multiple errosive ulcers present in oral mucosa along with some white streaks in surrounding mucosa. On genital examination, labia minora and introitus was bright red and raw. On the basis of above diagnosis, what is the primary treatment option?
   A. Clobetasol propionate ointment 0.05%
   B. Topical retinoids
   C. Prednisolone lmg/kg per day until improvement.
   D. Immunosuppresive agents
   E. PUVA therapy

Key: C
Ref: Rook (37.16)

7. A 45 years old man presented with multiple pruritic, shiny, polygonal 1-3mm papules with red to violet colour papules confined to shins of both legs for 1 year. Biopsy of the lesions show basal vacular degeneration with colloid bodies and band like lymphocytic infiltrate obliterating DEJ.
What is the 1st line treatment option in this patient?
   A. Clobetasol propionate ointment 0.05% once daily at night until remission
   B. Oral prednisolone 0.5mg/kg for 4-6 weeks
   C. Tacrolimus ointment
   D. PUVA therapy
   E. No treatment needed

Key: A
Ref: Rook (37.16)

8. A 5 years old girl was brought by her parents with the complaint of sudden appearance of small, discrete, pink, flat topped, lichenoid papules in a typical linear distribution on the left leg extending from buttock up to the ankle posteromedial. The lesions were asymptomatic. Keeping in mind the above senario, what is the 1st line management in this patient?
   A. Photodynamic therapy
   B. Topical tacrolimus
   C. Topical antibiotics
   D. Topical corticosteroids
   E. Observation and reassurance

Key: E
Ref: Rook (37.20)

9. A 6 years old boy is presented in opd with minute ,pinpoint to pinhead sized papules which are dome shaped having shiny surface predominantly on forearms and on dorsal surface of both hands. Biopsy of lesions shows focally dense infiltrate of lymphocytes with a few giant cells encircled by elongated rete ridges. All are true regarding the diagnosis EXCEPT:
   A. Eventually self-limiting
   B. No treatment is required
   C. Sun exposure is beneficial
   D. PUVA can be considered as a treatment option
   E. Fluorinated topical corticosteroids worsen the condition.

Key: E
Ref: Rook (37.18)

10. 35 years old man presented with symptomatic biopsy proven widespread cutaneous lichen planus.He is not willing to take oral corticosteroids for the condition. What is the most appropriate next treatment option?

A. PUVA 3 times a week
B. UVB 2 times a week
C. Oral acitretin 30 mg per day for 8 weeks
D. topical corticosteroids
E. No treatment required

Key: C
Ref: Rook (37.16)

11. A female after dental procedure developed white plaques on tounge and streaks with lace work on buccal mucosa. What is possible cause?

A. Asenic
B. Mercury
C. Aluminium
D. Gold
E. Iron

Key: B
Ref: Rook (37.3)

12. All are associated with Lichen planus except

A. Hepatitis B
B. Hepatitis C
C. VZV
D. HHV7
E. HHV8

Key: E
Ref: Rook (37.2)

13. Lichen planus like contact dermatitis occur in car industry workers due to

A. Ppd
B. Methyacrylic acidesters
C. Dimethylfumartae
D. Polyene glycol
E. Lanolin

Key: B
Ref: Rook (37.3)

14. A Hepatitis C pt developed polygonal pruritic purple papules over the shins. What is true regarding pathophysiology of lesion?

A. RANTES is secreted by T cell and cause relase of IL 8 from mast cells
B. Interferon type 1 is produced by keratinocytes
C. MMP are decreased
D. ICAM 1 is reduced
E. Granzyme B + Tcells are not present

Key: B
Ref: Rook (37.2)

15. Lp can develope in patient who recieved hepatitis B vaccination after

A. First dose
B. Second dose

C. Donot develope
D. Both doses

Key: B
Ref: Rook (37.2)

16. Annular LP is most common on which site
A. Scalp
B. Perianal area
C. Shaft of penis
D. Oral Mucosa
E. Dorsum of hand

Ref: Rook (37.3)

17. A middle aged man presents with 2 years history of hyper pigmented and Hypertrophic plaques on lower limbs, especially around ankles and complains of mild itching. All the following are it's complication except
A. SCC
B. B-atrophy
C. Cutaneous horn
D. Seborrheic keratosis
E. Keratoacanthoma

Key: D
Ref: Rook (37.7)

18. A middle aged female presents with 6 months history of itchy popular eruption on forearms and trunk. She also complains of burning sensation in mouth. Now there are sudden eruption of tense bullae on both involved and uninvolved skin.
What are the Direct Immunofluorescence findings in this case?
A- Linear BMZ deposition of Ig G and C3 in peri lesional skin
B- DIF is negative
C- Annular deposit of Ig A and C3 in peri lesional skin
D- Annular deposition of Ig G and C3
E- Reticular deposition of Ig G and C 3

Key: A
Ref: Rook (37.9)

19. A middle aged man presents with asymptomatic minute flesh colored papules on abdomen and chest. He also has nail pitting. All the following are associated with this condition except
A- Sweet Syndrome
B- Crohn's Disease
C- Trisomy 21
D- Congenital megacolon
E- Nieman pick disease

Key: A
Ref: Rook (37.10)

20. 22 year male presents with popular and nodular eruption on extensors of forearms and buttocks. It is symmetrical and arranged in Reticular pattern. He also has thick nails. Histopathology shows nonspecific chronic dermatitis with some lichenoid features. Regarding course of this disease, which statement is true?
A- It is a chronic, progressive disease and generally resistant to treatment
B- It is self-limiting and no treatment required in most cases

C- It responds well to topical and oral corticosteroids
D- Corticosteroids decreases the course of illness
E- It resolves in 2 to 3 yrs. without treatment and corticosteroids decreases symptoms

Key: A
Ref: Rook (37.11 and 37.18)

21. A 45 years old lady presented with history of burning sensation in mouth from last 1 year. On Examination white streaks forming a lacework were present on the buccal mucosa. On the tongue, there were fixed, white plaques; slightly depressed below the surrounding normal mucous membrane. Which of the following could not be associated/causative factor

A. Diabetes
B. Herpes virus 8
C. VZV
D. Hepatitis B vaccine
E. HCV

Key: B
Ref: Rook (37.2)

22. A 45 years old lady presented with history of burning sensation in mouth from last 1 year. On Examination white streaks forming a lacework were present on the buccal mucosa. On the tongue, there were fixed, white plaques; slightly depressed below the surrounding normal mucous membrane. Which of the following could not b associated/causative factor

A. Diabetes
B. Herpes virus 8
C. VZV
D. Hepatitis B vaccine
E. HCV

Key: B

23 In above mentioned case, which of the following is least likely treatment option?

A. Topical retinoid
B. Topical tacrolimus
C. Potent topical steroid
D. Oral steroid
E. Topical cyclosporine

Key: B
Ref: Rook (37.17)

Chapter 38

GRAFT-VERSUS-HOST DISEASE

1. A18 year old male presented to you with generalized dry, tight and itchy skin. On examination there are violaceous papules and plaques with some poikilodermatous changes on trunk and limbs. Patient describes oral discomfort while eating. Oral cavity examination revealed white lacy pattern on buccal mucosa. There is alopecia and nail dystrophy also present. Investigations revealed anemia. Chest x ray shows bilateral lung fibrosis. He had History of bone marrow transplantation for his aplastic anemia 1.5years ago. What is he suffering from?

A. Juvenile dermatomyositis
B. Chronic graft vs host disease
C. Sjogren syndrome
D. Morphea
E. Radiation induced dermatitis

Key: B
Ref: Rook (38.7)

2. A18 year old male presented to you with generalized dry, tight and itchy skin. On examination there are violaceous papules and plaques with some poikilodermatous changes on trunk and limbs. Patient describes oral discomfort while eating. Oral cavity examination revealed white lacy pattern on buccal mucosa. There is alopecia and nail dystrophy also present. Investigations revealed Hb 8.8g/dl. Chest x ray shows bilateral lung fibrosis. He had History of bone marrow transplantation for his aplastic anemia 1.5years ago. What is his survival rate at 2years?

A. 86%
B. 95%
C. 50%
D. 97%

Key: A
Ref: Rook (38.9)

3. A 15 year old male presents to you with alopecia snd widespread sclerotic skin lesions with some areas of dyspigmentation on trunk and limbs. On legs there is woody induration of skin and venous guttering. Patient feels discomfort during urination. Investigations revealed anemia and derranged LFTs 4times upper limit of normal. He had history of HSCT for his AML 3 years ago. How it can be prevented?

A. By recipient HLA matching,related donor match
B. 1mg/kg prednisolone for 2weeks
C. Ciclosporin
D. MMF

Key: A

4. A pt developed maculopaular rash involving less than 10% body surface area. He has dry eyes and wt loss of <5% after 3 years of bone marrow transplantaltion .What is treatement of choice

A. Topical steroids
B. Oral steroid 1 week
C. Tacrolimus
D. Methotreaxte
E. MMF

Key: A
Ref: Rook (38.11)

5. Which of the following is not a risk factor for chronic graft vs host disease?
   A. Gender mismatch
   B. Donor alloimmunization
   C. History of acute graft vs host disease
   D. Use of oral tacrolimus or methotrexate
   E. Old age of recipient

Key: D
Ref: Rook (38.11)

6. A 22 yr old male undergo HSCT for CLL 1 month ago now presented to opd with complaint of purpuric rash over body with bullae formation on trunk.nikolsky +ve.diagnosis
   A. TENS
   B. Acute graft vs host disease
   C. Chronic gvhd
   D. SSSS

Key: B
Ref: Rook (38.3)

7. A 35 yr old man with HSCT 2 months ago now presented maculopapular rash with abdominal pain, vomiting and diarrhea. On exam 40% BSA involved. And diarrhea 95ml/kg.bilirubin 4.5.you suspect which stage of acute GVHD
   A. Stage 1
   B. Stage 2
   C. Stage 3
   D. Stage 4
   E. Stage 5

Key: D
Ref: Rook (38.5)

8. Interface dermatitis is seen in all except.
   A. LP
   B. Acute GVHD
   C. Chronic GVHD
   D. psoriasis
   E. DLE

Key: D
Ref: Rook (38.2)

9. Mortality rate of stage 3 graft vs host disease
   A. 27%
   B. 43%
   C. 54%
   D. 68%

Key: D
Ref: Rook (38.5)

Chapter 39

ECZEMATOUS DISORDERS

1. A patient presented to you with lesions on forearms accompanied by itching. He is a farmer by occupation. On examination lichenified pigmented plaques were seen on both forearms in a symmetrical distribution. Surrounding skin was normal. Which test will you advise this patient?

A. No test needed
B. Skin scrapings with KOH
C. Patch testing
D. Skin biopsy
E. Serum IgE levelsv

Key: C
Ref: Rook (39.30)

2. 62 years male patient with no known comorbid presented with complain of redness of skin along with feeling of tightness and itching for few days. On further inquiry he had complain of dryness and itchy skin for many years. On cutaneous examination there was generalized erythema along with fine scaling.
What is the most likely underlying cause of his condition?

A. Drug intake.
B. Psoriasis
C. Atopic eczema
D. Scabies
E. Cutaneous T cell lymphoma

Key: C
Ref: Rook (39.31)

3. A 86 years elderly male presented to OPD with complain of dry, slighty scaly skin of arms & legs which was more marked in winter & improved in summer initially but now are persistant. previously he had Hx of generalized dry skin & cold intolerance. He is a diagnosed hypertensive & on regular medication for it. On examination there are prolonged depression on pulp of fingers and on legs, superficial markings are more marked and deeper, a few of them are haemorrhagic. Keeping in view the above findings, what is most likely diagnosis?

A. chronic eczema
B. infective eczema
C. eczema craquele
D. varicose eczema
E. malignacy

Key: C
Ref: Rook (39.10)

4. A 32 years female, housewife presented with complain of dry, cracked, painful fissures of fingers of dominant hand, preferentially involve thumb & forefinger. Keeping the diagnosis in mind, what is most useful investigation?

A. skin biopsy
B. blood c/s
C. latec prick testing
D. patch testing
E. scrapping for fungal hypahae

Key: D
Ref: Rook (39.14)

5. A middle aged female presented to OPD with complain of generalized redness and itching. She had past history red, itchy, plaques over scalp and seborrheic areas of body. On examination there was generalized erythema with bran like scale, no visceromegly or lymphadenopathy. She reports previous 2 episodes of same redness and itching for which she was treated and skin biopsy was done that showed spongiosis, parakeratosis and nonspecific inflammatory infiltrate.
Regarding her diagnosis what is the commonest cause of death in this condition?

A. Cardiac failure
B. Acute renal failure
C. Pneumonia
D. Stroke
E. Malgnancy

Key: C
Ref: Rook (39.34)

6. A middle aged female presented with complain of asymmetrical, irregular vesiculosquamous eruption of hands. She also complained of involvement of nails. What is most likely diagnosis?

A. pomphlyx
B. patchy vesiculosquamous eczema
C. hyperkeratotic eczema
D. psoriasis
E. chronic acral dermatitis

Key: B
Ref: Rook (39.15)

7. Morphological pattern of hand eczema include which of following

A. nummular dermatitis
B. Gut eczema
C. Ring eczema
D. wear & tear dermatitis
E. all of above

Key: E
Ref: Rook (39.13)

8. A 26 years newly married female presented with vesicular lesions over fingers. She noticed that lesion developed rapidly at site of wearing of ring & 2 to 3 discoid patches also present on arms and trunk .which of the following disease is most likely associated with the scenario?

A. xerosis
B. irritant contact dermatitis
C. allergic contact dermatitis
D. atopic eczema
E. nummular dermatitis

Key: D
Ref: Rook (39.12)

9. 52 years female known case of epilepsy visits to dermatologist with complain of generalized itching and redness for 6 days, it started as morbilliform erythema and progressed to more than 90 % of body surface. On examination there was generalized erythema along with scales, no visceromegly or lymphadenopathy. You suspect drug in the etiology of her condition.
What is the most likely culprit drug?

A. Levetiracetam
B. Sodium valporate
C. Clonazepam

D. Pregablin
E. Carbamazepine

Key: E
Ref: Rook (39.31)

10. 65 year male diabetic, hypertensive, post stroke bed bound was brought to OPD with complain of thinking and crusting of palms and soles along with thickened nails. He recently also developed generalized redness and scaling involving more than 90 % of his body Regarding his diagnosis , all are complications of his condition except ?
A. High output Cardiac failure
B. Peripheral edema
C. Hypothermia
D. Hypoalbuminemia
E. Hyperthermia

Key: E
Ref: Rook (39.34)

11. Elderly male patient presented with complain of redness of on trunk and limbs that initially started as red brown flat papules which became confluent on cutaneous examination you noticed sparing of abdominal flexures, what is this sign called?
A. Darier sign
B. Deck chair sign
C. Holster sign
D. Lesser trelat sign
E. Cullen's sign

Key: B
Ref: Rook (39.34)

12. A 40 yr alcoholic male with history of DVT and varicosities of left leg presented with an erythematous scaly plaque on the left lower leg with an indurated painful ulcer of 2×3 cm size above the medial malleolus for 1 month. The most likely cause is
A. Statis dermatitis
B. Venous eczema
C. Dermatitis artefacta
D. Asteototic eczema
E. Eczema sec to underlying systemic disease.

Key: B
Ref: Rook (39.19)

13. Which of following are treatment options for numular eczema.
A. Emollients, Topical steroids, topical or oral antibiotics.
B. Topical calcineurin inhibitors.
C. phototherapy (Narrow band UVB/PUVA)
D. Oral steroids or Methotrexate
E. All of above

Key: E
Ref: Rook (39.9)

14. 45 years old male presented with coin shaped lesion with central clearing on trunk.patch test performed. Positive patch tests commonest were to
A. Chromate

B. Nickle
C. Cobalt
D. (D)fragrance
E. All of above

Key: E
Ref: Rook (39.9)

15. 20 years old boy presented with coin shaped plaque of closely set, thin walled vesicles on an erythematous base on lower limbs. Which of following are clinical variants of this disease?
A. Exudative type
B. Dry type
C. Dermatitis of hands
D. Exudative discoid and lichenoid chronic dermatosis
E. All of above

Key: E
Ref: Rook (39.8)

16. 25 years old male presented with single oval erythematous plaque with a clearly demarcated edge on hand. What is the diagnosis?
A. Nummular eczema
B. Asteatotic eczema
C. Dermatitis and eczema of Hand
D. chronic acral dermatitis
E. None of above

Key: A
Ref: Rook (39.7)

17. 30 years old male with known case of atopy presented with two circular erythematous plaques with clearly demarcated edges on left leg.
Skin biopsy of lesion done .on histopatholigy sub a cute dermatitis with spongiotic vesicles and lymphohistiocytic infiltrate.eosinophils in upper dermis, intense intercellular oedema between cells of basal layer. What s diagnosis?
A. Discoid eczema
B. Tinea corporis
C. pityriasis alba
D. Chronic superficial dermatitis
E. prelymphomatous eruption

Key: A
Ref: Rook (39.7)

18. 45 year old obese diabetic lady presents with slightly swollen Rt lower limb veins and medially placed venous ulcer below, it has surrounding erythema with multiple areas of discharging pus surrounded by microvesicles. There is no hx if contact medicament, but a slight eczematous change around the moist wound with no defined margin. What is the likely dx?
A. Post traumatic eczema
B. Infective eczema
C. Infected eczema
D. Venous eczema
E. Contact eczema

Key: B
Ref: Rook (39.24)

19. 7 year old boy presents with oval, irregular hypopigmented patch over Rt cheek and shoulder. O/E:it's slightly erythematous, not well marginated with fine scaling and hypopigmentation. The patch is 1cm in diameter. What is the most common association?

A. Pitryasis Roscea
B. Atopic dematitis
C. Dermatophydite
D. Poriasis
E. P.Foliaceous

Key: B
Ref: Rook (39.25)

20. A young adult with vitiligo comes to you with itching on arm. On examination there is a mole surrounded by papulosquamous lesion. Histology shows a benign nevus surrounded by a dermal lymphocytic and eosinophilic infiltrate, with overlying acanthosis, spongiosis and parakeratosis. The patient is concerned that it might be a cancer. What will you tell him about the prognosis?

A. It might become cancerous so mohs surgery is needed
B. It might resolve in a few months alongwith the nevus
C. It might resolve in a few months without involution of nevus
D. He needs to visit annually so that doctors can see any new changes
E. This condition has nothing to do with his vitiligo

Key: C
Ref: Rook (39.27, 39.28)

21. A female patient presented with severe itching in perineal area. On examination, there was a plaque with a warty, cribriform surface. On palpation, plaques felt solid tumour-like. What is your diagnosis?

A. Pebbly lichenification
B. Genital warts
C. Giant condyloma of Buschke-Löwenstein
D. Giant lichenification of Pautrier

Key: D
Ref: Rook (39.29)

22. A female patient presented to you with an itchy lesion on the back of her neck. On examination, there was a psoriasiform scaly plaque extending to the fold behind the ear. Crusting and fissuring was evident. What is your first line treatment for this patient?

A. Occlusive zinc paste bandage
B. Self adhesive steroid impregnated tape
C. Sedative antihistamines
D. Patient education about her disease
E. Intralesional triamcinolone

Key: D
Ref: Rook (39.30)

23. A patient presented with a plaque on ankle associated with itching. The central area was scaly and thickened that was surrounded by licheoid papules. Histology showed gross acanthosis and hyperkeratosis. Rete ridges were irregularly and strikingly elongated and widened. What is your diagnosis?

A. Lichen planus
B. Actinic lentigo
C. Atopic eczema
D. Chronic Lichen simplex
E. Psoriasis

Key: D
Ref: Rook (39.29)

Chapter 40

SEBORRHEOEIC DERMATITIS

1. Raised levels of the following has been implicated in patients of seborrheic dermatitis.
   A. cathepsin
   B. histamine
   C. A and B
   D. Lipases
   E. A B and D

Key: E
Ref: Rook (40.2)

2. A 18 year old female with flat facies and bent 5 th finger of the right hand complains of itching on her scalp. On examination multiple scaly plaques were seen with thick scales. This has reduced her DLQI. Which of the following is true regarding the genetics of her skin condition.
   A. A.D HLA A*32 and HLA B*18
   B. A.R HLA A* 33 and HLA B*19
   C. A.D HLA B27
   D. All of the above
   E. X linked recessive with multiple HLA

Key: A
Ref: Rook (40.2)

3. A patient presented with a silver scaly pink rash on the parasternal and glabellar area with well circumscribed margins. Biopsy revealed hyperplasia of the epidermis with spongioform pustules in stratum corneum. Patient is suffering from a chronic condition namely.
   A. Seborrheic dermatitis
   B. Pustular dermatitis
   C. Seb psoriasis
   D. ILVEN
   E. ACD

Key: C
Ref: Rook (40.4)

4. Possible Malignancy associated with a 55 year old patient presenting with thick scaly pruritic plaques with a yellow hue on nasiolabial folds since 30 years of age.
   A. Adenocarcinoma lung
   B. Gastric ca
   C. Multiple myeloma
   D. Basal cell carcinoma
   E. Glioblastoma

Key: E

5. A young male 32 years of age presents with fine flaking of the skin at the glabellar area with localized erythema. There is conjunctival redness and irritation. Which of the following statements regarding this conditions holds true?
   A. Predilection towards infundibulam of sebaceous glands as aminoacids are present in abundance
   B. Increased secretion of proteases and phospholipases that disrupt epidermal barrier
   C. Malasezzin and indole 3 carbaldehyde detected on skin
   D. C, B and E
   E. Anti-inflammatory cytoines IL 6 8 12 and TNF a produced

Key: C
Ref: Rook (40.2)

Chapter 41

ATOPIC ECZEMA

1. A mother brings her 1 year old daughter to the OPD with complaints of dry erythematous skin more pronounced in flexural areas, with mild excoriation on the exposed parts. The delivery was uneventful, there is no history of collodion membrane, photosensitivity, swelling, or any drug intake. The family history is also inconclusive. Personal history includes episodes of wheeze and dry cough in spring time. Which of following is incorrect regarding pathophysiology of her condition?
   A. Flaggrin insufficiency predisposes to barrier dysfunction
   B. Genetic susceptibility loci in this condition overlaps with asthma to a greater extent than psoriasis
   C. Reduced extracellular lipids and impaired ceramide production are characteristic
   D. UV radiation has well established protective role in this disease
   E. Western affluent diet leads to increased risk

Key: B
Ref: Rook (41.5)

2. Role of Regulatory T cells in regulating allergic responses in various clinical allergy settings comprises all except:
   A. Inhibition of aeroallergen sensitivity
   B. Inhibition to cow's milk allergy
   C. Induction of tolerance to hymenoptera venom
   D. Allergic contact dermatitis to nickel
   E. Achieving remission in psoriasis

Key: E
Ref: Rook (41.10)

3. The term 'atopic march' describes progression within an individual from Atopic eczema to other atopic diseases including:
   A. Allergic rhinitis
   B. Post infectious eczema
   C. Hay fever
   D. Eosinophilia
   E. Urticaria

Key: A
Ref. Rook (41.11)

4. To induce B cell class switching of antibody production to make IgE the cells required is:
   A. Cytotoxic T cells
   B. Natural Killer cells
   C. Th1 Cells
   D. Antigen presenting cells
   E. Th2 Cells

Key: E
Ref. Rook (41.11)

5. In chronic atopic eczema growth and survival of eosinophil's and macrophages is regulated by:
   A. IFN Alpha
   B. IL-5 and GM-CSF
   C. IL- 22

D. IL-12
E. IL-31

Key: B
Ref: Rook (41.10)

6. A 35 years old male patient presented with history of excessive itching, erythema and crusting on body. Patient also had asthma. In past he has multiple episodes of relapses of eczema and got multiple admissions. 1st line and 2nd line drugs seem to be in effective to control his disease. Which of the following is not better option for him?
A. Azathioprine
B. Cyclosporine
C. Methotrexate
D. Omalizumab
E. Myclophenolate mofetil

Key is D
Ref. Rook (41.33)

7. A 10 year's old boy known case of atopic eczema for last 5 years came to opd with acute exacerbation of eczema. After 2 weeks of treatment, his condition is markedly improved. Which of the following will u advise him on follow-up?
A. Continuous use of mildly potent topical steroid
B. Addition of twice weekly application of potent topical steroids to the healed areas
C. Avoid precipitating factor and bath daily with antiseptic soap
D. Phototherapy to maintain remission
E. Daily use of topical calcineurin inhibitors on sensitive areas.

Key: B
Ref. Rook (41.31)

8. Which of the following is not an aggravating factor for atopic eczema?
A. Smoking
B. Food allergen
C. Sweating
D. Habitual scratching
E. Winter chapping

Key: A
Ref. Rook (41. 23)

9. A 7 year old boy presented with history of recurrent itching and erythema on body for last 3 years. On examination there was erythema, crusting, excoriation, hyper- and hypopigmentation, and warty Lichenification and vesiculation on body, predominately on flexures. His neck had reticulate pigmentation. What is the best treatment option for the boy?
A. Emollients+ Topical steroid
B. Emollients+ Topical steroid+ antibiotics
C. Topical calcineurin inhibitors
D. Wet wrap therapy
E. Oral corticosteroids (short course)

Key: B
Ref. Rook (41.24)

10. A 10 years old boy known case of atopic eczema for last 5 years came to opd with acute exacerbation of eczema. After 2 weeks of treatment, his condition is markedly improved. Which of the following will u advise him on follow-up?

A. Continuous use of mildly potent topical steroid
B. Addition of twice weekly application of potent topical steroids to the healed areas
C. Avoid precipitating factor and bath daily with antiseptic soap
D. Phototherapy to maintain remission
E. Daily use of topical calcineurin inhibitors on sensitive areas.

Key: B
Ref. Rook (41.31)

Chapter 42

URTICARIA

1. Which of the following doesn't suggest urticarial vasculitis over urticarial?
   A. Lesions lasting more than 24 hours
   B. Painful and tender lesions
   C. Association with recent infection
   D. Purpuric lesions
   E. Red dots and globules on Demoscopy

Key: B
Ref: Rook (42.14)

2. A middle aged patient presented in emergency with erythema and swelling of hands and lips, along with itching, headache and mild dizziness. There were no other sign and symptoms, on history inquiry you get to know that this episode is of half an hour duration....and he got 2 such episodes in past month....
His health is otherwise good, and he is a gardener in a college, by profession. What is the diagnosis?
   A. Solar urticarial
   B. Solar angioedema
   C. Vibratory urticaria
   D. Vibratory angioedema
   E. Delayed pressure urticaria

Key: D
Ref: Rook (42.10)

3. A 29 years old female came to skin opd with complain of skin eruption at few specific days in each month for last 2 years. On examination there were well demarcated erythematous edematous skin eruption involved most of her body .Keeping diagnosis in mind which of the following test will be confirmatory for it.
   A. Immune CAP
   B. Serum allergen Specific IgE
   C. Intradermal testing for progesterone sensitivity or skin prick sensitivity
   D. C4 complement
   E. Both A and D

Key: C
Ref: Rook (42.8)

4. A 45 years old male came in skin opd with new skin eruption on n off for last one month. He has previous history of starting new medicines for his cardiac issue. On examination there were erythematous edematous skin eruption mainly cover his trunk. There were no swelling of lips or genitalias. Keeping diagnosis in mind which one of the following responsible for it
   A. Leukotriene C4 synthetase gene
   B. E selectin
   C. FCERI inhibitor
   D. leukotrine C2 synthetase gene
   E. None of them

Key: A
Ref: Rook (42.7)

5. A 45 years old female came with complain of pruritus and skin eruption since 3 months which get subside in 24 hours spontaneously or after taking antihistamine. There was no burning or no history of any systemic involvement. On examination multiple erythematous edematous swelling at lower trunk and upper limbs with no purpura. Histopathology of skin eruption showed....

A. Dermal oedema with a moderate perivascular and interstitial mixed inflammatory infiltrate, including intravascular neutrophils with vasculitis.
B. Epidermal acanthosis , elongated rete ridges , dermal edema with thickening of collagen
C. Dermal oedema with a moderate perivascular and interstitial mixed inflammatory infiltrate, including intravascular neutrophils but no vasculitis.
D. Hyperkeratosis, acanthosis, saw tooth rete ridges, perivscular lymphocytic infiltrates
E. None of above

Key: C
Ref: Rook (42.6)

6. A 35 years old female came with complain of weight gain and constipation for last 5 months. On examination there were diffuse swelling in front of neck and multiple well demarcated erythematous edematous eruptions over trunk and flanks. Her TPO was also positive. Keeping diagnosis in mind which one can be use as marker of functional autoantibodies...

A. Neutrophil histamine release assay test
B. Eosinophil histamine release assay test
C. Basophil histamine release assay
D. Both A and B
E. Both B n C

Key: C
Ref: Rook (42.6)

7: 25 years old female came with complain of recurrent episode of skin eruption with pruritus since one month. She has history of sore throat few days back .On examination there were well demarcated erythematous swelling on her face, limbs and trunk which get subside by taking antihistamine. Keeping diagnosis in mind which one of the following is not an immunological stimuli for it

A. C5
B. Allergen only
C. AntiIgE
D. Anti FcERI
E. Both b and c

Key: A
Ref: Rook (42.4)

8. A patient presented with itchy red spots, off and on, since a month. These persist for an hour or 2 and then disappear, leaving no residual signs or scars. On history and exam you ascertain that these are small weals with marked flare and usually appear at the morning time when he has done with exercise and breakfast.

Which statement regarding this is not true?

A. Patient has increased histamine and decreased chymotrypsin levels
B. Stimuli include emotional distress and spicy food
C. Stimulation of post ganglionic parasympathetic nerve supply to sweat glands is thought to be underlying mechanism
D. Diagnosis is confirmed by provocation when core temp is raised to 0.7 to 1 degree
E. It may get worse in winter months

Key: C
Ref: Rook (42.11)

9. A young patient presented with itching and buring sensation of mouth since an hour,
He hasn't eaten anything spicy or street food except a glass of fresh apple juice in morning.
There are no weals or erythema.
Which of the statement is true?

A. Condition can progress to angioedema if not treated immediately
B. Immune CAP offers the diagnosis
C. He should avoid fresh and canned juices in future
D. It is due to the cross reaction between profilins and PR10
E. This condition confers immunity against respiratory allergies with pollens

Key: D
Ref: Rook (42.13)

Chapter 43

RECURRENT ANGIO-OEDEMA WITHOUT WEALS

1. A 18 year old male presented with complaint of recurrent non itching swelling of skin, lips and eyes for few years associated with nausea, abdominal colic and urinary symptoms. What is likely diagnosis?

A. Mast cell mediated angioedema
B. Ereditary angioedema
C. Utricarial vasculitis
D. Urticaria
E. None of above

Key: B
Ref: Rook (43.4)

2. On investigation of recurrent angioedema without weals there is low C4 along with low C1, INH, low C1INH function and low C1q. what is your diagnosis based on above investigation?

A. type 1 hereditary angioedema
B. type 2 hereditary angioedema
C. type 3 hereditary angioedema
D. acquired C1INH deficiency
E. idiopathic angioedema

Key: D
Ref: Rook (43.5 and 43.4)

3. A patient presented in emergency with angioedema without weals known case of hereditary angioedema what is treatment of choice.

A. Ffp
B. Catinab
C. Danazil
D. Epinephrine
E. Solucortif i/v

Key B
Ref: Rook (43.5)

Chapter 44

URTICARIAL VASCULITIS

1. A patient presented with H/o recurrent painful change in color of digits and net like lesions over his legs especially in winters.
He is known case of hepatitis C and essential cryoglobunemia.
On furthers inquiring he has h/o painful erythematous lesions on his limbs as well.
Keeping in mind your diagnosis, what will you expect in the biopsy of his cutaneous lesions?

A. Caseating granulomatous skin disease
B. Palisading necrobiosis
C. Haubner arteritis
D. Clumps of bacilli and perivascular neutrophillic infiltrate
E. Leukocytoclastic vasculitis with fibrinoid necrosis

Ref: Rook (44.2)

2. Regarding diagnostic criteria of Hypocomplemententemic urticarial vasculitis, following is not true?

A. arthritis
B. episcleritis
C. abdominal pain
D. decreased C H50
E. biopsy proven vasculitis

Key: D
Ref: Rook (44.3)

3. A 45 years old lady presented in skin opd with complain of painful erythematous patches over her trunk and limbs for last 2 days. There were some new erythematous patches as well as some older brownish patches. She also has complained of pain in her joints, blurring of vision and fever.
O/E: lymph nodes were enlarged and there was hepatosplenomegaly
What is your most probable diagnosis?

A. chronic urticaria
B. acute urticaria
C. Muckle well disease
D. Urticarial vasculitis
E. HUVS

Key: D
Ref: Rook (44.3)

4. A middle aged lady known case of SLE presented with c/o generalized fatigue, malaise, joint pain and abdominal pain. O/E: there were irregular patches and plaques on her trunk, thighs palms and soles.

A. Her work up revealed
B. Cbc: anaemia, neutrophilia
C. ESR: raised
D. LFTs and Rfts: deranged
E. Skin biopsy: vascular endothelial damage in superficial dermis
F. Immunofluorescence: IgG, IgM and C 3 at DEJ

5. What is most important associated complication?

A. Uveitis
B. Arthritis

C. Pulmonary involvement
D. Glomerulonephritis
E. Angioedema

Key: D
Ref: Rook (44.4)

Chapter 45 AUTO INFLAMMATORY DISEASES PRESENTING IN THE SKIN

1. A 48-year-old female with no significant medical history presented to the clinic with a two-year history of low-grade fevers, intermittent chills, night sweats, recurrent episodes of left eye pain with redness and edema, pleuritic chest pains, intermittent abdominal pain, diffuse myalgia skin exam showed pruritic rash on her right hand and right foot that began two days prior to presentation. History of malignancy, connective tissue disease, or any autoimmune disorder was negative.
Her physical exam revealed a temperature of 98.8°F, blood pressure of 136/94, and heart rate of 110. The recent range in temperatures from outpatient encounters was within the range of 98.8-99.9°F., Her left eye appeared injected and her neck was without adenopathy or thyromegaly. The skin exam revealed a erythematous patch of 5-centimeter diameter on the dorsum of the right foot which expanded centrifugally into edematous dermal plaques overlying area of local muscle tenderness, what is the underlying mutational defect of this disorder

A. TNFRSF1A gene mutation
B. CARD 15 gene mutation
C. MEFV gene mutation
D. NLPR3/CIAS1 gene mutation
E. PMS b8 gene mutation

Key: A
Ref: Rook (45.5)

2. 10-year-old boy initially presented with warm swollen erythema on dorsum of foot and around the right malleolar area, and complaints of bilateral joint pain of the hips, knees, and ankles and pain of the right shoulder. The child responded to daily naproxen. One year later, he continued to complain of hip, knee, ankle, and bilateral wrist pain. He also reported mild to moderate recurrent abdominal discomfort. Omeprazole provided intermittent relief. The patient continued to experience episodes of joint and abdominal pain thrice in a year, how ll you treat the above mentioned disorder

A. Iv steroids
B. No efficient treatment
C. Colchicine and anaconda
D. Will respond to nsaids only
E. Etenercept

Key: C
Ref: Rook (45.6)

3. 10yr old boy with fever abdominal pain myalgia arthralgia for last 10days on exam there was peri orbital edema and migratory erythematous patch and plaque with centrifugal spread over limbs history of similar episodes in past
What is the main complication of this disorder?

A. No serious complication besides joint deformities
B. b) Septic shock
C. Renal failure
D. Amyloidosis
E. Bleeding

Key: D

4. 12 yr. old boy presented with lancinating leg pains deafness polyarthritis along with fever and urticarial. He was diagnosed with muckle well syndrome
What is the treatment of choice?

A. Steroids
B. Inhibitors
C. Interleukin 1 inhibitor
D. Nsaids
E. Anti histamines nsaids and steroids

Key: C

Chapter 47

REACTIVE INFLAMMATORY ERYTHEMAS

1. A middle aged HIV positive male presented to skin OPD with complaints of pruritic rash on skin since 01 week. Examination shows erythematous annular & polycyclic plaques with scaling behind advancing edges mostly on arms thighs and buttocks. Keeping the diagnosis in mind what's the most common association among the following.

A. Malignancy
B. Infections
C. Drugs
D. Systemic disease
E. Idiopathic

Key: B
Ref: Rook (47.9)

2. A 32 years old lady presented to skin OPD with erythematous annular polycyclic plaque on arms and thighs since few days. On examination plaques were indurated with overlying scales. Further inquiry reveals she often takes painkillers for generalized body aches.
Keeping diagnosis in mind which of the following will be first management goal.

A. Identify and treat underlying condition.
B. Potent topical corticosteroids.
C. Topical calciprotriol.
D. Phototherapy.
E. Topical Tacrolimus

Key: A
Ref: Rook (47.10)

3. 58 years old male with erythematous, pruritic eruption since few days. On examination there were figurate eruption of concentric, palpable, erythematous wave like bands having peripheral scales. According to the patient these lesions are mobile. He is chronic smoker with history of weight loss cough and dyspnoea since 01 month. What's the diagnosis?

A. Erythema Annular Centrifuged
B. Erythema gyrate ripens
C. Erythema Marinate
D. Necrolysis Migratory erythema
E. None of the above.

Key: B
Ref: Rook (47.10)

4. A middle aged male known rheumatoid arthritis patient, presented with some pruritic eruption to skin opd since 02 weeks. On examination there were figurate concentric bands in a pattern resembling grains of wood, scaling also present at trailing edges. Keeping diagnosis in mind what will be the disease course and prognosis.

A. Progressive course but resolve in 2-3 years.
B. Chronic course, not curable.
C. Self-limiting
D. Dependent on underlying condition.
E. None of the above.

Key: D
Ref: Rook (47.11)

5. A 28 years old lady presented to skin opd with pruritic lesions on arm and feet. O/E there was a solitary, erythematous, 5*6cm, annular plaque with no surface changes on right upper arm. According to patient, about 2 weeks ago, lesion appeared first as erythematous papule which then enlarges to form ring with central area of clearing. Feet examination shows toe webs maceration bilaterally, which according to patient appeared 1 month back. Biopsy for histopathology was sent from arm lesion.
What will be the histopathological findings?

A. Dyskeratosis, acanthosis and dermal lymphocytic infiltrate.
B. Perivascular infiltrate of neutrophils and mononuclear cells in dermis.
C. Perivascular sleeve like lymph histiocytic infiltrate, melanophages and individual cell necrosis.
D. Vacuolar liquefactive degeneration of basal layer, lymphocytic epidermotropism.
E. None of above.

Key: C
Ref: Rook (47.9)

6. A 10 year old boy presented with erythematous rash over the body and had complain of joint pain.o/e it was noticed that he had some nodules over his bones and erythematous rush was serpiginous and polyclic on further inquiry he told that he had some throat infection few days back and after that all these started. He was also having some meaningless abrupt movement's .in view of above mentioned features what is diagnosis?

A. Erythema annular centrifuge
B. Erythema marinate
C. Necrolysis migratory erythema
D. Erythema gyrate ripens

Key: B
Ref: Rook (47.12)

7. A 15years old presented with serpiginous polycyclic annular eruption which was painless and non-pruritic/e he has subcutaneous nodules over bones and abrupt meaningless movements. On investigation he was diagnosed to have erythema marinate all of the following conditions are associated with this condition except?

A. Rheumatic fever
B. Psittacosis
C. Angioedema
D. Urticarial

Key: D
Ref: Rook (47.12)

8. What is the most common heart finding is present in rheumatic fever?

A. MR
B. MS
C. AR
D. AS

Key: A
Ref: Rook (47.12)

9. A 50 year old man presented in opd with complains of weight loss after he was diagnosed with diabetes mellitus. Further he told regarding the appearance of some rash over his genitalia and groin which was extending according to him. O/e it was annular erythematous lesion with crusted edge. there was postinflamatory hyperpigmentation in the centre.in view of the above mentioned features considering the diagnosis what is the 1st line tx of this condition?

A. Surgery

B. Somatostatin analogue
C. 5.fu
D. Decarbonize
E. Streotozocin

Key: A
Ref: Rook (47.15)

10. What is the prognosis of the above mentioned condition?
A. It will resolve spontaneously
B. It will never metastasize
C. 50% of patient will have metastatic disease at time of diagnosis
D. 10% will have metastatic disease at the time of diagnosis

Key: C
Ref: Rook (47.15)

11. A 6 months old child presented with erythematous maculopapular lesions enlarging and evolving into variable sized grouped annular plaques predominantly located to face, trunk and proximal limbs. Lesions last from 2 to several days and cyclic pattern of new lesions appearing every 5 to 6 weeks. Lesions are self-limiting and so systemic symptoms. Mode of inheritance of most likely dx is?
A. Autosomal dominant
B. Autosomal recessive
C. x linked dominant
D. x linked recessive

Key: A

12. Regarding management of erythema multiform which of following is used prophylactically in recurrent EM?
A. Prednisolone
B. Acyclovir
C. Dispone
D. Thalidomide
E. Both b and d

Key: E
Ref: Rook (47.6)

13. Recurrent erythema multiform has association with?
A. HLA B62
B. HLA B35
C. HLA DR53
D. All of above

Key: D
Ref: Rook (47.3)

14. Erythema multiform is self-limiting cytotoxic dermatitis which results due to which hypersensitivity reaction?
A. Type 1
B. Type 2
C. Type 3
D. Type 4

Key: D
Ref: Rook (47.1)

15. A young male presented in derma opd with skin rash of sudden onset. On examination there are multiple flat dull red macules and urticated lesions on various parts of body. Lesions on palms and soles are having central blisters with marginal zone of erythema. Both of his conjunctiva are red and having watery discharge. Most likely cause of disease is:

A. Viral infection
B. Bacterial infection
C. Fungal infection
D. Malignancy associated

Key A
Ref: Rook (47.3)

Chapter 48 ADAMANTIADES-BEHCET DISEASES

1. Pathergy test of Behcet's Disease is ideally interpreted at:
   - A. 6 hours
   - B. 12 hours
   - C. 24 hours
   - D. 48 hours
   - E. 72 hours

Key: D
Ref: Rook (48.7)

2. Treatment of ocular disease in Behcet Disease includes:
   - A. Topical corticosteroids
   - B. System corticosteroids
   - C. Anti TNF Alpha
   - D. Methotrexate
   - E. All of the above

Key: E
Ref: Rook (48.9)

3. Occular findings in Behcet Disease may include:
   - A. Anterior uveitis
   - B. Posterior uveitis
   - C. Hypopyon
   - D. Cataract
   - E. All of the above

Key: E
Ref: Rook (48.4)

4. Which of the following is a criterion for the diagnosis of Behcet Disease:
   - A. IBD
   - B. Conjunctivitis
   - C. Nasal septum perforation
   - D. Uveitis
   - E. Lobular Panniculitis

Key: D
Ref: Rook (48.4)

5. The arthritis of Behcet disease may characteristically be:
   - A. Symmetrical Erosive Polyarthritis
   - B. Asymmetrical Erosive Polyarthritis
   - C. Asymmetrical Erosive Monoarthritis
   - D. Asymmetrical Non-Erosive Polyarthritis
   - E. All of the above

Key: D
Ref: Rook (48.5)

6. A patient of Middle Eastern origin presents at your OPD with recurrent genital and oral ulceration and a diagnosis of posterior uveitis. What HLA type is associated with the diagnosis you suspect?
   A. HLA B27
   B. HLA DR3
   C. HLA DR4
   D. HLA B51
   E. HLA CW6

Key: D
Ref: Rook (48.3)

Chapter 49

NEUTROPHILIC DERMATOSES

1. A 27 years old male presented in derma OPD with complain of pustules on trunk from last 10 days. He also complain of pruritic lesions. Similar lesions appeared 5 months back. The progression of lesion is from flat to palpable lesions and now there's pus in it. His past surgical history is significant for Bowel resection 2 years back. He is diagnosed case of IBD for which he is taking medicine and the disease is controlled. He also complain of joint pains involving multiple joints started from wrist joint then small joints of fingers of hand and knee joint. There is no history of mucosal ulceration. Patient denies any recent abdominal pain, heart burn, dysphagia, painful defecation, blood in stool and no genitourinary complains.
What is most likely diagnosis?

A. Psoriatic arthritis
B. Bowel associated dermatitis arthritis syndrome
C. Reactive arthritis
D. Behcet's disease
E. Systemic lupus erythematous

Key: B

2. The pathophysiology of above mentioned disease is same as

A. Bee sting
B. Good Pasteur syndrome
C. I/V poison
D. Serum sickness
E. Penicillin reaction

Key: D

3. A 27 years old male presented in derma OPD with complain of pustules on trunk from last 10 days. He also complain of pruritic lesions. Similar lesions appeared 5 months back. The progression of lesion is from flat to palpable lesions and now there's pus in it. His past surgical history is significant for Bowel resection 2 years back. He is diagnosed case of IBD for which he is taking medicine and the disease is controlled. He also complain of joint pains involving multiple joints started from wrist joint then small joints of fingers of hand and knee joint. There is no history of mucosal ulceration. Patient denies any recent abdominal pain, heart burn, dysphagia, painful defecation, blood in stool and no genitourinary complains.
What is the mainstay treatment of this patient?

A. Immunosuppressant
B. Antimicrobials
C. Systemic steroids + Dispone
D. Antimicrobials + Antifungals
E. Antimicrobials + systematic steroids

Key: B

4. Sweet's syndrome caused by:

A. Bleomycin
B. Cytoxan
C. Granulocyte colony stimulating factor
D. Intravenous immune globulin

Key: C

5. Which of the following ocular finding is mainly consistent with classical sweet syndrome?
   A. Nodular episcleritis
   B. Conjunctivitis
   C. Pan uveitis
   D. Retinal artery occlusion
   E. Anterior uveitis

Key: B
Ref: Rook (49.7)

6. Which of the following is major diagnostic criteria of sweet syndrome
   A. Fever >38
   B. Associated with malignancy
   C. Excellent response to systemic corticosteroids or ki
   D. Acute onset of typical lesions
   E. Esr >20mm leucocytes >8000 neutrophils >70%

Key: D
Ref: Rook (49.11)

7. Middle age female known case of psoriasis for last 20 yrs taking multiple treatments. Now presented with erythematous plaques on forum of hands. Skin biopsy shows dense neutrophilic infiltrate. Which drug is responsible?
   A. A .methotrexate
   B. Oral retinoid
   C. NB UVB
   D. TNF a inhibitors
   E. Cyclosporine

Key: B
Ref: Rook (49.7)

8. Middle age lady presented with c/o painful skin lesions on hands and face along with high grade fever O/E erythematous plaques with pseudovesciles keep in mind diagnosis of this patient which statement is not correct regarding etiologic
   A. associated with URTI
   B. Drug hx must be asked
   C. IL-5 and TNF a play important role
   D. Dramatic improvement with steroids

Key: C

9. A 35 year old lady presents with a history of increasing pain and bleeding from a skin ulcer next to her stoma. She underwent proctocolectomy 3 years back for medically refractory colonic Crohn's disease. Her vitals and the rest of the skin is normal. What is the diagnosis?
   A. Squamous cell carcinoma
   B. Mucormycosis
   C. Pyoderma gangrenosom
   D. Acrodermatitis enteropathica
   E. None of the above

Key: C
Ref: Rook (49.4)

10. PG exhibits pathergy in
   A. 75% of cases

B. 25% of cases
C. 85% of cases
D. 50% of cases
E. 65% of cases

Key: B
Ref: Rook (49.3)

11. Associated diseases of PG include except
A. Inflammatory bowel diseases
B. Monoclonal gammopathy
C. Chronic active hepatitis
D. Acne conglobate
E. Sarcoidosis

Key: D
Ref: Rook (49.2)

12. In PG, anti TNF therapy healed in 4-8 weeks while prednisolone 38% healed in 1-3 months. Which biologic would likely render this result:
A. Etarnercept
B. Adalenumab
C. Infliximab
D. Ustekinumab
E. Canakinumab

Key: C
Ref: Rook (49.5)

13. A 45year female presented with a painful non healing ulcer for the fast 3weeks. Her biopsy revealed no organism, and ulceration of the epidermis and dermis associated with an intense neutrophilic infiltrate, neutrophilic pustules and abscess formation. What would be the diagnosis?
A. Pyoderma Gangrenous
B. Vascular occlusion
C. Caliphylaxis
D. Drug induced ulcers
E. None of the above

Key: A
Ref: Rook (49.4)

Chapter 50 IMMUNOBULLOUS DISEASES

1. 29-year-old female initially developed polyarthritis of the small joints in her hands. On the basis of several examinations, a diagnosis of SLE. She had been treated with oral prednisolone. 6 months later, she suddenly presented with a widespread blistering eruption on the trunk and neck. Which one of the following is a likely trigger factor for this presentation?

A. NSAIDs
B. Sunlight
C. Trauma
D. Penicillins
E. Stress

Key: B
Ref: Rook (50.48)

2. 35 year black lady presents multiple tense bullaes on her face for the last 1 month. Previously she had been getting treatment for an unknown disease that caused pain in her hands and feet. Considering the most likely diagnosis, antibodies to which one of the following antigens maybe found in this patient?

A. Desmoglein 1
B. Desmoglein 3
C. Laminin 332
D. Desmoplakin
E. LAD

Key: C
Ref: Rook (50.48)

3. 44 year old woman presents with multiple bullae over her face and trunk. The bulla are tense, contain clear fluid with few haemorrhagic bullae. Previously, she had been diagnosed with SLE and was treated with oral steroids and hydroxychloroquine.
Which of the following antibodies is most closely related to the severity of this eruption?

A. Serum anti-type VII collagen IgM levels
B. Serum anti-type VII collagen IgG levels
C. Serum anti-BP180 antigen IgM levels
D. Serum anti-BP180 antigen IgG levels
E. Serum anti-BP230 antigen IgG levels

Key: B
Ref: Rook (50.48)

4. 44 year old woman presents with multiple bullae over her face and trunk. The bulla are tense, contain clear fluid with few haemorrhagic bullae. Previously, she had been diagnosed with SLE and was treated with oral steroids and hydroxychloroquine.
Which of the following antibodies is most closely related to the severity of this eruption?

A. Serum anti-type VII collagen IgM levels
B. Serum anti-type VII collagen IgG levels
C. Serum anti-BP180 antigen IgM levels
D. Serum anti-BP180 antigen IgG levels
E. Serum anti-BP230 antigen IgG levels

Key: B
Ref: Rook (50.48)

5. 33 year old black male is diagnosed with bullous SLE. Previously he has been under treatment for hypertension and diabetes. He has a BMI of 35 and gives a history of yellowish discoloration a few times in childhood.
In addition to oral steroids, which of the following is the appropriate treatment?

A. Hydroxychloroquine
B. Dapsone
C. Ciclosporin
D. Azathioprine
E. Rituximab

Key: D
Ref: Rook (50.48)

6. Yellowish discoloration could indicate a history of G6PD deficiency. Next best immunosuppressant is Azathioprine.
26 year old girl has bullous eruption over her face and trunk. She previously had a history of pain in small joints of hands, frothing of urine and photosensitivity. Her labs reveal a high titre of ANA, a positive anti dsDNA, low haemoglobin and platelets and microalbuminuria.
Considering the most likely diagnosis, which disease has a similar target antigen?

A. Pemphigus vulgaris
B. Paraneoplastic pemphigus
C. Pemphigus erythematous
D. Pemphigus foilaceous
E. EBA

Key: E
Ref: Rook (50.48)

7. A 5 years male child known case of congenital mitral valve disease and MRSA positive, admitted in cardiology intensive care unit for valve surgery. He developed crusted erosions and tense vesicles in annular pattern for 3 days over limbs and trunk area associated with nasal crusting and few genital ulcers. On further inquiry it was told that some injectable drug was given few days back. No history of blisters in his family. Biopsy and immunofluorescence report awaited. What will be the first line treatment option in this case?

A. Doxycycline
B. Dapsone
C. Sulfapyridine
D. Nicotinamide
E. Ciclosporin

Key: B
Ref: Rook (50.38)

8. A 52 years female patient known case of diabetes and rheumatoid arthritis for 8 years came from village area presented in outpatient department having fragile skin, tense blisters, milias and scarring over elbows knees and oral musoca for 2 months. On further examination scarring alopecia and few nail loss were also present. No history of fever, photosensitivity, drug intake and similar lesions before. Histopathology with Immunofluorescence studies done, showed subepidermal cleft with neutrophilic and some eosinophilic infiltrate along with IgG deposit of u-serrated pattern at dermoepidermal junction. What is the most likely diagnosis?

A. Bullous Pemphigoid
B. Mucous membrane pemphigoid
C. Epidermolysis Bullosa Acquisita
D. Linear IgA disease
E. Porphyria Cutanea Tarda

Key: C
Ref: Rook (50.43)

9. A 35 years female patient known case of systemic lupus erythematous for 6 years suddenly developed tense vesicles and blisters on erythematous skin. Some containing hemorrhagic fluid while other having clear fluid on face, neck, upper trunk and proximal limbs. There was no itching but mild burning sensation. No history of recent intake of any drug. Biopsy and immunofluorescence studies done. Salt split skin test showed deposition of immunoglobulins at the floor of the basement membrane. What is the most likely diagnosis?

A. Bullous Drug Reaction
B. Bullous Pemphigoid
C. Bullous EM
D. Bullous SLE
E. Bullous Scabies

Key: D
Ref: Rook (50.48)

10. A young male patient developed intensely pruritic eruption on scalp, elbows and buttocks for 3 weeks. On further examination some patches of depigmentation were also appreciated on trunk and chest by birth. What will be the immunofluorescence studies in this case?

A. Deposit of IgA in granular pattern
B. Deposit of IgM in linear pattern
C. Deposit of IgG in granular pattern
D. Deposit of C3 in linear pattern
E. None of the above

Key: A
Ref: Rook (50.54)

11. A middle age man known case of treated hepatitis C infection, presented in outpatient department having partially ruptured erosions and blisters over dorsum of both feet for 10 days. Oral mucosa examination showed reticular pattern of white macules. While rest of the body has violaceous papules and plaques over wrist and ankle joint for 1 month. How will you treat him?

A. Wait and watch
B. Repeat HCV RNA PCR
C. Treat Lichen Planus first
D. Treat skin lesions first
E. None of the above

Key: C
Ref: Rook (50.49)

12. The diagnosis of LP pemphigoides is made by the presence of tense blisters at?

A. inside the lp lesions
B. after 2 days of lp lesions
C. outside the lp lesions
D. on face only

Key: C
Ref: Rook (50.49)

13. Brunsting-perry pemphigoid, is a heterogenous disorder with several target antigens. All of the following antigens are found in it except?

A. collagen 7
B. BP180
C. C)BP230
D. desmoglein 3
E. laminin332

Key: D

Ref: Rook (50.50)

14. In a patient with anti p200 pemphigoid, the immunodomimant region is?
    A. DEJ
    B. basement membrane
    C. C ternus of laminin ¥1
    D. type 7 collagen

Key: C
Ref: Rook (50.38)

Chapter 51 LUPUS ERYTHEMATOSUS

1. A 10 year old girl presented with symmetrically distributed circumscribed erythematous to violaceous plaques over dorsal and lateral aspect of hand and feet in cold damp weather. Similar lesions appeared last winter which were healed with rewarming and patient did not consult doctor. This time the lesions were more pruritic and painful. On further inquiry there was no history of oral ulcer, joint pain, frothing of urine or any systemic complaint. Lab revealed haemoglobin 10g/do, ESR 30, ANA positive, antids DNA positive, antiRO positive, LFT, RFT, urine RE were normal. Histopathology revealed focal basal cell vacuolation of epidermis and moderate perivascular and per adnexal lymphocytic infiltrate. What is the mode of inheritance in case of familial form of the disease?

A. Autosomal dominant
B. Autosomal recessive
C. Sporadic
D. X-Linked recessive
E. X-linked dominant

KEY: A
Ref: Rook (51.22)

2. A 10 year old girl presented with symmetrically distributed circumscribed erythematous to violaceous plaques over dorsal and lateral aspect of hand and feet in cold damp weather. Similar lesions appeared last winter which were healed with rewarming and patient did not consult doctor. This time the lesions were more pruritic and painful. On further inquiry there was no history of oral ulcer, joint pain, frothing of urine or any systemic complaint. Lab revealed haemoglobin 10g/do, ESR 30, ANA positive, antidsDNA positive, anti-RO positive, LFT, RFT, urine RE were normal. Histopathology revealed focal basal cell vacuolation of epidermis and moderate perivascular and per adnexal lymphocytic infiltrate. What gene mutation is found in this case?

A. SPINK1
B. TREX1
C. KRT1
D. KRT10
E. TTG1

Key: B
Ref: Rook (51.22)

3. A 45 year old female who was recently diagnosed as a case of hypertension and started on anti-hypertensive treatment. Now she presented in Dermatology OPD with erythematous scaly hyperkeratotic lesion predominantly involving butterfly distribution on the cheek and in Seborrheic distribution on the trunk. ANA was positive but anti DNA and ENA antibodies were not found. Antidesmoglian 1 and 3 antibodies were also positive.

Which drug can induce such condition?

A. Furosemide
B. Chlorothiazide
C. Captopril
D. Valsartan
E. Amlodipine

Key: C
Ref: Rook (51.26)

4. 30 year old female patient presented with vesiculobullous eruption present on the face and neck along with photosensitivity. Histopathology revealed subepidermal blister, neutrophilic upper dermal infiltrate. DIF demonstrated linear IgG at the basement membrane zone. What will be indirect immunofluorescence finding in this case?

A. Antibodies to BP180
B. Antibodies to LAD1
C. Antibodies to Laminin 332
D. Antibodies to type VII collagen
E. Antibodies to p200

Key: D
Ref: Rook (51.26)

5. 25 year old female presented with the history of diffuse hair loss, recurrent oral ulcers, low grade fever and arthralgia for 6 months. She developed broken fishnet type pattern with mottled red discoloration which blanched on pressure on lower legs. The appearance of this pattern may herald involvement of which system?

A. Pulmonary
B. Renal
C. Central nervous system
D. GI system
E. Rheumatic system

Key: C
Ref: Rook (51.24)

6. The most typical condition affecting pulmonary system in pts of SLE is

A. pulmonary hypertension
B. pulmonary fibrosis
C. shrinking lung syndrome
D. pneumothorax

Key: C

7. Following are the most common renal changes seen in SLE pts except

A. ESRF
B. Nephrotic syndrome
C. Membranous nephritis
D. Renal vein thrombosis
E. Nephritic syndrome

Key: E

8. A 23 yr old pregnant lady presented with 2-month history of fatigue, generalised weakness and joint pains. She also complains of oral ulcers and photosensitivity. Labs show pancytopenia. Following statements are true regarding SLE in pregnancy except

A. Azathioprine is safe in pregnancy
B. 20% are affected by pre-eclampsia and preterm delivery
C. Anti-phospholipid syndrome leads to fatal loss
D. Prednisolone is not safe in pregnancy

Key: D

9. A 40-years-old female having long history of photosensitivity and rash presented in dermatology opd for follow up visit. According to her she has been avoiding sun exposure and using high SPF sunblock but still not getting relief. She was also giving history of gritty sensation in her eyes. On examination there were

papulosqamous lesions with scaling. Her autoimmune antibody profile came to be positive. Systemic examination was normal.

Which of the following statement is most appropriate regarding pathogenesis of disease?

A. Increase expression of ANA on the surface of keratinocytes
B. Increase expression of Anti LA on the surface of lymphocytes
C. Increase expression of Anti RO on the surface of keratinocytes
D. Increase expression of Anticardilioin on the surface of keratinocytes
E. Increase expression of Anti RO/SSA on the surface of lymphocytes.

Key: C
Ref: Rook (51.12)

10. A 40-year-old female known case of Lupus erythematosus without any systemic involvement came for follow up visit. Her disease is well controlled on medication and no flare since one year.

Which of the following advice will u give to the patient?

A. You are free from disease, discontinue the treatment
B. 18% chances that u can develop systemic symptoms
C. You can never develop systemic symptoms
D. 79% chances that u can develop systemic symptoms
E. There are more chances of sudden mortality

Key: B
Ref: Rook (51.14)

11. On examination there were many erythematous papules some of them merge to form plagues with scaling. She has been returned from vacations 2 weeks back. Her family history was positive for photosensitivity. There were few blisters on buccal mucosa, nails and hairs were normal. Systemic examination was unremarkable. Histology reveals epidermal atrophy with basal layer vascular degeneration. Auto Antibody profile was positive.

Which of the following is most appropriate treatment?

A. Oral corticosteroid
B. Oral dapsone
C. Oral mepacrine
D. Oral chloroquine
E. Oral methotrexate

Key: C
Ref: Rook (51.14)

12. A 35-years-old female presented in dermatology opd with red papules and plagues over neck and shoulders. On examination there were many erythematous papules some of them merge to form plagues with scaling. She has been returned from vacations 2 weeks back. Her family history was positive for photosensitivity. Oral cavity, nails and hairs were normal. Systemic examination was unremarkable. Histology reveals epidermal atrophy with basal layer vascular degeneration.

Which of the following antibodies are more specific for diagnosis?

A. Anti-ANA
B. Anti RO antibody
C. Anti La antibody
D. Anti DsDNA
E. Anti la and ANA

Key: B
Ref: Rook (51.12)

13. A 30-years-old female known case of Diabetes mellitus, hypertension and ischemic heart disease presented with erythematous slightly itchy rash confined to chest, upper back and proximal limbs for 2 weeks. On cutaneous examination there were circular, erythematous lesions with central clearing. Few vesicles were noted over the active border. Oral examination revealed few ulcers on inner aspect of lips and palate. Scrapping was done for fungal infection which came out to be normal. Lab investigation showed ANA, anti-cardiolipin and SS-A positive.
Which of the following drug is most culprit?

A. Aspirin
B. Clopidogrel
C. Diuretics
D. Glibenclamide
E. Procainamide

Key: C
Ref: Rook (51.12)

14. 32 years old female smoker known case of dle presented in skin opd with complain of sudden eruption of multiple erythematous to violeceus papules on toes of both feet on exposure to cold which are painful. Considering diagnosis which of the statement is not true?

A. 15 % of patients with this condition may develop sle
B. Precipitated by pregnancy
C. Some patients may have cryofibrinogenemia
D. Patients are often ro antibody positive
E. Ana positive in 30 % of cases

Key: E
Ref: Rook (51.7)

15. 30 years old female presented to opd with hyperpigmented plaque with adherent scales on bridge of nose .on removal of scale under surface shows horny plugs.
Histopathology shows lymphocytic interface dermatitis with basement membrane thickening. Which of the following disease is associated with this rash?

A. Thymoma
B. Gunther disease
C. Myeloma
D. Diabetes
E. Addison disease

Key: A
Ref: Rook (51.2)

16. 35 years old female presented to opd with history of scarring alopecia, atrophic hypopigmented plaques on bilateral cheeks. And wide follicular pits on triangular fossa of right ear.
Considering the diagnosis which of the following statement is false?

A. Immunoglobulins and complements are present in uninvolved skin in dle
B. Most patients exposed to uv radiation stress trauma develop systemic disease
C. Dle has different genetic background as compared to sle
D. Patients with sle may develop typical lesions of dle in chronic disease
E. Patiennts with genotype solely for dle will never convert to sle even if exposed to environmental factors

Key: A
Ref: Rook (51.2)

17. 28 years old male presented to dermatology opd with 7 months history of skin lesion on vertex of scalp e patchy loss of hair not associated with itching or redness .no preceding history of trauma.
On cutaneous examination there is 3*4 cm well defined erythematous plaque e atrophy and mild scaling and loss of hairs present on vertex of scalp. There are also multiple wide follicular pits present on concha of right ear.
Her systemic inquiry is unremarkable
Her auto immune profile for ana was negative.
Considering the diagnosis following statements are true for the prognosis of the disease excpet?

A. Scarring is unusual if untreated
B. Disease is chronic and relapsing
C. It exacerbates in spring and summer
D. If the disease is untreated, it will continue episodically for many years
E. Some patients have mild disease that settles spontaneously

Key: A
Ref: Rook (51.10)

18. 26 years old female smoker presented to dermatology opd with history of scarring alopecia for last 3 years. Now for the past 6 months she is started having asymptomatic rash on left cheek and bilateral forearms.
On examination well defined erythematous plaque of size 3*4 cm with adherent scales present on left cheek and similar plaques of variable sizes present on bilateral forearms. Her ana is negative Systemic inquiry unremarkable. U r suspecting discoid lupus erythematous.
Considering the above scenario how much is the chance to convert into sle?

A. 22%
B. 6.5%
C. 16%
D. 5%
E. 1%

Key: A
Ref: Rook (51.1)

Chapter 52 ANTIPYHOSPHOLIPID SYNDROME

1. Young girl diagnosed case of She for last 3years. On her routine investigation she was found to be anemic and urine dr. showed proteinuria with cellular casts. Her renal biopsy was done which showed glomerulonephritis involving > 50% of all glomeruli. According to international society of nephrology what is her class of lupus nephritis?

A. Class2
B. Class 3
C. Class 4
D. Class 5
E. Class 6

Key: C

2. 27 years female presented with fatigue, joint pains and photosensitivity. On further inquiry she added that she also suffers from fevel and oral ulcers. Rest of the systemic inquiry was unremarkable. On routine investigations her bloods showed pancytopecia and urine DR showed 4-5 pus cells. Which of the following is characteristic feature of the disease?

A. Intraepidermal vesicle formation
B. HLA DR2& 3 are involved in antigent presentation to CD4 cells.
C. Microscopic feature pericarditis
D. Macroscopic feature is wire loop lesions in the kidneys
E. Mucin may be found in papillary dermis

Key: B

Chapter 53

DERMATOMYOSITS

1. Regarding antibodies to MDA 5, which statement is not correct?
   A. It is associated with vasculopathic ulcer
   B. Inverse gottron sign associated with these antibodies
   C. Higher incidence of clinically amyopathic dermatomyositis
   D. Almost 50 percent associated with progressive intestinal lung disease
   E. No risk of malignancy

Key E
Ref: Rook (53.11)

2. A 29 year male presented with purplish periorbital rash and proximal muscle weakness since last 1 year. Being his treating dermatologist, you have taken multidisciplinary on board for his management. You started him on oral corticosteroids 6 months back but his skin rash did not respond to treatment. He also developed difficulty in swallowing and recently developed exertional dyspnoea over last 1 month. Next treatment of choice you will offer him:
   A. Continue oral corticosteroids for another 6 months to achieve remission
   B. Pulsed IV Corticosteroids
   C. Azathioprine
   D. Mycophenolate mofetil
   E. IVIg

Key: B
Ref: Rook (53.11)

3. 65 years old female presented to derma opd with c/o marked weight loss, lower abdominal pain and skin rash over hands and face from last 1 year ,There is no significant associated h/o Shortness of breath, O/E lilac erythema present over eyelids,
Keeping in mind diagnosis of this patient, what would be the next appropriate investigation step for this patient which can alter her mortality rate?
   A. Ct chest
   B. Skin biopsy
   C. EMG
   D. MRI brain
   E. Ct abdomen /pelvis

Key: E
Ref: Rook (53.2)

4. An elderly man with weight loss, SOB, difficulty in climbing stairs and standing from sitting posture from last 6 months
On dermatological ex periorbital rash present while on systemic ex fine late inspiratory crept present
On pulmonary function test, what abnormality would we expect of this elderly patient?
   A. Obstructive lung defect
   B. Restrictive lung defect
   C. Both a and b
   D. Inconclusive result, will go for lung biopsy
   E. Will show high snip nasal inspiratory pressure

Key: B
Ref: Rook (53.10)

5. 07 years old female brought by her mother to derma opd with c/o skin rash over face and upper trunk from last 1 year, now she developed multiple subcutaneous nodules over extremities which are restricting her daily physical activities, her mother is concerned about these lesions
Keeping in view diagnosis of this patient, which autoantibody is the most specific for her current complaints?

A. Anti NXP2
B. Anti-Mi 2
C. Anti SUMO
D. U1 RNP
E. 52 kd RO

Key: A
Ref: Rook (53.9)

6. An elderly man, known smoker presented with h/o weight loss ,cough and shortness of breath from last 06 months ,he has h/o multiple visits to different GPs ,he took ATT for it but got no relief from these complaints, on further inquiry he has concurrent h/o multiple erythematous papules over bilateral dorsum of hands ,skin biopsy advised ,which of the following is most consistent findings with these papules on histopathology report

A. Hyperkeratosis
B. Acanthosis
C. Papillomatosis
D. A, b, c
E. Hypergranulosis

Key: D
Ref: Rook (53.3)

Chapter 56

SYSTEMATIC SCLEROSIS

1. A 50 years old female presented in opd with taught indurates and thickened skin. O/e he had reduced hair and sweating and had mask like faces. There was breaking of nose and furrowing of perioral skin with reduced perioral aperture. Considering the diagnosis which of the following investigations are advised annually?

   A. Echo
   B. Lung function test
   C. Thermography
   D. A and b
   E. Hrct

Key: D
Ref: Rook (56.18)

2. Which of the following regarding thermogram is correct?

   A. Immersion of fingers in water at 15c for 1min and recording thermogram after 10min
   B. Immersion of fingers in water at 10c for 5min and recording thermogram after 5min
   C. Immersion of fingers in water at 5c for 5min and recording thermogram after 20min
   D. Immersion of fingers in water at 15c for 5min and recording thermogram at 20min

Key: A
Ref: Rook (56.15)

3. A 55years old presented in opd with complains of dysphagia. o/e she had multiple skin coloured subcutaneous nodules on the body and various telangiectasias. She had taught indurated and thickened skin. We want to treat her skin condition which of the following group should be considered coz of strong ant fibrinolytic effect?

   A. Anti cd 20
   B. Tyrosine kinase inhibitors
   C. Calcineurin inhibitors
   D. Penicillamine

Key: B
Ref: Rook (56.19)

4. Which of the following drugs is most effective in patients of systemic sclerosis with inflammatory genre profile in their skin and show reduced MRSS?

   A. Mmf
   B. Cyclophosohamide
   C. Azathioprine
   D. Mtx

Key: A
Ref: Rook (56.19)

5. A patient of 40years presented in opd with complains of dry cough, breathlessness. He was having attacks of syncope and had peripheral edema. he had right heart catheterization few months back and had a mean pulmonary pressure of 25mm hg at rest and was diagnosed as PAH seci dary to ssc. He had painful joints.
In view of above feature which of the following medicine if he would have taken to reduce the risk of PAH and cardiopulmonary complications?

A. Cyclophosphamide
B. Tnf inhibitors
C. Mmf
D. Pde5inhibitors
E. Azathiporine

Key: D
Ref: Rook (56.21)

6. A 39 year old female, diagnosed case of systemic sclerosis, presents with progressive worsening of her condition. From laboured breathing to inability of flexion of her fingers, she is concerned over the possibility of it being genetically predisposed to her. Multiple susceptibility loci have been identified, which of the following is not related to SSc.
A. STAT4
B. CD247
C. BANK1
D. TNFSF4
E. None of the above

Key: E
Ref: Rook (56:11)

7. A 42 year old lady with characteristic beak nose and pinched lips presented with taut skin on her face and hands and arms for the face 4 years. She gives a history of vaccination antecedent to the disease. Which other environmental trigger is not related to this condition?
A. Viral infections
B. Exposure to silica
C. Exposure to vinyl chloride
D. Hair dyes
E. Chlorinated solvents

Key: D
Ref: Rook (56.13)

8. The following key pathological feature of SSc crosses multiple organ beds - except:
A. Proliferative vasculopathy
B. Neointimal hyperplasia
C. Luminal narrowing
D. Mucin deposition
E. Advential fibrosis

Key: D
Ref: Rook (56.11)

9. A 25yr old diagnosed case of systemic sclerosis biopsy revealed squared edges due to thickening of the dermis and extension of fibrosis into the subcutaneous septate. Which other feature would not be evident in this case:
A. Densely eosinophilic dermis
B. Homogenised dermis
C. Swollen eosinophilic collagen bundles running parallel to the epidermis
D. Dermal atrophy
E. None of the above

Key: D
Ref: Rook (56.10)

10. A 43 yr old female with pulmonary arterial hypertension associated with systemic sclerosis is admitted with increased breathlessness. The risk of her siblings having this disease is:

A. 10 fold increased risk
B. 50 fold increased
C. 13-15 fold increased
D. 18-20 fold increased
E. 5- 8 fold increase

Key: C
Ref: Rook (56:11)

11. Digital vascular disease in systemic sclerosis is associated with

A. Raynoud's phenomenon
B. Ischemia
C. Digital ulceration
D. Both A and B
E. All of the above

Key: E
Ref: Rook (56.18)

12. A 50years old female, being investigated for pulmonary hypertension, was referred to Dermatology OPD. On examination she had peri oral furrowing, skin thickening of fingers of both hands distal to MCP joints and abnormal nailfold capillaries. Her Anti-topoisomerase antibodies were positive what is the score of this patient according to the classification crieteria for systemic sclerosis?

A. 8
B. 9
C. 10
D. 11
E. 12

Key: B
Ref: Rook (56.1)

13. A 42 years old female is referred to Dermatology OPD. On examination she had dyspigmentation of the neck. There were few telangiectasia's on face and upper trunk. On examination of hands, digital tip ulcers were present on 2nd and 3rd fingers. Which of the following is true about Diffuse SSc?

A. Low risk scleroderma renal crisis and cardiac disease.
B. Slow onset and progressive skin changes.
C. Peak skin sclerosis score (MRSS) < 14.
D. ACA + in 50% of cases.
E. High risk of organ based complications Lung fibrosis,secondary PH.

Key: E
Ref: Rook (56.2)

14. A 45years old male presented in Dermatology opd with complaints of headache, fever and malaise for the last 01 week. His also had uncontrolled hypertension along with blurred vision and dyspnoea on exertion. On examination he had mat like telengiectasias on face and thickened skin of fingers. Which of the following is likely to be present in this patient?

A. Anti RNA polymerase III antibodies
B. Anti-centromere antibodies
C. Anti U3 RNP antibodies
D. Anti U1 RNP antibodies
E. Anti Ku antibodies

Key: A
Ref: Rook (56.3)

15. A 55 years old male presented in Dermatology opd with complaints of decreased opening of mouth and bluish discoloration of fingers on exposure to cold. He had small joints pain and early morning stiffness for which he was taking treatment. Diagnosed as a case of SSc Overlap syndrome. Which antibody is present in SLE overlap syndrome?

A. Anti-Centromere antibodies
B. Anti PmScl antibodies
C. Anti Ro antibodies
D. Anti U1 RNP antibodies
E. Anti CCP antibodies.

Key: D
Ref: Rook (56.8)

16. Which of the following is correct about overlap syndrome?

A. Earlier and more extensive musculoskeletal disease.
B. Pulmonary fibrosis and heart disease occur later than in lSSc.
C. Esophageal disease occur earlier than in lSSc.
D. Heart disease occur earlier then in dSSc.
E. Pulmonary Hypertension develop later than in lSSc.

Key: A
Ref: Rook (56.8)

17. A 46 years old female patient diagnosed case of pulmonary arterial hypertension referred from cardiology department with few months history of difficulty in opening her mouth, reduced sweating and difficulty in performing daily activities. O/E skin of fingers and hands was thickened, tight and fixed to deeper structures resulting in contractures. Skin of upper trunk and arms was also thickened and tight. There was also reduced radial furrowing of perioral skin with reduced oral aperture.
Regarding mortality in this case which statement is correct?

A. Mortality is higher in young males.
B. Low mortality in patients with low systolic BP.
C. High in those having high mean Right atrial pressure.
D. Mortality is high in idiopathic form of disease.
E. Mortality is low in patients with lower DLCO.

Key: C
Ref: Rook (56.18)

18. A middle age female patient presented to skin opd with history of change in colour of fingers on exposure to cold since few months. O/E skin of fingers and hands was tight, thickened and fixed to deeper structures. Facial skin was waxy and wrinkles were diminished.
Keeping diagnosis in mind which among following is not true?

A. Almost all patients will have associated gastrointestinal manifestation.
B. Digital vascular disease is almost universal.
C. Inflammatory muscle involvement never occurs.
D. Structural vascular damage associated with digital ulceration.
E. None of the above.

Key: C
Ref: Rook (56.18)

19. A 36 years old male patient referred from gastroenterology presented to skin opd with history of change of colour of fingers on exposure to cold. O/E skin of both hands, forearms and chest was thickened, indurated and tight. Digital ulcerations and pitting were also present. Further examination revealed nasal breaking and decreased oral aperture.

Regarding disease prognosis which among the following is correct?

A. Case specific mortality is low.
B. Mortality is Upto 20%
A. C.1/3rd of deaths are due to pulmonary fibrosis.
C. Half of deaths are due to pulmonary arterial hypertension.
B. E.1/3rd of deaths are due to cardiac diseases.

Key: C
Ref: Rook (56.18)

20. A 45 years old female patient presented with history of dryness and gritty sensation of her eyes and dryness of her mouth since few months. She also complains of limitation of movements of her digits. Further inquiry revealed decrease appetite and post parandial bloating.

O/E skin of upper, lower limbs and trunk was thickened and indurated. Mat like telangectasias was present on face.

Which among the following is not a complication of this disease?

A. Pulmonary fibrosis
B. Pulmonary arterial hypertension
C. Tendon contractures.
D. Renal disease.
E. Fatty liver disease.

Key: E
Ref: Rook (56.18)

Chapter 57 MORPHOEA AND ALLIED SCARRING AND SCLEROSING INFLAMMATION

1. 14 year old female presented with hyper pigmented, linear, macular and thickened lesions extending from the lateral aspect of left knee joint to lateral malleolus for the past 5 years. There were no systemic complaints. Physical examination revealed multiple, hyper-, hypo pigmented, indurated plaques with atrophic, shiny surface along lateral border of left leg. The lesions ranged from 1cm to 30cms in diameter. The lesion was atrophic in the proximal part and demonstrated induration in the distal part. Histopathology showed epidermal atrophy, a sparse superficial and predominantly deep, dermal and subcutaneous perivascular lymphocytic infiltrate and plasma cells, and the collagen bundles appeared thickened and closely packed with sparse adnexal structure. Anti-Scl-70 antibodies were negative.
Considering the diagnosis presence of which of the following antibodies is associated with severe disease?

A. Antifebrile 1
B. Anti MMP1
C. ANA and Anti histones
D. Anti-centromere antibody
E. ANA and anti U3RNP

Key: C
Ref: Rook (57.7)

2. 14 year old female presented with hyper pigmented, linear, macular and thickened lesions extending from the lateral aspect of left knee joint to lateral malleolus for the past 5 years. There were no systemic complaints. Physical examination revealed multiple, hyper-, hypo pigmented, indurated plaques with atrophic, shiny surface along lateral border of left leg. The lesions ranged from 1cm to 30cms in diameter. The lesion was atrophic in the proximal part and demonstrated induration in the distal part. Histopathology showed epidermal atrophy, a sparse superficial and predominantly deep, dermal and subcutaneous perivascular lymphocytic infiltrate and plasma cells, and the collagen bundles appeared thickened and closely packed with sparse adnexal structure. Anti-Scl-70 antibodies were negative.
Considering the diagnosis presence of which of the following antibodies is associated with severe disease?

A. Antifebrile 1
B. Anti MMP1
C. ANA and Anti histones
D. Anti-centromere antibody
E. ANA and anti U3RNP

Key: C
Ref: Rook (57.7)

3. A 30 year old female came with complaints of dark brown sclerotic plaque over the upper half of the right thigh with restriction of movements at the right hip joint. The skin biopsy showed an epidermal atrophy, a sparse superficial and predominantly deep dermal and subcutaneous perivascular infiltrate of lymphocytes and plasma cells, and the collagen bundles appeared thickened and closely packed with paucity of adnexal structures. His Anti MMP1 antibodies were positive.
Considering the diagnosis presence of which of the infection has been correlated with this condition?

A. Rickettsia
B. Trypanosome
C. Staphylococcus
D. Borrelia
E. Mycobacterium

Key: D
Ref: Rook (57.9)

4. A 46-year-old woman is presented with a 3-year history of dermatosis involving the trunk and extremities. The disease began as a discrete area of erythema and progressed steadily with induration of the plaques and affection of other body areas. The surface became smooth and shiny. Physical examination revealed multiple, hyper-, hypo pigmented and ivory-colored indurated plaques with atrophic, shiny surface on the upper and lower extremities, trunk, and buttocks. The lesions ranged from 1cm to 30cm in diameter and some of them were surrounded by violaceous border.
Considering the diagnosis which of the following condition is associated with this disease?

A. Rheumatoid arthritis
B. Sjogren
C. Lichen planus
D. Dermatomyositis
E. Type 2 diabetes

Key: A
Ref: Rook (57.9 & 57.10)

5. A 5-year-old girl had a solitary sclerotic plaque on the back of recent onset. The histopathology features showed Thickening and homogenization of collagen bundles in the dermis and subcutaneous tissues, admixed with a prominent lymphocytic and plasma cell inflammatory infiltrate. She was negative for Anti centromere antibodies but antifebrile were positive.
Considering the diagnosis this condition is associated with which of the following vaccination?

A. DPT
B. Hepatitis a
C. Typhoid
D. Chickenpox
E. IPV

Key: A
Ref: Rook (57.10)

6. Which of the following is predisposing factor for morphea?

A. UVR
B. smoking
C. Radiation therapy
D. Staphylococcus infection
E. OCP

Key: C
Ref: Rook (57.6)

7. Regarding scoring system in morphoea, which is component of modified localized scleroderma skin index?

A. Dermal atrophy
B. Subcutaneous atrophy
C. Depigmentation
D. Erythema
E. Epidermal Atrophy

Key: D

8. Treatment in progressive disease and in patients with linear or deep morphoea methotrexate can be combined with?

A. Pulse I/V methylprednisolone
B. Azathioprine
C. Tacrolimus

D. Acetretin
E. Infliximab

Key: A

9. Regarding phototherapy in morphoea which is false?
A. Treatment of choice for deep morphoea
B. UVA-1 is less erytemogenic and penetrates deeper than UVA-2
C. Current recommendation is medium dose UVA-1
D. BB-UVB, NB-UVB, PUVA therapy can be used if UVA-1 is not available
E. Ant fibrotic effects of UVA-1 were determined by skin type as suggested by wang et all

Key: A
Ref: Rook (57.26, 57.27)

10. 35 years old man presented with thickened and waxy plaque at lateral side of his thigh surrounded by erythematous to violaceous ring. What is the most common subtype of this disease?
A. Plaque
B. Linear
C. Generalized
D. Deep

Key: A
Ref: Rook (57.4)

11.40 years old female presented with multiple small less than 1 cm erythematous to yellowish white mildly indurated with shiny and crinkled surfaces with no scales on trunk.the most likely diagnosis is
A. Guttate psoriasis
B. Guttate morphea
C. Pitryiasis versicolor
D. Lichen planus
E. Paederus dermatitis

Key: B
Ref: Rook (57.2)

12. The term deep morphea implies when it involves
A. Sup and deep dermis
B. Subcutis
C. Both A and B
D. Fasicia and muscle
E. A b and D

Key: E
Ref: Rook (57.3)

13. 40 years old female presented in the opd with widespread thickened skin .on examination there was waxy plaques with crinkled hyperkeratosis surface present around the waist and inframammary areas. The most common variant of this disease in childhood is
A. Plaque
B. Generalised type
C. Linear type
D. Mixed type
E. Overlap

Key: C
Ref: Rook (57.3)

14. A 40 yrs. female patient presented with multiple plaques of morphea on different areas of the body, especially plaques coalesce in the inflammatory area and bra line, waistband, and around the hips and inguinal region at sites of repeated trauma from clothing. This z a type of morphea called as?

A. Non isomorphic pattern
B. Isomorphic pattern
C. Eoisonophillic fascitis
D. Linear morphea
E. pansclerotic morphea

Key: B
Ref: Rook (57.3)

15. All of the following are components of parry-romberg syndrome except?

A. Areas affected are supplied by branches of trigeminal nerve
B. Follow blaschko's lines
C. Patient suffer from renal complications
D. Pts suffer from neurological complications
E. There may be hemiatrophy of the tongue

Key: C
Ref: Rook (57.18)

16. A 24 yrs. old patient, who usually does severe exercise developed painful, burning erythema and pitting edema of the limbs, which later replaced by induration and fibrosis resulting in a peaud' orange appearance. A significant eosinophilia infiltrate present in deep fascia. Biopsy shows thickening of deep fascia. The probable diagnosis is?

A. Eosinophilic cellulitis
B. Pansclerotic morphea
C. Keloid formation
D. Shulman syndrome
E. Linear atrophoderma of moulin

Key: D
Ref: Rook (57.17)

17. Following points favour the diagnosis of atrophoderma of pasini-pierini except?

A. Usually occurs in adolescence n young adults
B. Typical lesions are non-indurated blue grey hyperpigmented, sharply dematcated patcheswith a cliff drop border
C. It's never congenital
D. There may be mild lymphocytic infiltrates histologically

Key: C
Ref: Rook (57.11)

18. 8 years old girl presented with new onset partial complex seizures and skin lesions. Her EEG was done which was abnormal and she was started on anticonvulsants. You are asked to review the patient in Dermatology Department for skin lesion. On/E there is a 10 cm linear brown atrophic plaque on the forehead. The lesion extends onto the scalp with resulting scarring alopecia. Keeping in view the diagnosis which of the following statement is true

A. Neurological complications are the most common systemic association
B. Complex partial seizures have been reported most frequently
C. Radiological abnormalities are predominantly ipsilateral to the skin lesions
D. Abnormalities of MRI and ct scan can occur even in the absence of neurological disease
E. All of the above

Key: E
Ref: Rook (57.18 and 57.22)

19. 45 years old female presented with c/o hypopigmentation and atrophy of skin overlying her left temple and lower jaw. She noticed progressive change in the facial contours for the last 2 years with mouth and nose deviated towards the left side. On/e there was atrophic smooth longitudinal patch on left side of the tongue. There was no family history of similar lesions, neither h/o specific trauma. Her MRI brain revealed no gross white matter changes. Lab testing including ANA was negative. What is the most likely diagnosis?

A. Idiopathic facial palsy
B. Parry Romberg Syndrome
C. Rasmussen Encephalopathy
D. Partial Acquired Lipodystrophy
E. Encoupe de Sabre Syndrome

Key: B
Ref: Rook (57.18)

20. 35 years old female presented with unilateral depressed hyper pigmented blaschkoid plaque on her left thigh since 3 years. The lesion was preceded by generalized arthralgia and Edema of the involved extremity. Regarding diagnosis which of the following is not true

A. Lesions extending joints result in flexion contractures
B. It is associated with muscle atrophy leading to weakness of the involved and adjacent muscle
C. The condition coexists or is preceded by pansclerotic morphea
D. A majority of linear lesions are unilateral
E. None of the above

Key: C
Ref: Rook (57.19)

21. 25 years old lady presents with 5 cm hyper pigmented lesion over her right shoulder. The lesion is a firm oval plaque with shiny smooth surface and purple edge. Over time it feels thickened compared to surrounding skin. New areas have also appeared on the trunk and right thigh. 8 months ago she was admitted to the hospital following a motorcycle accident. Her skin biopsy showed atrophic epidermis and a thickened dermis composed of abundant collagen bundles. There were few inflammatory cells the histopathological findings were consistent with scleroderma. Regarding disease course which statement is correct?

A. The duration of disease activity was usually 5-10 years
B. In limited plaque group 50% resolution occurred on average 5 years and 2.7 years for generalized group
C. The mean disease duration of adult onset disease was twice as long as that for childhood onset morphea
D. Reactivation of disease was infrequent after affective course of methotrexate and corticosteroids
E. Transition from morphea to SSc was reported in 0.13-1.3% of morphea

Key: E
Ref: Rook (57.23)

22. 10 year old boy presented with linear band of Alopecia and Atrophy on scalp at frontoparietal area, following Balshko lines, histopathology shows epidermal atrophy, hyalinization of dermis, atrophy of sweat glands, keeping in mind the diagnosis what is false regarding investigations?

A. MRI can provide useful tool for assesing depth and extend of involvement.
B. MRI can be repeated every 2-3 yearly, since CNS involvement can occur
C. Serial ultrasonography can be used to evaluate skin thickness and loos of muscle and fat.
D. Durometer is hand held instrument that measure tissue blood flow
E. Eosinophilia may occur in active disease.

Key: D

23. A 20 years old female presented with history of blistering and tense bullae formation at Sun exposed sites, on back of hands and face and also of phtoonycholysis. The blustering started 2 years ago. The blisters heal with scarring, pigmentation and sclerodermatous changes. What can be the possible dx?

A. Porphyria cutanea TARDA
B. Congenital erythopoetic protoporphyria.
C. Systemic SCLEROSIS.
D. Variegate porphyria.
E. Sle

Key: A

24. 35 years old man presented with thickened and waxy plaque at lateral side of his thigh surrounded by erythematous to violaceous ring. What is the most common subtype of this disease?

A. Plaque
B. Linear
C. Generalized
D. Deep

Key: A
Ref: Rook (57.4)

25.40 years old female presented with multiple small less than 1 cm erythematous to yellowish white mildly indurated with shiny and crinkled surfaces with no scales on trunk. The most likely diagnosis is

A. Guttate psoriasis
B. Guttate morphea
C. Pitryiasis versicolor
D. Lichen planus
E. Paederus dermatitis

Key: B
Ref: Rook (57.2)

26. The term deep morphea implies when it involves

A. Sup and deep dermis
B. Subcutis
C. Both A and B
D. Fasicia and muscle
E. A b and D

Key: E
Ref: Rook (57.3)

27. 40 years old female presented in the opd with widespread thickened skin .on examination there was waxy plaques with crinkled hyperkeratosis surface present around the waist and inframammary areas. The most common variant of this disease in childhood is

A. Plaque
B. Generalized type
C. Linear type
D. Mixed type
E. Overlap

Key: E
Ref: Rook (57.3)

Chapter 58 CUTANEOUS AMYLOIDOSES

1. 40 years old female, presented with 6 months history of brown colored papules on legs, forearm and trunk. There is moderate pruritus. On histology the following stains can specifically be used except

A. Congo red
B. Thioflavin T
C. Crystal violet
D. Methyl violet
E. Vonkossa stain

Key: E
Ref: Rook (58.3)

2. 50 years old female presents with 1 year history of hyper pigmented, well demarcated macules in the interscapular region with some itching. Which of the following is true regarding the pathophysiology of her disease?

A. Amyloid K is the key feature for localized cutaneous amyloidosis
B. In popular and macular PLCA, cytokeratin 15 is the major constituent.
C. Transglutaminase does not play any role in pathogenesis of PLCA
D. There is increase in oncostatin M (OSM) and IL-31 signaling
E. Pruritus which provokes scratching of the skin reduces amyloid K deposition

Key: A

3. 50 year's old female presented with 7 months history of multiple nodules on feet, they were asymptomatic, red-brown in colour. After work up diagnosis of Nodular Primary localized Cutaneous Amyloidosis was made. All the following are its disease associated except

A. Diabetes Mellitus
B. Rheumatoid arthritis
C. Sjogren's Syndrome
D. CREST syndrome
E. Primary Biliary cirrhosis

Key: B
Ref: Rook (58.6)

Chapter 59 CUTANEOUS MUCINOSES

1. A 60 year old civil servant a known hypertensive of 10 years duration and uncontrolled insulin dependent diabetic since 15 years, presented with wood like thickening of the skin of the upper back with obvious peaud' orange changes in the same region, considering the diagnosis, what is correct as pathophysiology of disease?

A. An increase of type 1 collagen syn-thesis by dysfunctional fibroblasts has been demonstrated in the affected skin.
B. In diabetic scleroderma, the accumulation of collagen may be due to irreversible non-enzymatic glycosylation of collagen and resistance to degradation by collagenase.
C. Excess stimulation by insulin, micro vascular damage and hypoxia may induce the abnormal synthesis of collagen and mucin.
D. Immunological response has also been postulated, but the lack of lymphocytic infiltrate in the dermal lesions seems to rule out a T-cell-mediated etiologic mechanism
E. All of the above

Key: E
Ref: Rook (59.10)

2. A 45-year-old man with type 2 diabetes visited hospital and told that his posterior neck and upper back had progressive thickening and wooden induration for 5 years. A skin biopsy showed an expanded reticular dermis and thickened collagen bundles. Epidermal thickness was 8.7 mm, considering the diagnosis, which of the option is incorrect?

A. It has been diagnosed in 2.5–14% of diabetes.
B. The diabetic type is considered the most common type accounting for 25–50% of cases.
C. The form that is associated with diabetes is more prevalent in men (10: 1)
D. The diabetic type occurs mainly in obese middle-aged men with poorly controlled insulin-dependent diabetes
E. The diabetic type is considered the most common type accounting for 60–70% of cases.

Key: E
Ref: Rook (59.9)

3. A 63- year old woman K/c of hyperthyroidism presented to the dermatology clinic with a six-month history of indurated skin lesion involving both shins. The initial lesion started as asymptomatic, erythematous papules, which slowly coalesced and formed an infiltrative indurated plaque. Over the ensuing months the lesion enlarged to cover the entire lower two-third of the pretibial region, causing associated edema, itching and discomfort. Considering the diagnosis following are variants of the disease except:

A. Diffuse non-pitting oedema
B. Plaque type
C. Nodular
D. Elephantiasis
E. Diffuse pitting edema

Key: E
Ref: Rook (59.11)

4. 82-year-old female, presented with a 1-year history of large, irregular nodular swollen lesions present over both her legs and feet. She suffered a hip fracture a year before presentation without receiving any treatment. As a result, her movement was severely impaired. Her limited walking movement resulted in

gradual swelling of the legs. Raised, plaque-like lesions appeared over the anterior aspects of the tibia bilaterally, extending to involve both feet but sparing toes. The patient stated that she had been treated with levothyroxine (100 μg/day) for over 30 years. She had neither taken a thyroid function test nor changed the dose in the past year. She was a nonsmoker. She was taking amlodipine (5 mg) for high blood pressure. Regarding the treatment, what is the first line therapy?

A. Medium to high potency corticosteroids applied under occlusive dressings or delivered by intralesional injection and compression stockings
B. Octreotide
C. Rituximab
D. Plasmaphresis
E. I/V immunoglobulins

Key: A
Ref: Rook (59.13)

5. A 57-year-old woman presented with a 12-month history of lower leg pain and pruritus aggravated by sitting or standing. She had bilateral, nonpitting edema of the anterior shins, and slight periorlitol edema without exophthalmos. Since treatment of Graves's disease with radioactive iodine a year previously, the patient had remained euthyroid with thyroid-stimulating hormone (TSH) levels in the normal range on levothyroxine prescribed for postradioiodine hypothyroidism. A punch biopsy of the dorsal foot is consistent with pretibial myedema. All are correct except:

A. Infiltrative dermopathy due to mucin deposition
B. Seen in grave's disease
C. Women are affected more often than men (3: 1)
D. Peak of incidence at age 50–60 years
E. Cannot be associated with Hashimoto thyroiditis and euthyroidism

Key: E
Ref: Rook (59.11)

6. A 45-year-old male presented with a skin eruption of closely spaced firm waxy dome shaped papules on his hands, upper limbs, trunk and thighs with surrounding shiny skin. His axillary and pubic hair were sparse. His skin biopsy revealed diffuse dermal deposition, fibroblast proliferation and fibrotic collagen. A diagnosis of scleromyxoedema was made. Treatment options include

A. Thalidomide
B. Intravenous Immunoglobulin
C. Systemic steroids
D. Hydroxycholoroquine
E. Bortezomib
F. All of above

Key: D

7. A 45 year old male presented with erythematous macules and indurated plaque like lesions with a reticular configuration in the midline of his chest. On examination there was no scaling or any other surface changes on these lesions. On histopathology there was deposition of mucin in upper dermis and a perivascular T cell infiltrate. Epidermis was normal. Direct immunofluorescence may reveal the following

A. Granular deposits of IgM, IgG and C3 at dermoepidermal junction.
B. Linear deposits of IgM, IgA and C3 at dermoepidermal junction.
C. Granular deposits of IgM, IgA and C3 at dermoepidermal junction.
D. Granular deposits of IgM, IgG and C2at dermoepidermal junction.
E. Linear deposits of IgM, IgG and C4 at dermoepidermal junction.

Key: C

8. A 50 year old female presented with erythematous macules and indurated plaque like lesions with a reticular configuration in the midline of her chest and her arms. On examination there was no scaling or any other surface changes on these lesions. On histopathology there was deposition of mucin in upper dermis and a perivascular T cell infiltrate. She is hypothyroid and also suffers from diabetes Mellitus. A diagnosis of reticular erythematous mucinosis was made.
First line treatment for this condition is

A. Topical steroids
B. Systemic steroids
C. Hydroxycholoroquine
D. Phototherapy
E. Topical Tacrolimus

Key: C

9. A 49 year Old male presented with widespread eruption on his limbs and trunk which consisted of firm waxy closely spaced, dome shaped papules in a linear pattern with surrounding thick and shiny skin. On investigation his ANA, anticentromere, and AntiScl70 antibody were negative. His thyroid function test also came out to be normal. On histopathology which stains can be used to confirm the diagnosis

A. Alcian blue at pH 2.5
B. Alcian blue at pH 0.4
C. Colloidal iron
D. Toluidine blue

Key: E

10. A 60-year-old woman presented with a skin eruption of firm waxy flat topped papules involving the dorsal aspect of upper limbs, head and neck, upper trunk. She had tight shiny skin of her hands with restricted movement of joints of hands and reduced mobility of mouth. On investigation her thyroid function tests were normal and her ANA, HbA1c were normal.
Hematological malignancies associated with this condition are all except

A. Monoclonal gammopathy
B. Myeloma
C. Hodgkin lymphoma
D. Macroglobulinaemia
E. Acute lymphocytic leukemia

Key: E

Chapter 60 CUTANEOUS PORPHYRIAS

1. A 20 years old female presented with history of blistering and tense bullae formation at Sun exposed sites, on back of hands and face and also of phtoonycholysis. The blustering started 2 years ago. The blisters heal with scarring, pigmentation and sclerodermatous changes. What can be the possible dx?

A. Porphyria cutanea TARDA
B. Congenital erythopoetic protoporphyria.
C. Systemic SCLEROSIS.
D. Variegate porphyria.
E. Sle

Key: A

2. What is dx test for above disease??

A. ENA profile.
B. URINE coproporhyrinogen
C. Plasma spectroflumetry.
D. Histology.
E. Faecal protoporphyrinogen level

Key: C

3. A 19 year old male presented with recurrent attacks of burning and itching along with oedema of hands and face 1-2 hours after exposure to sunlight since childhood. Skin examination revealed vermicular waxy scars over the nose, cheeks, forehead on the background of erythema and pebbly textured skin. Which investigation is most relevant to the above scenario?

A. Peak plasma flourimetery at 624 -627 nm
B. Peak plasma flourimetery at 615-620nm
C. C)Peak plasma fluorimetry at 639nm
D. Peak plasma flourimetry at 633nm
E. Peak plasma fluorimetry at 610nm

Key: D
Ref: Rook (EPP)

4. A 1 year old boy starts crying in his pram in sunny weather. On examination baby has oedema of face, dorsal hands and feet Urinary porphyrin levels are normal but increased decal protoporphyrin concentration .Keep the diagnosis in mind, which enzyme activity is deficient in this baby

A. Uroporphyrinogen 3 cosynthase
B. Urocorporphyrinogen decarboxylase
C. Ferrochelatase
D. Corproporphyrinogen oxidase
E. Protoporphyrinogen oxidase

Key: C
Ref: Rook (EPP)

5. A 7 year old girl complain of oedema and toxic reaction upon sunlight exposure especially of face and dorsal of hands along with itching and tingling Sensation. On examination slight skin thickening of metacarpopharyngeal and interphalangeal joints and vermicular waxy scarring on nose and radial scars on lips .Which is not the complication of above scenario?

A. Vit D deficiency
B. Hypochromic microcytic anaemia

C. Liver failure
D. Gallstones leading to choleastasis
E. HCC

Key: E
Ref: Rook (EPP)

6. A 18 years old girl has history of discomfort and tingling sensation on exposure to sunlight more on dorsal of hands and face on examination of skin of nose, forehead and cheeks shows roughened and pebbly in texture. Keratoderma also seen. Protoporphyrin is seen peak at 633nm on plasma flourimetry scanning.Keep the disease in mind .how the pregnancy can affect the disease in her future.
   A. Symptoms worse during pregnancy
   B. Symptoms will improve and porphyrin level fall down
   C. No effect of pregnancy
   D. This girl will never conceive
   E. Pregnancy will be complicated by anaemia in this pt

Key: B

7. A 18 year old boy presented in ER with abdominal pain and yellowish discoloration of conjunctiva. On examination pt has jaundice and some skin thickening of metacarpophalangeal and interphalangeal joints. Roughened and pebbly skin surface of nose and forehead. He has past history of photosensitivity and now complaining of increased photosensitivity keep the diagnosis in mind. What is the cause of jaundice and abdominal pain in this pt
   A. Severe or total choleastasis
   B. Liver cirrhosis due to protoporphyrin Accumulation
   C. Iron deficiency anaemia
   D. Iron replacement in iron deficiency anaemia
   E. All of the above

Key: E

8. What is treatment of PCT in chronic renal failure?
   A. Venesection
   B. Erythropoeitin
   C. Iron supplementation
   D. Chloroquine
   E. Heparin

Key: B
Ref: Rook (60.13)

9. What is true regarding the PCT?
   A. Isocoproporrphyrin accumulate in faeces
   B. Urinary porphyrin level is sufficient for diagnosis
   C. Urinary porphyrins are used in renal failure
   D. Plasma porphyrins are decreased by hemodialysis

Key: A
Ref: Rook (60.12)

10. What is true regarding the hepatic erythropoetic porphyria?
   A. Symptoms are like CEP
   B. Life expectancy is normal
   C. Hemolysis is milder than CEP
   D. All are true

Key: D
Ref: Rook (60.12)

11. A farmer after spray in the farm developed skin fragility, painful bulla on light exposed areas healing with milia atrophic scaring. Urinary porphyrins are increased. What is diagnosis?

A. PLE
B. Hydroa vaccineforme
C. HEP
D. PCT

Key: D
Ref: Rook (60.11)

12. Pseudoprophyria is common in pt of??

A. Renal transplant
B. b. Acute renal failure
C. c. Interstitial nephritis.
D. Pts undergoing haemodialysis.
E. liver failure

Key: D

13. A 3yr old male child brought to derma Opd having hx of mutilating photosensitivity since early infancy. On examination there was mutilating scarring of face and hands. Hypertrichosis is found on upper arms, temple and malar regions. Mother also had noticed brown staining of nappies in early infancy. Regarding his diagnosis, what is mode of inheritance in this disease?

A. Autosomal recessive
B. Autosomal dominant
C. X.linked dominant
D. X.linked recessive

Key: A
Ref: Rook (60.9)

14. A 3yr old male child brought to derma Opd having hx of mutilating photosensitivity since early infancy. On examination there was mutilating scarring of face and hands. Hypertrichosis is found on upper arms, temple and malar regions. Mother also had noticed brown staining of nappies in early infancy. Considering his condition, diagnosis can be made in utero by measuring uroporphyrin 1concentration as early as

A. 12wks
B. 16wks
C. 20wks
D. 8wks

Key: B
Ref: Rook (60.11)

15. A 4yr old child presented in opd with blisters on exposed areas since age of 5months.Blisters healed with scarring. On examination photo mutilation associated with erosions of terminal phalanges, onycholysis, destructive changes of pinnae and nose. A diffuse pseudosclerodermatous appearance of exposed skin. Regarding his dx, on investigations we will see red cells and urine contain large amount of

A. Uro and coproporphyrin 1
B. Uro n coproporphyrin 3
C. Iso coproporphyrin
D. Protoporphyrin

Key: A
Ref: Rook (60.10)

16. A 5yr old female presented in derma old with mutilating photosensitivity and haematological disease since early infancy. On examination having a diffuse pseudo sclerodermatous thickening of exposed skin. Parents are concerned about disease in future offspring. Considering her dx, what is chance of each future offspring having disease?

A. 50%
B. 20%
C. 25%
D. 10%

Key: C
Ref: Rook (60.11)

17. A 8days old infant developed blisters after photo therapy for neonatal jaundice. On investigations red cells and urine contain large amount of uro and coproporphyrin 1. Feces contain increased coproporphyrin 1.A plasma Spector fluorimetry peak seen at 615-620nm.Regarding his diagnosis, which enzyme deficiency cause this condition

A. porphobilinogen deaminase
B. Uroporphyrinogin 3 cosynthase
C. Uroporphyrinogen decorboxylase
D. Ferrochelatase

Key: B
Ref: Rook (60.9)

Chapter 61 CALCIFICATION OF THE SKIN AND SUBCUTANEOUS TISSUE

1. A female presents with a chronic disease of muscle weakness, oesopgageal dysfunction, telangiectasia, bluish discolouration of hands on change of weather, already taking some treatment for her this problem, now she is having ulcerated white yellow nodules on her trunk, with discharging chalky material, what do u think her problem is caused by

    A. Pox virus
    B. HSV
    C. Taenia solium
    D. Wucheria Bancrofti

Key: C
Ref: Rook (61.1)

2. In above mentioned scenario, what will be the 1st line treatment?

    A. Oral sodium thiosulphate
    B. Intralesional sodium thiosulphate
    C. Topical steroids
    D. Oral steroids
    E. Bisphosphonates

Key: B
Ref: Rook (61.2)

3. Metastatic calcification is rarely associated with

    A. hyperpatathyroidism
    B. Hypervitaminosis D
    C. Sarcoidosis
    D. Milk Alkali Syndrome
    E. Hyperphosphataemia

Key: E
Ref: Rook (61.5)

4. What is the prognosis of heel prick calcinosis?

    A. May resolve without treatment
    B. All lesions need excision
    C. If untreated rarely regress
    D. Resolve once underlying hyperphosphatemia has been corrected

Key: A
Ref: Rook (61.3)

5. Calcium deposits will stain blue with

    A. Giemsa stain
    B. H&E stain
    C. Gram stain
    D. Von kossa stain
    E. Romanowsky stain

Key: B
Ref: Rook (61.6)

6. A 15-year-old boy on a vegetarian diet presented with severe macrocytic anaemia (haemoglobin, 5.1 g/dL; mean corpuscular volume, 116 FL) in addition to leukopenia and thrombocytopenia (pancytopenia), icterus secondary to haemolysis and splenomegaly. Skin exam revealed hyperpigmentation in flexures and palmer creases along with glossitis and angular chelates Laboratory investigations revealed hyper segmented neutrophils on peripheral film

Keeping the diagnosis in mind how you ll treat this disorder

A. Pyridoxine 100mg once daily
B. Cobalamin 2mg daily
C. Folic acid 5mg daily
D. Folic acid plus vitamin b6 supplementation
E. Cobalamin plus folic acid supplementation

Key: B
Ref: Rook (61.23)

7. A 55 year old obese and diabetic patient brought to ER with uremic encephalopathy. O/E of lower extremities, multiple stellate purpuric lesions and livedo remosa seen. On H/P of lesions, most likely finding will be

A. Medial calcification in arterioles
B. Fibrin thrombi small venules
C. Hyaline arteriosclerosis intimal thickening
D. Medial calcification in arterioles, intimal thickening, intraluminal thrombi, extracellular ca deposition

Key: D

8. An old female diabetic for 30 years has been undergoing dialysis for 1 year. Her relative brought her to derma opd for complain of severe pain in thighs. O/E you notice fixed non-blanchable dusky mottled erythema on thighs. Apart from correcting the Ca homeostasis and optimizing her renal treatment what is next best step

A. Sodium thiosulphate
B. Thrombolysis
C. Anticoagulation
D. Cinacalcet
E. Para thyroidectomy

Key: A

9. A patient with ongoing treatment for CA thyroid has presented with painful necrotic ulcers on lower legs. Patient has been admitted and treatment started for calcify axis. Which treatment option has improvement in survival of patient?

A. Sodium thiosulphate
B. Thrombolysis anticoagulation
C. Local debridement
D. Para thyroidectomy
E. None of above

Key: C

10. A 63 year old man brought to ER with severe pain in the lower legs .O/E you notice extensive purpuric indurated plagues with stellate borders and ulceration on thighs and feet; surrounding skin livedo and firm subcutaneous nodules present. What is the most common association with this condition?

A. Renal failure and dialysis
B. Malignancy
C. Hyperparathyroidism

D. Diabetes

Key: A

11. Regarding the etiopathogenesis of above mentioned condition; which option is true?
    A. Hyperglycaemia stimulates osteopontin
    B. Vit d inhibits patathormone related peptide
    C. Warfarin inhibits matrix gla protein
    D. Vit d inhibits fetuin a
    E. All of above

Key: E

Chapter 62 XANTHOMAS AND ABNORMALITIES OR LIPID METABOLISM

1. A 50 year old male presented to you with a tender immobile subcutaneous skin colored nodule overlying the patella since 2 years. The nodule was gradually inc in size. On onvestigation his lipid profile was raised with serum cholesterol above 300 mg/dl and LDL-cholesterol above 255 mg/dl, while HDL-cholesterol was within normal range.
The most likely diagnosis is
A. Tuberous xanthoma
B. Tendon xanthoma
C. Tubero eruptive xanthoma
D. Eruptive xanthoma
E. Planar xanthoma

Key: B
Ref: Rook (62.2)

2. Giving the diagnosis in above scenario, the most likely outcome in the patient for his pathology is
A. Complete resolution on withdrawal of cholesterol diet
B. Do not resolve completely
C. Chronic recurring course
D. Joint immobility in 10 years' time
E. Have a metastatic potential.

Key: B
Ref: Rook (62.3)

3. A patient presented with a painless firm yellow red nodule at the heel for past 2 months. The lesion was small smooth and round at first but has become exophytic quickly. The lesion is surrounded with multiple small similar colored lesions. What is the diagnosis?
A. Tuberous xanthoma
B. Tendon xanthoma
C. Plane xanthoma
D. Xanthelesma
E. Tuberoeruptive xanthoma

Key: E
Ref: Rook (62.3)

4. The above patient should be evaluated for
A. Type 1 hyoerlipidemia
B. Type 2 hyperlipidemia
C. Type 3 hyperlipdemia
D. Hyperglycedimeia
E. Cholesterimia

Key is C
Ref: Rook (62.3)

5. A pt presented with multiple small yellow colored papules on an erythematous base on the buttocks, legs and arms for 3 months. His trigycleride levels are elevated. The most common association of the underlying diagnosis is
A. Lipidemia retinalis

B. Xanthelesma palpebrun
C. Cholestrol emboli
D. Normolipidemic xanthomatosis
E. Necrobiotic xanthogranuloma

Key: A
Ref: Rook (62.4)

6. A patient comes to you with abnormal lipid profile. He has raised VLDL levels. His fasting TGs are 5.5 mmol/L. Apart from abnormal labs, he has no cutaneous findaings. He was advised some dietary fat restriction and was given Statins after his 10 year CVD risk. Your diagnosis of his condition is:

A. Type 1 hyperlipoproteinaemia
B. Type 3 hyperlipoproteinaemia
C. Type 4 hyperlipoproteinaemia
D. Type 5 hyperlipoproteinaemia
E. Sitosterolaemia

Key: C
Ref: Rook (62.10)

7. A patient presented with multiple small papules over buttocks. He gives history of pancreatitis. On examination liver and spleen both are enlarged. His Uric acid levels, VLDL and Chylomicron levels are raised. He was given fibrates for his condition. Which of the following factors is not associated with this condition?

A. Obesity
B. Pregnancy
C. Thiazide diuretics
D. Hyperthyroidism
E. Renal failure

Key: D
Ref: Rook (62.9)

8. A 20 year old patient presented with yellow lesions on face. On examination you found them to be planar xanthomas. Rest of the skin examination was normal. Labs showed total cholesterol 8 mmol/L. He remembered his mother also had same total cholesterol levels when checked some weeks back. Your likely diagnosis will be:

A. Definite Familial hypercholesterolaemia
B. Possible Familial Hypercholesterolaemia
C. Could be both
D. None of the above
E. This patient needs more investigations for a diagnosis to be made

Key: B
Ref: Rook (62.7)

9. A patient in his teens came to see you for some hard mass on his leg. On examination you note subcutaneous firm nodules. He tells you that these have been present since he was born. He is recently diagnosed as having coronary heart disease. His total cholesterol levels are 16 mmol/L. What treatment will you advise?

A. Statins
B. Gemfibrozil
C. Ezetimibe
D. LDL apharesis

Key: D
Ref: Rook (62.7)

10. A 15 year old presented in ER and was diagnosed with Coronary vascular disease. He was referred to you due to Achilles tendon xanthoma. His TGs levels were normal. However Total Cholesterol levels and LDL levels were raised. Which receptor mutation in this disease is Receptor negative?
   A. Type 1
   B. Type 2
   C. Type 3
   D. Type 4
   E. Type 5

Key: A
Ref: Rook (62.6)

11. A 39 years male known Case of IHD presented with complain of yellowish-orange palmer creases and yellowish painless nodules on extensors.
On investigation: increase in plasma total cholesterol and triglycerides.
Further investigation showed lipoprotein electrophoretic pattern.
Keeping the diagnosis in mind, following are complications except?
   A. Premature CVD
   B. Gout
   C. Lipoprotein glomerulopathy
   D. Acute pancreatitis
   E. Peripheral vascular disease.

Key: D

12. A 40 year female presented to OPD with complain of yellowish painless nodules on elbows and knees. She had history of MI 2 years back. On cutaneous examination firm yellow- red non tender nodules on elbows and knees. On further examination you noticed yellowish orange palmer creases.
What will be most likely findings on investigation?
   A. Increase VLDL, increase IDL, Decrease LDL
   B. Increase VLDL, Increase IDL, increase LDL
   C. Decrease VLDL, Increase LDL, increase HDL
   D. Decrease VLDL,
   E. Decrease IDL, increase LDL
   F. Increase LDL only

Key: A

13. A 14 yrs old boy presented to you with history of seizures and peripheral neuropathy for one month. On cutaneous examination u see yellowish coloured plaques around both eyes along with one plaque on knee joint. Further examination revealed early stage cataract in right eye. What would you expect in lipid profile of the patient?
   A. High serum cholesterol level
   B. High cholestenol concentration
   C. Both a and b
   D. Hyper triglyceridemia

Key: B

14. Which statement is true about cerebrotendinous xanthomatosis?
   A. Serum cholesterol level is markedly high in this condition
   B. It is an autosomal dominant condition
   C. It is caused by deficiency of sterol 10 hydroxylase
   D. Chenodeoxycholate is the treatment of choice

Key: D

15. Treatment of choice in sitosterolaemia is?
   A. lifestyle and dietary modification
   B. Chenodeoxycholate
   C. Ezetimibe
   D. Statins

Key: C

16. 39 years patient presented with multiple small papules over extensor surfaces.
On cutaneous examination there were 5mm yellowish papules in large number present on buttocks, legs and back.
On examination of fundus creamy yellow discoloration of retinal blood vessels was present. All are true regarding this disease except?
   A. Increase risk of acute pancreatitis.
   B. There can be hepatomegaly and splenomegaly
   C. Extremely elevated serum triglycerides > 20 mmol/ L.
   D. It is due to deficiency of lipoprotein lipase.
   E. Treatment includes bile acid sequestration.

Key: E

17. A 40 yrs old HIV patient currently on treatment with antiretrovirals came to you clinic with weight loss and progressive proportionate thinning of arms and legs for 2 months. You got his baselines done .u found that his lipid profile is markedly derranged .what would be ur first step of managemen?
   A. Lifestyle modification
   B. Start statins and fibrates
   C. Daily physiotherapy
   D. Optimization of drug regimen

Key: A

18. A 45 year male presented to Emergency department with complain of acute abdominal pain and multiple small papules over buttocks, back and arms. On cutaneous examination yellowish papules of 2-5mm size on erythematous base were seen.
Investigations showed increase in triglycerides and increase amylase.
What is mode of inheritance of the underlying disease?
   A. Autosomal dominant
   B. Autosomal recessive
   C. X linked dominant
   D. X linked recessive
   E. None of above.

Key: B

19. Effect of corticosteroids on lipid profile mainly involves?
   A. Increased total LDL and HDL cholesterol
   B. Type 2 hyperlipoproteinemia
   C. Hyper triglyceridemia
   D. It does not cause any effect

Key: A

20. A patient presented with complain of yellowish palmer creases and yellow nodules on knees and elbows.
He is taking treatment for gout and IHD.
Regarding his disease what is underlying defect?
   A. Abnormal Apo E
   B. Deficiency of lipoprotein lipase
   C. Mutation in gene ABCG5

D. Defect in sterol - 27- hydroxylase
E. Mutation in LDL receptor gene.

Key: A

21. A young male patient presents with LDL 600 mg/dl, triglycerides 160 mg/dl. On palpation s/c nodules attached to the achilles tendon but the overlying skin had no yellow hue. What would be the most likely finding on physical examination?
A. Tendon xanthoma
B. Lipemia retinalis
C. Eruptive tuberous xanthomas
D. Xanthelasma

Key: A

22. A 32-year-old, mentally retarded female presented with gait instability and right malar eminence swelling as well as swelling along the posterior aspect of both ankle joints. Patient had undergone surgery for cataracts in both eyes 10 years back. On examination patient was found to have ataxia, soft, non-tender swelling along the posterior aspect of both ankle joints, as well as right malar emminence
Lipid profile revealed total cholesterol of 306 mg/dl (LDL 205 mg/dl, VLDL 46mg/dl, HDL 55 mg/dl) and triglycerides of 526 mg/dl. MRI brain revealed hyperintensity of bilateral dentate nuclei, deep cerebellar white matter with hyperintensity of posterior limbs of internal capsules on T2W and FLAIR images with corresponding hypointensity on T1W images. Considering above what could be probable diagnosis?
A. Niemann-Pick Disease Type C
B. Hypercholesterolemia type II
C. Cerebrotendinous Xanthomatosis
D. Cholesterol Ester Storage/Wolman Disease
E. Sitosterolaemia

Key: C

23. A five-month-old girl presented with a three-week history of a rash and mucositis unresponsive to a variety of topical medications. She also had symptoms of irritability, vomiting, and diarrhea. Her diet consisted almost exclusively of breast milk. Physical examination showed acral edema and petechialike macules on the trunk. The most dramatic findings were large desquamating shiny hyperpigmented plaques on the extensor extremities, over the time more generalised erythema on body starting from face and groin area with generalised exfoliation! What could be probable diagnosis?
A. Protein energy malnutrition (kwashiorkor)
B. Drug eruption
C. Staph Scalded skin
D. Omenn syndrome
E. Congenital icthyosis

Key: A

24. 14-month-old African boy and hyperkeratotic papules and plaques, Patches initially arise on the back of the elbows and the front of the knees, and can spread to involve the extremities, upper forearms and thighs. On histopathology shows Enlarged hair follicles containing keratin plug, Lamellated hyperkeratosis next to the hair follicles, Atrophy of the sebaceous glands! Lab evaluation shows normal blood count but decrease Albumin.
What is probable diagnosis?
A. Keratosis pilaris
B. Lichen spinolusis
C. Keratosis circumsripta
D. Phrynoderma
E. Darier disease

Key: D

Chapter 63

NUTRITIONAL DISORDERS AFFECTING THE SKIN

1. A 60 old lady, known case of Parkinson's disease, pulmonary tuberculosis on ATT and stage 4 chronic renal failure not on hd. She experienced a sudden onset of seizure-like attacks with upper limb jerking, head tilting back and eyeballs rolling up. She had five episodes within 24 hours on examination of skin there was seborrheic dermatitis like rash on face scalp and shoulders and angular chelitis was also seen keeping the diagnosis in mind which drug is likely interacted and leads to this condition

A. Pyrazinamide
B. Isoniazid
C. Ethambutol
D. Levodopa/carbidopa
E. Loop diuretics

Key: B
Ref: Rook (63.12)

2. A 20 year-old vegetarian boy born to non-consanguineous parents presented with easy fatigue, breathlessness and pain in the legs on walking, noted during the past few weeks. On skin examination there was hyperpigmentation of face flexures and palmer creases and diffuse hair depigmentation. Paleness and icterus in the sclerae and angular chelitis had been noted by the parents. The vegetarian patient had not consumed any food of animal origin for many years. Besides, the family only rarely ate fresh fruits or vegetables.

The patient had a history of an upper respiratory tract infection that began about 15 days earlier and resolved 1 week later. No fever was noted. In the physical examination, the patient looked pale and weak, and his sclerae were icteric. His heart rate was 96 bpm, and a 2/6 mesocardiac systolic murmur was heard.

Laboratory investigations revealed (haemoglobin 5.1 g/dL; mean corpuscular volume (MCV), 116 fL), leucopenia (white cell count 2540/μL; neutrophil count 1230/μL) and thrombocytopaenia (107 000/mm3). Reticulocyte percentage was 0.8%. Serum indirect bilirubin, lactate dehydrogenase (LDH), aspartate and alanine aminotransferases and uric acid levels were 4 mg/dL (0–0., 5565 U/L (135–225), 150 U/L (8–40), 51 U/L (8–41) and 8.5 mg/dL (2.4–8), respectively. C reactive protein, direct Coombs and testing for glucose-6-phosphate dehydrogenase (G6PD) deficiency (screening test) were all negative.Plasma homocysteine level was markedly elevated (>50 μmol/L; normal 5–12 μmol/L). Epstein-Barr virus and cytomegalovirus serologies were both indicative of a past infection (no recent infection).

What is the likely diagnosis?

A. Vitamin b6 def
B. Cobalamin defeciency
C. Riboflavin defeciency
D. Folic acid defeincy
E. Iron defeciency

Key: D
Ref: Rook (63.18)

Chapter 64

SKIN DISORDERS IN DIABETES MELLITUS

1. With regards to DM and Skin which is the most accurate:
   A. Diabetic aeropathy is most commonly expressed on forearms and feet
   B. Scleroderma most often presents on the tibia surfaces
   C. Scleroderma is most common manifestation of DM
   D. Less than 5% of patients with DM have Necrobiosis lipoidica
   E. Less than 5% of patients with Necrobiosis lipoidica have DM

Key: D
Ref: Rook (64.5)

2. Which of the following is characteristic of Diabetic Skin:
   A. Approximately 20% of Diabetes have Necrobiosis lipoidica Diabeticorum
   B. The level of cleavage in Bullous Diabeticorum is mostly sub-corneal
   C. Candida Tropicalis is the most common cause of angular cheilitis
   D. Yellow skin may occur in upto or even more than 10% of Diabetics
   E. There is well established association between Granuloma Annulare and DM

Key: D
Ref: Rook (64.7)

3. All of the following are true regarding Diabetes and Skin EXCEPT:
   A. Yellow skin and nails have been reported to be more frequent in patients Diabetes or Glucose intolerance
   B. Necrobiosis lipoidica Diabeticorum may be associated with cutaneous anesthesia
   C. There is no impact of tight glucose control on developing Necrobiosis lipoidica Diabeticorum
   D. Necrobiosis lipoidica Diabeticorum is associated with increased dermal mucin
   E. 0.3% to 3% of Diabetics have this skin condition

Key: D
Ref: Rook (64)

4. Which of the following BEST describes the relationship between Diabetes and Skin:
   A. Bullae are common on thighs
   B. Yellow skin affects majority of Diabetes
   C. Diabetic dermopathy mainly affects upper back
   D. DIF is negative in Bullous Diabeticorum
   E. Necrobiosis lipoidica Diabeticorum may affect upto 20% of Diabetics

Key: D
Ref: Rook (64.7)

5. Eruptive xanthomas in Diabetics may pose a significant risk of:
   A. Myocarditis
   B. Atherosclerosis
   C. Stroke
   D. Pancreatitis
   E. Infections

Key: D
Ref: Rook (64.3)

6. Diabetes is a feature of which of the following genetic diseases:
   A. Werner Syndrome
   B. Lipoid Proteinases
   C. Haemochromatosis
   D. Acromegaly
   E. All of the above

Key: E
Ref: Rook (64.4)

Chapter 65

INHERITED DISORDERS OF COMIFICATION

1. 6-year-old girl, the first child of no consanguineous marriage, delivered full term by the vaginal route presented with limb defects involving the right side of the body. Within a few days of birth, she developed reddish scaly lesion over the right groin with strict midline demarcation. It then gradually progressed to involve the right neck, axilla, and popliteal fossa within a few months. Because of lower limb asymmetry, walking was very difficult and developed contractures of both lower limbs. Cutaneous examination revealed multiple patchy sharply demarcated, erythematous, hyperkeratotic, scaly plaques on the right side of the neck, axilla, buttock, popliteal fossa, groin, and hand and foot. Nail plates were dystrophic. No history of similar skin and limb abnormalities was in either parents or siblings. Nail plates were dystrophic. Rest skin and mucosal examination were normal. Her mental development, ophthalmological and hearing was normal. Her physical growth, social, and adaptive behavior was normal.
Which treatment will produce excellent clinical response in for the cutaneous lesions in this disease?

A. Low dose oral isotretinoin
B. Paraffin based ointments
C. Topical corticosteroid cream
D. Topical cholesterol cream
E. Topical tacrolimus ointment

Key: D
Ref: Rooks (65.22)

2. A 15 year old boy presented with well demarcated hyperkeratotic and erythematous plaques, in a map like distribution on the trunk and buttocks, which extend and regress in area of thickness and erythema. He has been using topical medications but not responding to any of them. Histopathological examination shows papillomatosis, moderate to severe acanthosis, hypergranulosis composed of two to four layer cells, compact hyperkeratosis and follicular plugging. In papillary dermis, there are dilated, elongated capillaries with a variable perivascular inflammatory infiltrate. A "church spire" configuration of the epidermis is noted. Ultrastructural studies show a decreased number of lamellar bodies in the granular layer. What is the diagnosis?

A. Acrokeratosis verruciformis of hope
B. Gottron syndrome
C. Happle syndrome
D. Mendes DA Costa syndrome
E. Symmetrical acrokeratoderma

Key: D
Ref: Rooks (65.18)

3. 11-year-old boy presented with transient redness and brownish-crusty lesions. He had these lesions since age 2 years. He was seen by several physicians and he was treated with different treatments including salicylic acid, and corticosteroids that were ineffective. Erythematous lesions appeared from time to time that worsened with physical activities and heat, and disappeared spontaneously. However, the brownish crusty lesions did not recover. His parent was a second-degree relative. His sister had similar symptoms.
Which of the following junction is defective in this disease?

A. Desmosomes
B. Gap junctions
C. Hemidesmosomes
D. Tight junctions

E. Zonula adheres

Key: B
Ref: Rooks (65.18)

4. A 2 months old female child was brought in the opd by her mother with the complain of linear scaling with a swirling pattern following the lines of blashko, on the body involving the upper and lower limbs. There is presence of facial Asymmetry, palmo plantar hyperkeratosis, and nail dystrophy. Scalp and eyebrow hair are sparse and lusterless. Asymmetrical shortening of limbs are also present. What is the defect in this disease?

A. Elevated 8-dehydrocholestrol
B. Elevated 7-dehydrocholestrol
C. Decrease 8-dehydrocholestrol
D. Deficiency of steroid sulfatase
E. Deficiency of beta hydroxysteroid dehydrogenase

Key: A
Ref: Rooks (65.21)

5. A 2 months old female child was brought in the opd by her mother with the complain of linear scaling with a swirling pattern following the lines of blashko, on the body involving the upper and lower limbs. There is presence of facial Asymmetry, palmo plantar hyperkeratosis, and nail dystrophy. Scalp and eyebrow hair are sparse and lusterless. Asymmetrical shortening of limbs are also present. What is the diagnosis?

A. Congenital hemi dysplasia ichthyoses nevus limb defect syndrome
B. Klick syndrome
C. MEND syndrome
D. Gauche syndrome
E. X-linked dominant chondrodysplasia type II

Key: E
Ref: Rooks (65.20)

6. Mother brought her 3 months old baby with complain of dryness and scaling of the body mostly involving extensor surfaces of the extremities and trunk. Flexures and groins are spared and there are accentuated palmer crease. On histopathology, there is orthohyperkeratosis with absent granular layer. Diagnosis:

A. Lamellar ichthyosis
B. Ichthyosis vulgaris
C. Bathing suit ichthyosis
D. X-linked ichthyosis
E. Epidermolysis

Key: B
Ref: Rooks (65.4)

7. Which investigation would support the diagnosis of Ichthyosis vulgaris?

A. Serum TSH
B. Serum bilirubin
C. Serum IgE level
D. Serum creatinine
E. Serum ferritin

Key: C

8. 5 years old boy presented with dark brown colored scaling since birth covering trunk, extremities and neck. Palms and soles are spared. Family history is positive for similar condition. Histopathology reveals orthohyperkeratosis with thickened stratum granulosum. This condition is caused by mutation in:

A. Lipoxygenase E3 & 12B
B. Steriod sulfatase
C. Transglutaminase-1
D. Acid lipase
E. Patalin like phospholipase

Key: B
Ref: Rooks (65.4)

9. IV can be differentiated from RXLI by:

A. IV usually present at birth
B. Palms and soles unaffected in IV
C. Dark hyperkeratosis giving dirty look usually seen in IV
D. Scales tendes to be larger in IV
E. Antecubital folds and popliteal folds spared in IV.

Key: E
Ref: Rook (65.3)

10. Frequent ophthalmological examination findings in patient with RXLI:

A. Keratitis
B. Deep stromal corneal opacity
C. Corneal ulcers
D. Keratoconus
E. Corneal abrasion

Key: B
Ref: Rooks (65.6)

11: A 5 year old child presented with rerecurrent episodes of lip swelling, especially after taking nuts. On examination he has multiple polycyclic patches with double edge scales. There is hair shaft abnormality as well, what is the term used for hair abnormality in this condition.

A. Monilethrix (beaded appearance)
B. Trichorrhexis nodosa
C. Trichotillomania
D. Trichorrhexis invagination (Bamboo appearance)
E. Alopecia areata

Key: D
Ref: Rooks (65.24)

12: A 6 year old boy born of a consanguineous marriage under care of neurophysician was referred to the dermatology department , there was history of generalized scaly & pruritic skin lesion, The lesions were over the forehead, trunk, forearm and legs with accentuation at flexures and umbilicus. Hair, nail and mucosal surface were spared, the child had a seizure at the age of 4 months and developed spastic diplegia affecting lower limbs at the age of 3 years. What is the diagnosis?

A. Refsums disease
B. XLD ichthyoses
C. Netherton syndrome
D. Sjogren's larsson syndrome
E. icthyosis hystrix

Key: D

Ref: Rooks (55.5)

13: A 3 years old child presents to you with dryness of skin since birth & rash for the past six months, He has been treated previously for flexural eczema but showed no improvement. On examination the trunk shows multiple annular plaques with scaly, double edged margins, he has sparse brittle, luster less hair whereas the nails are normal. What is the mode of inheritance of this disease?

A. AD
B. AR
C. XLR
D. XLD
E. None of the above

Key: B
Ref: Rooks (65.24)

14: Sjogren syndrome, which of the following option is correct

A. Mutation in ALDH3A2 gene that results in deficiency of (FALDH)
B. Spink5 defect
C. Defect in ECM Protein 1
D. Mutation in LMNA gene
E. TGM1 gene

Key: A

15. A 55 years old woman presented with decrease vision and hearing loss .Collecting medical history, a diagnosis of Retinitis Pigmentosa associated with cataract made at the age of 50 years, sensorimotor polyneuropathy with elevated CSF protein was present. Physical examination shows decrease vision, anosmia, impaired taste, sensorineural deafness, postural instability and sensorimotor polyneuropathy. Cutaneous examination shows mild ichthyosis. Histological examination shows vacuolated basal cells and fat globules within the basal cell layer seen with Oil red O stain. Keeping in mind the diagnosis, best treatment is

A. Retinoid therapy
B. Green vegetables and weight Loss
C. Lipid apheresis and phytanic acid rich diet
D. Lipid apheresis with retinoids.
E. Lipid apheresis and phytanic acid poor diet

Key: E
Ref: Rooks (65.29)

16. Two siblings, presented with fragile and brittle hair since birth associated with extreme sensitivity in sun-exposed areas. Both were born preterm at 32 weeks after a pregnancy complicated by pregnancy-induced hypertension with a low birth weight .Their one another brother was born normal with no anomalies. At 2 year of age, she presented with fragile small nails, pulp atrophy, brittle hair, teeth discolouration, and palmoplantar hyperkeratosis and skin dryness with an ichthyosiform pattern. Scalp and eyebrow hair are fragile, sparse and short. On polarizing microscopy, it shows "Tiger tail pattern". The most probable diagnosis is

A. Refsum disease
B. Gaucher syndrome
C. Tay syndrome
D. Sjogren Larsson syndrome

Key: C
Ref: Rooks (65.33)

17. A 58 years old woman presented with decrease vision and hearing loss .Collecting medical history, a diagnosis of Retinitis Pigmentosa associated with cataract made at the age of 52 years, sensorimotor polyneuropathy with elevated CSF protein was present. Physical examination shows decrease vision, anosmia, impaired taste, sensorineural deafness, postural instability and sonsorimotor polyneuropathy. Cutaneous examination shows mild ichthyosis .Histolological examinatiin shows vacuolated basal cells and fat globules within the basal cell layer seen with Oil red O stain. Keeping in mind the diagnosis, which one is correct?

A. Autosomal dominant inheritance and mutation in PHYH
B. Autosomal recessive inheritance and mutation in SUMF1
C. Autosomal recessive inheritance and mutation in PHYH
D. X Linked recessive inheritance and mutation in PHYH

Key: C
Ref: Rooks (65.28)

18. An 18 year old female presented with fragile and brittle hair since birth associated with extreme sensitivity in sun-exposed areas. She was born as a collodion baby. At 1 year of age, she presented with fragile small nails, pulp atrophy, brittle hair, teeth discolouration, palmoplanter hyperkeratosis and skin dryness with an ichthyosiform pattern. Some episodes of seizure also reported. Polarizing microscopy shows "Tiger tail pattern ". Keeping in mind the diagnosis, true regarding the genetic of disease is

A. DNA repair defect with mutation in C7ORF11
B. DNA repair defect involving TFIIH
C. No DNA repair defect but with mutation in C7ORF11
D. DNA repair defect with mutation in ABHD5

Key: B
Ref: Rooks (65.33)

19. 35 year old unmarried female, presented with a history of increasing weakness of limbs and ataxia for three months, rapidly worsening for 8 days before admission. There were no limb pains and there was no subjective loss of sensation. She was barely able to walk without support. She had 'always' had difficulty in perceiving odors, and had been aware of night-blindness since early childhood. Her skin had always been dry and scaly. Keeping in mind the diagnosis, histology of the disease will show?

A. Sub corneal splitting and enhanced detachment of coenocytes
B. Hyperkeratosis, parakeratosis and eosinophilic material below the stratum carenum
C. Vacuolated basal cells and numerous fat globules within the basal cell layer with special lipid stain
D. Deadhesion of keratinocytes with widening of intercellular spaces with special lipid stain

Key: C
Ref: Rooks (65.29)

20. A 5 years old boy presented in the opd with history of toe nail dystrophy, Focal palmoplantar keratoderma, patchy white thickened areas on tongue for last 4 years. He also presented with erupted teeth at birth. What is the most likely diagnosis?

A. Onychomycosis
B. Pachyonychia congenita
C. Frizzled 6 gene dystrophy
D. Cloustan syndrome
E. Painful hereditary callositie

Key: B
Ref: Rooks (65.44)

21. A 2 year old boy presented in the opd with history of plantar keratoderma, Plantar pain, toenail dystrophy, follicular hyperkeratosis on knees and elbows, Oral leuko keratosis, palmoplantar hyperhidrosis and cysts. Which of the following statement is false

A. Treatment with retinoid is satisfactory
B. Treatment of hyperhidrosis may reduce blistering
C. Incision and drainage in patients with cysts
D. Mechanical reduction of hyperkeratosis of nails
E. All of the above

Key: A
Ref: Rooks (65.45)

22. Pachyonychia congenita, autosomal dominant disorder, is associated with which of the following keratin gene mutation

A. KRT6A
B. KRT16
C. KRT6B
D. KRT6C
E. All of the above

Key: E
Ref: Rooks (65.44)

23. A 65 years old man presented in the opd with history of multiple circular sharply defined hyper pigmented patches of dry skin with icthyosis form scaling present on back, upper arms, buttocks, thighs and abdomen for last 6 months. He has been diagnosed with Hepatocellular carcinoma. What is the most likely diagnosis?

A. Dermatophytosis
B. Pitriyasis Versiclor
C. Pitriyasis Rotunda
D. Nummular Eczema
E. Leprosy

Key: C
Ref: Rooks (65.41)

24. A 25 years old boy presented in the opd with history of multiple circular sharply defined hyper pigmented patches of dry skin with icthyosis form scaling present on the back and upper arms, buttocks, thighs and abdomen for last 1 year. What is the most important investigation of choice to diagnose the condition?

A. Clinical diagnosis
B. Biopsy
C. Electron microscopy
D. Immunohistochemically studies
E. Mutational Analysis

Key: B
Ref: Rooks (65.41)

25. 18 yr. old boy presents with patch of waxy, yellow hyperkeratosis which is extending along whole surface of Palms and soles. Onset is since early childhood. There is hyperhidrosis of Palms and soles with maceration and malodour. He also has angular cheilitis, thickened nails and pseudo ainhum. What is the gene involved?

A. SLURP 1
B. KRT1

C. KRT6 & KRT16
D. KRT9
E. PEX7

Key: A
Ref: Rooks (65.48)

26. Regarding above scenario, what is false regarding the treatment:
A. Oral retinoids are effective
B. Split thickness skin grafts can relieve functional impairment
C. There is no risk of malignancy
D. Patients with long history should be foll
E. Owed up regularly for secondary malignancy

Key: C
Ref: Rooks (65.48)hats

27. A child presents with diffuse honey comb hyperkeratosis of Palms, there are also cicatricle bands along the little finger. He has a generalized dry skin since birth. Which of the following is true about its Histopathology findings
A- Hyperkeratosis, hypergranulosis, parakeratosis
B- Hyperkeratosis, absent granular layer and thick upper dermis
C- Hyperkeratosis, hypergranulosis, lympho-histiocytic infiltrate in upper dermis
D- Hyperkeratosis, hypergranulosis. There are vaculated cells below granular layer
E- Atrophic epidermis, thickened superficial and deep dermis

Key: A
Ref: Rooks (65.49)

28. A 16 yr old male presents with history since infancy, of diffuse honey comb keratosis on Palms and soles. He has a generalized dry skin since birth. He also has cicatricial bands around fifth finger.
What is true regarding pathophysiology for his disease?
A. It is caused by SPINK5 mutation
B. It is caused by mutations in LOR gene encoding a glycine rich cornified envelope protein
C. It is caused by mutations in GJB2
D. It is caused by KRT1 & KRT9 mutations
E. It is caused by FALDH mutations

Key: B
Ref: Rooks (65.49)

29. A 2 yr. old girl presents with thick hyperkeratosis of whole surface of hands and feet. She developed them since age of 3 months. She also has hyperhidrosis. She has developed fungal infections few times in last 1 year. Her nail, hair and teeth are normal. Her differential diagnosis includes all the following except:
A. Mal de Melada
B. Nagashima NEPPK
C. Kimonis NEPPK
D. Bothnia NEPPK
E. Keratoelastoides marginalis

Key: E
Ref: Rooks (65.46)

30. A 2 months old baby girl is presented to OPD, accompanied by her mother, complain of thick plates like skin with fissuring since birth continuous, now progressive and limitation of body movements. Baby having breathing difficulty. Mother denies any family history of similar complaints. Parents are cousins.

On examination: Baby girl has bilateral ectropions. What is most likely diagnosis?

A. Self-improving congenital icthyosis
B. Bathing suit icthyosis
C. Herliquin icthyosis
D. Lamellar icthyosis
E. RXLI

Key: C

31. A 2 months old baby girl is presented to OPD, accompanied by her mother, complain of thick plates like skin with fissuring since birth continuous, now progressive and limitation of body movements. Baby having breathing difficulty. Mother denies any family history of similar complaints. Parents are cousins.
On examination: Baby girl has bilateral ectropions. Skin biopsy sent. What is most likely findings?

A. Thickened stratum corneum displaying multiple cholesterol clefts
B. Orthohyperkeratosis, thickened stratum granulosum, marked follicular plugging
C. Defects in Lamellar bodies in stratum granulosum
D. Hyper granulose, abnormally large keratohyaline granuloma

Key: C

32. A 28 days old female neonate is brought to Derma OPD by her mother complains of sudden onset if fluid filled lesions all over body since age of day 2, gradually, progressive, baby cries, and these lesions are increased on axilla and other body folds. After rupture of these lesions, baby skin is looking like burnt.
On examination: There are numerous blisters on her body most prominent on folds, large erosions (like burn) and few scattered spiny hyperkeratotic lesions on lower legs and knees.
What is most likely diagnosis?

A. Congenital reticular icthosiform erythroderma.
B. Epidermolytic icthyosis
C. Icthyosis Curth - Macklin
D. Annular Epidermolytic icthyosis
E. Exfoliative icthosis

Key: B

33. A 28 days old female neonate is brought to Derma OPD by her mother complains of sudden onset if fluid filled lesions all over body since age of day 2, gradually, progressive, baby cries, and these lesions are increased on axilla and other body folds. After rupture of these lesions, baby skin is looking like burnt.
On examination: There are numerous blisters on her body most prominent on folds, large erosions (like burn) and few scattered spiny hyperkeratotic lesions on lower legs and knees.
The mode of inheritance of disease is?

A. AR
B. X- Linked
C. AD
D. Multifactorial

Key: C

34. The disturbed epidermal barrier of collodion babies result in transepidermal water loss, which may result in hypothermia.to overcome this problem ,the collodion babies are kept in a high humidity incubator with close monitoring of body temp. Typically it is recommended to start with humidity in the range of ?

A. 10 to 30%
B. 30 to 40 %
C. 40 to 50%
D. 50 to 60%
E. 60 to 80%

Key: E

35. Apart from history and examination, following are the tests helpful in the diagnosis of collodion baby except?

A. Target testing of family members
B. Prenatal diagnosis
C. Steroid sulphatase activity
D. Hair shaft microscopy
E. ct brain

Key: E

36. For a collodion baby, after bath and soaking the skin for around 20 to 30 min, the mechanical scale removal z done by sponge, microfibre cloth to rub the skin, then a variety of topical emollients can be used to hydrate the stratum corneum. All of the following keratolytic agents and moisturizers are used except?

A. petrolatum like ointments
B. Topical betamethason
C. dexapanthenol
D. Glycerol
E. Urea based ointments

Key: B

37. The connexins are membrane proteins, that form inter and intracellular channels for ion n molecule transfer, the mutations in connexin expression leads to abnormal cellular and calcium homeostasis,.snd cell dysfunction, lysis n death. The mutations in gap junction protein in KID syn (keratitis -icthyosis deafness) found is?

A. GjB2 encoding connexin 26
B. GjB2 ecoding connexin 30
C. Steroid sulphase
D. Connexin 31
E. None of the above

Key: A

38. Following serious complications are associated with KID Syn except?

A. Fatal malignant fibrous histiocytoma
B. Metastatic malignant pilar tumors
C. Malignant melanoma
D. tricholemmal tumours
E. scc of tongue

Key: C

39. A 15 year old boy presented with linear pattern of skin thickening on the palms and flexor aspects of fingers. It was associated with pain and hyperhidrosis of hands and focal thickening of soles of feet. On examination mild thickening of skin over knees was observed. On histopathology disadhesion of keratinocytes with widening of intercellular spaces was found. The most important association to rule out in this case is.

A. Colonic carcinoma
B. Cardiomyopathy
C. Calcinosis cutis
D. Cystic fibrosis
E. Nephropathy

Key: B

40. A two year old child was brought in by his parents to skin OPD. On examination he has mild punctate thickening of skin of his palms. On further examination multiple sharply demarcated irregular hypo pigmented macules were observed on his upper and lower limbs along with a hard yellow /white nodule on his right upper limb. On histopathology there is hyperkeratosis hypergranulosis and acanthodians . There is reduction of melanin content of keratinocytes. There number of Melanocytes is normal. The gene involved in this disease is

A. KRT1
B. JUP
C. DSP
D. DSG1
E. ENPP1

Key: E

41. A three-year-old child was brought in skin OPD due to linear pattern of skin thickening on his palms and flexor aspects of his fingers. There was also skin thickening of soles in a confluent pattern. The parents were concerned because of the pain he was experiencing in these lesions. A diagnosis of striate palmoplantar keratoderma was made. In gene analysis which gene would be involved in SPPK1?

A. Desmoplakin
B. KRT1
C. Plakoglobin
D. ENPP1
E. Desmoglein 1

Key: E

42. A 16-year-old boy presented to cardiac unit with symptoms of shortness of breath on physical exertion, dizziness, lightheadedness. On examination he has swelling on his ankles and feet. On further examination diffuse thickening of skin of soles and linear keratoderma on palms and fingers was observed. Echocardiography showed dilated cardiomyopathy. A diagnosis of Nexos syndrome was made after doing gene analysis. The affected gene in this disease is also implicated in the following disease

A. Severe dermatitis
B. Striate palmoplantar keratoderma 2
C. Atopy
D. Acantholytic Epidermolysis bullosa
E. Atopy

Key: D

43. A 25-year-old construction worker presented with extensive pinpoint keratitis papules with central depression on his palms and soles. Some warty and opaque lesions were also observed. On histopathology of punctate lesion there was orthohyperkeratosis and compact acanthosis with hypergranulosis, with the depression in the centre of lesion. The most appropriate management for this is the following

A. Topical steroids
B. Topical retinoid
C. Proper choice of foot ware and regular use of pomice stone
D. Topical calcipotriol
E. Urea creams

Key: C

44. A one month old baby girl presented to Derma OPD by her parents with complain of large plate like dark brown scales covering entire body. There is no erythrodermas but beneath the thick scales there's mild erythema. On further inquiry there is another baby of similar disease in maternal side of patient and her

parents are also cousins. Patient is afebrile with no other complaints. Which of the following is most likely mutation seen in this patient?

A. Transglutaminase 1
B. Cytochrome P450
C. Acid Lipase
D. Epidermal lipoxygenases E3 and 12 B

Key: A

45. A mother of 5 year old child came in dermatology clinic and gave history of hyperkeratotic papules on knuckles and dorsum of his child's hands since few months after birth. Now gradually increasing in size with prominent spikes onto normal skin along with cicatricle band around little finger and mild hearing problem. No history of collodion baby at birth. Rest of the hairs, eyes, nails, teeth and mucosae examinations were unremarkable. What is the most likely diagnosis?

A. Loricrin Keratoderma
B. Vohwinkel syndrome
C. Bart Pumphrey syndrome
D. KID syndrome
E. Papillon Lefevre syndrome

Key: B
Ref: Rooks (65.57)

46. A 65 years male patient came with progressive weight loss, dysphagia and persistent cough for last 2 years. Biospy report revealed poorly differentiated squamous cell carcinoma grade lll. On further examination he had keratoderma on pressure points of sole without any nail changes. Oral mucosa showed white thick patches. Rest of the cutaneous examination was normal. History similar skin lesions in his siblings also. Which syndrome is most responsible for his condition?

A. Howel Evans Syndrome
B. Huriez Syndrome
C. Clouston Syndrome
D. Pachonychia Congenita
E. Olmsted Syndrome

Key: A
Ref: Rooks (65.59)

47. A young boy known case of Marfan syndrome developed asymptomatic keratotic papules on his left forearms for few days. Some coalescing to form arcuate pattern. No history of any prior infection, trauma and insect bite. Similar lesions in his siblings also with ocular involvement. On Histopathology amorphous substance that binds with elastic tissue stain can be seen, traversing the epidermis. What is the most likely diagnosis?

A. Tinea Corporis
B. Annular Sarcoidosis
C. Erythema Annulare Centrifugum
D. Elastosis Perforans Serpiginosa
E. Granuloma Annulare

Key: C
Ref: Rooks (65.69)

48. A 5 years male child came with congenital hair loss on scalp, diffuse follicular hyperkeratosis associated with photophobia. Her elder sister has follicular ichthyosis on her right arm along the lines of blaschko. What is the trait of this disease?

A. X-linked Dominant

B. X-linked Recessive
C. Autosomal Dominant
D. Autosomal Recessive
E. Mitochondrial

Key: B
Ref: Rooks (68.15)

49. A 7 years boy presented with multiple yellowish papules over face, scalp margins, ears and neck. Some flat papules on dorsum of hands associated with nail fragility, longitudinal splits and distal v shaped nick. Biopsy of flat papules showed church spire pattern of hyperkeratosis. What is the most likely diagnosis?
A. Plane warts
B. EDV
C. Acrokeratosis verruciformis
D. Lichen Nitidus
E. All of the above

Key: C
Ref: Rooks (65.6)

50. 45 year old obese female presented with complaints of difficulty in walking. O/E there is erythema, hyperkeratosis and fissuring of pressure areas. Keeping in mind diagnosis, which is not true
A. Symptoms worse in winter
B. Obesity & HTN are associated
C. High vitamin A levels
D. Topical 0.05% oestradiol can be used as treatment

Key: C

51. Regarding bureau- barriere syndrome which is not correct
A. Autonomic disturbances
B. Polyneuropathy
C. Painless ulcer
D. Diffuse keratoderma & osteolysis in forefoot

Key: A

52. All of the following can cause acquired keratoderma except
A. Secondary syphilis
B. Reactive arthritis
C. Halogenated weed killer
D. Hyperthyroidism

Key: D

53. Patient presented wjgh brownish to reddish macules and plaque surrounded by raised keratitis border confined to body folds. What is true about diagnosis??
A. Highly pruritic
B. Confined to male
C. Histology shows multiple coronoid lamella
D. B & C
E. All of the above

Key: E

54. Which variant of parakeratosis has highest malignant potential?
A. Porokeratosis of mantoux

B. Porokeratosis ptychotropica
C. Porokeratosis of mibellk
D. Giant porokeratosis

Key: D

55. A 35 year old man presented with 2-3 mm multiple asymptomatic red brown papules with discrete irregular margins on both legs and arms. Similar lesions were present in the concha also. There was no involvement elsewhere. Similar illness was found in the younger brother aged 30 years with the duration of illness for the past 5 years. Histopathology shows hyperkeratosis with a focal parakeratosis overlying a thinner flat epidermis with loss of keratohyalin granules. In the periphery of lesions, the epidermis is acanthotic with collarets like elongated rete ridges. What is the treatment of choice in this case??

A. Methotrexate
B. Cyclosporin
C. Systemic retinoids
D. Dapsone
E. CO2 laser

Key: C

56. A 2 year old male born by non-consanguineous marriage presented with dry rough skin & loss of hair on scalp. There was history of photophobia, redness, watering of eyes since birth. No sweating defect, hearing deficit, nail dystrophy. No systemic involvement. No similar complaint in family members. He was born with collodion baby. On dermatological examination - hyperkeratotic spiny follicular papules having sand paper like texture of the skin & alopecia Universalist. There was no erythema and scarring. Teeth, genital and oral mucosa were in normal limits. General examination was within normal limits. What is the diagnosis?

A. Hereditary mucoepithelial dysplasia
B. Ichthyosis folliculairs atrichia photophobia syndrome
C. Conradi-hunermann happle syndrome
D. Ichthyosis Curth macklin

Key: B

57. A 35 year old female patient presented with a 3-month history of a pruritic eruption of multiple, keratotic papules. The patient had a history of chronic renal failure. Dermatological examination revealed erythematous papules exhibiting a central depression with keratotic plugging over the extensor surfaces of knees and shins. Histopathology shows follicular and non-follicular lesions. Degenerate collagen, elastic tissue and keratin. All of the following are treatment EXCEPT:

A. Intrelesional steroid
B. Narrow band UVB phototherapy
C. Topical tretinoin
D. Allopurinol
E. Methotrexate

Key: E

58. A 50 years old diabetic patient with chronic kidney disease on dialysis presents with 4 months history of multiple keratitis papules.
Diagnosis of perforting keratotic disorder was made.
All of the following are included EXCEPT:

A. kyrle disease
B. Reactive perforting collagenosis
C. Elastosis Perforans serpiginosa
D. Necrotizing infundiular crystalline folliculitis

E. Digitate keratosis

Key: E

59. A 65 year old male patient presenting with multiple hyperkeratotic lesions localized on the forehead, neck and back. Histopathological analysis of one of the lesions revealed a follicular invagination containing cellular debris and keratin lamellae containing filamentous mucinous material and numerous crystals birefringent in polarized light microscopy. What is the treatment of choice?

A. Retinoid
B. Steroids
C. Antimycotics
D. Dapsone

Key: C

60. 8 year old girl presents with the complaints of redness and thickening of the palms and soles, associated with loss of few teeth and frequent skin infections. Her brother is also reported to have similar symptoms. Which gene is most likely mutated in this patient?

A. TRPV3
B. CTSC
C. Transient receptor potential vanilloid
D. Cathepsin C
E. Gap junction β-6

Key: B
Ref: Rooks (65.61)

61. Year old boy presents to Derma OPD with symmetrical sharply defined palmar and plantar keratoderma surrounded by erythema, flexion deformities and constriction of the digits since childhood. He also has perioroficial and perianal hyperkaratotic plaques. Considering the diagnosis, what would be the most likely family history of this disease?

A. No one else in his family most likely has this disorder
B. Half of his siblings would most likely be affected by this disorder
C. Half of his siblings would most likely be carriers of this disorder
D. His maternal uncle would most likely have this disorder
E. His mother and brothers would most likely have this disorder

Key: A
Ref: Rooks (65.62)

62. 10 year old boy presents with mutilating palmoplantar keratoderma with perioroficial and perianal involvement. Laboratory investigations show that the patient also had a raised IgE level. There was no family history of similar disorder however his father gave a history of psoriasis. Which of the following is the closest differential diagnosis of the disorder described above?

A. Bart Pumphrey
B. Acrodermatitis enteropathica
C. Chanarin dorfmann syndrome
D. IFAP
E. Comel Netherton

Key: B
Ref: Rooks (65.62)

63. Two siblings have developed diffuse palmoplantar keratoderma since childhood with severe fissuring and now are even unable to walk because of pain and usually use wheelchair to move about. Their nails also show some degree of dystrophy with increased curvature of nail plate. You notice that they recently received some antibiotics and painkillers during a visit to dentist. Detailed history reveals a long history of

recurrent skin abscess and folliculitis. Which of following would be most effective to improve the skin condition of these siblings?

A. Topical salicylic acid dressing
B. Emollients
C. Sodium bicarbonate baths
D. Oral Retinoids
E. Surgical debridement keratoderma

Key: D
Ref: Rooks (65.61)

64. 35 year old has decreased hair on scalp, nail fragility, palmoplantar keratoderma and multiple hydrocystomas of the eyelids. On detailed history taking, he also mentions that he lost his deciduous teeth earlier than his age mates. Which of the following is the most likely gene mutation in this disorder?

A. CTSC
B. TPVR3
C. WNT10A
D. D.GJB6
E. Connexion 32

Key: C
Ref: Rooks (65.61)

Chapter 66 INHERITED ACANTHOLYTIC DISORDERS

1. A 40 year old female presented with complain of burning sensation of mouth for 15 years, that is aggravated by eating spicy foods, on oral examination there were multiple umblicated and coblestone papules were present on hard palat. Extra oral exam show widespread waxy paules involving face, scalp, post auricular region, pinna, and external auditory meatus. What is pathophysiology of the disease?
   - A. Due to mutation in SPCA2 gene
   - B. Mutation in ATP2C1
   - C. Mutation in TRPC1
   - D. Mutation in ATP2A2
   - E. Mutation in SPCA1

Key: D
Ref: Rook (66.1)

2. A 20 year old woman presented with complain of multiple pruritic skin lesions on left breast for 5 years that extended to left axilla, her symptoms were aggravated by exposure to high environment temperature. No involvement of scalp, nails, and mucous membranes. Punch biopsy were performed for histopath that revealed hyperkeratosis, suprabasal acantholysis and dyskeratosis, how to manage her condition?
   - A. Oral methotrexate
   - B. Azithromycin
   - C. Potent topical corticosteroids
   - D. UVB
   - E. Puva therapy

Key: C
Ref: Rook (66.9)

3. A 42 years old female known case of darier disease presented with aggravation of her skin lesions, which is not complcation of disease from following?
   - A. Herpes simplex infection
   - B. Cowpox
   - C. SCC of skin
   - D. Renal failure
   - E. Extramummary pagets disease

Key: D
Ref: Rook (66.8)

4. A 33 year old woman with 10 year history of keratotic papules on back of her hands and feet, her nails of hands and feet were also affected. Histopath shows suprabasal acantholysis and dyskeratosis. she is concerned about prognosis of her disease, what is false regarding prognosis?
   - A. Disease is chronic
   - B. Having relapsing coarse
   - C. Unpredictable severity
   - D. Deteriorate in old age
   - E. Early onset of disease has better prognosis

Key: E
Ref: Rook (66.9)

Chapter 67 ECTODERMAL DYSPLASIAS

1. A 10 year old boy presented with knee pain, locking, instability and inability to straighten the knee and proteinuria along with triangular lunula. What is true regarding this disease?
   A. ESRD occur in 30 % patients
   B. ESRD occur in 5 % patients
   C. ESRD does not occur
   D. Renal hypertension is not a feature
   E. ESRD in 10% parients

Key: B

2. A 13 year old female presented with Ocular Hypertension,open angle glaucoma ,elbow deformity and triangular lunula .What are other features of this disease
   A. Kidney involvement, Joint subluxation,illiac horns
   B. kidney involvement, Coloboma, osteosarcoma
   C. crumbled teeth, cardiac defects, multiple fractures
   D. nail pitting, spliting, Hair loss,cardiac defects
   E. None of above

Key: A

3. A boy presented with white forelock with hypopigmented lesions on anterior chest since birth. Hands feet and back are normally pigmented. What is true regarding its pathogenisis
   A. There is absence of melanocytes in hypopigmented area
   B. There is reduced number of abnormally large melanocytes
   C. There are normal melanocytes in hypermelanotic area of skin
   D. None is correct
   E. All are correct

Key: E

4. A pt presented with v shaped hypopigmented area on forehead. Pt also had mental retardation. What is the genetic mutation of this disease?
   A. C KIT
   B. LEKTI 1
   C. EDNRB
   D. OCA1
   E. PAX3

Key: A

5. A 10 year old girl presented with history of knee pain. she is unable to straighten her knee joint. She had a past history of multiple fractures. Her nails are ridged and pitted. On radiological examination of knee joint there is a small patella. Keeping in mind the diagnosis how will you monitor this patient?
   A. 6 monthly monitoring of RFTs and hypertension
   B. Annual monitoring for hypertension, urinalysis and glaucoma
   C. Annual DEXA scan

D. Both B and C

Key: B

6. A 7 year old girl presented with ocular hypertension, crumbled teeth, pitting of nails, absent patella. What is pathognomic of this disease?

A. Elbow involement
B. Finger nail involement
C. knee involvement
D. Illiac horns
E. Toe nail involvement

Key: D

7. A 17 year old female presented with soft lesion over the buttocks for past 5 years. on examination she had linear atrophic and telengactatic lesions on both thighs, her left little and mid finger were fused together. after diagnosis and involving a multidisciplinary team for the management parents are concerned inheritance of the disease. what will councel the parents?

A. 50% of her male children ll be normal
B. All her female children ll be diseased
C. All of her male children ll be aborted
D. All her female children ll be normal
E. 25% of her female children ll be diseased

Key: A
Ref: Rook (67.23)

8. A 16 years old male presented in skin OPD with generalized hypotrichois, dystrophic nails, hyperkeratotic palms and soles, normal looking teeth. on inquiry sweating is normal. which of the following eye change is not associated with the disease?

A. cataract
B. Photophobia
C. Strabismus
D. Glucoma
E. photophobia

Key: D
Ref Rook (67.21)

9. A 35 year old male presented with short thick brittle nails, diffuse hyperkeratosis of palms and soles. on examination brittle hair on body with prominent dermal ridges on finger pulps. which mutation is involved in disease?

A. Connexin 26
B. Connexin 30
C. Keratin 6A
D. PORCN gene
E. connexin 31

Key: B
Ref Rook (67.21)

10. Which of the following is not a feature of H syndrome?

A. hypertrichosis
B. hyperpigmentation

C. hearing loss
D. hypopigmentation
E. hypogonadism

Key: D
Ref: Rook (67.12)

11. A 12 year old boy with linear enamel hypoplasia referred to dermatology OPD by dentist for evaluation of cribriform atrophic lesions in linear blashkoid pattern on trunk and extermities with swelling over buttocks. Which of the following is the not the feature of the disease?

A. Periorifical pappiloma
B. Coloboma
C. Syndactyly
D. Retinal detachment

Key: D
Ref: Rook (67.24)

12. A 12 years boy came to OPD with his mother with complain of sparse, dry, lusterless scalp hairs as well as eyebrows & heat intolerance. Further inquiry revealed he had delayed dentition .both deciduous and permanent teeth are affected & impaired sweating with recurrent episodes of eczema. On examination he had small widely spaces peg shaped teeth. periorbital hyperpigmentation & milia like lesions present on face & spock ears. keeping in view the clinical features & examination findings what is most likely diagnosis

A. Hidrotic ectoderma dysplasia
B. Hypohidrotic ectodermal dysplasia
C. Ectodermal dysplasia with immunodeficiency
D. Hay wells syndrome
E. Sicca syndrome

Key: B
Ref: Rook (67.13)

13. You are asked to see a neonate who had collodion membrane & eroded skin at birth that resolve in almost 2 weeks leaving behind dry skin. On examination, there are multiple scalp erosions and sparse hairs, severe erosive dermatitis with secondary super infection with conjuctivitis & dystrophic nails. Hypospadiasis & mid facial hypoplasia with high forehead also present.

Which of following is most likely diagnosis in this case?

A. Ankyloblepharon- ectodermal defect cleft lip/ palate syndrome
B. Ectrodactyly- ectodermal dyspasis- cleft lip/ palate syndrome
C. Hypohidrotic ectodermal dysplasia
D. Epidermolysis bullosa simplex
E. X- linked hypohidrotic dysplasia with immunodeficiency

Key: A
Ref: Rook (67.15)

14. A 08 months boy presented to you in OPD with history of pear-shaped nose and decreased hair since birth and delayed milestones. On examination he had bullous nose, high arched palate

with sparse scalp, eyebrow, eyelashes. Nails are brittle & dystrophic with racket nail appearance and has short metacarpals and phalanges. What is most likely diagnosis

A. Ectodermal dysplasia 2
B. Tricho dento- osseous syndrome
C. Tricho- rhino- phalangeal syndrome
D. Langer- Giedion syndrome
E. Goltz syndrome

Key: C
Ref: Rook (67.20)

15. A 11 month baby girl brought to you in OPD with history of severe growth retardation. On examination, she has short stature, severe brachydactyly & abnormal metacarpal & phalanges. eyebrows are normal. keeping in mind the most likely diagnosis she has which of following genetic defect

A. WNT10A mutation
B. TRPS1 with missense mutation
C. TRPS1 with nonsense mutation
D. TRPS1 with deletion
E. TRAF 6 mutation

Key: B
Ref: Rook (67.21)

16. A neonate with collodion like membrane admitted in NICU with redimentary eyelashes & absent finger and toe nails. he had icthyosiform scaling & hyperkeratosis of trunk and extremities and curly hair as well as lacrimal duct atresia. consistent with diagnosis what complications he developed

A. Chronic otitis media
B. Chronic conjuctivitis
C. Chronic scalp infection
D. Secondary hearing loss
E. All of above

Key: E
Ref: Rook (67.16)

Chapter 68 INHERITED HAIR DISORDERS

1. A 2yr old child presented with pale and sparse hair with mottled discoloration and exaggerated cubed bow. On microscopic exam hair shows 180° twist. This classic hair shaft defect is known as
   A. Trichorrhexis nodosa
   B. Pili torti
   C. Trichorrhexis invaginata
   D. Monelithrix

Key: B

2. A 6 yr. old child presented with short brittle scalp and eyebrow hair, born as a collodion baby, now presented with polycyclic serpingous eruption on body. On microscopy the hallmark hair shaft defect present in this pt. is known as
   A. Trichorrhexis nodosa
   B. Trichorrhexis invagination
   C. Pili torti
   D. Monelithrix

Key: B

3. A 5 yr. old child born as a collodion baby presents with short brittle sparse hair. The boy has a short stature/o photosenstivity, intellectual impairment, cataract and IUGR. Characteristic hair shaft defect present is
   A. Trichorrhexis nodosa
   B. Trichothiodystrophy
   C. Pili torti
   D. Monelithrix

Key: B

4. A 13 yr. old boy presents with brownish discoloration on neck and thigh for 6 yrs. O/E involved skin has reticulate pigmentation with atrophy and telangiectasia. He also has dystrophic nails and white plaque on tongue. Most common cause of death in this pt. is
   A. Pulmonary fibrosis
   B. Bone marrow failure
   C. Liver cirrhosis
   D. Squamous cell carcinoma

Key: B

5. Mostly the above disease is inherited as
   A. Autosomal dominant
   B. X linked recessive
   C. Autosommal recessive
   D. X linked dominant

Key: B

Chapter 69

GENETIC DEFECTS OF NAILS AND NAIL GROWTH

1. 12 year old boy presents with reticulated dusky brown hyperpigmentation on face, neck, shoulders, upper back and thighs. His nails are dystrophic and oral examination reveals leukoplaikia. Keeping in view the diagnosis, which malignancy is most common in these patients?

A. laryngeal carcinoma
B. Squamous cell carcinoma of tongue
C. Basal cell carcinoma of tongue
D. oesophageal carcinoma

Key: B
Ref: Rook (69.14)

2. 12 year old boy presents with reticulated dusky brown hyperpigmentation on face, neck, shoulders, upper back and thighs. His nails are dystrophic and oral examination reveals leukoplaikia. Keeping in view the diagnosis, which is most common cause of death in these patients?

A. Malignany
B. Pulmonary disease
C. bone marrow failure
D. neurological involvement.

Key: C
Ref Rook (69.15)

Chapter 70

GENETIC DISORDERS OF PIGMENTATION

1. A 5 years old girl is brought to you in opd with complete absence of pigmentation with white hairs and pink skin. She also has nystagmus and photophobia.
Keeping in mind the most likely diagnosis, she has which of the following genetic defect?

A. Mutations in TYR
B. Mutations in OCA2 gene
C. Mutations in TYRP1
D. Mutations in SLC45A2
E. Mutations in SLC24A5

Key: A
Ref: Rook (70.7)

2. A 10 years old albino boy is brought to the opd with easy brusing while playing and recurrent epistaxis. He complains of recurrent abdominal pain.
He also has photophobia and nystagmus. Keeping in mind the most likely diagnosis, which of the following is standard diagnostic test;

A. Ct scan chest for pulmonary fibrosis
B. Endoscopy for oesophageal varices
C. Electron microscopy of platelets showing absence of dense bodies
D. Pulmonary function tests
E. MRI abdomen

Key: C
Ref: Rook (70.8)

3. A 2 years old boy is brought to the opd with high grade fever, diarhea and abdominal distension for the last 7 days.
O/E he was mild paler, having oral trush, photophobia.
Skin examination shows patchy hypopigmentation.
Past history was positive for recurrent chest infections.
On laboratory investigations, lymphocytes were large and contain large round inclusion body in cytoplasm.
What is the mode of inheritance of above disease?

A. Autosomal dominant
B. Autosomal recessive
C. X linked dominant
D. X linked recessive
E. Sporadic

Key: B
Ref: Rook (70.8)

4. 6 years old boy presented in eye opd with nystagmus. He was also having generalized hypopigmentation. On further history taking, parents gave history of easy brusing while playing.There was no history of any recurrent infections and neurological abnormalities.
Before strabismus surgery, what necessary investigation should be done most importantly?

A. total leucocyte count
B. platelet aggregation studies
C. compliment levels

D. Optical coherence tomography
E. light microscopy of hairs

Key: B
Ref: Rook (70.8)

5. A 3 years old male Albino child was brought to opd by his parents with the complaint of recurrent chest infections since 6 months of age. He was having one brother who was normal and 1 brother died at the age of 2 months due to unknown reasons.
The child was also having nystagmus and photophobia.
Keeping in mind the diagnosis, what is the 1st line diagnostic test;
A. light microscopy of hairs
B. Examination of leukocytes for giant inclusions
C. Optical coherent tomography
D. platelet aggregation studies
E. Total leucocyte count

Key: B
Ref: Rook (70.9)

6. A 6 year old boy presented with a reticular hyperpigmention on the trunk for past 6 months. He also says that he is intolerant to heat with reduced sweating. His dentition is poor and palms and soles show absence of dermatoglyphics and moderate keratoderma. Considering the diagnosis what is the mode of inheritance in thus disease
A. AR
B. AD
C. X linked dominant
D. X linked recessive
E. sporadic

Key: B
Ref: Rook (70.13)

7. A young girl presents to you with generalized reticulate hyperpigmentation with non cicatrial alopecia, abscense of dermatoglyphics and onychodystrophy.This typical presentation is of:
A. dowling degos disease
B. dyskeratosis congenita
C. dermathopathia pigmentosa reticularia
D. dyschromatosis symmetrica hereditaria

Key: C
Ref: Rook (70.14)

8. A 15 year old girl presented with hyperpigmented macules primarily involving the flexural areas since 3 months. Few comedo like lesions and perioral acne form scarring is also seen on examination. The most likely diagnosis is
A. flexural dowling degos
B. generalized degos disease
C. degos disease
D. naegeli franschetti jadasohn
E. dyschrmoica symmetrica hereditarian

Key: A
Ref: Rook (70.14)

9. In the above scenario the underlying gene mutation in this pt is
A. ADAM10

B. STK11
C. POFUTI
D. POGLUTI
E. KRT5

Key: E
Ref: Rook (70.14)

10. A 18 year old boy is having problem in finger scanning and is referred to you. On examination you find palmoplantar pits along with reticulate hyperpigmented strophic macules on the dorsum. Of hands which he says has darkened over time. The most likely pathology is
A. naegelli franschetti jadassohn
B. dermatopathia pigmentosa
C. galli galli disease
D. reticulate acropigmentation of kitamura
E. dyschromatosis universalis hereditaria

Key: D
Ref: Rook (70.14)

11. A 2 yrs old boy presented in derma opd with white forelock, white patches on body n deafness. On examination hypopigmented patches on Trunk n limbs, dystopia acanthorum iris colour difference., dysmorphic facial features with broad nasal root n medial hyperplasia of eyebrows. He is most probably suffering from
A. Oculicutaneous albinism
B. Hermansky pudlak syndrome
C. Waardenburg syndrome
D. Woolf syndrome

Key: C
Ref: Rook (70. 4)

12. An infant presented with white forelock, sensorineural deafness, piebaldism and dysmorphic facial features. A syndrome is diagnosed. Regarding diagnosis which one is not true.
A. All types are AD
B. Type 1,2.3 r AD
C. Type 4 is AR
D. Caused by mutation in PAX3. MITF. SLUG. n EDNRB genes
E. Hearing loss is non progressive

Key: A
Ref: Rook (70.4)

13. A 6 yrs old boy presented with toenail abnormalities since birth now severe pain on standing n walking n thickened soles. O/e dystrophic toe nails, plantar keratoderma i. E focal, hoarness n oral leukokeratosis, focal hyperkaratosis of knees n elbows. He is suffering from.
A. DKC
B. Clouston syndrome
C. Pachyonychia congenita
D. Mal de meleda

Key: C

14. A pt presented with toenail dystrophy, severe plantar pain n focal plantar keratoderma. Regarding diagnosis which is true
A. AD inheritance

B. KRT. Gene mutation
C. KRT 17 gene mutation is ass with natal teeth
D. Pilisebaceous cysts found in KRT 6a. 6b..n 17 mutations
E. All of the above

Key: E

15. Regarding treatment of pt in above scenario wth nal dystrophy, plantar keratoderma n plain. Which is not true
A. Mechanical reduction of hyperkeratosis n nails useful
B. Surgical removal of cysts
C. Emolients n keratolytics in mild cases
D. Oral retinoids are most effective
E. Antibiotics n antifungals for sec infecyions

Key: D

16. A female child presents with linear verrucous plaques mainly on the limbs. On further examination, she has cone shaped teeth, onychodystrophy, motor impairment and microcephaly. What is the likely diagnosis?
A. incontinentia pigmenti
B. hypomelanosis of ito
C. Chediak-Higashi syndrome
D. Griscelli syndrome

Key: A
Ref: Rook (70.11)

17. An infant presents with seizures, and decrease in muscle tone. On examination, patient has silvery hair, eyebrows and eye lashes, hepatospleenomegaly, lymphadenopathy and eye examination reveals partial ocular albinism. Complete blood picture reveals pancytopenia. What is the mode of inheritance of this disorder?
A. Autosomal Dominant
B. Autosomal Recessive
C. Chromosomal Mosaicism
D. X-linked dominant

Key: B
Ref: Rook (70.9)

18. A female child presents with linear verrucous plaques mainly on the limbs. She gives the history of vesicular eruptions in her limbs in the past that have evolved into verrucous plaques. On further examination, she has cone shaped teeth, onychodystrophy, motor impairment and microcephaly. Keeping in view the diagnosis, the disease can present in males in which of the following condition?
A. Down syndrome
B. Turner syndrome
C. Klinefelter syndrome
D. Noonan syndrome

Key: C
Ref: Rook (70.11)

Chapter 71 GENETIC BLISTERING DISEASES

1. A mother brings her one month old child to urology opd with c/o urinary retention and pain in abdomen with distention from last 3 days, further she gives h/o extensive blistering with erosions over whole body since birth and bulbous changes of finger tips, O/E non healing crusted erosions containing exuberant granulation tissue over nose, mouth and trunk
What will be the most appropriate diagnosis for this patient?

A. generalized severe junctional EB
B. Dominant dystrophic EB generalized
C. generalized intermediate junctional EB
D. dominant dystrophic EB pruriginosa
E. recessive dystrophic bullous dermolysis of the new-born

Key: A
Ref: Rook (71.12)

2. A 13 years old boy came with complain of photosensitivity and difficulty in passing urine. On cutaneous examination multiple hypo and hyperpigmented macules were present at face and dorsal surface of hands and feet with overall thin skin ,his lips and gums were also red and swollen. Genital examination showed scarring at external uretheral meatus. Mother told that he has history of blistering since neonatal age. Keeping diagnosis in mind which of the following gene responsible for it.

A. ITGA3
B. LAMININ 322
C. COL XVII
D. DYSTONIN BP230
E. KINDLIN/FERMT1

Key: E
Ref: Rook (71.18)

3. A 1year old girl brought by parents in emergency department with complain of multiple grouped vesicle on trunk, limbs and neck on and off since birth. Her oral mucosa show extensive erosions. Area of atrophic scarring were seen at dorsal hands and limbs. Nails were absent. Ultrastructure study of skin showed split at intraepidermal and ball like clumping of tonofilament in basal keratinocyte. Keeping diagnosis in mind which of the following gene is responsible for it.

A. Laminin 322
B. KERATIN 5/14
C. COLXVII
D. TGM 5
E. PLECTIN

Key: B
Ref: Rook (71.21)

4. A 2 years old boy brought up by parents in dermatology opd with complain of pruritus, dysphagia, constipation and skin erosion. On examination there were absent skin at lower legs. knee showed thick scars. Few area of skin showed crusted erosions and atrophic scarring. His fingers and toes were fused and showed mitten like deformity. Oral cavity showed microstomia, with eroded gums. While perianal area showed scarring. Keeping diagnosis in mind which of the following antigen is reduced on immunolabelling

A. Type VII collagen
B. 6B4

C. Laminin 322
D. Type XVII collagen
E. Kindlin

Key: A
Ref: Rook (71.22)

6. A 13 years old boy came with complain of photosensitivity and difficulty in passing urine. On cutaneous examination multiple hypo and hyperpigmented macules were present at face and dorsal surface of hands and feet with overall thin skin, his lips and gums were also red and swollen. Genital examination showed scarring at external uretheral meatus. Mother told that he has history of blistering since neonatal age. Keeping diagnosis in mind all of the following includes in its complications except
A. Mucocutaneous Scc
B. Colitis
C. Psudoosyndactyly
D. Ectropion
E. Melanoma

Key: E
Ref: Rook (71.19)

7. A 2 years old boy brought up by parents in dermatology opd with complain of pruritus, dysphagia, constipation and skin erosion and multiple blisters. On examination there were absent skin at lower legs. knee showed thick scars. Few area of skin showed crusted erosions and atrophic scarring. His fingers and toes were fused and showed mitten like deformity. Oral cavity showed microstomia, with eroded gums. While perianal area showed scarring. Keeping diagnosis in mind what is ideal type and site for biopsy
A. Punch biopsy from blister more than 12hours
B. B.Shave biopsy from lesional skin
C. Shave biopsy from rubbed non lesional skin
D. Punch biopsy from well-formed blister containing blood
E. Both A n D

Key: C
Ref: Rook (71.19)

8. 2 years old child presented to dermatology opd by her father with c/o blistering involving lower legs and feet leading to erosions, these are very painful acc to attendant even she can't sleep at night and cries. O /E tender erosions associated with hyperkeratosis present on lower legs and soles.
What will be the most appropriate step in management of pain of this child?
A. systemic opiate
B. NSAIDS
C. c)benzodiazepine
D. amitriptyline
E. cognitive behavioral therapy

Key: D
Ref: Rook (71.27)

9. A 30 yr old male presented with complaint of intense itching on his shins with a few lesions for few weeks, he states that itching is so strong that he tends to scratch it with comb or any nearby thing. then it results in scarring.
On examination you find few violaceous hypertrophic papules, atrophic scars with milia and few intact blisters on his shins bilaterally. Nails are dystrophic and there are no mucosal lesions, however he gives history of mucosal ulcers off and on.
Rest of the body is clear with no involvement.

What is the probable diagnosis?

A. DEB pretibial
B. DEB pruriginosa
C. LP pemphigoides
D. prurigo nodularis
E. DEB acral

Key: B

10. A 2 yr old baby boy presented with blisters on his body. According to his parents, his skin is so fragile that he can hardly play with his siblings as trauma during playing results in blistering of his skin, and then blisters heal with scarring.
On examination you find blisters and scars on his body specially on elbows, knees and lumber area. His nails are dystrophic and there are oral ulcers as well.
Parents don't remember history of any such disease in their family, but they have a consanginous marriage.
What could be the cause of this disease?

A. COL7A1 mutation
B. LAMA 3 mutation
C. LAMC 2 mutation
D. LAMB 3 mutation
E. all of the above can be implicated

Key: A

11. A 20 yr old patient presented with blistering and scarring in axillae and groins and few blisters in neck fold. He says that the blistering was initially generalized and very mild, so he didn't bother his problem. But since a few months it has become more localized to the above sites and increased in severity.
Few of his nails are dystrophic but mucosa and teeth are normal.
He gives history of severe pain in eyes few months back for which he consulted an ophthalmologist.
Patient is having an increased risk of?

A. BCC
B. SCC
C. blindness
D. CA esophagus
E. both A and B

Key: B

12. A 3 yr old boy presented with complaint of skin fragility and skin blisters since a few months of age.
On examination there are few blisters on elbows and dorsal hands mainly shins are involved with few atrophic scars along with milia and few intact blisters. There is dystrophy of nails of hands and feet. teeth and hair are normal.
What could be the diagnosis?

A. DEB pretibial
B. DEB pruriginosa
C. Generalized intermediate DEB
D. DEB acral variant
E. junctional EB

Key: A

13. Regarding dystrophic EB, which one is NOT true?

A. Results from mutation in collagen 7
B. Mutations include nonsense, missense, insertions, deletions.
C. Most common cause is replacement of glycine within type 7 collagen triple helix.

D. collagen 7 is component of anchoring filaments in lamina lucida
E. Level of split is beneath lamina dense.

Key: D

14. 6 months old child presented to derma opd by her mother with c/o blistering since birth O/E widespread atrophic scarring present over whole body, enamel defect and nails are dystrophic, there is associated h/o recurrent vomiting after every feed, mother also gives h/o pregnancy complication with polyhydromnios prior to birth of this child.
What is the underlying pathology involving mutation of which gene?
A. COL17A1 gene
B. Alpha 6 beta 4 integrin
C. Alpha 3 integrin
D. Mutation in exophilin 5
E. LAMA3A gene mutation

Key: B
Ref: Rook (71.13)

15. A 10 years old boy presented with history of recurrent leg ulcers for 2 years. Patient had history of delayed milestone development. On examination there was prominent eyes with hypertelorism, a high forehead, saddle nose and micrognathia. What is the least effective management option?
A. oral proline
B. topical 5% proline alone
C. topical 5% proline and 5% glycine
D. pulsed steroid
E. Dapsone

Key: A

16. A 14 years old girl presented with history of recurrent leg ulcers and photosensitivity for last 4 years. On examination the skin was spongy, with pitting and scarring, especially on the legs, telangiectasia on face, and splenomegaly. Labs showed anemia and thrombocytopenia. What is the true statement?
A. Most effective treatment is oral proline
B. 10% risk of systemic lupus erythematosus
C. SLE could occur due to antibodies against lupus antigen
D. 20% Risk of developing SCC
E. Mostly patients have normal IQ

Key: B

17. What is not true regarding management of Ehler Danlos Syndrome?
A. pregnancy should be avoided in vEDS
B. high dose ascorbic acid improves wound healing
C. wound should be closed with tension, in 2 layers to avoid stretching of scar
D. deep stitches should be applied generously
E. sunexposure should be avoided

Key: C

18. Which statement is incorrect about laryngo onycho cutaneous syndrome?
A. it has autosomal recessive inheritance
B. hoarseness is universal feature of this disease
C. starts in infancy with chronic erosions affecting the face mainly around the nose and mouth
D. teeth notching and periungual and subungal inflammation of nails
E. result from LAMA3 gene mutation

Key: E
Ref: Rook (71.14)

19. What is not true regarding Ehler Danlos Syndrome?
    A. Dorsiflexion of L and R 5th finger >90°
    B. Apposition L and R thumb to forearm
    C. Hyperextend L and R elbow >10°
    D. Hyperextend L and R knee >20°
    E. Palms to floor

Key: D

20. A 7 years old boy presented with history of easy bruisability, hypermobile joints, and skin laxity. He had blue sclera. Gorlin sign was positive. There were multiple cigarette paper scars. What is the probable diagnosis?
    A. Marfan syndrome
    B. secondary cutis laxa
    C. classical ehler Danlos syndrome
    D. osteogensis imperfecta
    E. Turner syndrome

Key: C

21. Mother brings her 5 years child with h/o blistering and fragility since childhood.There is associated h/o nail dystrophy and sparse hair over scalp, eyebrows and eyelashes O/E post inflammatory hypopigmentation and hyperpigmentation present in area of scarring. On further inquiry mother tells that there is spontaneous improvement of the patches of skin that don't blister now this characteristics phenomenon is found in which type of epidermolysis bullosa
    A. generalized intermediate junctional EB
    B. generalized late onset junctional EB
    C. localized EB inverse
    D. dominant dystrophic EB generalized
    E. dominant or recessive dystrophic EB pruriginosa

Key: A
Ref: Rook (71.13)

22. For management of a neonate with epidermolysis bullosa all are true accept:
    A. Hospitalisation and extensive workup
    B. Nursing babies on thick foam pads
    C. Covering erosions in non-adherent dressings after washing with normal saline
    D. Total parenteral Nutrition in early days of life
    E. Topical antiseptic cream

Key: D
Ref: Rook (71.24)

22. General measures of EB simplex include:
    A. Warm insoles
    B. Well-fitting comfortable footwear
    C. Wool socks preferred over cotton socks
    D. Dressings are preferred to avoid secondary infections
    E. There is no role of corn flour in management of EB simplex

Key B
Ref: Rook (71.25)

23. Regarding genetic blistering disorders, pick the false statement:
    A. Patients with generalised severe junctional EB have poor prognosis

B. Patients with generalised severe recessive dystrophic EB will often survive into middle age
C. All patients with recessive dystrophic EB are anaemic
D. Basal cell carcinomas associated with generalised recessive dystrophic EB
E. Autologous split thickness graft have short to long-term benefit in generalised recessive dystrophic EB

Key: D
Ref: Rook (71.27)

24. Among innovative therapies for genetic blistering disorders which of following is most appropriate:
A. Genetic editing utilises properties of engineered transcriptases
B. Recombinant protein therapy encompasses intradermal injections of human recombinant type VII collagen
C. Recessive blistering genodermatosis associated with loss-of-function mutations in one of alleles
D. SMaRT works on the principal of removing a mutated gene while increasing a normal protein production
E. Cell therapy with intradermal fibroblasts increases laminin 332 expression at dermal epidermal junction

Key: B
Ref: Rook (71.28 - 71.29)

25. Gene therapy for dominant EB involves following principles except:
A. In autosomal dominant EB there is one defective allele
B. The main therapeutic strategy is to silence the mutant allele to allow the wild type allele to restore function without any interference
C. Techniques involve silencing mutant allele with a small interfering RNA (SiRNA)
D. Splicesosome mediated RNA trans-splicing (SMaRT) utilises endogenous transcription machinery to splice out mutant exons
E. Recessive genetic blistering diseases can be treated with introduction of non-functioning gene with synthetic copy of functioning gene via retroviral vector

Key: D
Ref: Rook (71.28)

Chapter 72

GENETIC DISORDERS OF COLLAGEN, ELASTIN AND DERMAL MATRIX

1. A 15years old male presented in Dermatology opd with complaints of multiple bruises on body. He had history of multiple fractures since childhood. On examination of face blue sclera were present. Keeping in view the diagnosis which of the following is true about its various types.

A. Type 1: sclera are not blue, deafness is rare.
B. Type 2: Blue sclera, easy bruisability, early onset deafness.
C. Type 3: Fractures of long bones cause crippling deformities.
D. Type 4: Radiography shows beaded ribs, crumpled femora, little skull calcification.
E. Type 5: Dentinogenesis imperfecta is not seen

Key: C
Ref: Rook (72.10)

2. An 8years old child, known case of mitral valve prolapse, presented in Dermatology opd with complaints of easy bruisability. He was being managed for shortness of breath and lower limbs edema. On examination various skeletal deformities were present. Considering the diagnosis what are the commonest causes of premature death?

A. Multiple long bone fractures leading to crippling deformities
B. Mitral valve prolapse leading to cardiac complications.
C. Respiratory failure and accidental trauma.
D. Microvascular fragility leading to thin fragile skin.
E. Repeated cutest infections.

Key: C
Ref: Rook (72.10)

3. A 13years old referred to Dermatology with laxity of skin. He has history of multiple admissions in previous years for bronchiectasisd pulmonary emphysema. He was operated for umblicated hernia 2 months back. On cutaneous examination his skin was soft and redundant food were visible in neck and inguinal region. Which of the following syndrome related to this disease had the same defect as that of Menkes Syndrome?

A. Costello syndrome
B. Lenz-Majewski Syndrome
C. Arterial tortuosity Syndrome
D. Occipital Horn Syndrome
E. SCARF Syndrome.

Key: D
Ref: Rook (72.12)

4. A 5years old diagnosed case of craniosynostosis presented to Dermatology opd with complaint of low hairline. On examination he was found to have ptosis and facial asymmetry .Which of the following is most likely diagnosis in this case?

A. Apert syndrome
B. Pfeiffer Syndrome
C. Seathre chotzen syndrome
D. Beare- sterenson syndrome
E. Chrouzon syndrome.

Key: C
Ref: Rook (72.14)

5. A 4 years old girl presented with loose skin affecting the trunk. On examination of the fact there were downward slanting palpebral fissures, a broad float nose and large ears. Which of the following is correct about investigations of this disease?

A. Skin biopsy is necessary in all types
B. Neurological Examination and imaging is mandatory in autosomal recessive type.
C. Molecular testing is essential in all types to establish diagnosis.
D. Cardiovascular examination and imaging is mandatory in autosomal dominant type
E. Cardiovascular examination and imaging is mandatory in autosomal recessive type

Key: B
Ref: Rook (72.14)

6. A 22 years old female patient presented to skin opd with some lesions on neck and axilla. O/E there were plaques of multiple yellowish coloured papules in linear pattern. Numerous comedonal lesions were also present on neck and axilla bilaterally. She also complaint of aching pain in both legs while walking.
Keeping diagnosis in mind, angiographic findings in this disease can be

A. Angiomatosis malformation
B. Aneurysmal dilatation
C. Narrowing of peripheral arteries
D. Occlusion of visceral arteries
E. All of the above

Key: E
Ref: Rook (72.29)

7. A 1 year old female baby presented to skin opd with dry and wrinkled skin over hands and feet. Her mother was much concerned as her face appeared pinched with hollow cheeked appearance. O/E there was beaked nose and thin lips.
Regarding histopathology in this case which among the following is not true

A. Dermis is atrophic.
B. Sparse collagen bundles.
C. Absent subcutaneous fats.
D. Decrease elastin.
E. Elastin appears clumped.

Key: D
Ref: Rook (72.24)

8. A 52 years old male patient presented to skin opd with plaques of yellowish coloured papules with pebbly surface on neck, axillae and abdomen. O/E similar changes were also present on soft palate and inside of lips. His skin was soft, lax and wrinkled. Patient also complaint of decreased vision.
Visual impairment in this patient might be due to

A. Macular atrophy
B. Choroidal rupture and haemorrhage
C. retinal dysfunction
D. D)All of the above
E. None of the above

Key: D
Ref: Rook (72.29)

Q4: Regarding pseudoxanthoma elasticum, which among the following is true

A. Peaud orange fundus more evident with age.
B. 20% of patients develop gastrointestinal bleeding
C. Intermittent claudication and angina occurs in old age.

D. Calcification of Internal elastic lamina of arteries lead to vascular occlusion.
E. Increased risk of 2nd trimester miscarriages.

Key: D
Ref: Rook (72.29)

9. A middle aged female patient presented to skin opd with complaint of yellowish coloured papules on neck. O/E papules were arranged in reticular pattern. Reticulate pigmentation was also present on abdomen. She also gives history of two 1st trimester miscarriages.
Regarding investigations in this case which among the following is not true

A. Calcium and phosphate levels should be checked.
B. Skin biopsy from side of neck can be helpful.
C. A baseline echocardiogram is not required.
D. Soft tissue calcification may be detected radiologically.
E. Definitive diagnosis is made by molecular analysis.

Key: C
Ref: Rook (72.30)

10. A 1 week old premature baby presented with complaint of stiffness of joints with shiny taut skin since birth. On examination skin is tight, red and shiny with erosions in flexures. Joints were fixed in flexion posture and mouth was open and fixed on examination. Most common mutation leading to this disorder is due to?

A. LMNA gene
B. ZMPSTE 24 gene
C. FBN1 gene
D. TWIST gene

Key: B
Ref: Rook (72.20)

11. Most common cause of death in restrictive dermopathy is due to?

A. respiratory insufficiency
B. infections
C. malnutrition
D. malignancies

Key: A
Ref: Rook (72.20)

12. A 6 year old child presented with a droopy and aged appearance of skin particularly in flexures. On examination skin lacks elasticity and there is increased wrinkling predominantly in flexures. There is inguinal hernia and a diastolic murmur on auscultation. What is the likely diagnosis?

A. Bloom syndrome
B. Cutis laxa
C. marfan syndrome
D. werner syndrome
E. progeria

Key: B

13. Werner syndrome is an autosomal recessive disorder causing death in mid fifties usually due to?

A. malignancies
B. cardiovascular compliance
C. respiratory insufficiency
D. infections

E. both a and b

Key: E

14. An 8 year old child presented with sclerodermatous changes of skin of trunk with pigmentation. His parents also complain that their childs hand turn blue in winters and he hasn't loose his deciduous teeth till yet with permanent teeth growing behind the primary teeth. There is growth retardation and difficulty in hearing. What is the mode of inheritance of this disorder?

A. autosomal recessive
B. autosomal dominant
C. x linked dominant
D. x linked recessive

Key: B

15. A 10 years old boy presented in ops with scars on face and body. o/e he was found to have waxy and hyperkeratotic papules. There were beaded papules along the margin of eyelid. He had hoarseness of voice along with enlarged tongue. He also had acneform, pock like scars on face.in view of above mentioned features what is the diagnosis?

A. lipoid proteinosis
B. pxeudoxanthoma elasticum
C. amyloidosis
D. lichen myxoedematosis

Key: A
Ref: Rook (72.33)

16. A 15 years old patient presented in opd with complaints of hyperkeratotic waxy papules. There were beaded papules along eye margin. He had pock like scaring. His parents were worried about his further complications of this disease. Which of the following can occur?

A. stroke
B. epilepsy
C. intracranial mass
D. MI

Key: B
Ref: Rook (72.33)

17. What is the mode of inheritance of lipoid proteinosis?

A. autosomal recessive
B. autosomal dominant
C. x linked recessive
D. x linked dominant

Key: A
Ref: Rook (72.32)

18. A 22 year old female presented to dermatology outdoor with skin hyperextensibility. The patient had diminished vision for which she had consulted an ophthalmologist. The patient was tall, had slender limbs, thin body and with an increased arm span-to-height ratio. She had long and slender fingers, chest deformity, and abnormal curvature of the spine, tempero-mandibular joint hypermobility and flat feet. The patient Demonstrated a positive wrist sign and positive thumb sign. Ophthalmological examination reveals ectopia lentis and myopia. The intra-oral findings were small mouth, incompetent lips, forwardly placed upper incisor teeth with a high palatal vault.

Keeping in mind the diagnosis, most common cause of mortality in these patients is

A. Aortic dissection

B. Myocardial infarction
C. Pulmonary hypertension
D. Sepsis

Key: A
Ref: Rook (72.17)

19. A eight month old female child, presented to dermatology outdoor with multiple, symmetric, deep, circumferential skin folds on the upper and lower limbs .The folds were present since birth and were asymptomatic without causing any physical discomfort to the child. The patient had microcephaly with small anterior fontanelle. Bilateral epicanthic folds, low set ears, cleft palate, and lips with hypoplastic teeth are also present. The most probable diagnosis is

A. Cutis laxa
B. Michelin tyre baby
C. Williams beuren syndrome
D. Progeria

Key: B
Ref: Rook (72.18)

20. A 5 year old girl with an unremarkable medical and family history presented with firm thick skin that started on the right leg for 1 year. She had thickened skin with overlying hyperpigmentation that involved her buttocks lower back, lateral thighs, and entire legs. There was also increased dense hair growth over the lumbosacral area. She has a short stature. Skin biopsy reveals Lattice like array of thickened, horizontally oriented collagen bundles in the absence of inflammation. the most probable diagnosis is

A. Mulvihil smith syndrome
B. Stiff skin syndrome
C. Autosomal recessive cutis laxa
D. Neonatal progeroid syndrome

Key: B
Ref: Rook (72.18)

21. A 7 year old boy presented with thickened skin since infancy. His parents noted thickened skin on his right thigh at 2 year of age that subsequently spread to the right buttocks, trunk, and recently to the left thigh. He began walking at 10 months of age with a limp that never resolved. He had progressively impaired mobility and required physical therapy and a wheelchair. He has had no visceral symptoms, no Raynaud phenomena, and no intellectual Impairment. There were no affected family members. On physical examination, he had a much thickened skin, reduced join mobility and flexion contractures. There is hypertrichosis, short stature, muscle weakness and some cutaneous nodules are present over distal interphalengeal joints. Keeping in mind the diagnosis mode of inheritance and mutation in gene is

A. Autosomal recessive and FBN2
A. b. Autosomal dominant and FBN2
B. Autosomal dominant and FBN1
C. X linked recessive and FBN1

Key: C
Ref: Rook (72.18)

22. A 32 year old female presented to dermatology outdoor with complaint of skin hyperextensibility. The patient had diminished vision for which she had consulted an ophthalmologist.The patient was tall, had slender limbs, thin body and with an increased arm span-to-height ratio. She had long and slender fingers, chest deformity, and abnormal curvature of the spine, tempero-mandibular joint hypermobility and flat feet. The patient demonstrated a positive wrist sign and positive thumb sign. Ophthalmological examination reveals ectopia lentis and myopia. The intra-oral findings were small mouth, incompetent lips, forwardly placed upper incisor teeth with a high palatal vault.

Keeping in mind the diagnosis, the disease has association with which of the following

A. Michelin tyre baby
B. Ehlers Danlos syndrome
C. Lipoid proteinosis
D. Osteogenesis imperfecta

Key: B
Ref: Rook (72.16)

Chapter 73

DISORDERS AFFECTING CUTANEOUS VASCULATURE

1. An infant presented in the opd having a pink/purple flat lesion with geaographic border on the neck. According to parents lesion is increasing in size as the infant is growing. Considering the diagnosis which of the following gene is involved in this?

A. ATM
B. ECM1
C. TYP
D. GNAQ

Key: D
Ref: Rook (73.1)

2. Which of the following is true regarding sturge weber syndrome?

A. A.75% of children with intra cranial vascukar anomaly develop seizures before age of 2years with contralateral neurological deficit.
B. B.75% of children with intracranial vascular anomaly develop seizures before age of 4years with contralateral neurological deficit.
C. C.80% of children with intracranial vascular anomaly develop seizures before age of 4yrs with contralateral neurological deficit.
D. D.90% of children with intracranial vascular anomaly develop seizurea before age of 2years with contralateral neurological deficit

Key: A
Ref: Rook (73.3)

3. A 20 yrs old male presents with history of recurrent epistaxis. He also has few macular lesions on face and in his oral cavity for the last 5 years. He also complains of headache off and on. All the following can be used for his treatment except

A. Blood transfusion
B. VEGF-A
C. Thalidomide
D. nasal humidifiers
E. I/V Ig

Key: E
Ref: Rook (73.8)

4. Regarding PTEN Hamartoma Syndrome which of the following statement is correct

A. It regroups patients with Bannayan Riley Ruvalcaba Syndrome RRRS and Cowden Syndrome CS
B. Heterozygous PTEN mutations are identified in about 60% of CS and 81% of BRRS
C. Rapamycin does not seem to be effective in clinical trials
D. Measurement of head circumference does not help to diagnose a patient with atypical vascular lesion
E. Most vascular anomalies are slow flowing

Key: A
Ref: Rook (73.8)

5. 15 old female presents with few bluish plaques on her right foot. There was one plaque during infancy age and now increased in number gradually. It is hyperkeratotic and painful. She also had 2 episodes of hematemesis in last 3 years.
Following is the disease association

A. SLE
B. Localised intravascular coagulopathy
C. Bean Syndrome
D. Glomus tumor
E. Hereditary Haemorrhagic Telangiectasia

Key: B
Ref: Rook (73.12)

6. 18 years old female presents with red macular lesion on neck and face since infancy. She also had 4 episodes of epistaxis in last 2 years. She complains of abdominal pain off and on along with headaches.
All the following genes are involved in causing this disease except

A. ENG
B. ACVRL1
C. SMAD4
D. GDF2
E. HHT3,4
F. AKVP

Key: F

7. A 22 years old female presents with purple plaque on her hand. She has this plaque since infancy. It is hyperkeratotic. She also complains pain off and on in the plaque. 1wk back she had an episode of hematemesis after which she panicked and came to OPD. What is the mode of inheritance of her condition?

A. AD
B. AR
C. C-XLR
D. XLD
E. sporadic

Key: E
Ref: Rook (73.12)

8. A 29 Yr old female presented to dermatology opd with bilateral odema of lower legs n double rows of eye lashes. She also is diagnosed case of bilateral renal cysts and hypertension. keeping in mind diagnosis ,disease is caused by mutation in

A. SOX 18
B. FOXC2
C. CCBE1
D. FAT4

Key: B
Ref: Rook (73.18)

9. A young female presented to dermatology opd with bilateral lymphoedema, double rows of eyelashes, corneal ulceration, ptosis and yellow. Considering her condition, mode of inheritance is

A. Autosomal dominant
B. Autosomal recessive
C. X.linked dominant
D. X linked recessive

Key: A

Ref: Rook (73.18)

10. A 2yr male child presented to dermatology opd with bilateral lower limbs swelling since birth with history of recurrent eye infections. After hereditary lymphoedema type1, most frequently genetic cause of primary lymphoedema is

A. Turner syndrome
B. Noonan syndrome
C. Costello syndrome
D. Lymphoedema distichiasis syndrome

Key: D
Ref: Rook (73.18)

11. A 13yr old boy presented to dermatology opd with history of lower legs oedema bilaterally along with genitalia. He had this complaint since birth. On examination having flat face, low nasal bridge, hypertelorism, epicanthal folds, and small mouth. He had also having hx of diarrhoea for last six month. Keeping in mind diagnosis ,diarrhea treatment should include all except

A. Fat restriction
B. medium chain TG
C. Octreotide administration
D. anti-diarrheal

Key: D
Ref: Rook (73.19)

12. A 13yr old boy presented to dermatology opd with history of lower legs oedema bilaterally along with genitalia. He had this complaint since birth. On examination having flat face, low nasal bridge, hypertelorism, epicanthal folds, and small mouth. He had also having hx of diarrhea for last six month. Keeping in mind diagnosis, features present in syndrome include all except

A. Hyperthyroidism
B. Syndactyly
C. Craniosynostosis
D. Ectopic kidney

Key: A
Ref: Rook (73.19)

13. Mode of inheritance of Rendu-osler-weber Syndrome is

A. Autosomal recessive
B. Autosomal dominant
C. X- linked dominant
D. X-linked recessive
E. None of the above

Key: B

14. Curacao Criteria for diagnose of Hereditary haemorrhagic telangiectasia includes all except

A. Telangiectasias
B. Epistaxis
C. visceral fast flow lesions
D. Family History
E. Facial trichilemmomas

Key: E

15. Regarding surveillance of patients with cowden syndrome, which statement is incorrect.

A. Mammography in women age > 30
B. Cerebral MRI above 40
C. Colonoscopy above age of 35
D. Renal MRI above age of 45
E. Baseline thyroid ultrasound

Key: B

16. All of the following are included in pathogonomic Criteria for cowden disease except
A. Hamartomatous intestinal polyps
B. Acral Keratosis
C. Trichilemmomas
D. Oral mucosa papillomatosis
E. both a &b

Key: A

17. Regarding venous malformations, which statement is incorrect?
A. Localized intravascular coagulopathy is 96% specific for venous malformations.
B. D- Dimers are elevated in 42% patients.
C. 20% have low level of fibrinogen.
D. Patients with low fibrinogen level are at high risk of DIC during surgical procedure.
E. D- Dimer level is more than twice the normal range in 25% patients

Key: C

18. HHT in combination with juvenile polyposis is due to ------ Gene mutation?
A. ENG
B. SMAD4
C. ACVRLI
D. GDF2
E. None of the above

Key: B

19. A 10yrs old child has to undergo surgery for appendix. His medical record reveals venous malformation involving R lower extremity. What treatment you will offer to prevent bleeding during surgical procedure
A. Aspirin
B. LMW- Heparin
C. Sclerotherapy
D. pulse-dye laser
E. No treatment is required

Key: B

20. Regarding prognosis of venous malformations, which statement is incorrect?
A. Never regress spontaneously
B. functional impairment worsen with time
C. can be life threatening
D. improve spontaneously with time
E. None of the above.

Key: D

Chapter 75

CONGENITAL NAEVI AND DEVELOPMENT ABNORMALITIES

1. A mother brought her one week old infant for evaluation of spots on his body. On examination pt was having erythematous spots on the chest, upper limbs, hypogastrium, and a large area of the dorsum after birth. Besides these, well demarcated greyish-blue hyperpigmentation with clear-cut edges on the back region of the shoulder, dorsum, buttocks, and lower limbs were also noticed. These lesions were unchanged and asymptomatic since the time of presentation.
Considering the probable diagnosis what other association you will look for?

A. Hemihypertrophy
B. Congenital lipomas
C. Mucinous nevus
D. Ichthyosis
E. retinoblastoma

Key: A
Ref: Rook (75.23)

Chapter 76

CHROMOSOMAL DISORDERS

1. A 14-years-old girl presented with complaint of excessive dryness and rashes on upper arm and front of thigh. According to mother previously her skin was soft and fine but now from last 1-2 years she started developing these complaints. On examining the girl, she was found to be having prominent epicanthal folds of eyes, depressed nasal bridge, protruded tongue and the fingers are short and webbed. On dermatological examination patient was having generalized xerosis along with lichenified patches on front of thigh, upper arm and back of neck.
Considering the diagnosis which of the following is an association?

A. CML
B. Lewy body dementia
C. Hyperthyroidism
D. AML
E. Impaired B cell function

Key: D
Ref: Rook (76.1)

2. You received a call from gynecology department to examine a boy born few hours back for his unusual features. On examination he was having small head, flat face, short nose and small mishappen ear. There is also slanting palpebral fissures. His dermatoglyphics showed single palmer crease.
Considering the diagnosis which of the following congenital anomaly you will look for in this pt?

A. Hypoplastic femur
B. Small left colon syndrome
C. Pyloric atresia
D. Cystic kidney
E. Endo cardial cushion defect

Key: E
Ref: Rook (76.2)

3. A 18-years-old girl with history of failure of growth at the time of birth presented with primary amenorrhoea and failure to develop secondary sexual characteristics. On physical examination her height was 90 cm, sparse axillary & genital hair, a broad shield-shaped chest with widely spaced nipples, pterygium colli. She is also found to be having kyphoscoliosis.
Considering the diagnosis which of the following option is important diagnostic clue?

A. Chromatin negative buccal smear
B. Increased urinary testosterone
C. Small testes
D. Chromatin positive buccal smear
E. Increased urinary estrogen

Key: A
Ref: Rook (76.3)

4. All of the following is associated with turner's syndrome except;

A. Hypoplasia of cutaneous lymphatics
B. Elastosis perforans serpiginosa
C. Melanocytic nevi
D. Alopecia areata
E. Psoriasis

Key: B
Ref: Rook (76.3)

5. A 25 year old male comes to your Opd who has been married since 1 year but is having problems in trying to have a child. On initial physical examination you notice he has less facial and body hairs. He has longer arms and legs with wide hips and BMI of 30. He has normal looking genitalia, however you notice enlarged breast tissue. He gives history that he had hard time making friends and was always shy, he was also taller than rest of his family members. You order a urine test which showed increased urinary excretion of gonadotrophins. In order to confirm the diagnosis, you perform chromosomal studies. What will be the result of buccal smear in this case?

A. XXYY
B. XYY
C. XXY
D. X0

Key C
Ref: Rook (76.4)

6. A 25 year old male comes to your Opd who has been married since 1 year but is having problems in trying to have a child. On initial physical examination you notice he has less facial and body hairs. He has longer arms and legs with wide hips and BMI of 30. He has normal looking genitalia, however you notice enlarged breast tissue. He gives history that he had hard time making friends and was always shy, he was also taller than rest of his family members. You order a urine test which showed increased urinary excretion of gonadotrophins. A diagnosis of Klinefelter syndrome is made. Which of the following statements is incorrect?

A. Men with klinefelter seem to have Sle of same degree of severity as women
B. Men have Sle that is more severe than found among women
C. After treatment with testosterone to adult male range haematological and serological abnormalities will return to normal
D. Testosterone replacement will improve secondary sexual characteristics but infertility is the rule
E. Taller heavier and less fertile male have more risk of developing leg ulcers

Key B
Ref: Rook (76.4)

Chapter 77

POIKILODERMA SYNDROME

1. You are asked to examine a 10 years old child with small stature with slender delicate limbs. He has small hands and short fingers. The child has bird like facial features with premature aging skin. His scalp hairs along with body hairs are sparse. You notice rough warty lesions on feet ankle, hands and wrists with surrounding atrophic skin. The child has bilateral cataract since 6 years of age. Keeping in view the diagnosis which malignancy will not be associated with this syndrome

A. Malignant eccrine Poroma
B. Myelodysplastic syndrome
C. Squamous cell Carcinoma
D. Basal cell carcinoma
E. Pancreatic Carcinoma

Key: E
Ref: Rook (77.5)

2. A 5 year old child is brought to opd with her mother. She tells you that his skin was normal at birth but at the age of 2 years he developed plaques of erythema on his cheeks. He is sensitive to light exposure and once developed blisters on his face, hands and forearms. On/e you notice fine pink or red lines on the face and hands. There is also thinning of skin along with brown coloured irregular macular pigmentation on lower legs, buttocks and thighs. He has sparse hairs and dystrophic nails. Keeping in mind the diagnosis, this defect occurs in which of the following mutated genes

A. RECQL3
B. RECQL2
C. RECQL4
D. RECQL1

Key: C
Ref: Rook (77.5)

Chapter 78

DNA REPAIR DISORDERS WITH CUTANEOUS FEATURES

1. A 32 year old patient who has previously undergone a pancolectomy with ileo-rectal anastomosis presents with multiple epidermoid cysts on face scalp and extremities. Other features include a recurrent abdominal desmoid tumour, lipomas, osteomas of the mandible and skull, and dental abnormalities. What is the diagnosis??

A. Cowden syndrome
B. Gardner syndrome
C. Turcot syndrome
D. Werner syndrome

Key: B

2. A 42 year old woman presented to the out-patient clinic with a 3 cm diameter lump near the left arm, which was excised. The histopathologist reported this as a sebaceous adenoma and also raised the possibility of the association of these lesions with visceral neoplasms. The patient had undergone hysterectomy for endometrial cancer at the age of 32 years. She also had an actinic keratosis and a basal cell carcinoma previously.
What is the diagnosis??

A. Cowden syndrome
B. Gardner syndrome
C. Turcot syndrome
D. Muir torre syndrome

Key: D
Ref: Rook (78.12)

3. A three years old girl with a history of failure to thrive, pancytopenia for six months. On physical examination, her height was 72 cm consistent with short stature. Cutaneous examination include reticulate hyperpigmentation. She has hyperpigmented lesions (Café-au-lait spots). She has also been noted to have absent thumb in the right hand.
What is the diagnosis??

A. Cockayne syndrome
B. Louis Bar syndrome
C. Fanconi anaemia
D. Bloom syndrome

Key: C

4. All of the following are features of Gardner syndrome EXCEPT:

A. Epidermoid cyst
B. Osteomas
C. Fibromas
D. Leiomyosarcoma
E. Fibrosarcomas

Key: D

5. All of the following carcinomas are associated with fanconi anaemia EXCEPT:

A. Acute myeloid leukaemia
B. Lymphoma
C. Urinary bladder carcinoma

D. Liver carcinoma
E. Brain tumor

Key: C

6. A mother brings 15 years old child to your opd who has abnormal uncoordinated movements. Mother gives history of recurrent episodes of URTI. The child has premature greying of hairs and recently mother noticed small dull red punctuate lesions involving face and conjunctiva. Keeping in view the diagnosis what other problems is the child likely to suffer

A. Hypogonadism
B. Insulin resistance
C. Increase chances of breast cancer
D. Piokiloderma and pigmentary changes
E. All of the above

Key: E
Ref: Rook (78.11)

7. In the above scenario which statement is true?

A. Telangectasia present at 1 year of age
B. X-rays and Radiotherapy can be given
C. First clinical presentation is neurological
D. There is no increased risk of cancer
E. Prognosis is usually good

Key: C
Ref: Rook (78.11)

8. 6 year old child who was normal at birth had now presented with multiple lentigines all over sun exposed areas. The child is currently wearing thick glasses and the mother reports severe sun burn whenever they go to the beach or have a picnic outdoors. On examination, in addition to multiple irregular lentigines, he has periocular scarring. Other than skin malignancies, which cancer is he at most risk for?

A. Cardiac rhabdomyoma
B. Medulloblastoma
C. Renal angiomyolipoma
D. Colon adenocarcinoma
E. Nasopharyngeal carcinoma

Key: B
Ref: Rook (78.4)

9. 12 year and 16 year old brother and sister are regular visitors of dermatology OPD. They have a history of eruption of many lentigines since childhood and have progressively increased in size and number. Both wear thick glasses and have decreased vision while the elder sister is in wheel chair. They have had few abnormal growths on their face and hands that have been removed with topical treatment and surgery in the past. Which one of the following is the strongest predictor of their disease severity?

A. Number of lentigines
B. Family history
C. Neurological involvement
D. Ocular involvement
E. Mucosal involvement

Key: C
Ref: Rook (78.6)

10. An 8 year old child with a history of multiple lentigines and squamous cell carcinoma arising on his face is diagnosed to have xeroderma pigmentosa. He is advised to have strict UVR protection and guided to

wear UV protected clothes, window films and UV filters on florescent lamps. Other than UV protection, which of the following can decrease malignancy risk in this patient?

A. Vitamin D supplements
B. Topical imiquimod
C. Topical 5-flourouracil
D. Oral retinoids
E. Photodynamic therapy

Key: D
Ref: Rook (78.7)

11. 15 year old boy complains of short stature and burning of skin on sun exposure. On examination, he seems to have a small head with sunken eyes and prominent thin nose. Based on the history and examination, you consider a provisional diagnosis. Which of the following findings maybe be found on cerebral imaging of this patient?

A. Calcification of falx cerebri
B. Calcification of dural ligament
C. Calcification of choroid plexus
D. Calcification of temporal lobe
E. Calcification of basal ganglia

Key: E
Ref: Rook (78.9)

12. A 3 year old child is diagnosed with Cockayne syndrome and develops severe photosensitivity since birth and severe cataracts at the age of 2. Considering the type of Cockayne syndrome, what is the gene mutation?

A. ERCC6
B. NEMO
C. ATM
D. XPA
E. FANC

Key: A
Ref: Rook (78.8)

Chapter 80 HAMARTANEOPLASTIC SYNDROMES

1. An 8 year old boy presented in opd with multiple cafe au leit macules, axillary freckling and neurofibromas have started to form on trunk and limbs, for past 1 year. On eye examination pt is having lisch nodules on iris, there is also and orange papule on right eye since 1 year of life. What's the disease which can develop in such patients?
   A. Chronic myeloid leukaemia.
   B. Bowel tumor.
   C. Acute lymphocytic leukaemia.
   D. Juvenile myeloid leukaemia
   E. Lung cancer

Key: D

2. A pt presented in opd, on examination pt was having multiple cafe au leit macules and axillary freckling along with macrocephaly, bt no neurofibromas and slit lamp examination was also normal on genetic examination NF_1 gene was absent but SPRED 1 gene was present. What could be the disease this pt is having?
   A. Noonan syndrome.
   B. Rasopathies.
   C. Legius syndrome.
   D. Costello syndrome.
   E. Tuberous sclerosis

Key: C

3. A pt presented with h/o epilepsy since childhood, on examination pt is having hypomelanltic macules which are 5 in number, multiple angiofibromas on face, and retinal hamartomas on slit lamp exam. What would be the life expectancy in this pt.?
   A. 1 year.
   B. 2 year.
   C. 3 years.
   D. 4 years.
   E. 5 years

Key: A

4. Following is not a criteria for dx of tuberous sclerosis complex?
   A. Renal angiomyolipoma.
   B. Renal carcinoma.
   C. Renal cyst.
   D. Non retinal hamartoma.
   E. Retinal achromic patch

Key: B

5. What's the pattern of inheritance of above disease??
   A. Autosomal dominant.
   B. Autosomal recessive.
   C. X linked dominant.
   D. X linked recessive.
   E. Non familial

Key: A

6. A 21 years old patient with uterine fibroids and menstrual irregularity has been referred to dermaopd from gynae dept for assessment of skin lesions. O/E you notice multiple skin coloured coalescing lichenoid papules (giving cobblestone appearance) around the eyes and mouth. On the dorsae of hands and wrists multiple plane-wart like pigmented lesions are present. In the oral cavity a verrucous papillomatous lesion was present on the Rt buccal mucosa. Regarding this disease associations how should you counsel the patient

   A. Pt should have breast screening at 30
   B. Pt should have renal MRI over 40
   C. Pt should have colonoscopy above 35
   D. Pt should have baseline thyroid ultrasound examination
   E. All of above

Key: E
Ref: Rook (80.13)

7. A 7 years old girl presents to dermaopd with C/O hypopigmented patch on the nose and right cheek. At first look on the patient you notice that girl has adenoid facies. Examination reveals 3 lipomatous sweeling of upper limbs and 2 fibromas on neck and trunk.
O/E of oral cavity you notice high arched palate and papillomatous lesion on left buccal mucosa. Further you notice she has hoarse voice. On questioning, her mother reports poor performance of her daughter at school.
What is the most common extracutaneous finding in this disease?

   A. Intestinal polyposis
   B. Thyroid and breast abnormalities
   C. Genitourinary malformation
   D. Uterine fibroids.
   E. None of above

Key: B

8. A 35 years old female patient diagnosed with CA breast has been admitted in oncology ward. You are requested to examine the patient for her skin lesions. After detailed cutaneous examination, you suspect cowden syndrome in the patient. This patient is accompanied by her 1st cousin in the hospital. You notice 1 small skin coloured lichenoid papule near the eye of her cousin as well. Her cousin is most likely to have cowden if she has

   A. Enlarged thyroid and intellectual disability
   B. Cutaneous lipomas
   C. Cutaneous fibromas
   D. Biopsy proven fibrocystic disease of breast

Key: A

9. A 14 years old boy develops multiple dark red telangeictatic macules and papules on the lower trunk, inner thighs and buttocks over a period of six months. There is history of episodic severe burning pain in the palms and soles since the age of 10 years after playing for long hours outdoors with friends. GPE reveals left lower limb lymphedema extending upto knee. How will you confirm the likely disease in this patient?

   A. Skin histology
   B. slit lamp examination of cornea
   C. demonstrating enzyme deficiency in leukocytes
   D. Molecular analysis

Key: C

10. A 16 months old boy is brought by his parents to derma opd for eczematous skin lesions. O/E you notice boy has blonde hair and blue irides while both of his patents having dark brown irides and dark hair. There is hx of 2 episodes of seizures since the age of 10 months. During the examination the baby is irritable and cries a lot. Which statement is true regarding this disease?

A. x-linked dominant inheritance
1. B.50% patients have defects in synthesis of tetrahydrobiopterin
B. Semi synthetic diet throughout life
C. plasma amino acid is first line investigation

Key: D

Chapter 81

INHERITED METABOLIC DISEASES

1. A 5-year-old girl presented with thin dry brittle hairs, and learning difficulties, mother gives history of seizures too.
Keeping in mind the diagnosis of the patient, what is the gene affected in this case?

A. ATP7A
B. P63
C. ASL
D. Connexin 30
E. Ectodysplastin A

Key: A
Ref: Rook (81.15)

2. A 4 yr old child presented to you in opd with red scaly light sensitive rash on face, arms, extremities and inheritance exposed areas of skin. On detailed examination pt is having unsteady walk which started after rash. Also, pt is impaired muscle coordination, impaired articulation of speech and delayed cognitive development.
What is the diagnosis?

A. Lesch-Nyhan syndrome
B. Mevalonate kinase deficiency
C. Tays syndrome
D. Hartnup disease
E. Prolidase deficiency

Key: D
Ref: Rook (81.15)

3. A 65 yr old male admitted with history of blueish grey pigmentation of skin and long-standing arthritis. Medical history is significant for valve replacement for aortic stenosis. And there is also history of renal calculi. After deciding about the diagnosis, recall what is the mode of inheritance of this disease.

A. autosomal dominant
B. autosomal recessive
C. X linked recessive
D. X linked dominanat
E. AR / AD pattern

Key: B
Ref: Rook (81.13)

4. A 40 year old patient with cardiac problem and backache presented to ENT surgeon with observation of change of color of ear wax to black. On examination surgeon noted pigmentation of ear and nose.
Wats the probable diagnosis?

A. alkaptonuria
B. addisons disease
C. phenulyketonuria
D. pellagra
E. hemochromotosis

Key: A
Ref: Rook (81.13)

5. A 52 yr old Male patient, sought medical assistance complaining about progressive appearance of hyperchromic papules on the lateral edge of the second finger of both hands for a period of 2 years. He also complained about darkening of urine, sperm and underwear for 20 years with recent worsening. He is obese and hypertensive, currently using enalapril. He already underwent knee arthropathy five years ago. According to his family history his sister presented Coca-Cola color in her diapers during infancy.
On further examination grayish spot in the sclera is noted.
What's the most likely diagnosis?

A. Fabrys disease
B. Gauchers disease
C. Homocystineuria
D. phenylketonuria
E. Alkaptonuria

Key: E
Ref: Rook (81.13)

6. A baby presented with hypotonia and seizures since 3 months of age. His hairs are sparse and brittle . Trichoscopy reveals pillitorti. Regarding pathophysiology transport of which mineral is defective

A. Fe
B. Cu
C. Al
D. K
E. none of above

Key: B
Ref: Rook (81.18)

7. A 7 year old boy presented with exostosis over occiput and learning difficulty. There are no neurological signs. Hair microscopy is normal. There is history of diarrhoea. What is diagnosis

A. Menkes disease
B. Occipital horn syndrome
C. Cutis laxa
D. Familial tumoral calcinosis
E. Lesch nyhan syndrome

Key: B

8. A girl presented with perioral and perianal dermatitis along with alopecia. Pt was diagnosed as acrodermatitis enteropathoca. Pt was given zinc. Monitoring of which element should be done while giving zinc

A. Fe
B. Cu
C. Mg
D. K
E. Phosphorous

Key: B

9. Pt presented with dysarthria and detriorating handwriting along with blue lunula and hyperpigmentation over the leg. What is treatment of this condition

A. Hydralazine
B. phenytoin
C. zinc
D. Carbamezapine
E. EDTA

Key: C

10. A child presented with perioral dermatitis along with rash in perianal area. Pt also had diahorrhea and alopecia. What will help in making diagnosis?

   A. increased AST level
   B. decreased alkaline phosphatase
   C. C)increased Br level
   D. D)increased zn level
   E. E) none

Key: B

Chapter 82 INHERITED IMMUNODEFICIENCY

1. Investigations at birth showed he had normal platelet size. His family history revealed two early neonatal deaths in maternal uncles. Spontaneous bleeding was only seen at the age of 3 months. He was initially treated for immune thrombocytopenic purpura and was started on intravenously administered immunoglobulin. His clinical deterioration and poor response to the immunoglobulin raised suspicion for a different underlying pathology. Molecular analysis of the WAS gene revealed a missense mutation in exon 10. Considering the diagnosis, what is the mode of inheritance of this disease?

A. Autosomal dominant
B. Autosomal recessive
C. X linked recessive
D. D Mitochondrial
E. X linked dominant

Key: C
Ref: Rook (82.9)

2. A 7-year-old boy was referred to allergy clinic with complaints of wheezing, dry skin and infection. He was the first child born to consanguineous parents. At age 2, he was hospitalized for the first time with high grade fever due to severe cold, followed by respiratory distress and ecchymosis. PLT count was 30000/mL. A bone marrow biopsy was performed to evaluate underlying etiology of thrombocytopenia. Idiopathic thrombocytopenic purpura (ITP) and asthma were diagnosed and he was treated with prednisolone and oral beclomethasone spray. During the age 3 to 6, he was suffering from asthma attacks and admitted to ICU for several times. Also, he developed generalized eczema when he was 6 years old. Two of his uncles were reported to have died in childhood after experiencing similar symptoms. Physical examination revealed generalized eczema and normal growth. Laboratory tests showed microcytic thrombocytopenia with PLT count of 30000/mL and WBC 6000/ml with 50% neutrophils, 38% lymphocytes and 5% eosinophils. On examination, no hepatosplenomegaly, no lymphadenopathy but a moderate eczema was seen in physical exam. Considering the diagnosis following are treatment options except:

A. Platelet transfusion
B. Haematopoietic stem cell transplantation (HSCT)
C. Systemic steroids and splenectomy
D. Intravenous immunoglobulin
E. Prophylactic antibiotics

Key: C
Ref: Rook (82.9)

3. The male patient suffered from itchy skin and diarrhea since the first year of life. Eczema and asthma due to food allergies were also seen. At the age of 4 years, left leg arterial thrombosis led to the amputation of the left first toe. The patient was hospitalized three times because of septicemia, dysentery, and osteomyelitis. Subsequently, aortic and abdominal aneurysms were diagnosed by Doppler sonography. At the age of 8 years, the patient died due to the rupture of the aortic aneurysm. Considering the diagnosis, following cutaneous viral infections common in these patients:

A. HSV
B. Human papillomavirus
C. Molluscum contagiosum
D. varicella-zoster virus
E. All of the above

Key: E
Ref: Rook (82.9)

4. A 3-month-old girl was referred for recurrent fever, pneumonia, diarrhea, chronic dermatitis, failure to thrive, and motor retardation. The patient was the daughter of consanguineous parents and had a female sibling who had died due to recurrent infections. On a physical examination, her weight, height, and head circumference were all less than the third percentile. She suffered from oral thrush and a diffuse brownish colored macular rash on the trunk. Chest auscultation revealed bilateral crackles at the lower zones. Chest X-ray, indicated the absence of thymus shadow; a para-cardiac infiltration and an inferolateral squaring scapula were demonstrated. Laboratory tests revealed mild anaemia with profound lymphocytopenia, and hypogammaglobulinemia. A lymphocyte subgroup analysis revealed a severe combined immunodeficiency. Regarding histopathological findings of disease following is correct:

A. Dense dermal perivascular lym-phohistiocytic infiltrate, comprising activated T lymphocytes, with numerous eosinophils.
B. S100-positive Langerhans cells are usually absent and there is no epidermotropism.
C. Lymph node architecture is disordered, being replaced by a massive infiltrate of S100- positive interdigitating reticulum cells with absence of germinal centres, absent B cells and paucity of T lymphocytes.
D. All of the above

Key: E
Ref: Rook (82.8)

5. A 14 years old female child was brought to the OPD by the grandmother, with the complaints of discharge from left side of nose since birth. There was history of hard of hearing both ears, difficulty in speech, defective vision on left eye. Otherwise, the perinatal and developmental history was normal. On examination, pt had unilateral choanal atresia, sensorineural hearing loss on both side. Eye examination revealed left eye micro cornea with typical coloboma choroid involving optic disc and iris, squint, spontaneous nystagmus, loss of left eye vision. General examination of the patient showed facial asymmetry , polydactyly , poor breast development on left side, systemic examination revealed, wide fixed split on auscultation, abdominal and respiratory systems are normal. Child was investigated. Diagnostic nasal endoscopy showed complete choanal atresia on left side. Severe sensorineural hearing loss on both sides on Pure Tone Audiogram. CT PNS and temporal bone showed posterior coloboma left eye, left osseous choanal atresia . Ultra sonogram of abdomen showed Left side extra renal pelvis. On echocardiogram moderate size 5 mm ostium secondum type of atrial septal defect with less than 2:1 left to right shunt. Child has choanal atresia, coloboma of eyes.
What is the diagnosis?

A. Omenn syndrome
B. DiGeorge syndrome
C. CHARGE Syndome
D. Adenosine deaminase deficiency
E. Calcium channel deficiencies

Key: B
Ref: Rook (82.8)

6. 2yr old child presented with diarrhea, failure to thrive and congenital icthyosis. On examination polycyclic scaly migratory plaques present on skin trichoscopy shows bamboo hair. Considering diagnosis most likely immunodeficiency associated is

A. Hypergammaglobulinaemia
B. Pancytopenia
C. Lymphopenia and polysaccharide antibody deficiency
D. Defect in neutrophil phagocytosis

Key: C
Ref: Rook (82.11)

7. Genetic mutation in above mentioned scenerio is
   A. DKC 1 mutation
   B. SPINK5
   C. NSDHL
   D. Gene encoding tyrosinase kinase enzyme

Key: B
Ref: Rook (82.11)

8. Netherton syndrome hv spink5 and lekti mutation a 4yr old boy presented to derma opd with complaint of nonspecific eczematous rash since 1st yr of life, had h/o recurrent admissions in paeds due to recurrent pulmonary and other infections. On examination nonspecific eczematous rash present and some cold abscesses present on skin.chest Xray show multiple pneumatocoels most likely diagnosis
   A. Jobs syndrome
   B. SCID
   C. Wiscot aldrich syndrome
   D. Fanconi anemia

Key: A
Ref: Rook (82.17)

9. A 5 yr child present with easy bruisibility. On examination boy is small for age elfin like features and skin shows reticulate hyper and hypopigmentation. labs show pancytopenia, aplastic bone marrow, most likely diagnosis
   A. fanconi anemia
   B. Ataxic telangiectasia
   C. Netherton syndrome
   D. Wiskot aldrich syndrome

Key: A
Ref: Rook (82.12)

10. A 5 yr old had h/o recurrent bacterial skin infections. He also had h/o sinopulmonary infections pyoderma and gastroenteritis. Labs show normal T lymphocytes count but nȯ B lymphocytes present. Lymph nodes show absent germinal centre. Most likely defect will b
   A. BTK gene defect
   B. CD 40 defect
   C. Mu chain defect
   D. LEKTI gene defect

Key: A
Ref: Rook (82.12)

11. A 5 year old child was brought to OPD with the complain of recurrent episodes of pyogenic infections particularly meningococcal meningitis and pneumococcal pneumonia, he also had history of persistent candidiasis of mouth and nails. You are suspecting immunodeficiency in this patient and ordered lab workup which showed a deficiency in complement. What is the most common deficiency in these patients?
   A. C1q
   B. C 2
   C. C 3
   D. C 4
   E. C 5- 9

Key: C
Ref: Rook (82.17)

12. A child was brought by parents to OPD with complain of rash around mouth, nostrils and ears. On examination it was impetiginized rash around periorificial areas.
He also had history of neonatal pustulosis and subcutaneous nodule formation at vaccination site.
There was history of past hospital admissions due to lung abscess and perianal abscess.
What disease you are suspecting in this child?

A. WHIM syndrome
B. Job syndrome
C. Comel netherton syndrome
D. Wiskot Aldrich syndrome
E. Chronic granulomatous disease.

Key: E
Ref: Rook (82.15)

13. A neonate was brought to OPD with complain of failure of umbilical cord shrinkage and separation at age of 3 weeks. On examination of cord there was omphalitis.
Also there was rapidly progressive erosive perianal ulcers. His CBC was done that showed marked leucocytosis.
What defect is most likely in this patient?

A. Neutrophil adhesion defect
B. Complement deficiency
C. DOCK8 deficiency
D. Hyper IgM deficiency
E. Hyper IgE deficiency

Key: A
Ref: Rook (82.16)

14. A child was brought to OPD with complain of generalized erythematous rash, dry, scaly skin. The rash started few weeks after birth. He also had dysmorphic features along with cardiac anomalies and hypoplastic thymus. Workup showed hypocalcemia and TBX1 gene defect.
What is the most likely diagnosis?

A. Omen syndrome
B. Di - George syndrome
C. Wiskot Aldrich syndrome
D. CHARGE syndrome
E. Comel netherton syndrome

Key: B
Ref: Rook (82.8)

15. Infant presented to you with complain of generalized erythema since birth. On examination there was lymphadenopathy and eczema.
The other findings were cardiac and oesophageal anomalies. Further workup showed thymic aplasia and absence of T lymphocytes.
What gene defect you are suspecting?

A. WAS
B. DOCK8
C. CHD7
D. SPINK5
E. BTK

Key: C
Ref: Rook (82.4 / 8)

Chapter 83 PRURITUS, PRURIGO AND LICHEN SIMPLEX

1. A 4 yrs old boy with history of rhinitis n itching. N infected plaques more on flexures n gen body itching. History of atopy in mother n brotjer. Based on diagnosis mediators of this disease are.
   A. Acetylcholine
   B. IL-31
   A. C.NGF
   C. Tryptase n substance p
   D. A. B n c
   E. All of the above

Key: F

2. A 41 yr old female with history of itching presented in opd with circumscribed lichenified plaque on neck. She was a treated case of hepatitis. She has itching in lower legs n ankles too with redness n edema. Oral cavity, nails normal. On histopathology epidermal hyperplasia, hyperkeratosis n lengthend rete ridges. Demis show chronic inflammatory infiltrate. Based on diagnosis. Which is true
   A. It is reaction pattern to scratching
   B. Pt usually have history of atopic dermatitis
   C. Increases nerve fibres n mast cell r present
   D. Gabapentin is useful in v chronic cases
   E. A, b, c
   F. All of the above

Key: F
Ref: Rook (83.18)

3. Which is not true regarding mediators of itching.
   A. Psoriasis by NGF. n substance P
   B. Cut. Mastocytosis. Histamine n tryptase
   C. Atopic eczema.acetlvholine
   D. Mastocytosis. Acrtylcholine
   E. Urticaria. Histamine,

Key: D

4. A 63 yr old female presented in derma opd with generalized itching history. Now complain of symmetrical n bilateral multie pink nodules on legs n thighs. Some nodules r hyperkeratotic n eroded. A few papules also present. Sparing of face palms n soles n central back. Her two siblings were diagnosed case of atopic eczema. She took multiple treatment but minimal response. She is diabetic n have gastric ulcer. She is most probably having
   A. Hypertrophic LP
   B. Mastocytoma
   C. Nodular scabies
   D. Lymphomatoid paulosis
   E. Prurigo nodularis

Key: E

5. Treatment option for above. All true except
   A. Topical emoliemts n topical steroids
   B. Gabapentin, pregabalin, nalteraxone
   C. Thalidomide is highly recomended
   D. Cryotherapy, intralesional steroids n excimer laser invasive treatment of nodules

Key: C

Chapter 84

MUCOCUTANEOUS PAIN SYNDROMES

1. A 61-year-old female patient presented to dermatology department with episodes of erythematous dyschromia along the outer side of the left foot for the last 1-year patient was having 2-3 episodes per month each one lasting for hours to maximum of 2 days.
The condition was accampanied by nonspecific local discomfort, which used to get releived by raising the limb. On further investigations, she was diagnosed with polycythemia vera. What dermatological condition she is suffering from?

A. Erythromelalgia
B. Perephral neuropathy
C. Post herpetic neuralgia
D. B and c
E. Venous stasis dermatitis

Key: A
Ref: Rook (84.10)

2. A 60 years old women with major depression presented in opd with the complaints of burning in mouth, pain, xerostomia and unpleasant and strange feeling of taste and itching in mouth.
On examination and investigation, no demonstrable neurological deficit was found. What is the 1st line treatment option in this patient?

A. Clonazepam
B. Lidicaine gel
C. Benzydamine
D. Alpha lipoic acid
E. A,b and c

Key: E
Ref: Rook (84.3)

3. A62 year old man with a history of meningioma resection 18 years prior with an intractable ulceration around his left nasolabial fold. Pain and light touch sensations around the ulcer were decreased.
He admitted to frequent manipulation due to crawling sensation.
Skin biopsy showed acanthotic changes and a decreased number of peripheral nerve fibres.
What is the most likely diagnosis?

A. Post herpetic neuralgia
B. Trigeminal trophic syndrome
C. Delution of parasitosis
D. Dermatitis artefacta
E. Atypical trigeminal trophic syndrome

Key: B.
Ref: Rook (84.7)

4. A 55-year-old female had come with a complaint of burning sensation in the mouth and slightly on face.
On examination, oral cavity was having normal findings.
On investigations, autiantibody screen, hematology, blood glucose, and allergy testing, all were negative.
On further history, she was stressed out and depressed.
What is the most likely diagnosis?

A. Allergic contact stomatitis

B. Candida infection
C. Burning mouth syndrome
D. Parafunctional habits
E. Gastro oesophagial reflex

Key: C
Ref: Rook (84.2)

5. A 73 year old female patient presented in opd and was diagnosed with herpes zooster along the left ophthalmic branch of trigeminal nerve with associated cutaneous vesicles.
The patient subsequently developed post herpetic neuralgia in the same dermatome.
What is the major predisposing factor leading to PHN?

A. Male gender
B. Old age
C. Severe or disseminated rash
D. Trigeminal nerve ophthalmic division
E. B,C and D

Key: E
Ref: Rook (84.3)

Chapter 85 NEUROLOGICAL CONDITIONS AFFECTING THE SKIN

1. A 20-year-old male patient having short neck and a low hairline presents with painless cuts and burns on the forearm and hands. He is also complaining of dyshydrosis on his face on consumption of hot /spicy foods. What is the likely diagnosis?
   A. Spinal Dysraphism
   B. Freys Syndrome
   C. HSMN-111
   D. Syringomyelia

Key: D
Ref: Rook (85.7)

2. A 20 year old male patient having short neck and a low hairline presents with painless cuts and burns on the forearm and hands. He is also complaining of dyshydrosis on his face on consumption of hot /spicy foods. Keeping in view the diagnosis which one of the following is the likely complication of this disease?
   A. Sepsis
   B. Loss of taste and tongue wasting
   C. Osteomyelitis
   D. Malignant hyperthermia

Key: B
Ref: Rook (85.8)

3. A middle aged male presents with an irresistible pain/itch /burning sensation which is only relieved by deeply traumatizing the affected area of the face or neck. Keeping in mind the diagnosis of Atypical Trigeminal trophic syndrome, which of the following differentiates it from trigeminal trophic syndrome?
   A. It involves all branches of trigeminal nerve
   B. Ulceration is unilateral
   C. Ulceration is bilateral
   D. IT INVOLVES ONLY ONE AREA OF TRIGEMINAL NERVE.

Key: C
Ref: Rook (84.8)

4. A child presents with recurrent fevers, anhidrosis, absence of nociception, self-mutilation and learning difficulties. He is hypotonic and areflexic. There is also history of seizures associated with high grade fever. What is the most common cause of mortality in this patient?
   A. Osteomyelitis
   B. Joint deformities
   C. Malignant Hyperthermia
   D. Corneal Scarring

Key: C
Ref: Rook (85.12)

5. A 50-year-old Diabetic patient who is on Haemodialysis for last 4 years presents with a painless ulcer with well-defined margins on the heel of foot. On examination his foot is anaesthetic, warm with palpable pulses and dilated veins. The skin is dry and hyperkeratotic under the heel. What is the best predictor of osteomyelitis in this patient?
   A. Plain Xray
   B. Radio isotope bone scan
   C. Palpable bone at base of ulcer on wound probing
   D. Sinogram

Key: C
Ref: Rook (85.5)

Chapter 86 PSYCHODERMATOLOGY AND PHSYCHOCUTANEOUS DISEASE

1. A 20 year old male presented with asymptomatic pigmented hyperkeratotic papules on the trunk .some of which coalesce to form plaques which were confluent in the centre and reticulate towards the periphery .fungal stains frequently show malassezia. Keeping in view the diagnosis on H/P what are the epidermal changes?

A. Hypergranulosis
B. Decrease on melanin in basal layer
C. Hypergranulosis
D. Acanthosis

Key: C

2. A 35 year old lady presented to the opd with symmetrical dark thick scaly skin .she is a diagnosed case of kaposis sarcoma and is under treatment. She was weak and lethargic. on examination there is palmoplantar hyperkeratosis with fissuring. She has complained of pruritus…what is the likely diagnosis?

A. Xerosis cutis
B. Acquired ichthyosis
C. Drug induced
D. Atopic eczema

Key: B

3. A 45 years old obese patient presented to the opd with no comorbids.on examination there were symmetrical velvety dark patches most commonly in the axilla, grown and back. These patches were asymptomatic. There were also some skin tages in the affected areas. She was diagnosed with benign acanthosis Nigerians.

What is the management of the patient?

A. Treat the underlying condition
B. Counsel to reduce weight
C. Oral isofredinoin
D. Refer to oncologist.

Key: B

4. 50 year old lady presented to the opd diagnosed case of hyperlipidaemia is on statins for the last 10 months. On examination her skin was dry and there were symmetrical dark thick brown scales on the upper and lower limbs. The skin resembled more like fish. Flexures were relatively spared. Same scales were present on the scalp. She had complained of pruritus. Face was spared.

What is the first line treatment?

A. Salicylic acid
B. Lactic acid
C. Topical retinoid
D. Glycolic acid

Key: C

5. 74 year old man presented to the ER with abdominal pain, loss of appetite and heart burn…he has lost 10 kg in a month. On examination there were symmetrical hyper pigmented, rugose velvety plaques on bilateral axilla areolar area and nape of the neck. He was complaining of generalized pruritus and his palms were thick and velvety. What is the most likely diagnosis?

A. Benign acanthosis nagricans
B. Malignant acanthosis nagricans
C. HAIR-AN syndrome
D. Drug abuse…

Key: B

6. A 55 year-old female businesswoman describes a clinical history of five years of visual hallucinations, depressive symptoms, and generalized pruritus, along with the use of toxic substances to "clean" her skin and cloths. Erosions and excoriations were seen on skin. She reports similar symptoms in some relatives but they were not evaluated. Blood tests and analyses of the "specimen" brought by the patient were performed, yielding negative results. The patient had never been assessed by any specialist, and showed disoriented during the consultation. Follow-up was not possible due to the reluctance of the patient to follow the indications and seek psychiatric treatment. What is the diagnosis?

A. Morgellons syndrome
B. Delusional infestation
C. Ocd
D. Depression
E. None of the above

Key: B
Ref: Rook (86.6)

7. A: 26 year-old woman, presented 6 months before the time of this report with an illness of 10 years' duration with repetitive thoughts and preoccupation related to short stature and facial deformity. She was repeatedly checking the mirror and seeking assurance about her presumed facial deformity and height and focus specifically on her skin of face nose Her appetite and sleep were reduced, and she had preferred staying at home because of doubts that people were looking at her and mocking her ugliness.
After she was married, she was critical of the attributes of her husband and felt that his face was disproportionately big. With the fear that her baby would also share her physical ugliness, she even attempted an abortion, though unsuccessful. Since the birth of her daughter, she indulged in frequent checking and assurance seeking for her daughter's assumed deformity of face. She used to feel guilty for passing along ugliness to her daughter.
There was no family history of any significant psychiatric or medical illness, and her general physical examinations revealed no abnormalities. Which scale is used to assess the above mentioned condition?

A. Scored score
B. Generalized anxiety disorder score
C. Family dermatology life quality index
D. Skindex 16 and 29
E. Yale-brown obsessive compulsive scale

Key: E
Ref: Rook (86.11)

8. 19-year-old male with Body dysmorphic disorder who had delusional-intensity beliefs about facial disfigurement that had gradually intensified over a 2-year period. However, he was initially misdiagnosed with depression partly because he was admitted immediately after a suicide attempt that was associated with depressive symptoms and social withdrawal, symptoms that subsequently proved to be secondary to his BDD. The symptoms resolved completely and his social functioning returned to normal after 8 weeks of inpatient treatment with fluoxetine and cognitive behavioural therapy which one of the following is associated condition

A. Chronic skin pricking
B. Depression
C. Substance abuse

D. Deliberate self-harm
E. All of the above

Key: E
Ref: Rook (86.11)

9. Young lady presented with one year history of itchy erythematous pustular and scarring facial lesions, associated with burning sensation. There were visible excoriations with no comedowns, involving the lower cheeks and chin and hairline, she mainly scratches at night time.
This has been unresponsive to various topical and oral treatment isofredinoin was also given but deemed unfit due to suicidal thoughts.
Her medications included ssri she was under a psychiatrist for years
What is the diagnosis of above mentioned condition?

A. Facial pricking disorder
B. Trigeminal trophic syndrome
C. Dermatitis artifact
D. Acne exocrine
E. None of the above

Key: D
Ref: Rook (86.16)

10. 20yrs old lady presented with severe urge to pick and gouge at her skin she spends 3hrs per day pricking, thinking about pricking and resisting the urge to prick. Lesions were quite deep and more commonly distributed within the reach of dominant hand. Older lesions show pink or red scars (atrophic)
What is the diagnosis?

A. Acne exocrine
B. Magellan syndrome
C. Lichen planus
D. Skin pricking disorder
E. Dermatitis artefact

Key: D
Ref: Rook (86.14)

11. A 8 year-old boy was brought by his parents with a history of recurrent abnormal body movement and shaking of his body. It was initially misconstrued as seizure or dystonic reaction without the loss of consciousness for 3 days. It was of abrupt onset and a fluctuating pattern. The pt had no history of drugs usage such as antipsychotic or antiemetic that could cause abnormal body movement or dystonia. There were intervals of normal movement and behaviour. He was said to be having 4–5 episodes of abnormal body movements per day. There was no history of muscle spasm, tongue thrusting, stridor, or dysphonia. There was no history of seizure at any time. There was no history of use of anticonvulsant at any time and electroencephalogram done was normal. The physical and neurological examination done on him was normal. His cognitive functions and psychometric evaluation test was normal. Laboratory results, including a full blood count, blood film for malaria parasite, and blood chemistry (serum calcium, sodium, potassium, and bicarbonate), were essentially normal. He was sleeping well and was fully interactive and energetic in the ward. The child was initially managed as a case of dystonia even though, no history of the use of drug that can cause dystonia. He was placed on iv fluid and diazepam 2.5 mg twice daily for 2 days. On the 3rd day, repeated abnormal body movement persisted even while walking without any fall. There was curiosity to look at diagnosis in the child because of abnormal movement and gyration while walking without any fall which is not consistent with features of seizure disorder, pseudo seizure, or dystonia. The need to consider interaction with the child was encouraged to explore a positive outcome. The child was then instructed to display that movement voluntarily, and to amazement, he was able to display the movement repeatedly and was able to abort the movement voluntarily. He was able to repeat this symptom and abort

severally when instructed. Further history at this point revealed that child elder sister had epilepsy. On close discussion with the child, revealed that passion for the body movement learnt from his sister. Adopting a non-judgmental approach and gentle persuasion, the pt was encouraged to tell the full story, and he expressed that he enjoyed mimicking the abnormal body movement because of the attention he gets from the parents any time he displayed .what is the diagnosis?

A. Psudologia fantastic
B. Malingering
C. Fabricated and induced illness
D. Witchcraft syndrome

Key: B

12. A 15-year-old woman along with her mother entered in dermatology OPD with stacks of investigative reports and bag of medication presented with complaint of multiple painful erosions with some pustules and scarring over her accessible body parts. There was no evidence of insect bite, or drug or food allergy. She denied any self-inflictive nature of her injury such as scratching or rubbing with any object. While during the interview session there was constant rubbing and picking of the lesions with Mona Lisa smile. The lesions were bizarre, with a tapering end at various stages of healing, and were not compatible with any known dermatological disorder. The Gram stain and Tzanck smear were found to be negative from the pustules. Her histopathological findings were nonspecific. Patient appears to be cooperative, unconcerned about /her painful and puzzling lesions, while her mother was very anxious and frustrated .Her psychiatric evaluation revealed marital discord. She was admitted in ward under strict observation and treatment with occlusive therapy completely healed the lesions within 2 weeks. What is the diagnosis?

A. Dermatitis artefecta
B. Dermatitis simulata
C. Dermatological pathomimicry
D. Dermatitis passivata

Key: A

13. A 48-year-old lady sought consultation for multiple skin lesions having features of chemical burn over her face, back, inframammary region, arm, and abdomen .She gave a hollow history regarding the causation. Complete amnesia or indifference to the presenting symptoms (belle indifference) was noted. She is now under the observation of the psychiatric department. Keeping the diagnosis in mind what complications can occur in this pt.

A. Fistulae
B. Scarring
C. Osteomilitis
D. Abcess
E. All of the above

Key: E

14. A 28-year-old man presented to the Dermatology Outpatient Department with a complaint of a burning sensation and soreness over his left cheek and left ear of 10 days duration. It had started suddenly one morning when he woke up from sleep. He noticed a large blister with intense redness over his left cheek, associated with a burning sensation. There was a history of similar episodes over the past year, and all were sudden in onset, involved the cheeks, and were noticed after waking up from sleep. The patient volunteered that the episodes were always associated with a drinking spree the previous night. The individual was a healthy man with a wife and two children. The patient had been dependent on alcohol for the past year, and had been consuming alcohol for many years. On examination, there was an eschar occupying almost the entire cheek, with a few scattered lesions over the left tragus and left external ear. Peripheral scarring was noted with hyperpigmentation. While the angle of the mouth was superficially involved on the left side, the oral mucosa was normal. The right cheek also showed a few areas of scarring. There were no similar

lesions elsewhere on the body. The peculiar history and the morphology of the lesion, that defied any classical diagnosis description, prompted us to interrogate both the man and his wife with regard to any serious differences. After much persuasion and on assurance of secrecy, the wife admitted that her husband was an alcoholic and was neglecting his family. When her efforts to prevent his drinking failed, she resorted to this drastic measure. Each time he passed out after a drinking bout, she poured acid on his cheek, hoping that the sequelae would frighten him from drinking. The acid was readily available to her as she used it for domestic cleaning. The couple were sent for psychiatric evaluation. Detailed psychiatric evaluation, together with psychometric assessment, revealed that the patient had an alcohol dependence. Severe marital discord due to alcohol dependence had been present for the past 2 years. Evaluation of the patient's wife revealed that she was under significant psychologic distress. She showed major depressive symptoms with a histrionic personality. She revealed that she had resorted to using the corrosive out of frustration and anger over the behaviour of the patient while he was in an inebriated state. The couple are currently undergoing psychiatric treatment. What is the diagnosis?

A. Malingering
B. Witchcraft syndrome
C. Munchausen syndrome
D. Terre firme forme

Key: B

15. 23 years old girl was taking isofredinoin for acne treatment for last 6 months. She presented with complaint of fatigue, headache, confusion, poor concentration, tearfulness, depression, ruminations of guilt and psychosis. Her Beck depression inventory score is more than 10.what will be your next step.

A. Reassuring the pt
B. Continue the treatment with psychiatrist help
C. Withdraw the drug and referral to psychiatry
D. None of the above

Key: C

Chapter **87**

ACQUIRED DISORDERS OF EPIDERMAL KERATINIZATION

1. A 65 years old female presented in OPD with acute swelling of her lower limbs after withdrawal of diuretic therapy. On examination there was formation of a tense unilocular, non-pruritic bullae appearing in the areas of acute oedema on the left leg.
What is the diagnosis of her disease?

A. Acute oedema blisters
B. Bullous pemphigoid
C. Diabetic bullae
D. Linear IgA disease
E. Pemphigus Vulgaris

Key: A
Ref: Rook (87.27)

Chapter 88

ACQUIRED PIGMENTARY DISORDERS

1. A 41 years old traffic police man presented with orange brown pigmented plaques irregular in shape and size for last 2 months. The plaques are not itchy. Which of the following statement is true regarding the above-mentioned scenario?

A. Dyspigmentation associated with hemosiderosis is due to haemosiderin
B. May be secondary to drug reactions or contact dermatitis due to clothing
C. Cutaneous hemosiderosis may arise due to congenital hemolytic anemias only
D. Prognosis does not depend on the management of primary cause
E. All of the above

Key: B
Ref: Rook (88.49)

2. Neonatal jaundice is routinely treated with visible light

A. 470-480nm
B. B)460-490nm
C. 480-490nm
D. D)450-490nm
E. E)460-470nm

Key: B
Ref: Rook (88.50)

3. A 31 years old obese female presented in the opd with history of yellowish discoloration of skin. Sclera and mucosae were normal color. Carotene level in blood was 290ug/dl. She was on diet since 1 month. What is the most likely diagnosis?

A. Primary Carotenoderma
B. Secondary Carotenoderma
C. Tertiary Carotenoderma
D. Cutaneous Hemosiderosis
E. Ochronosis

Key: A
Ref: Rook (88.50)

4. A 7 years old boy presented with darkening of ear cartilage, sclera and conjuctiva, and axillary folds. There is also brown mottled pigmentation of face, neck and trunk. Which of the following statement is true?

A. Alkaptonuria is autosomal dominant trait
B. Alkaptonuria is autosomal recessive trait
C. Endogenous ochronosis is present in about 85% of patients with Alkaptonuria
D. Treatment with retinoids
E. All of the above

Key: B
Ref: Rook (88.51)

5. A 35 years old female presented with grey brown discoloration of face, neck and back and extensor surface of limbs. She was using hydroquinone for last 2 months. Patient also complains of photosensitivity. What is the most likely diagnosis?

A. Addison disease

B. PCT
C. Exogenous ochronosis
D. Haemochromatosis
E. Hyperthyroidism

Key: C
Ref: Rook (88.51)

6. A 35years old female referred to Dermatology opd with complaints of face, nack and trunk for last 01year.Slowly extending. On examination there were numerous macules grey colored, coalescing at places to form patches? On face margins of the lesions were red with palpable infiltrated margins. What is first line treatment in this case?
A. Dapsone 100mg/day for 03months
B. Clofazimine 100mg/day for 03 months
C. UV therapy
D. Oral corticosteroids threat
E. Topical corticosteroids therapy.

Key: B
Ref: Rook (88.32)

7. A 25 years old pregnant female, presented in OPD with hyperpigmented patches on the malar regions, forehead and chin area of her face. Keeping diagnosis in mind all of the following are true accept?
A. UV exposure and hormonal factors are most significant factors.
B. Pregnancy has been linked to increase skin pigmentation
C. OCPs do not have role in causing skin pigmentation
D. Melasma is common in third trimester of pregnancy
E. Pigmentation usually fades after parturition but may persist for many months.

Key: C
Ref: Rook (88.10)

8. A 25 years old pregnant female, presented in OPD with hyperpigmented patches on the malar regions, forehead and chin area of her face. Keeping diagnosis in mind, which is the first line treatment of this disease?
A. Sun protection/broad spectrum sunscreen (SPF>30)
B. Chemical peels
C. Azealic acid (15-20%)
D. Laser therapy
E. IPL

Key: A
Ref: Rook (88.12)

9. A 30 year old female presented in OPD with complain of reticulate Hyperpigmentation of face and neck symmetrically, along with telengiectasis and dermal atrophy. What is the diagnosis of her disease?
A. Melasma
B. Riel Melanosis
C. Addison disease
D. Poikloderma of Civatte
E. Dry the one manos is follicular is facei et colli

Key: D
Ref: Rook (88.13)

10. A 30 year old female presented in OPD with complain of reticulate Hyperpigmentation of face and neck symmetrically, along with telengiectasis and dermal atrophy. Her condition had exacerbated by use of cosmetics and sun exposure. Keeping the diagnosis in mind, what is the course and prognosis of her disease?
   A. The pigmentation usually fades away.
   B. Slowly progressive and irreversible
   C. Dermatological manifestations increase with time
   D. Normalization of pigmentation occurs with treatment of deficiency
   E. None of the above

Key: B
Ref: Rook (88.14)

11. A 58 years old diabetic male presented to you with complaint of abnormal skin pigmentation. Examination showed, a generalized bluish grey pigmentation over the body, also involving the oral mucosa. Systemic examination revealed a palpable liver. What is your diagnosis?
   A. Drug induced pigmentation
   B. Addison disease
   C. Amyloidosis
   D. Hemochromatosis
   E. Wilson's disease

Key: D

12. A 60 years old female with skin type 1 known case of ischemic heart disease on treatment, presented with slate grey or purple discoloration mainly on the sun exposed skin, pigmentation is more pronounced over nose and ears, what is the most likely drug causing hyperpigmentation.
   A. Propranolol
   B. Captopril
   C. Verapamil
   D. Amiodarone.
   E. None of the above

Key: D

13. Topical cytostatic drugs that produce localized hyperpigmentation include
   A. Carmustine
   B. Mechlorethamine
   C. Fluorouracil
   D. All of the above
   E. None of the above

Key: D

14. A 55 years old male presented with darkening of skin along with fatigue and lassitude. Examination revealed blotchy areas of slate grey pigmentation on whole trunk and hepatosplenomegaly, lab investigations revealed hyperglycemia and glycosuria. What is the inheritance of disease?
   A. AD
   B. AR
   C. XLD
   D. XLR
   E. None of the above

Key: B

15. A 62 yrs old female presents with darkening of skin, dizziness, fatigue, nausea vomiting and progressive weight loss since 8 months, medical history unremarkable. On examination elderly lady with generalized

hyperpigmentation especially on face, oral mucosa, palmar creases and knuckles, pulse was 106bpm regular, and Bp was 90/60, clinical diagnosis of addison's disease was made, what is the key diagnostic test for this disease.

A. Serum electrolytes
B. Short Synacthen test
C. U/s abdomen
D. Random serum cortisol level

Key: B

16. A 13 years old girl presented with progressive expanded depigmented patches on her face for the past 6 months. The mother is considered over the disease progression. Following treatment options are opted accept:

A. PUVA
A. potent topical steroids
B. topical calcineurin inhibitors
C. melanocytes transplant/ grafting
D. none of the above

Key: D
Ref: Rook (88.39)

17. A 21 year old male with presents with a hypopigmented patch over a pigmented naevi on the trunk for the past few weeks. Which differential should be ruled out in this condition?

A. Halo naevi
B. Vitiligo
C. Malignant melanoma
D. Punctate leukoderma
E. None of the above

Key: C

18. A 35year female presents with pain in the eyes and redness, patchy loss of hair on the scalp, streaks of white hair on head and discrete depigmented patches on her trunk. What condition should be considered in her case?

A. Post inflammatory hypomelanosis
B. Idiopathic guttate hypomelanosis
C. Chemical induced hypomelanisis
D. Vogt koyanagi harada syndrome
E. Alezzandrini syndrome

Key: D
Ref: Rook (88.43)

19. A 10year old boy presents with hypopigmeted patches on the face for the past month. The mother is concerned over it progressing to vitiligo. What conditions are to be considered in this case to reassure the mother that it is not vitiligo except:

A. pityriasis Alba
B. post inflammatory hypopigmentation
C. pityriasis versicolor
D. progressive macular hypomelanosis
E. halo Nevis

Key: E
Ref: Rook (88.44)

20. A 52 year old female presents with desecrate hypopigmented patches on her dorsal aspect of the hands for the past 6 months. Histopathology reveals slight basket weave hyperkeratosis with epidermal atrophy and flattening of the rete pegs. What is the probable diagnosis?

A. Punctate leukoderma
B. Idiopathic guttate hypomelanosis
C. Chemical induced hypomelanosis
D. Post inflammatory hypopigmentation
E. Vitiligo

Key: B
Ref: Rook (88.45)

Chapter 89

ACQUIRED DISORDERS OF HAIR

1. 6 year old female patient, accompanied by her mother, reported hair loss for the past 4 months. The mother noted that, when the patient was nervous, she had an uncontrollable urge to manipulate the scalp, confirmed by the accumulation of hair around her. Dermatological examination revealed diffuse thinning with short and broken hairs, and negative tensile test. At dermoscopy, we noticed different hair lengths with broken shafts and vellus hair. There are no exclamation point hairs, nor yellow dots. Patient refused for scalp biopsy. The most probable diagnosis is

A. Alopecia areata
B. Androgenic alopecia
C. Trichophagia
D. Trichotillomania

Key: D
Ref: Rook (89.46)

2. A 32 year old woman presented for evaluation of hair loss on the scalp. She reported wearing tight microbraids and using hair straightening heat instruments over the last 7 years. She was counseled to discontinue hairstyling practices that contributed to hair loss, the patient continued to wear hair extensions to hide the bald patches on her scalp. On examination of scalp, there is loss of hair along frontotemporal anterior hairline. The most probable diagnosis is

A. Trichotillomania
B. Traction alopecia
C. Cosmetic alopecia
D. Monilithrix

Key: B
Ref: Rook (89.44)

3. A 16 year old female patient, accompanied by her mother, reported hair loss for the past 4 months. The mother noted that, when the patient was nervous, she had an uncontrollable urge to manipulate the scalp, confirmed by the accumulation of hair around her. Dermatological examination revealed diffuse thinning with short and broken hairs, and negative tensile test .At dermoscopy, we noticed different hair lengths with broken shafts and vellus hair. There are no exclamation point hairs, nor yellow dots. Best management plan for her is

A. Refer to physician
B. Habit reversal therapy
C. SSRI
D. Contact with fellow sufferers

Key: B
Ref: Rook (89.47)

4. 23 yr old female presented to skin outpatient department with complain of nonprogressive patch of hair loss over the right side of scalp since birth. She uses oral medications, hair oil, and shampoo but no improvement. No history of itching, contact with chemicals, or dandruff over scalp. No significant past and family history or any comorbidities present. Cutaneous examination showed single, well-defined, triangular patch of alopecia measuring approximately 3 cm × 2 cm with sparse hair in between over right frontotemporal region. Dermoscopy showed normal follicular openings with vellus hairs with no inflammation or atrophy. This is the case of

A. Alopecia areata

B. cosmetic alopecia
C. Aplasia cutis congenita
D. Triangular alopecia

Key: D
Ref: Rook (89.49)

5. A 54 yr old woman presented for evaluation of scalp alopecia. She was diagnosed with invasive ductal carcinoma of the right breast diagnosed 12 months earlier.
She had been treated with bilateral lumpectomy with right sided sentinel lymph node biopsy and started chemotherapy 8 months earlier. Three weeks after completing taxane chemotherapy, she was also treated with radiation therapy and is currently on neratinib 240 mg daily. She noted hair loss beginning after her first course of systemic chemotherapy. It became more extensive throughout the remainder of her treatment. She had not experienced any regrowth of scalp hair since the completion of chemotherapy. Cutaneous examination revealed alopecia of the scalp. There is diffuse and nearly complete hair loss on the central and vertex region with retention of hair on the temporal region of scalp. There was also loss of hair on the eyebrows, axillae, pubic region, and upper lip. The most probable diagnosis is
A. Alopecia areata
B. uncombable hair syndrome
C. Traction alopecia
D. Chemotherapy alopecia

Key: D
Ref: Rook (89.49)

6. A 40yr old female presented to dermatology OPD with history of patchy hair loss on vertex for last 2yrs.Initial lesion was 2yrs back but in last 6months disease was progressive. No hx of any local or systemic illness. On examination irregular but well defined hair loss patches on vertex with mild epidermal atrophy. On biopsy the section showed atrophy of epidermis with the absence of viable pilosebaceous follicles, replaced by fibrosis, elastic fibers around lower part of follicle most likely DX is
A. Pseudopelade of Brocq
B. Folliculitis decalvans
C. Artefactual alopecia
D. Central centrifugal cicatricial alopecia

Key: A

7. A 40yr old female presented to dermatology OPD with history of patchy hair loss on vertex for last 2yrs.Initial lesion was 2yrs back but in last 6months disease was progressive. No hx of any local or systemic illness. On examination irregular but well defined hair loss patches on vertex with mild epidermal atrophy. On biopsy the section showed atrophy of epidermis with the absence of viable pilosebaceous follicles, replaced by fibrosis, elastic fibers around lower part of follicle. Considering DX clinical criteria include all except
A. long course (more than 2yrs)
B. female yo male ratio 3:1
C. severe atrophy
D. irregular, defined patches of alopecia

Key: C

8. A 24 yrs old male presented to dermatology opd with hx of recurrent infection of scalp which lead to scarring alopecia n keloid formation for last 10yrs.On examination rounded patches of alopecia on vertex of scalp. lesions were characterized by flat-elevated erythematous on the surface of which several hair tufts of 10-30 normal-looking hairs arising from a single dilated follicular ostium, and red papules with adherent yellow-white crusts scattered nearby. Skin biopsy was taken from the margin site of the lesion. Studies

showed perifollicular inflammation of lymphocyte, neutrophils and plasma cells, a few foreign body giant cells around the upper portions of the follicles. Fibrosis was seen in the upper dermis and around follicles grouped. Considering DX tufted folliculitis can be seen in following conditions except

A. Folliculitis Decalvans
B. Central centrifugal cicatricial alopecia
C. Pemphigus vulgaris
D. Artefactual alopecia

Key: D

9. A 50yr old female presented to dermatology Opd with hx of hair loss for last 10yr which started from crown of scalp n progressive in nature. She also had hx of using chemical for hair straightening in her youth. On examination a central alopecic patch on vertex n numerous interconnected patched on occipital n parietal areas. Considering her DX which feature is not present on skin biopsy

A. perifollicular lymphocytic infiltrate
B. Eccrine glands are lost
C. premature disintegration of inner root sheath epithelium
D. prominent concentric lamellar fibrosis

Key: B

10. A 24 yrs old male presented to dermatology opd with hx of recurrent infection of scalp which lead to scarring alopecia n keloid formation for last 10yrs.On examination rounded patches of alopecia on vertex of scalp. lesions were characterized by flat-elevated erythematous on the surface of which several hair tufts of 10-30 normal-looking hairs arising from a single dilated follicular ostium, and red papules with adherent yellow-white crusts scattered nearby. Skin biopsy was taken from the margin site of the lesion. Studies showed perifollicular inflammation of lymphocyte, neutrophils and plasma cells, a few foreign body giant cells around the upper portions of the follicles. Fibrosis was seen in the upper dermis and around follicles grouped. Considering DX, treatment to induce prolonged remission is

A. use of tar shampoo n topical keratolytics
B. prolong use of antibiotics
C. Rifampicin with antibiotics
D. Oral zinc

Key: C
Ref: Rook (89.44)

11. A 33 years old male presents with two patches of hair loss on his scalp. The patches were circumscribed, hair less, smooth skin, short and easily extractable broken hair were seen at the margin of the patch. History is of 1 month duration

Which of the following is true regarding pathology of his condition?

A. Inflammatory cell infiltrate is concentrated in and around hair bulb.
B. Decreased number of follicles are found in established bald patches
C. pigmented and white hair are involved equally
D. Inflammatory infiltrate is predominantly composed of neutrophils
E. Inflammatory infiltrate is seen around the isthmus of the hair follicles

Key: A
Ref: Rook (89.29)

12. 25 years old female presents with a patch of hair loss on scalp, it has some erythema and scaling and some Follicular plugging at margins.

All the following can be used in the management except

A. Hydroxychloroquin
B. Ciclosporin
C. Thalidomide

D. Acetretin
E. Pioglitazone

Key: E
Ref: Rook (89.37)

13. 55 years old female patient presents with complains of hair fall from frontal area of her scalp. There was recession of frontal hair line and posterior hair line. She was also losing hair from her eye brow. There was mild erythema present. She also had few scattered papules on forehead and cheeks.
Regarding the prognosis of her disease what is true

A. It is a rapidly progressive disease to complete baldness
B. Slowly progressive over many years to complete baldness
C. Slowly progressive over many yrs, recession eventually stops but cannot be predicted
D. Slowly progressive to patchy hair loss over many years which may spontaneous regrow in next few years
E. Rapidly progressive to patchy hair loss all over scalp which will eventually regrow in next few years

Key: C
Ref: Rook (89.39)

14. A 50 years old female patient presents with scarring alopecia of scalp, she also complained of loss of public and axillary hair, along with Papular eruption.
Which treatment options cannot be given?

A. Oral corticosteroids
B. Hydroxychloroquin
C. Thalidomide
D. Ciclosporin
E. Isotretinoin

Key: E

15. 35 years old female presented with a bald patch of hair loss on her scalp, skin was smooth, there was no scaling, no erythema.
All the following are associated with her disease except

A. Thyroiditis
B. LE
C. Vitiligo
D. Psoriasis
E. Porokeratosis

Key: E
Ref: Rook (89.29)

16. A pregnant woman had a history of fragile hairs which improved spontaneously during pregnancy. Her new born baby also developed same complaint along with keratosis pilaris on nape of the neck. Rest of the cutaneous examination was normal. What will be the most likely mutation leading to the apparent hypertrichosis.

A. KRT 5,14
B. KRT 81,83,86
C. KRT 85
D. DSP
E. SPINK5

Key: B
Ref: Rook (89.50)

17. A newborn baby after 3 days developed erythroderma. On close examination of skin there were scaly annular patches covering whole body. Scalp hairs, eyebrows and eyelashes were sparse. He was admitted in ICU. What will be the complications of this disease?

A. Hypernatremic dehydration
B. Failure to thrive
C. Dermopathic enteropathy
D. Severe infections
E. All of the above

Key: E
Ref: Rook (89.53)

18. A 6 months baby developed sparse scalp hairs. At birth his hairs were normal. No associated any other skin and systemic problem. Microscopic examination of hair sample revealed flat hairs having irregular intervals rotated at 180° around their long axis. Keeping in mind that this isolated condition will improve in adulthood. What will be the most likely diagnosis?

A. Pili annulati
B. Pili bifurcati
C. Pili trianguli
D. Pili torti
E. None of the above

Key: D
Ref: Rook (89.51)

19. A pregnant female patient suddenly developed high B.P associated with decreased fetal movements for which emergency caesarean section was done. Newborn baby was microcephalic, small for age and unable to breath due to shiny taut membrane over whole skin, for which he was urgently referred to ICU. After few days mild light grey small sized scales were visible on trunk and sparse, fragile scalp hairs. At the age of 4 years his mother noticed gait problems and intellectual impairment. CT Brain showed basal ganglia calcification. On further examination he had an aged appearance of face, premature bilateral cataract and small nails. What will be the most likely associated syndrome?

A. Itin syndrome
B. Politt Syndrome
C. PIBIDS Syndrome
D. Sabinas Syndrome
E. Tay Syndrome

Key: E
Ref: Rook (89.55, 68.22)

20. 6 year old child was brought to the OPD by his mother with the complaints of generalized increased growth of hair all over his body. On examination, he has terminal hair growth all over his body including have, trunk and limbs which have replaced normal vellus hair. Height, right, neurological examination and cognition is normal. Considering the causes of generalized hypertrichosis, which of the following maybe be present in this patient?

A. Enlarged liver
B. Bifid kidneys
C. Calcification of falx cerebri
D. Renal stones
E. MVP

Key: A
Ref: Rook (89.61)

21. 23 year old college student presents in OPD with the complains of fine thin hair growing on her arms and trunk for the last 6 months. On examination, she has normally distributed terminal hair, no male pattern hair growth however fine brown hair growth can be appreciated all over her trunk. Which of the following causes is the most likely cause in this patient?

A. Her history of epilepsy
B. Her history of decreased food intake and low BMI
C. Goitre and slow reflexes seen on her examination
D. Her treatment of psoriasis
E. Her history of difficulty in climbing stairs and periorbital rash

Key: A
Ref: Rook (89.62)

22. 20 year old girl presents to Derma OPD with the complains of thick terminal hair in male pattern distribution around her chin, beard area and abdomen. Along with depilatory method of hair removal, she is prescribed some oral medication considering her history of irregular menstruation. Which of the following is not a mechanism of action of drugs prescribed for hirsutism?

A. Reduces the bioavailability of the tosterone by interfering with its production and increases its meta bolic clearance.
B. Inhibits the type 2 isoenzyme of 5α-reductase
C. Reduce levels of insulin, increase insulin sen sitivity
D. Inhibiting the enzyme ornithine decarboxylase
E. Reduces androgen production, increases the metabolic clearance of testosterone and binds to the androgen receptor.

Key: D
Ref: Rook (89.67)

23. 35 year old woman with hirsutism presents to OPD and is recommended laser hair removal. She is of type IV skin type. Which of following lasers will be the most appropriate?

A. IPL
B. Nd-Yag
C. Alexandrite
D. PDL
E. Q switch

Key: B
Ref: Rook (89.67)

24. 25 year old woman with hirsutism is depressed considering her facial look and wants to get her hair removed permanently. She is currently married and had 3 children. She is recommended oral treatment. Which of the following can be a contraindication?

A. Her history of taking thyroxine
B. Pregnancy
C. Liver function derangement
D. Acute infection
E. Cardiac failure

Key: B
Ref: Rook (89.67)

25. The characteristic hairs in syphilis are:

A. Wooly hair
B. cock screw hair

C. Moth-Eaten hair
D. Pili torti
E. Spun glass hair

Key: C
Ref: Rook (89.47)

26. Trichodysplasia spinulosa is caused by.
A. Herpes virus
B. Adenovirus
C. EBV
D. Polyoma virus
E. Rota virus

Key: D
Ref: Rook (89.47)

27. Treatment of trichodysplasia spinulosa is
A. Acyclovir
B. Cidofovir
C. Famiclovir
D. Adefovir
E. Ribavirin

Key: B
Ref: Rook (89.47)

28. Which one of the following drugs causes more chemotherapy alopecia?
A. Carboplatin
B. Carmustine
C. Paclitexal
D. 5-FU
E. VinBlastin

Key: C
Ref: Rook (89.48)

29. A 14 years old boy known case of AML with Bone Marrow transplantation 2 years back presents with permanent alopecia. Which of the following drug is output?
A. Bleomycin
B. Thiotopa
C. VinBlastine
D. Busulphan
E. Carboplatin

Key: D
Ref: Rook (89.49)

30. A 4 years old girl presented with 1 year history of asymptomatic localised alopecia. Examination revealed a 3.5 x 3.0 cm area of alopecia over the right front temporal region of scalp with its apex towards the vertex. There was no scaling or erythema. Her father had a h/o androgenic alopecia. Dermatoscopy of the scalp showed the presence of a 'carpet' of vellus hair over area. What is the diagnosis?
A. Sutural alopecia
B. Trichotillomania
C. Trianglan alopecia
D. Alopecia ameata
E. Cicatricial alopecia

Key: C

Ref: Rook (89.49)

31. A 6 years old girl Born of a non-consanguimeous manige. She had two healthy sisters. Her normal hairs had progessively been replaced by abnormal one during the early months of life. In fact, she never had a haircut due to its easily fragmentation and consequently short length. On examination: - Diffuse hypitrichosis of the scalp, as a well as coarse hair. Keratotic follicular apples were mainly observed in occipital region. The hair shaft is beaded, what is diagnosis?

A. Tigertail
B. Trichorhexis Nodosa
C. Monilethrix
D. Pilitorti
E. Tricholasis

Key: C
Ref: Rook (89.50)

32. All of the following have Pili torti except.

A. Menkes syndrome
B. Bjornstad syndrome
C. Hallermann-streiff syndrome
D. Crandall syndrome
E. Bazex syndrome

Key: C
Ref: Rook (89.52)

33. A 6-year-old white female patient with light brown hair reported. 1 year history of difficulty in combing her hair and the appearance of weak and brittle hair strands. The child had age adequate psychomotor development and no history of illness and hospitalization. She denied similar cases in the family. Dermatological examination revealed thick, coarse and brittle hairs in the left occipitotemporal region. The skin and its annexes showed no abnormalities. Polarized light microscopy revealed a flattered hair shaft, twisted 180° along its axis at irregular intervals. What is the diagnosis?

A. Pili multigemia
B. Trichorhexis Nodosa
C. Pili annulati
D. Pilitarti
E. Monilethrix

Key: D

34. Woolly hairs is caused by

A. Dapsone
B. Methotrexate
C. Azathioprine
D. Retinoids
E. Cyclosporin

Key: D
Ref: Rook (89.57)

35. A healthy 13-year-old boy with black coloured hair presented with a patch of hair thinning that did not grow over time. The symptom started at the age of 5 years. His parents having normal hair and scalp. On examination, a patch of hair thinning was observed on frontal scalp. Within the patch, there was no scalp lesion. No hair shaft abnormality such as brittleness and lusterness was observed. The hairs in the patch were easily pulled by gentle fraction.
Microscopy of plucked hairs gives appearance of floppy sock. What is the diagnosis?

A. Loose anagen hair syndrome
B. Trichostans spinulosa
C. Uncombable hair syndrome
D. Pili multigemini
E. Pili annulati

Key: A
Ref: Rook (89. 58)

36. In the above scenario, it is associated with all. EXCEPT
A. Hypohidrotic Ectodermal dysplasia
B. Ocular Coloboma
C. Epidermolysis Bullosa
D. Fabry disease
E. Noonan syndrome

Key: D
Ref: Rook (89.59)

37. A 24 years old male known case of NF-1 was observed to have Blonde, unruly and unmanageable hair. His mother state that his hair had always had that texture since first few months of his life and that his hairs not only seemed to grow slowly but also difficult to comb.
Hair microscopy shows: - longitudinal grooving. What is the diagnosis?
A. Pili multigemni
B. Woolly hair
C. Trichostaris spinulosa
D. Uncombable hair syndrome
E. Pili annulati

Key: D
Ref: Rook (89.57)

38. Trichothiodystrophy is associated with
A. Low magnesium content
B. Low calcium content
C. Low sulphur content
D. Low iron content
E. Low selenium content

Key: C
Ref: Rook (89.55)

39. Shape of the hair shaft is control by which one of following structure;
A. Dermal sheath
B. Inner root sheath
C. Outer root sheath
D. Medulla
E. None of the above

Key: B

40. The final length of hair is determined by which part of hair cycle?
A. Anagen
B. Catagen
C. Telogen
D. Kenogen

Key: A

41. Which part of the body shows obvious hair changes under the influence of androgen firstly?
    A. Axilla
    B. Facial
    C. Pubic
    D. trunk

Key: C

42. Which isoform of 5a- reductax plays a key role in regulating androgen dependent hair growth?
    a) Type 1
    b) Type 2
    c) Type 3
    d) All of the above

Key: B

43. Primary target of androgen action in hair follicle is which one of the following:
    a) Dermal sheath
    b) Hexle layer
    c) Henle layer
    d) Medulla.
    e) Dermal papilla

Key: E

44. The characteristic hairs in syphilis are: -
    A. Wodly hair
    B. cock screw hair
    C. Moth-Eaten hair
    D. Pili torti
    E. Spun glass hair

Key: C
Ref: Rook (89.47)

45. Trichodysplasia spinulosa is caused by.
    A. Herpes virus
    B. Adenovirus
    C. EBV
    D. Polyomavira
    E. Rota virus

Key: D
Ref: Rook (89.47)

46. Treatment of trichodysplasia spinulosa is
    A. Acyclovir
    B. Cidofovir
    C. Famiclovir
    D. Adefovir
    E. Ribawrin

Key: B
Ref: Rook (89.47)

47. Which one of the following drugs causes more chemotherapy alopecia?

A. Carboplatin
B. Carmutine
C. Paclitexal
D. 5-FU
E. VinBlastin

Key: C
Ref: Rook (89.48)

48. A 14 years old boy known case of AML with Bone Marrow transplantation 2 years back presents with permanent alopecia. Which of the following drug is output?
A. Bleomycin
B. Thiotopa
C. VinBlastine
D. Busulphan
E. Carboplatin

Key: D
Ref: Rook (89.49)

49. A 4 years old girl presented with 1 year history of asymptomatic localised alopecia. Examination revealed a 3.5 x 3.0 cm area of alopecia over the right front temporal region of scalp with its apex towards the vertex. There was no scaling or erythema. Her father had a H10 androgenic alopecia. Dermatoscopy of the scalp showed the presence of a 'carpet' of vellus hair over area. What is the diagnosis?
A. Sutural alopecia
B. Trichotillomania
C. Trianglan alopecia
D. Alopecia ameata
E. Cicotncial alopecia

Key: C
Ref: Rook (89.49)

50. A 6 years old girl Born of a non-consanguimeous manige. She had two healthy sisters.
Her normal hairs had progessively been replaced by abnormal one during the early months of life. In fact, she never had a haircut due to its easily fragmentation and consequently short length.
On examination: - Diffuse hypitrichosis of the scalp, as a ouell as coarse hair. Keratotic follicular apples were mainly observed in occipital region. The hair shaft is beaded, what is diagnosis?
A. Tigertail
B. Trichorhexis Nodosa
C. Monilethrix
D. Pilitorti
E. Tricholasis

Key: C
Ref: Rook (89.50)

51. All of the following hare Pili torti except.
A. Menkes syndrome
B. Bjornstad syndrome
C. Hallermann-slreiff syndrome
D. Crandall syndrome
E. Bazex syndrome

Key: C
Ref: Rook (89.52)

52. A 6-year-old white female patient with light brown hair reported. 1 year history of difficulty in combing her hair and the appearance of weak and brittle hair strands. The child had age adequate psychomotor development and no history of illness and hospitalization. She denied similar cases in the family. Dermatological examination revealed thick, coarse and brittle hairs in the left occipitotemporal region. The skin and its annexes showed no abnormalities. Polarized light microscopy revealed a flattered hair shaft, twisted 180° along its axis at irregular intervals. What is the diagnosis?

A. Pili multigemia
B. Trichorhexis Nodosa
C. Pili annulati
D. Pilitarti
E. Monilethrix

Key: D

53. Wood hairs is caused by

A. Dapsone
B. Methotrexate
C. Azathioprine
D. Retinoide
E. Cyclosporin

Key: D
Ref: Rook (89.57)

54. A healthy 13-year-old boy with black coloured hair presented with a patch of hair thinning that did not grow over time. The symptom started at the age of 5 years. His parents having normal hair and scalp. On examination, a patch of hair thinning was observed on frontal scalp. Within the patch, there was no scalp lesion. No hair shaft abnormality such as brittleness and lusterness was observed. The hairs in the patch were easily pulled by gentle fraction.
Microscopy of plucked hairs gives appearance of floppy sock. What is the diagnosis?

A. Loose anagen hair syndrome
B. Trichostans spinulosa
C. Uncombable hair syndrome
D. Pili multimni
E. Pili annulati

Key: A
Ref: Rook (89.58)

55. In the above scenario, it is associated with all. EXCEPT

A. Hypohidrotic Etodermal dysplasia
B. Oclar Coloboma
C. Epidermolysis Bllosa
D. Fabry disease
E. Noonan syndrome

Key: D
Ref: Rook (89.59)

56. A 24 years old male known case of NF-1 was observed to have Blonde, unruly and unmanageable hair. His mother state that his hair had always had that texture since first few months of his life and that his hairs not only seemed to grow slowly but also difficult to comb.
Hair microscopy shows: - longitudinal groonng. What is the diagnosis?

A. Pili multigemni

B. Woolly hair
C. Trichostaris spinulosa
D. Uncombable hair syndrome
E. Pili annulati

Key: D
Ref: Rook (89.57)

57. Trichothiodystrophy is as
A. Low magnesium content
B. Low calcium content
C. Low sulphur content
D. Low iron content
E. Low selenium content

Key: C
Ref: Rook (89.55)

58. In telogen effluvium positive hair pull finding?
A. Increase in telogen hair from affected areas
B. Increase in telogen hairs extracted from all areas
C. Painless extraction of dysplastic anagen hair, lacking root sheaths
D. Increase in anagen hairs extracted
E. None of above

Key: B

59. Trichogram technique has been used exclusively in some countries to access
A. Telogen effluvium
B. Androgenic alopecia
C. Alopecia areata
D. Primary cicatricial alopecia
E. Loose anagen syndrome

Key: A

60. In scarring alopecia scalp biopsy is taken
A. One biopsy is sectioned vertically and second horizontally
B. Both horizontally
C. Both vertically
D. All of above
E. None of above

Key: A

61. Male pattern balding is associated ē
A. Diabetes mellitus
B. Stroke
C. Coronary artery disease
D. Celiac disease
E. Vitiligo

Key: C

62. FPHL is associated ē
A. Hyperaldosteronism
B. Hypertension

C. Hyperandrogenim
D. Polycystic wary disease
E. All of above

Key: E

63. In telogen effluvium positive hair pull fingernail?
A. Increase in telogen hair from affected areas
B. Increase in telogen hairs extracted from all areas
C. Painless extraction of dysplastic anagen hair, lacking root sheaths
D. Increase in anagen hairs extracted
E. None of above

Key: B

64. Trichogram technique has been used exclusively in some countries to access
A. Talogen effluvium
B. Androgenic alopecia
C. Alopecia areata
D. Primary cicatricial
E. Loose anagen syndrome

Key: A

65. In scarring alopecia scalp biopsy is taken
A. One biopsy is seclioned vertically and second horizontally
B. Both horizontally
C. Both vertically
D. All of above
E. None of above

Key: A

66. Male pattern salding is associated ē
A. Diabetes mellitus
B. Stroke
C. Coronary artery disease
D. Celiac disease
E. Vitiligo

Key: C

67. FPHL is associated ē
A. Hyperaldo stermiom
B. Hypertension
C. Hyperandrogenim
D. Polycystic wary disease
E. All of above

Key: E

Chapter 90

ACNE

1. The 'endocrine acne' are associated with each of the following conditions except?
   A. Hyperthyroidism
   B. Pcos
   C. Late onset adrenocongenital syndrome
   D. Cushing disease

Key: A
Ref: Rook (90.3)

2. A 26 yrs old married woman presents to you with signs of androgen excess (hirsutism, ane, alopecia), with history of anovulatory cycles, keeping in mind the diagnosis, at laboratory parameter u wud expect to be raised?
   A. TSH
   B. Estrogen
   C. Dheas
   D. Cortisol
   E. Growth hormone

Key: C
Ref: Rook (90.3)

3. Rotterdam diagnostic criteria for PCOs comprises of all of the following postulates except?
   A. Oligo or anovulation
   B. Raised serum acth levels
   C. Clinical n biochemical signs of hyperanfrogenism
   D. Polycystic ovaries

Key: B
Ref: Rook (90.5)

4. A 21 yrs girl presented to you with nodulocystic acne, patient is on isotretinoine, This girl should not be given tetracycline (eg doxycycline) concomitantly as both can cause?
   A. Vomiting
   B. Arthritis
   C. C)deafness
   D. Raised benign intracranial hypertension
   E. Renal failure

Key: D
Ref: Rook (90.46)

5. Regarding the predisposing factors of acne, a small randomized dietary intervention study suggested that omega -3 fatty acids and gamma-linoleic acid supplementation independently shown to?
   A. Increase the acne incidence
   B. Reduce the acne incidence
   C. No effect on acne
   D. Caused complications in already present acne

Key: B
Ref: Rook (90.13)

6. 1 year old baby presented ē complains of inflamed papules & pustules ē open & closed comedones distributed all over face predominantly on central cheeks. Differential diagnosis you will consider in this patient includes all of following except?
   A. Infantile acne
   B. Acne venerate infertum

C. Chloracre
D. Heperandrogenison
E. Childhood granlumatrns Rosares

Key: E

7. 1 year old baby presented ē complain of inflamed papules & pustules ē open & closed comedones present predominantly on central cheeks. predictive factors for severity & persistence of these lesion include all of following except?
A. High # of comedones
B. Early development of comedones
C. High levels of dheas
D. Distribution on cheeks
E. ↑ face & total testosteume

Key: D

8. 10 days old baby presented ē multiple inflammatory papules, pustules presnt on B/L cheeks. There are no open & closed comedones present. What will be your diagnosis?
A. Neonatal acne
B. Neonatal cephalic pushiloris
C. Acne unglobata
D. Exyrtena toxicum nematoum.

Key: B

9. For above senecio, if the lesion do not heal sporatremry in 1-3 months, & if the lesion are widespread, what will be you treatment option?
A. Topical ketoconazole
B. Topical BPO
C. Oral isotretinoin
D. Systemic sterids
E. Topical clindamycin

Key: A

10. 25 years old male, farmer by occupation, presented ē yo. inflammatory papules, nodules, multiple straw-colored cysts & Temporal crmedones presnt on B/L cheeks, forehead & retroauricular area. On H/P there is epidermal hyperplasia, follicular hyperplasia & abrceme of sebaceous glands.what is you diagnosis?
A. Acne vulgaris
B. Chlovacne
C. Acne venenata
D. Coal tar acne

Key: B

11. In above senerio, management of above condition is?
A. Olestra potato chips
B. Tetracycline Antibiotics
C. Oral Isoheterosin
D. Topical BPO
E. Topical Dapnre gel

Key: A

Chapter 91

ROSACEA

1. A young pregnant female presented opd with gradual onset of marked facial erythema with nodular abscess, and indurated haemorrhagic plaques. on further examination, trunk is spared and no comedies are noted.
Wats is the most likely diagnosis?

A. Rosacea conglobata
B. roseacea fulminans
C. idiopatheic aseptic facial granuloma
D. Acne vulgaris

Key: A
Ref: Rook (91.15)

2. A pt came to you in opd with c/o facial swelling. this facial swelling is characterised by persistent erythema & non tender firm putting edema of upper 2/3rd of face, affecting more eyelids, cheeks, nose, globally.
There is no marked history of any allergy, or body aches or sun exposure.
What probable diagnosis can u think?

A. Acne vulgaris
B. Pyoderma faciale
C. Morbihan disease
D. Rosacea fulminans

Key: C
Ref: Rook (91.16)

3. A elderly male who works in an office, presented with unusual type of facial swelling and erythema.
After excluding other possibilities, he was labelled as lymohedematous rosacea and was given 60 mg of isotretinioin for more than a year.
What other drug can b advocated in this case??

A. tetracyclin
B. propanolol
C. thalidomide
D. clindamycin
E. azelaic acid

Key: C
Ref: Rook (91.16)

4. An elderly female patient Came to opd with c/o itching, burning and intense redness of face after using some cortocosteroid nasal spray for her allergic rhinitis by local GP.
She is also using some topical ointment for her small chalky white patch on right cheeks since last few weeks, similar patches appear on her foot too.
Keeping in mind the diagnosis, what's will be your most imp step of management?

A. Avoid sunexposure and apply sunblock
B. topical antibiotic therapy
C. Systemic antibiotic therapy
D. Less potent topical steroid
E. withdrawl of the causative topical steroid

Key: E
Ref: Rook (91.17)

5. A young women with oily skin, gestational amenorrhoea of 30+ weeks, presented with abrupt onset of severe facial inflammation with extensive pustules formation over her face, along with some inflammatory haemorrhagic plaques.
Probable Diagnosis in this scenario would be??

A. roseacea conglobata
B. rosecea fulminans
C. acne vulgaris
D. idiopathic facialnaspetic granuloma

Key: B
Ref: Rook (91.16)

6. An 18 years old male presented to you with multiple comedones in groups over face and papules, pustules, cysts and draining sinuses over face limbs and trunk for past 6 months, what will be the treatment of choice in this case?
A. Oral treitnoin with oral steroids to reduce inflammation and systemic antibiotics.
B. Topical retinoids and topical steroids.
C. Topical antibiotics.
D. Dapsone.
E. Minocycline

Key: A

7. In a pt of acne conglobata what are the complications?
A. DISFIGURING SCARRING.
B. MALIGNANCY.
C. RENAL AMYLOIDOSIS
D. Psychosocial impairment
E. All of the above

Key: E

8. A male patient of 27 years presented with multiple grouped comedones, acne cysts and inflammatory papules over face and trunk along with discharging sinuses and disfiguring scarring in axilla and groin for past 2 years, pt also gives hx of joint pains in knee and elbow joints for past some time, what will be the diagnosis?
A. Hair a syndrome
B. Sapho syndrome.
C. PASS
D. Inflammatory bowel disease
E. Malignancy

Key: C

9. Acne conglobata is associated with?
A. Down syndrome
B. Kline filter syndrome.
C. Turner syndrome.
D. Edward syndrome.
E. Patau syndrome

Key: B

10. Following are associated with Acne conglobata except.
A. Pilonidal sinus.
B. Folliculitis decalvans of scalp.
C. Hidradinitis Suppurativa.
D. Pyoderma gangrenosum.
E. all of the above

Key: B

Chapter 92 HIDRADENITIS SUPPURATIVE

1. A pt presented with history of multiple discharging sinuses and abcesses since last 4 years. Pt was diagnosed as Hidradenitis suppurativa. Pt has undergone wide local excision 1 year back and now developed recalcitrant disease. What is treatment of choice

A. radiotherapy with 12Gy
B. Radiontherapy with 10 Gy
C. Surgical excison
D. Nd yag laser

Key: A
Ref: Rook (92.11)

2. A female presented with history of fluctuating abcess in the axilla along with sinus tract formation in inframammary areas. She was diagnosed as Hidradenitis suppurativa. What is treatment of choice in this case

A. Incision and drainage
B. Excision and deroofing
C. surgery
D. CO2 laser

Key: A
Ref: Rook (92.10)

3. A patient presented with history of painful subcutaneous nodules and interconnected abcesses in groin with sinus tracts and cicatrization for last 5 years. He was diagnosed as HS. He has taken multiple treatments for this purpose. He has developed SCC of anogenital region. Which of following is the poor prognostic factor in this patient?

A. chronicity of disease
B. anogenital region
C. male gender
D. hypogammaglobulinemia
E. both b and c

Key: E
Ref: Rook (92.9)

4. A pt presented with history of multiple interconnected abcesses and sinus tract in axilla and groin for last 2 years. He was diagnosed as hidradenitis supurativa. What is treatment of choice ?

A. Co2 laser
B. excision and deroofing
C. Extensive surgery
D. Nd yag laser

Key: C
Ref: Rook (92.11)

5. A pt presented with multiple abcesses and sinus tract in axilla and groin for last 4 months. Which of the following is not a predisposing factor of this condition?

A. Female sex
B. Smoking
C. Alcohol
D. Obesity

Key: C
Ref: Rook (92.2)

6. A pt presented with acne over the face along with multiple draining sinuses and abcesses. He was diagnosed as Hidradenitis suppurativa. Follicular occlusion triad consists of all of the following except:

A. Hidradenitis suppurativa
B. Folliculitis decalvans
C. Acne
D. Dissecting cellulitis of scalp

Key: B
Ref: Rook (92.2)

7. A female developed multiple abesses in inframammary area along with sinus tracts. Which of the following regarding this condition is true

A. Has infectious etiology
B. Close comedones are present
C. Obesity correlates with disease severity
D. Regional lymphadenopathy is Hallmark of the disease

Key: C
Ref: Rook (92.2)

Chapter 93 OTHER ACQUIRED DISORDERS OF THE PILOSEBACEAOUS UNIT

1. 27 years old Japanese male with no known comorbids presented with complains of recurrent crops of itchy follicular papules and pustules on his face which colaesce to form inflammatory annular plaques with central clearing
These lesions settle without treatment in 10 days and then reappears
Some similar follicular papules also present on upper outer arms. There are no other systemic symptoms
On histopathology of skin there is infiltration of pilosebaceous follicles with eosinophils
Regarding management of disease which of the following is not a first line treatment option?

A. Potent topical steroids
B. Nsaids
C. Oral isotretinoin
D. Nb uvb
E. Dapsone

Key: C
Ref: Rook (93.8)

2. 35 years old HIV positive man presented with complain of intensely pruritic follicular papules present on anterior chest upper limbs and back for last 3 months.
On histopathology there is heavy infiltration of eosinophils in the outer root sheath of hair and sebaceous glands with scattered neutrophils.
His cbc reveals peripheral eosinophilia cd4 count is 184 which of the following statement regarding the disease is not true?

A. Clustering of papules into plaques is a characteristic feature
B. Pustules are often not seen
C. Facial skin is less commonly involved
D. Multiple biopsies are required to confirm diagnosis

Key: A
Ref: Rook (93.8)

3. 25 years old male presented with history of recurrent follicular papules and pustules on nape of neck.
On examination there are multiple papules pustules present some of the papules coalese to form irregular plaques and some of these lesions are healed with hypertrophic scarring
He has previous history of short courses of oral antibiotics and topical antiseptics for his skin complains on and off. Skin swabs for pustules shows growth of s aureus. on histopathology there is perifollicular inflammation with destroyed follicles and absence of sebaceous glands. considering diagnosis which of the following is predisposing factor of the disease?

A. Frequent haircuts at less than 2 weeks interval
B. Acne
C. Hidradenitis suppurativa
D. Friction from collar
E. All of above are true

Key: E
Ref: Rook (93.3)

4. 28 years old male army officer presented with complains of recurrent episodes of multiple small papules and pustules on beard area for last 1 year which get settles temporarily with some topical treatment. Some of the lesions heal with scarring and some leave residual hyperpigmentation
On histopathology there is microabsseces and foreign body giant cell granulomas present.
Regarding management of his disease which of the following statement is false?
A. Stop shaving the affected area for 6 weeks
B. Apply combination of steroid and antibacterial
C. Shave hairs 2 or 3 times per week
D. Use physical hair removal methods
E. Laser hair removal in affected area

Key: D
Ref: Rook (93.2)

5. 28 years old female presented to dermatology opd with complains of recurrent crops of multiple small reddish-brown papules some of them are umbilicate present on frontal hairline which heal with varioloform scarring.
The episodes are aggravated in summer season.
On skin biopsy lymphocytic perifollicular infiltrate along with necrosis of follicular epithelium is noted.
What is diagnosis?
A. Folliculitis keloidalis
B. Papulonecrotic tuberculid
C. Pyogenic bacterial folliculitis
D. Necrotizing lymphocytic folliculitis
E. Molluscum contagiosum

Key: D
Ref: Rook (93.4)

6. A 20-year-old man presented with multiple pruritic papules and pustules on nape of neck just below the hairline. Some of them are coalescing to form plaques for last 6 months. What is the curative treatment?
A. Close shaving to nape of neck
B. Intralesional steroids
C. Topical Retinoids
D. Nd yag laser

Key: D
Ref: Rook (93.4)

7. A patient presented with papules and pustules on shaven skin for last 2 months. Diagnosis of pseudofolliculits barbae was made. What is true regarding treatment?
A. Patient should stop shaving for 4 to 6weeks
B. Patient should keep length upto 1mm
C. Shaving should be restricted to 2 to 3 times per week
D. All are true
E. Both a and b

Key: D
Ref: Rook (93.2)

8. A patient presented with history of multiple pustules with surrounding erythema and overlying crusting for last one week. Patient complains of intense itching. What is the causative organism of this condition?
A. P acnes
B. Staphylococcus aureus
C. Streptococcus species

D. Staphylococcus epidermidis

Key: A
Ref: Rook (93.5)

9. A young black male c/o multiple small papules to pastilles on beard area adjacent new area had to same problem in also o/E coiled hairs & hair entrapped bonus skin surface are seen. He is suffering from
   A. Folliculitis
   B. Pseudo filiation's
   C. Sycosis blare
   D. Dermatophytosis.

Key: B.

10. Following is true for above war's pievieto folliculitis
   A. After puberty common
   B. Africans & males
   C. In females, common in lower lips & pubic
   D. It is acute inflammatory follicular Perifollicular foreign body reaction
   E. can occur as adverse reaction to oral minoxidil
   F. All of the above.

Key: F.
Ref: Rook (93.1 - 93.13)

11. Following is true for R of Pseudo folliculitis are all except
   A. Stop shaving for 6 was at least
   B. Shave area daily
   C. To pical antibacterial & stencil combination
   D. Chemical depilatories
   E. Laser hair removal.

Key: B.

12. A 21yr old black male h/o severe acne a now presented c/o papules k pustules on nape of neck below 4 at hairline. O/E Folliculate papules A pustules & hand Keloidal papules, some papules coalesce to form irregular plaques I bands. Hypertrophic scaling is also present. He is suffering from
   A. Pseudo Hollandite's
   B. Folliculitis Keloidal
   C. Scalp folliculitis Actinic heliotails.

Key: B
Ref: Rook (93.1→ 93.13)

13. Regarding treatment of Acne relei delis nuchae
   A. Avoid close shaving in affected aloe
   B. Topical antibacterial & steroids.
   C. I/L steroids
   D. ND: YAG laser
   E. Excisim + grafting, heeling by secondary intention.
   F. All of the above.

Key: F

14. A young girl with H/0 gradual onset of papules in frontal hair line ē mild itching a soreness. now aggravation in summer season.
O/E > Red brown papules, few ambulocetid ē focal necrosis & crusts over lesions. She is suffering from.

A. Repetitive excoriation
B. Folliculitis decabians
C. Papulonewolie tubulin.
D. Ne cotising lymphocytic folliculitis of scalp margin.

Key: D
Ref: Rook (93.193.13)

15. A 30 ye old male ĕ H/o acne 40 recruitment multiple small pustules in scalp with itching "O/E= minute postages in scalp with excoriation to crusting healing without scarring. He is suffering from.
A. Scalp folliculitis
B. Acne necrotic varioliform
C. Pseudo folliculitis
D. Actinic folliculitis.

Key: A

16. A 35 yr. old male working in outdoor in summer 40 papules & pustules on face neck supper aum shoulder & upper chest. ē mild itching a burning. O/E Monomorphic follicular papules & pustules: had same complaint some time ago after working in sunny area which reeled after about to diagnosis:
A. Miliacea
B. Acne vulgaris photogenerated
C. PLE
D. Actinic folliculitis

Key: D
Ref: Rook (93.1 → 93.13)

17. Following is true for Actinic follicles excepts
A. Follicular provocation test to support
B. Avoid dine exposure by using hat as screens.
C. oral antibiotics are beneficial
D. Isotretitine in suspensive in severe cases.
E. UVB photo therapy.

Key: C

18. An African 16 yr old boy c/o persistent itchy papules on taenia a Limbos (flexile scales C/E: Sheets of small monomorphic punicic papules H/P: - spongiotic dermatitis involving infundibula of multiple adjacent follies. He is suffering from.
A. Miliala pustulosa
B. Disseminated a recruitment infundibulum,
C. Folliculitis kebidalis
D. ICD.

Key: B
Ref: Rook (93.1 - 93.13)

19. A middle aged female came in OPD ē 40 multiple smooth creamy while well demarcated papules on vermillion border
of lips buccal mucosa in tabia minora. (She is most probably suffering from. No H/o burning on itching or walts.
A. Leucoplakia
B. Fordyce spots
C. Post herpetic changes
D. HPV infection.

Key: B

20. A 40 yr. old, kidney transplant pt. é immuno suppressive:40 asymptomatic flesh colored to yellow pink umbilicate prpules on
forehead, temples & cheeks. He is suffering from
    A. Fordyce spots
    B. Milia
    C. MCs
    D. Syringas
    E. Sebaceous gland hyperplasia

Key: E
Ref: Rook (93.1 - 93.13)

21. A Japanese 19yr young girl 40 well defined, dark erythematous annular plague on face é numerous pustules & ceusts HIP: - Dense accumulation of Eosinophils within follicular canal.
She is suffering from.
    A. Eosinophilic fasciitis
    B. Classical adult eosinophilic pustular folliculitis
    C. Immunosupression ass.
    D. Infantile cosinophilic pustular folliculitis

Key: B

22. 1st live Rx of Eosinophilic pustular folliculitis are all except?
Potent topical steroids
    A. Topical pimeccolimus/Taccolimus
    B. Indomethacin
    C. NB-UVB
    D. oral antimicrobials

Key: E
Ref: Rook (93.1 - 93:13)

23. A 8-month-old baby yo requirement crops of itchy sterile pustules on scalp cervical lymph nodes are enlarged pustules resolve spontaneously without scaling =HP folliculitis é dense infiltrate of, spongiosis & microbuses within follicles. CBC - ↑ Eos.
    A. Transient
    B. Infantile
    C. LCH
    D. Infantile accopustulosis

Key: B

24. A young black male c/o multiple small papules to pustules on beard area and adjacent area had same problem in past. o/E coiled hairs & hair entrapped beneath skin surface are seen. He is suffering from
    A. Folliculitis
    B. Pseudo folliculitis
    C. Sycosis blare
    D. Dermatophytosis.

Key: B.

25. Following is true for above scenario (pseudo folliculitis)
    A. After puberty common
    B. Africans & males
    C. In females, common in lower lips & pubic
    D. It is acute inflammatory follicular Perifollicular foreign body reaction

E. can occur as adverse reaction to oral minoxidil
F. All of the above.

Key: F.
Ref: Rook (93.1 - 93.13)

26. All Following are true for diagnosis of Pseudo folliculitis except
A. Stop shaving for 6 was at least
B. Shave area daily
C. Topical antibacterial & stencil combination
D. chemical depilatories
E. Laser hair removal.

Key: B.

27. A 21yr old black male h/o severe acne a now presented with c/o papules k pustules on nape of neck below and at hairline. O/E Follicular papules and pustules & hard Keloidal papules, some papules coalesce to form ir-regular plaques I bands. Hypertrophic scarring is also present. He is suffering from
A. Pseudo folliculitis
B. Folliculitis Keloidalis
C. scalp folliculitis
D. Actinic heliotails.

Key: B
Ref: Rook (93.1 → 93.13)

28. Regarding treatment of Acne Keloidali nuchae
A. Avoid close shaving in affected area
B. Topical antibacterial & steroids.
C. I/L steroids
D. ND: YAG laser
E. Excisim + grafting, heeling by secondary intention.
F. All of the above.

Key: F

29. A young girl with H/0 gradual onset of papules in frontal hair line ē mild itching and soreness. now aggravation in summer season.
O/E > Red brown papules, few ambulicatid ē focal necrosis & crusts over lesions. She is suffering from.
A. Repetitive excoriation
B. Folliculitis decalvans
C. Papulonecrotic tuberculids
D. Necrotising lymphocytic folliculitis of scalp margin.

Key: D
Ref: Rook (93.193.13)

30. A 30 ye old male presented ĕ H/o acne c/o recurrent, multiple small pustules in scalp with itching "O/E= minute pustules in scalp with excoriation and crusting, healing without scarring. He is suffering from.
A. Scalp folliculitis
B. Acne necrotic varioliform
C. Pseudo folliculitis
D. Actinic folliculitis.

Key: A

31. A 35 yr. old male working in outdoor in summer presented with c/o papules & pustules on face neck upper arm shoulder & upper chest. ē mild itching and burning. O/E Monomorphic follicular papules & pustules, had same complaint some time ago after working in sunny area which heeled after about 10 days. diagnosis is

A. Miliarea
B. Acne vulgaris photogenerated
C. PLE
D. Actinic folliculitis

Key: D
Ref: Rook (93.1 → 93.13)

32. Following is true for Actinic folliculitis except

A. Follicular provocation test to support
B. Avoid direct sun exposure by using hat as screens.
C. oral antibiotics are beneficial
D. Isotretinoine is responsive in severe cases.
E. UVB photo therapy.

Key: C

33. An African 16 yr old boy c/o persistent itchy papules on trunk and limbs (flexures spare) O/E: Sheets of small monomorphic pruritic papules. OnH/P: - spongiotic dermatitis involving infundibula of multiple adjacent follies. He is suffering from.

A. Miliaria pustulosis
B. Disseminated and recruitment infundibulum,
C. Folliculitis keloidalis
D. ICD.

Key: B
Ref: Rook (93.1 - 93.13)

34. A middle aged female came in OPD ē C/o multiple smooth creamy white well demarcated papules on vermillion border of lips and buccal mucosa and labia minora. . No H/o burning or itching or warts
She is most probably suffering from

A. Leucoplakia
B. Fordyce spots
C. Post herpetic changes
D. HPV infection.

Key: B

35. A 40 yr. old, kidney transplant pt. on immuno suppressive therapy presented with c/o asymptomatic flesh colored to yellow pink umbilicate papules on
forehead, temples & cheeks. He is suffering from

F. Fordyce spots
G. Milia
H. MCs
I. Syringas
J. Sebaceous gland hyperplasia

Key: E
Ref: Rook (93.1 - 93.13)

36. A Japanese 19yr young girl presented with c/o well defined, dark erythematous annular plague on face é numerous pustules & ceusts HIP: - Dense accumulation of Eosinophils within follicular canal.

She is suffering from.

F. Eosinophilic fasciitis
G. Classical adult eosinophilic pustular folliculitis
H. Immunosupression ass.
I. Infantile cosinophilic pustular folliculitis

Key: B

37. 1st live Rx of Eosinophilic pustular folliculitis are all except?
Potent topical steroids

A. Topical pimeccolimus/Taccolimus
B. Indomethacin
C. NB-UVB
D. oral antimicrobials

Key: E
Ref: Rook (93.1 - 93:13)

38. A 8-month-old baby yo requirement crops of itchy sterile pustules on scalp cervical lymph nodes are enlarged pustules resolve spontaneously without scaling =HP folliculitis é dense infiltrate of, spongiosis & microbuses within follicles. CBC - ↑ Eos.

A. Transient
B. Infantile
C. LCH
D. Infantile accopustulosis

Key: B

Chapter 94 DISORDERS OF THE SWEAT GLANDS

1. A 24yr old male pt presented with h/o excessive sweating since puberty now c/o macerated and foul odour with shallow circular lesions with punched out appearance coalescing to form irregular erosion on pressure areas of foot. keeping in mind diagnosis most likely causative organism is

A. Kytococcus sedentarius
B. Cornybacterium tenuis
C. Minutissium
D. Diphtheria
E. Erysipelothrix rusiopathiae

Key: A
Ref: Rook (94.6)

2. A 12 yrs old boy presented with h/o kyphoscoliosis, vulgus deformity, high arached palate previous h/o poor feeding and difficulty in sucking. Most likely cause of hyperhidrosis is

A. Heat induced hyperhidrosis
B. Cold induced hyperhidrosis
C. Gustatory hyperhidrosis
D. Emotions induced hyperhidrosis

Key: B
Ref: Rook (94.7)

3. A 52 yr old male pt presented with hypertension, paroxysmal sweating, tachycardia and headache, most likely diagnosis

A. Cushing syndrome
B. Carcinoid syndrome
C. Phaeochromocytoma
D. Frey syndrome

Key: C
Ref: Rooks (94.6)

4. A 24yr old pt with palmoplantar hyperhidrosis taking treatment with topical aluminium hydroxide but not improved next best step is

A. Botulinum toxin
B. Oral atropine
C. Sympethectomy
D. Topical anticholinergic

Key: A
Ref: Rook (94.10)

5. A pt with generalised hyperhidrosis plan to start with oral treatment with oral anticholinergic, most unlikely side effect

A. Galucoma
B. Hyperthermia
C. Convulsions
D. Cataract
E. Urinary retention

Key: D
Ref: Rook (94.9)

6. A 20 year old girl is presented in opd with the complaints of hyperhidrosis on both palmer and planter areas for the last 3 years.
It was decided to perform iodine Test on her.
What is the purpose of this test?

A. Iodine test is used to detect starch from a sample
B. Iodine test is of no use in this condition
C. iodine test should not be done in females
D. Iodine test is used to detect protein in sweat
E. None of the above

Key: A
Ref: Rook (94.3)

7. A 25 year old man presented with yellow discolouration of his clothes and undergarments since last 3 years.
The condition is more pronounced after exercise.
After all investigations, he was diagnosed as having chromhidrosis.
What is the findings of cytological examination of apocrine sweat secretion?

A. Secretion of starch in apocrine sweat
B. Secretion of lipofusin in apocrine sweat
C. Secretion of large amount of sodium chloride in sweat
D. Presence of porphyrins in sweat
E. None of the above

Key: B
Ref: Rook 94.17

8. A 32 year old female patient presented with 2 months history of multiple mildly pruritic yellowish brown papules in both armpits.
Histological examination showed dilation of follicular infundibulum with corneal plug,as well as inflammatory lymphohistiocytic infiltrate with xanthomatous cells surrounding the infundibulum.
Immunohistochemistry showed perifollicular cells strongly positive for CD68.
What is the likely diagnosis?

A. Hideradinitis suppurativa
B. Fox-fordyce disease
C. Hailey hailey disease
D. Follicular lichen planus
E. Flexural darier disease

Key: B
Ref: Rook (94.18)

9. A 22 year old female patient presented with intensely pruritic papules in both armpits and genital area fir last 2 years.
Patient has not improved with antihistamines and emollients.
She also has 6 year history of comedogenic acne on face and trunk.
Ultrasound pelvis shows pcos.
On h/E, there was dilated follicular infundibulum with hyperkeratosis as well as xanthomatous hiatiocytosis.
Keeping in mind the above scenario, what treatment option should we consider?

A. Topical terbinafine
B. Oral Itraconazole
C. Combined Oral contraceptive pills and topical hydrocortisone
D. Intravenous steroids
E. Intralesional botulinum toxin

Key: C
Ref: Rook (94.18)

10. A 52-year-old man presented with greenish discoloration of his hands and feet since the last six days. He was a worker in electrical equipment industry.
He did not take any other systemic medication and no exposure to any chemicals or dyes. The greenish tinge first appeared over the dorsum of his hands and then gradually progressed to involve the palms, forearms, arms, legs, and feet.
The patient also noticed slight greenish coloration of undergarments. The patient's blood copper level at presentation was slightly raised and 0.5 ml of sweat was collected which detect the presence of copper.
Keeping in mind the above scenario what is the likely diagnosis?
A. Chromhiderosis
B. Pseudochromohyderosis
C. Trimethylaminuria
D. Hyperhidrosis
E. Bromhidrosis

Key: B
Ref: Rook (94.17)

11. 14 yr old child presents with history of excessive sweating over tip of his nose. On examination, there are erythematous papules, vesicles and telangiectasias on nose, cheeks and upper lip. There is associated palmoplantar hyperhidrosis.
What is the likely diagnosis?
A. Ross syndrome
B. Rosacea
C. Shydrager Syndrome
D. Granulosis rubra nasi.

Key: D
Ref: Rook (94.10)

12. 14 yr old child presents with history of excessive sweating over tip of his nose. On examination, there are erythematous papules, vesicles and telangiectasias on nose, cheeks and upper lip. There is associated palmoplantar hyperhidrosis. Keeping in view the diagnosis what is the mode of inheritance?
A. Autosomal Recessive
B. Autosomal Dominant
C. X linked Dominant
D. X linked Recessive

Key: B
Ref: Rook (94.10)

13. A patient presents to opd with history of heat intolerance and socially disabling compensatory hyperhidrosis. On examination, there is segmental anhydrosis, absent deep tendon reflexes and tonic pupils. What is the likely diagnosis?
A. Ross syndrome
B. Granulosis rubra nasi
C. Bazex syndrome
D. Sjogren syndrome

Key: A
Ref: Rook (94.11)

14. A 20 year old male patient presents with history of rotting fish smell to the sufferers. Patient is a known case of chronic liver disease. He further tells that the unpleasant odour worsens after eating sea food and during periods of stress. What is the diagnosis?
A. Chromohydrosis
B. Bromohydrosis

C. Trimethylaminuria
D. Miliria

Key: C
Ref: Rook (94.16)

15. 20 year old male patient presents with history of rotting fish smell to the sufferers. Patient is a known case of chronic liver disease. He further tells that the unpleasant odour worsens after eating sea food and during periods of stress. Keeping in view the diagnosis what is the recommended treatment?

A. Diet low in cobalt and selenium
B. Diet low in carnitine and cobalt
C. Diet low in carnitine and choline
D. Diet high in choline and carnitine.

Key: C
Ref: Rook (94.16)

Chapter 95 ACQUIRED DISORDERS OF THE NAILS AND NAIL UNIT

1. A 35 years old female patient presented to skin opd seeking advice regarding a painless red lesion on her right toe since 3 weeks, after a trauma from aggressive pedicure. She also complaint of recurrent bleeding from the lesion after mild irritation. O/E there was a glistering red papule on proximal nail fold of right toe. Regarding this condition which among the following is true?

A. It is always located on proximal nail fold.
B. It is never associated with onycholysis.
C. Local infection can be a complication.
D. Multiple digits are never involved.
E. Drugs are the most common cause

Key: C.
Ref: Rook (95.22)

2. A middle aged female patient presented to skin opd with pulsating pain in right index finger nail. According to patient, the pain is aggrevated by cold weather. O/E there was small area of bluish discoloration of nail.
Keeping diagnosis in mind which among the following investigations has highest sensitivity.

A. Excisional biopsy
B. Ultrasonography.
C. Arteriography.
D. Thermography.
E. MRI nail unit.

Key: E.
Ref: Rook (95.23)

3. A 20 years old male patient presented to skin opd with multiple painful fleshy red nodules on lateral nail folds of middle 3 digits of left hand since 2 weeks. Patient also complaint of occasional bleeding from these lesions. On further inquiry he revealed that he has been taking oral isotretinoin for nodulocystic acne since 4 months.
Keeping in mind the diagnosis, what will be the initial step in management in this patient

A. Potent topical corticosteroids under occlusion.
B. Curettage under local anesthesia.
C. Stop oral isotretinoin.
D. Intralesional steroid.
E. Surgical removal.

Key: A.
Ref: Rook (95.22)

4. Regarding subungual exostosis which among the following is not true

A. It most commonly affects young people
B. Trauma is the most important etiological factor.
C. Thumb nail is affected in three quarters of cases.
D. Radiological examination is the corner stone in diagnosis.
E. Treatment is resection of outgrowth under full anesthetic conditions.

Key: C.
Ref: Rook (95.24)

5. A 50 years old female patient presented to skin opd with pain in right middle finger nail. According to her, pain is worst at night. O/E there was a longitudinal erythematous band with overlying fissuring. After thorough investigations diagnosis of glomus tumour was made.
How will you treat this patient?

A. CO2 laser
B. Surgical excision of tumour
C. Nd- YAG laser
D. Radiation therapy
E. Sclerotherapy with hypertonic saline

Key: B.
Ref: Rook (95.23)

6. A 50years old man presented in opd with complaints of thickening of nail plate.o/e it was noticed that along with thickening there was sparing of part of nail with transverse and longitudinal overcurvature and xanonychia of effected nail. There was wood worm cavity at free edge. What is the diagnosis?

A. Onchomatricoma
B. Onychomycosis
C. Bowen disease
A. Onychogryohosis

Key: A.
Ref: Rook (95.29)

7. Which of the following types of scc is associated with scc of nail?

A. Hpv 6
B. Hpv 16
C. Hpv 11
D. Hpv 18

Key: B
Ref: Rook (95.32)

8. A 50 years old male presented in opd with complains of discolouration of nail which was increasing over time.o/e he was found to have longitudinal melanonychia extending to nail folds. Diagnosis of melanoma was made. Which of the following is true regarding its treatment?

A. Removal of nail unit with 5-10mm margin
B. Removal of nail unit with 10-15 mm margin
C. Removal of nail unit with 15-20mm margin
D. Removal of nail unit with 20-25 mm margin

Key: A
Ref: Rook (95.34)

9. A 42years old malr presented with complians of pain in his right thumb nail. o/e of nail there was an isolated pink longitudinal streak extending from distal matrix to free edge along with distal onycholysis? What is the most likely diagnosis?

A. Onychopapilloma
B. Superficial acral fibromyxoma
C. Onychomatricoma
D. Digital myxoid pseudocyst

Key: A
Ref: Rook (95.31)

10. Which of the following statement is incorrect about melanoma of nail?
   A. 5year survival rate for in-situ melanoma is 100%
   B. 5year survival rate is 88% if Breslow thickness is less than 2.5
   C. 5year survival rate us 90% present for Breslow thickness more than 2.5
   D. None of the above

Key: C
Ref: Rook (95.34)

11. 14year old girl concerned about her grey nails of her hand for the last month presented to the opd. Her history was inconclusive. What other question would help the diagnosis?
   A. Drug history of anti-malarias
   B. History of self-tanners
   C. Any contact with particular dyes
   D. History of smoking
   E. None of the above

Key: A
Ref: Rook (95.13)

12. 38year old male in the icu diagnosed with infective endocarditis had nail changes. which of these would be evident in this patient nails when examined -
   A. Splinter haemorrhage
   B. Brown longitudinal streak
   C. Green discolouration
   D. Bright red nails
   E. White discolouration

Key: A
Ref: Rook (95.13)

13. 15 year old boy presented with whole porcelain white nails since birth. What is his diagnosis.
   A. Subtotal leukonychia
   B. Total leukonychia
   C. Mees lines
   D. Punctate leukonychia
   E. Terry's nail

Key: B
Ref: Rook (95.13)

14. 10year old girl presented with history of all her 20 nails being infected with associated pain for the past year and transverse ridging, thickened yellow nails on examination. Other complains are repeated nasal sinus disease. What is the probable diagnosis?
   A. Half and half nails
   B. Terry's nails
   C. Yellow nails syndrome
   D. Drug history of tetracycline
   E. None of the above

Key: C
Ref: Rook (95.15)

15. Most common site of splinter haemorrhages in nails is?
   A. Proximal nail bed

B. Distal nail bed
C. Fingers of dominant hand
D. Both a and c
E. Both b and c

Key: E

16. All of following are associated with median canaliform dystrophy of Heller except?
A. External trauma
B. Viral warts
C. Myxoid cysts
D. Oral retinoids
E. methotrexate

Key: E

17. A 50 yr old female presented with complaint of long standing longitudinal groove on left thumb nail showing irregularity and a small keratotic plug protruding from proximal nail fold. What is the likely diagnosis?
A. Amelanotic melanoma
B. Fibrokeratoma
C. Subungual exostosis
D. Myxoid pseudocyst

Key: D

18. Regarding acquired ungual fibrokeratoma all are correct except?
A. Histology is mandatory to rule out bowen disease
B. Trauma is the major causative factor
C. Lesions present on multiple digits are called koenen tumors
D. There is marked histological difference btween koenen tumor and fibrokeratoma
E. All are true

Key: D

19. A 40 yr old female presented with a rapidly growing painful lesion on distal part of thumb nail. On examination there is a keratotic nodular lesion with central keratinous material present. Likely diagnosis is?
A. Squamous cell carcinoma
B. Subungual keratoacanthoma
C. Subungual wart
D. Epidermoid implantation cyst

Key: B

20. A 15 years old child presented to the ER with index nail trauma .on examination the nail was completely separated from the nail bed.dressing was done and patient was sent home with assurance .After 3 months he reviewed in opd ,trauma was healed and the nail regrowth was in progress.What is the main component involve in nail regrowth.
A. Nail plate
B. Nail fols
C. Nail matrix
D. Nail cuticle

Key: C

21. A 35 year old male presented to the dermatology opd with generalized erythematous well demarcated thick silvery adherent-scaly plaques. On examination of the nails there were distal separation of the nails from the nail bed. Salman patch was also present on the nail bed. At the border the separated nails were

reddish brown reflecting underlying inflammatory process. Diagnosis of psoriasis was made. This sign of the nail is called??

A. Nail pitting
B. Nail shedding
C. Pterygium
D. Onycholysis

Key: D

22. A 9 year girl presented to the opd with nail deformity. On examination the nail was split in the mid line with a fir tree like appearance. Bilateral thumb nails were involved with cuticles sparing. median canaliform dystrophy of heller was made.
what is the underlying disease?

A. Psoriasis
B. Lichen planus
C. Diabetes
D. Periungual fibroma

Key: D

23. A 45 year old female was admitted in icu with pneumonia for the last 10 days.on examination of her nails there were transverse grooves developed across the nails.all the 20 nails were involved but were most prominent on the thumb and great toe nails.
These nails are referred to as??

A. Trachyonychia
B. Beaus lines
C. Nail pitting
D. Anonychia

Key: B

24. A 35 year old male presented to the opd with generalized pruritus.On examination there were multiple firm, shiny, flat topped, polygonal papules and plaques. On oral mucosa white streaks was present. On examination of the nails there were winged appearance with a central fibrotic band divides the nail into two. Keeping the diagnosis of the disease what is the nail deformity.

A. Nail pterygium
B. beaus lines
C. nail pitting
D. pincer nail

Key: A

25. 13 year old male presents with rough and lustre less nails. Most of his nails of his hand and feet were involved. Regarding his condition which of the following statement is not true

A. It can be seen in a range of autoimmune diseases
B. It has an overall good prognosis if treated early
C. On histopathology, there is granular layer in nail bed and metrix with marked spongiosis
D. It does not need to be treated and improves with age gradually in several years
E. Topical, intralesional, or oral steroids can be given as treatment

Key: D
Ref: Rook (95.45)

26. 16 year old male presents with history of 2 days of pain and swelling in right index finger, in the lateral paronychial area. It is pointing close to the nail, tender and appears to be superficial. What should be his treatment

A. It can be drained by incision with a pointed scalpel without anaesthesia
B. Surgical intervention under local anaesthesia by removal of the nail plate
C. It should be incised and drained and nail plate removed
D. A trial of oral antibiotics should be given for 1 week before any intervention

Key: A.
Ref: Rook (95.35)

27. A mother brought her one and a half year old baby girl to dermatology OPD with grouped small vesicles on her middle finger close to the nail. It had honey comb appearance. History is of 10 days duration. Baby cries frequently due to it and seems to be in pain.
All the following can be complications of her condition except

A. meningitis
B. lymphedema
C. Numbness of fingers
D. Systemic spread
E. Pleural effusion

Key: E
Ref: Rook (95.35)

28. A chef, 45 yr old male, comes to dermatology OPD with complains of 3 yrs history of gradual swelling of sides of nails of hands along with rough nails, irregular transverse ridges, 1 year back he had pus coming out from sides, his sides of nails have also turned dark gradually and the nail growth is also disturbed.
What is the diagnosis

A. Orf paronychia
B. Chronic paronychia
C. Acute paronychia
D. Herpetic paronychia
E. Acrodermatitis continua of Hallopeau

Key: B,.
Ref: Rook (95.36)

29. A 20 Yr old female presents with 3 days history of swelling of lateral paronychial area of left index finger. Swelling was painful, red and tender.
All the following can be complications of her condition except

A. Osteitis
B. Amputation
C. Acquired periungual fibrokeratoma
D. Superinfection
E. Scc

Key: E
Ref: Rook (95.35)

Chapter 96

ACQUIRED DISORDERS OF DERMAL CONNECTIVE TISSUE

1. A young male patient known case of Marfan Syndrome developed multiple umbilicate papules arranged in circles having elevated margins over both thighs. Histopathology showed acanthotic epidermis engulfing elastotic debris. What would be the suitable options for management of this condition.

A. Cryotherapy
B. Curettage
C. Imiquimod
D. Calcipotriol
E. All of the above

Key: E
Ref: Rook (96.53)

2. You get a call from nephrology department of an old age female patient, known case of chronic renal failure and on dialysis for 20 years, developed firm nodules on proximal thighs, distal hands and feet associated with skin tightness and hardness for 2 months. Face and trunk spared. No associated raynaud's, sclerodactyly and nail fold capillary changes. Her pre-dialysis GFR 13 ml/min/1.73m, serum creatinine 7.2, urea 52. What were the possible risk factors predisposing her skin condition?

A. High dose Erythropoietin
B. Procoagulant state
C. Intravenous Iron
D. Gadolinium based contrast use
E. All of the above

Key: E
Ref: Rook (96.41)

3. A 49 years female patient presented with linear pattern of hyperkeratotic skin-colored papules along the radial side of her index finger. Keeping in mind the diagnosis, what would be the possible varieties of it.

A. Actinic comedonal plaque
B. Elastotic marginal plaque
C. Elastotic ear nodule
D. Both B and C
E. All of the above

Key: E
Ref: Rook (96.5)

4. A 20 years old African girl comes to you in opd with c/o swelling on the left ear lobe since 1 year. She is giving history that she developed the lesion after ear piercing. She sometimes experiences puritis and pain. On /e the swelling is firm, non-tender, measures 3 cm in diameter. The lesion extends beyond the border of the original wound. What is the most likely diagnosis?

A. DFSP
B. Fibrosarcoma
C. Dumb- bell keloid
D. Scar Sarcoid
E. Nodular Bcc

Key: C
Ref: Rook (96.48)

5. A 55 years old female underwent mitral valve replacement surgery. The procedure and post op recovery was uncomplicated. However, 1 year later she came to her GP with c/o increasing pain and thickness of the sternotomy scar. She was given Silicone gel sheet for 3 months but with little relief. Now the GP intends to start new treatment. Which amongst the following will be least helpful in this case?

A. I/L Triamcinolone
B. Topical Mitomycin C
C. Topical Isotretinoin
D. I/L bleomycin 0.375IU + triamcinolone 4mg
E. Topical Imiquimod

Key: C
Ref: Rook (96.48 & 96.49)

6. A 40 years old male from sudan gives history of painful fissuring and hyperkeratosis on the medial aspect of left 5th toe. He recalls having suffered some trauma from walking barefoot almost 2 months ago. Now his toe has become dorsiflexed at MCP joint. He also complains of resting pain and bluish discolouration of the digit distal to the grove. Keeping in mind the diagnosis all of the following can cause this condition in adults except

A. Leprosy
B. Chronic Psoriasis
C. Systemic sclerosis
D. Trauma and cold injury
E. Linear Morphea

Key: E
Ref: Rook (96.45)

7. A 26 years old female comes to derma opd for evaluation of firm skin-coloured nodules on her arms and legs bilaterally. The lesions continued to grow in size over the time. Apart from this she has thin fragile and prematurely aged skin. She also has history of poor wound healing and easy bruising. Her obstetric history is significant for delivery at 32 weeks due to preterm rupture of membranes. Keeping in view the skin lesions what is the most likely diagnosis

A. Cutix Laxa
B. Ehler danlos syndrome type 4
C. Enter Danlos syndrome type 1
D. Dubowitz syndrome

Key: B
Ref: Rook (72.5)

8. A 30-year-old male presents to your opd with c/0 multiple skin-coloured nodules over the chest. He does not give history of any trauma or burn. However, he recalls having severe acne in teenage for which he was treated with isotretinoin and later some laser treatment. The lesions are asymptomatic however they are cosmetically disfiguring. Which amongst the following treatment given for treatment of keloid will inhibit DNA and RNA synthesis

A. I/L triamcinolone
B. Topical Immiquimod
C. I/L 5 Fluorouracil
D. IR light emitting diodes

Key: C
Ref: Rook (96.49)

9. A 62-year-old female, gravida 6, presented with itchy pigmented lesions over the abdomen of 2 years duration with an occasional discharge of white particles from the lesion. She had no other comorbidities,

and her family history was unremarkable. She was treated with antifungals and topical corticosteroids with no improvement. Her BMI was 21.11 kg/m2. Cutaneous examination revealed the presence of a well-defined, hyperpigmented, atrophic periumbilical plaque with keratotic papules at the margins as well as few discrete keratotic papules over the abdomen. The surrounding skin was lax with multiple striae. Histopathology of the keratotic papule revealed hyperkeratosis with irregular acanthosis. Dermis showed many fragmented, thick, short, and curly eosinophilic fibers with granular basophilic material and transepidermal elimination of calcified elastic fibers on haemotoxylin and eosin staining.
What is the most probable diagnosis?

A. Elastosis perforans serpiginosa
B. Actinomycosis
C. Nocardiosis
D. Perforating PXE
E. None of the above

Key D
Ref: Rook (96.28)

10. A white man in his 60s was referred to our dermatology clinic for the evaluation of new, progressive, lesions on his back. He stated that the skin lesions began 1 year after starting a rigorous, swimming exercise program. The lesions were asymptomatic, yellow, palpable lines extending horizontally and first appeared on his mid-upper back followed by his lower back. Ultrastructural studies reveal active elastogenesis. What is the most probable diagnosis?

A. Granulomatous slack skin
B. Striae distensae
C. Linear focal elastosis
D. Linear xanthoma
E. Pseudoxanthoma elasticum

Key: C
Ref: Rook (96.29)

11. A 52-year-old woman presented with a feeling of stretching in the palm and soles and pain in walking on the soles of the feet. He has had complaints for about 3 months. He is type 2 diabetic and is on insulin He had no other known illness and medication. ON examination patient is having nodular thickening more pronounced over his 3rd and 4th finger palmar side bilaterally with flexion contracture. Patient is also having nodule on his medial expect of both plantar surfaces having some ulceration.
Keeping the diagnosis in mind which one of the following is not a risk factor for developing this condition?

A. Epilepsy
B. Diabetes
C. Occupational exposure to vibrating devices
D. Rheumatoid arthritis
E. Chronic lung disease

Key: E
Ref: Rook (96.31)

12. which one of the following is not a component of polyfibromatosis syndrome?

A. Dupuytren contracture
B. Keloid
C. Peyronie
D. Knuckle pad
E. Linear subcutaneous bands

Key: E
Ref: Rook (96.31)

13. A 38-year-old female patient presented with multiple, normochromic or slightly yellowish papules measuring 2-5 mm in diameter, with a keratotic, glossy surface, clustered symmetrically on the margins of her hands and feet. The lesions were asymptomatic, had appeared in childhood and had been stable ever since. The patient had had no previous treatment. Her mother and maternal grandmother had the same clinical condition at the same anatomical sites, also beginning before they reached ten years of age. Histopathology of skin revealed hyperkeratosis, acanthosis and some fragmentation of elastic fibre.
What is the most probable diagnosis?

A. Ichthyosis curth macklin
B. Hysterix-ichthyosis-deafness syndrome
C. Flegel disease
D. Ackerokeratoelastoidosis
E. Spiny keratoderma

Key: D
Ref: Rook (96.28)

14. A 15-year-old girl was presented with painless swelling of both upper eyelids, each episode lasting several days, for past 12 months. There was no history of lip trauma. She did not have lip-sucking habit. She did not have family history of similar complaints. On examination, her upper lip was bulky. When she smiled, a horizontal sulcus appeared in the upper lip making it appear as if she had two upper lips. Skin over both upper eyelids was thin, boggy and flaccid. Blepharochalasis was present more on right side. she also had goitre. The most probable diagnosis is

A. Ehlers denlos syndrome
B. Ascher syndrome
C. Mid dermal elastolysis
D. Upper dermal elastolysis

Key: B.
Ref: Rook (96.25)

15. A 30-year-old man presented with a 2-year history of asymptomatic erythematous annular plaques on his upper chest, neck, upper back and dorsum of hands. The lesions started as small papules, which slowly expanded centrifugally to form annular plaques with atrophic centres. Histopathology shows actinic elastosis in the external normal skin and histiocytic and giant cells in the thickened annulus region. Centre has no elastic tissue. Keeping in mind the diagnosis, the clinical variant associated with this disease is

A. Granuloma annulare
B. Erythema multiforme
C. Annular form of sarcoidosis
D. Acrokeratoelastoidosis

Key: C.
Ref: Rook (96.27)

16. A 35-year-old female presented with progressive asymptomatic plaques on the trunk and limbs, which started 2 years before consultation. She did not complain about any other local (itch, redness or blistering) or systemic symptoms. Physical examination revealed multiple small and soft, symmetrically distributed skin-coloured patches of cigarette paper like fine wrinkled skin, mainly on the upper abdominal anterior wall and proximal upper extremities. Biopsy was obtained from a wrinkled area. Histopathological examination disclosed a mild superficial perivascular lymphocytic infiltrate with scattered histiocytes and multinucleated giant cells on the upper and mid-dermis. Stain demonstrated the complete absence of elastic fibres along the mid-dermis. Keeping in mind the diagnosis, the disease has association with

A. Diabetes
B. Prothrombotic state
C. Tuberculosis

D. Sarcoidosis

Key: B.
Ref: Rook (96.23)

17. A 35-year-old female presented with progressive asymptomatic plaques on the trunk and limbs, which started 2 years before consultation. She did not complain about any other local (itch, redness or blistering) or systemic symptoms. Physical examination revealed multiple small and soft, symmetrically distributed skin-coloured patches of cigarette paper like fine wrinkled skin, mainly on the upper abdominal anterior wall and proximal upper extremities. Biopsy was obtained from a wrinkled area. Histopathological examination disclosed a mild superficial perivascular lymphocytic infiltrate with scattered histiocytes and multinucleated giant cells on the upper and mid-dermis. Stain demonstrated the complete absence of elastic fibres along the mid-dermis. The most probable diagnosis is

A. Acquired pseudoxanthoma elasticum
B. Mid dermal elastolysis
C. Anetoderma
D. Linear atrophoderma
E. Elastoderma

Key: B
Ref: Rook (96.23)

18. 28-year-old female was observed for evaluation of white spots and papules on her neck, upper limbs, and trunk, that had developed gradually within the last 2 year without any symptoms. The initial lesions were macules. Some of them appeared pouched out. On examination, multiple, grouped, round well-defined, hypopigmented atrophic macules, papules, and plaques were found distributed on the neck, shoulders, upper limbs, scapular region. The skin surface appeared thinned and wrinkled. Rest of the examination is normal. histology shows fragmentation and disappearance of elastic tissues in the subpapillary zone. Dermal collagen is also diminished. Keeping in mind the diagnosis, true regarding disease course and prognosis

A. Lesions resolve spontaneously after few years
B. Lesions remain unchanged throughout life
C. Lesions enlarge to maximum size and then regress
D. Lesions heal with hypopigmentation

Key: B
Ref: Rook (96.22)

19. For the treatment of striae, the patient z usually reassured that they will become less conspicuous, but few unproven remedies are available. which of the following laser z claimed to respond to erythema of younger striae?

A. q swiched laser
B. pulsed dye laser 585nm
C. C)argon laser
D. CO2

Key: B
Ref: Rook (96.10)

20. All of the following inherited disorders have poikloderma as a feature except?

A. dyskeratosis congenita
B. rothmund thomson syndrome
C. weary syndrome
D. kindler syndrome
E. down syndrome

Key: E

Ref: Rook (96.10)

21. A 21 yrs old obese girl developed obesity related striae on the outer aspect of thighs, buttocks and breast, Initially the lesions r raised n irritable, but then become flat, livid red n bluish in color.
Which of the following complication can occur in these striae?

A. striae may ulcerate or tear, when traumatized
B. contratures may develop
C. lymphedema
D. cyanosis occurs
E. hypertrophy

Key: A

22. A 15 yrs old boy known case of atopic eczema on treatment with steroids, developed skin atrophy. All of the following mechanisms may be involved in the process of skin atrophy except.?

A. type lll collagen z reduced in fibroblast cultures
B. steroids inhibit the formation of glucosaminoglycans
C. the no of fibroblasts z decreased
D. the fibroblasts become shrunken
E. hyaluronate receptors CD44 are deplted

Key: C

23. Which one of the following z true regarding skin atrophy caused by corticosteroids?

A. atrophy z seen markedly with mild steroids
B. most marked effect when potent topical steroids are applied under an occlusive dressing
C. atrophy with oral steroids
D. there z no change in skin texture with steroids

Key: B

24. A 50-year-old male, known case of porphyrea cutan tarda presented in opd with yellowish discoloration and thickening of skin of forehead and bald scalp. Histopathology report shows reduction in collagen and aggregates of amorphous material in papillary and upper reticular dermis.
What types of wrinkles will be present in this patient?

A. Crinkles
B. Linear furrows
C. Glyphic wrinkles
D. Cigratte paper wrinkling
E. Fine lines

Key: C
Ref: Rook (96.2 ,96.3)

25. A 49-year-old farmer presented in opd with multiple papules and plaques around the first finger web space, ulnar aspect of thumb and the radial aspect of index finger. He also gave history of UVB session for his psoriasis treatment for past 3 months.
What is the likely diagnosis?

A. Psoariasis
B. Solar elastosis
C. Hand eczema
D. Keratoelastoidosis marginalis
E. Acrodermatitis of hallopeau

Key: D
Ref: Rook (96.4)

26. A 50-year-old male, known case of porphyrea cutan tarda presented in opd with yellowish discoloration and thickening of skin of forehead and around the one eye. On examination there were plaques which were coalescing, having multiple comedones and cyst around the periorbital area of left eye.
He had 20 pack years smoking history.
What is the most likely diagnosis?

A. Chronic actinic dermatitis
B. Polymorphuc light eruption
C. Nevus comedonicus
D. Favre -Racouchot syndrome
E. Acne

Key: D

Chapter 97 GRANUULOMATOUS DISORDERS OF THE SKIN

1. An elderly woman presented to derma opd with c/o ring of small, smooth, flesh-coloured erythematous papules over hands, O/E stretching of skin makes papules more prominent, there is no scaling, no associated h/o itching and pain
On histopathology, what would be the most differentiating features of this disease?
   A. Dense collection of neutrophils
   B. Naked granulomas
   C. Touton giant cells
   D. Necrobiotic granulomas
   E. Epidermotropism

Key: D
Ref: Rook (97.3)

2. 35 years old man presented with c/o multiple erythematous annular papules and plaques over whole body, diffusely distributed over hands, face and trunk, there is associated h/o mild itching, O/E no surface changes visible and no scaling, what is the most common history point to reach the association of following mention disease
   A. Occupational history
   B. Family history of itching
   C. H/o bullous disorder
   D. Sexual history
   E. H/o photosensitivity

Key: D
Ref: Rook (97.4)

3. An elderly woman presented with c/o multiple annular plaques, overlying skin is intact and there is no scaling, these lesions enlarge centrifugally before clearing, regarding prognosis of this condition, which statement is not correct
   A. 50 percent lesion resolve within 02 years
   B. 40 percent of those lesions cleared had recurrence
   C. Generalized granuloma annulare has good prognosis
   D. Anetoderma can develop secondary to generalized ga
   E. In disseminated ga, investigate for thyroid disease and hyperlipidemia in exceptional cases

Key: C
Ref: Rook (97.7)

4. 5 years old child presented to derma opd with c/o multiple papules and nodules on scalp and legs from last 3 months, mother explains that some of these lesions enlarge centrifugally before clearing, these lesions are asymptomatic, what would be the most appropriate step in management of this condition
   A. Reassurance
   B. Cryotherapy
   C. Topical tacrolimus
   D. Pdt
   E. Oral dapsone

Key: A
Ref: Rook (97.7)

5. Distinguishing features on histopathology of granuloma annulare include all except
   A. Extensive area of necrobiosis that are less well defined
   B. Small deposit of lipids
   C. Mucin deposition
   D. Absence of elastic fibers
   E. Absence of plasma cells

Key: A
Ref: Rook (97.2)

6. A 35 yrs old diabetic female presented with plaques on her shins for a few months.
On examination you see bilateral yellowish atrophic plaques with erythematous edges, surface was glazed with prominent telangiectatic vessels.
What is the first line treatment of this disease?
   A. Puva
   B. Topical and intralesional steroids
   C. Pdt
   D. Cryotherapy
   E. Imiquimod

Key: B

7. A 45 yr old diabetic male presented with complaint of reddish brown plaques on his shins, these are well demarcated, bilateral and have an atrophic centre and erythematous edge.
You suspect the diagnosis and order biopsy for H/P.
What would you expect?
   A. Superficial and deep perivascular infiltrate and a prominent septal panniculitis
   B. Atophic epidermis with lymphohistiocytic infiltrate and nacked granulomas
   C. Full thickness formal lymphohistiocytic infiltrate with extensive areas of necrobiosis
   D. Altered collagen and elastic fibres surrounded by lymphocytes
   E. All of the above can be seen

Key: E
Ref: Rook (97.9)

8. A 30 yrs old patient was referred to you from a gastroenterologist, from whom patient is taking treatment of his active bowel disease, and now having few cutaneous lesions for which he is referred.
On examination she is having indurated nodules and plaques around nipples, there was also vulval swelling and abscess.
What diagnosis would you suspect?
   A. Paget's disease
   B. Extrammary paget's disease
   C. Sarcoidosis
   D. Crohn's disease
   E. Metastatic CD

Key: E

9. You are a doctor in pathology dept, and received a sample of biopsy for reporting...the history which the form provides is not very adequate, it just says few aymptomatic plaques on limbs.
While reporting you are confused between Granulma annulare and necrobiosis lipoidica.
Which of the following features doesn't help to distinguish between these two correctly?
   A. Presence of mucin is more prominent in GA than in NL
   B. Histiocytes express marker PGMI in GA
   C. Perivascular infiltrate of eosinophils and plasma cells is seen in NL in contrast to GA

D. In NL areas of necrobiosis are usually more extensive and less well defined than in GA
E. There is marked reduction of collagen and elastin in GA but none in NL

Key: E

10. A patient presented with perianal abscess and fistulas, he is otherwise unwell too, weight loss, fatigue, he says that he often has abdominal pain with episodes of diarrhoea.
Your diagnosis is cutaneous CD. Which of the following statement is not true regarding CD?

A. It may present in skin as Pyoderma Gangrenosum or Erythema nodosum
B. Treatment of intestinal disease leads to resolution of skin lesions
C. Histopathology shows granulomatous infiltrate and septal panniculitis
D. If the lesions are at distant site and not continue with intestinal tract, it is called metastatic CD
E. Cutaneous disease may precede the intestinal disease

Key: B

Chapter 98 SARCOIDOSIS

1. A 45 years old male came with complain of redness of eyes, cough, dyspnea and skin lesion at forearm since 3 months. He has history of tattoo at same site of forearm since many years ago. On cutaneous examination there were reddish brown indurated plaque with identical shape of tattoo. Diascopy showed apply jelly colored nodule. Skin biopsy of nodule will suggest.

A. Caseating granuloma with positive AFB
B. Caseating granuloma with >25% lymphocytes
C. Non caseating granuloma with sparse lymphocytes
D. Caseating granuloma with polarizable foreign body
E. None of above

Key: C
Ref: Rook (98.2)

2. A 42 year old man with shortness of breath on exertion, presented with erythematous papular eruption on the face more prominently on periocular areas, nasolabial folds and few on dorsum aspects of both hands. These lesions coalesed to form plaques at exposed areas. On diascopy the lesions revealed apple jelly nodules. Regarding this condition following is most appropriate:

A. High serum triglycerides in such patients is a routine finding
B. May resolve spontaneously with scarring in 2 weeks
C. Not associated with hilar lymphadenopathy, acute uveitis and parotid enlargement
D. Grouped papules in popliteal fossa are a common finding
E. Polarizable foreign bodies are present in a high proportion of biopsies

Key: E
Ref: Rook (98.7)

3. A 25 years old male came with complain facial and neck swelling since 1 year. On examination there were small reddish brown infiltrated patches with few discrete papules less than 10mm over nasolabial fold and cheek. There were bilateral parotid swelling and cervical lymphadenopathy also noted. Biopsy of skin lesion showed non caseating granuloma with negative AFB and fungal culture. Keeping diagnosis in mind all of the following are associated with this disease except

A. Hogkin lymphoma
B. Sjogren syndrome
C. Systemic sclerosis
D. Grave disease
E. Hepatits A

Key: E
Ref: Rook (98.2)

4. A 38 year old male comes to you in opd for removal of a tattoo on his upper arm due to formation of erythematous plaque around this tattoo. According to the history given to you, the patient has history of chest congestion off and on since last few months and on treatment for his condition. The rash is non tender non-itchy, non-discharging, slightly indurated and progressively increasing in size over past few weeks. Pick the most appropriate statement regarding evolution of his new lesions:

A. Not associated with long-lasting pulmonary and mediastinal involvement, uveitis, peripheral lymphadenopathy
B. May lead to bony cysts formation and parotid infiltration

C. Secondary infections frequently followed after scars can act as an antigenic stimulus for the induction of granuloma formation
D. It is foreign-body reaction to tattoo pigment
E. Histopathology may yeild PAS positive branching hyphae

Key: B
Ref: Rook (98.9)

5. A 35 years old male known case of Hepatitis C on treatment came in OPD with complain of skin lesion at face since 6 months. On examination there were infiltrated erytematoviolaceous plaque involving his left cheek, left ala of nose and upper lip. With no signs of any ulcerations, talengactiasia and scaling. Skin biopsy showed dermal granuloma. Keeping diagnosis in mind which of the following is main culprit

A. Foreign body reaction
B. HLA DQB1 0401
C. INF a induced sarcoidosis
D. Hep C and EBV antigenicity
E. Idiopathic

Key: C
Ref: Rook (98.4)

6. A 55 year black female presented to your opd seeking advice for a reddish brown papular lesion on tip of the nose since past few months which is not responding to regular treatment for rosacea. There are no exacerbating or relieving factors associated with her condition and with time the lesion has become bit distorted. There are also infiltrated erythematoviolaceous plaques on the cheeks and forehead. On the cheeks, a prominent telangiectatic component is appreciated. Best treatment options to treat her condition is:

A. Oral Hydroxychloroquine
B. Demodex eradication
C. Topical Brimonidine
D. Cryosurgery
E. Pulsed-dye laser (PDL) and oxymetazoline 1.0% cream

Key: A
Ref: Rook (98.17)

7. A 25 years old male came with complain facial and neck swelling since 1 year. On examination there were small reddish brown infiltrated patches with few discrete papules less than 10mm over nasolabial fold and cheek. There were bilateral parotid swelling and cervical lymphadenopathy also noted. Biopsy of skin lesion showed non caseating granuloma with negative AFB and fungal culture. Keeping diagnosis in mind all of the following granulomas can be seen in it except

A. Naked granuloma
B. Tuberculoid granuloma Non caseating
C. Foreign body granuloma
D. Pallisading necrobiotic granuloma
E. Caseating Granuloma

Key: E
Ref: Rook (97.2)

8. A 42 year old man with shortness of breath on exertion, presented with erythematous papular eruption on the face more prominently on periocular areas, nasolabial folds and few on dorsum aspects of both hands. These lesions coalesed to form plaques at exposed areas. On diascopy the lesions revealed apple jelly nodules. Recommended basic assessment of patients with this condition includes all except:

A. History (including occupational and environmental exposure), Physical examination • Ophthalmological examination (slit-lamp and ophthalmoscopic examination)

B. Investigations: Chest radiograph, biochemistry profiles (including urine and serum calcium level and serum angiotensin-converting enzyme level)
C. ECG, Pulmonary function tests (including spirometry and DLco)
D. ETT, Bronchoscopy, Endoscopy to rule out differentials
E. Infectious screen including: Tuberculin skin test, Biopsies (including culture for mycobacteria and fungus)

Key: D
Ref: Rook (98.1 page 98.1**6)**

9. A 35 years old male known case of liver disease on INF a came in OPD with complain of skin lesion at face since 6 months. On examination there were infiltrated erytematoviolaceous plaque involving his left cheek, left ala of nose and upper lip. With no signs of any ulcerations and scaling. Skin biopsy showed dermal granuloma. Keeping diagnosis in mind what should be next step

A. Stop treatment start another antiviral
B. Stop treatment as it has malignant course
C. Do not stop treatment, 85%has benign course
D. Do not stop treatment, INF a has good role in skin lesions
E. None of above

Key: C
Ref: Rook (98.2)

Chapter 100 OTHER ACQUIRED DISORDERS OF SUBCUTANEOUS FAT

1. A 62-year-old female came in with a chief complaint of palpable mass present in shoulder and upper back regions. Images showed diffuse non-encapsulated adipose tissue in the subcutaneous layer of the sub occipital, posterior neck area. The patient wanted to remove the mass for cosmetic reasons and discomfort. Excisional biopsy was planned. Detailed history taking revealed that she consumed highly levels of alcohol. Lipectomy was performed and the histological findings demonstrated large dystrophic adipocyte morphology. The patient was recovered uneventfully.
What is the likely diagnosis?
   A. dercum disease
   B. Acquired partial lipodystrophy
   C. benign symmetrical lipomatosis
   D. Lipoedema
   E. localized lipodystrophy

Key: C
Ref: Rook (100.14)

2. A 54-year-old obese woman complained of multiple painful "lumps" in the extremities. The diagnosis of Dercum's disease was established by excisional biopsy of four tumours.
What is false regarding the disease?
   A. Its other name is adiposis dolorosa
   B. Disease has local defect in lipid metabolism
   C. There are no chances of recurrence after surgical excision
   D. Intralisional lidocaine can be used as a treatment option
   E. none of the above

Key: C
Ref: Rook (100.16)

3. A 50 years old women presented in opd with multiple lumps in both thighs with intense pain around then. She also complained of generalized pain in her arms and shoulders.
The physical examination showed obesity, with a body mass index of 32kg/m2.
Firm, mobile, painful lumps were felt in both thighs.
Ultrasound scanning of lumps showed that the lumps were composed of adipose tissue. The erythrocyte sedimentation rate was 10 mm/h and the C–reactive protein level was 6 mg/l. Serum lipid levels were normal.
What clinical variant of dercum disease she is having?
   A. Generalized diffuse form
   B. Generalized nodular form
   C. Localized nodular form
   D. juxta-articular form
   E. None of the above

Key: B
Ref: Rook (100.16)

4. A 43-year-old male presented to the dermatology out-patient dept with complaints of painless, slowly progressive, disfiguring swellings over his shoulders, arms and upper trunk since childhood. There was no history of dyspnoea or dysphagia, drug use or other medical conditions. He was a light drinker, taking four

units of alcohol per week for the past 10 years. The patient was operated twice before, but the lesions used to recur in a few years. On examination, there were diffuse, soft to firm, skin colored subcutaneous masses over his shoulders, arms and upper trunk. The lesions were non-tender and freely mobile.
Excisional biopsy was done. Histopathological examination showed clusters of mature adipocytes.
What is the major association of the above disease?

A. Dyslipidaemia
B. Gynaecomastia
C. Arterial hypertension
D. COPD
E. Type 2 diabetes

Key: A
Ref: Rook (100.14)

5. A 54 years old man visited the outpatient clinic complaining of bulging masses in the posterior upper part of the thorax, the occipital area, and the neck. The masses grew over a period of 2 years. The physical examination and imaging study revealed the presence of symmetric lipomatosis. A two-step surgical treatment was undertaken for the excision of the lipomatous tissue.
Histology revealed unencapsulated fatty tissue deposits.
What is false regarding the disease?

A. It is also called madelung disease
B. It is more common in females than males
C. It is associated with dyslipidaemia
D. Fatty growths in BSL are non-tender.
E. Genetic alterations are in mitochondrial DNA

Key: B
Ref: Rook (100.14)

6. 20 years old female patient presented to dermatology opd with history of symmetrical gradual enlargement of both limbs with sparing of both feet. There is no history of ulceration and cellulitis and it is tender touch. There is minimal effect from limb elevation. What is the likely diagnosis???

A. LYMPHEDEMA
B. LIPOEDMA
C. LIPPPLYMEDMA
D. OBESITY.

Key: B
Ref: Rook (100.19)

7. 20 years old female patient presented to dermatology opd with the history of symmetrical gradual enlargement of both limbs with sparing of both feet. There is no history of ulceration and cellulitis and it is tender touch. There is minimal effect from limb elevation.
On further Examination, there is a sharp demarcation between the normal and abnormal tissue at the ankles, with sparing of feet, normal to minimal pitting edema. Keeping in view the diagnosis what is the nature of disease?

A. chronic and lifelong
B. Acute /Subacute
C. chronic and ulcerative
D. Chronic and resolves in few years.

Key: A
Ref: Rook (100.21)

8. 20 years old female patient presented to dermatology opd with the history of symmetrical gradual enlargement of both limbs with sparing of both feet. There is no history of ulceration and cellulitis and it is tender touch. There is minimal effect from limb elevation.
On further Examination, there is a sharp demarcation between the normal and abnormal tissue at the ankles, with sparing of feet, normal to minimal pitting edema. Which of the following clinical signs helps to distinguish this condition from lymphedema?

A. Darier sign
B. Cuff sign
C. Stemmer's sign
D. none of above

Key: C
Ref: Rook (100.20)

9. A male patient presents to dermatology opd with progressive enlargement of his bilateral lower limbs starting from buttock area and extending till ankle joint with the sparing of his feet. He is diabetic as well as alcoholic. He is on treatment for some carcinoma from last 2 years. Lipedema can occur in a male patient in which of the following conditions?

A. Hypertensive and diabetic male
B. At the onset of puberty
C. Hormonal therapy for prostate cancer
D. Alcoholic

Key: C
Ref: Rook (100.20)

10. A male patient presents to dermatology opd with progressive enlargement of his bilateral lower limbs starting from buttock area and extending till ankle joint with the sparing of his feet.He is diabetic as well as alcoholic. He is on treatment for some carcinoma from last 2 years. His edema is relieved partially on limb elevation. Stemmer's sign is also positive. His Ct scan reveals diffuse and homogenous lipomatous hypertrophy of subcutaneous tissue. His Lymphangiogram is abnormal.
What is the likely diagnosis?

A. lipoedema
B. lipolymphedema
C. lymphedema
D. Cellulitis

Key: B
Ref: Rook (100.22)

Chapter 101 PURPURA

1. A 50 year diabetic male presented with itchy orange to red macules with cayenne pepper spots on a yellow brown background bilaterally on the lower legs for the past 6 months. The most likely diagnosis will be

A. Pigmented purpuric dermatosis
B. Hemosiderosis
C. Dermatitis secondary to infections
D. Thrombocytopenia induced vasculitis
A. E contact dermatitis

PKey: A
Ref: Rook (101.9)

2. You are called to asses a middle age man suffering from ischemic heart disease who has undergone a major cardiac surgery a week back. On examination you notice a sharply demarcated purpuric tender plaques in the abdomen and upper thigh with few showing needle prick mark in the center. The most likely diagnosis is

A. Warfarin necrosis
B. Heparin induced thrombocytopenia
C. Heparin associated thrombocytopenia
D. Drug induced coagulaopathy
E. Idiopathic thrombocytopenia

Key: B
Ref: Rook (101.10)

3. What is the most likely culprit in the above scenario?

A. Low molecular weight heparin
B. Unfractioned heparin, porcine variety
C. Unfractioned heparin, bovine variety
D. Warfarin
E. Clopidogrel

Key: C.
Ref: Rook (101.10)

4. A 30 yr old female who had lost her husband in a car accident 6 months back presented with painful recurrent erythematous and edematous plaques on the upper shoulders and torso for past 4 months. She says these lesions begin as plaques, enlarge in size and become purpler and gradually fade away. She has felt fatigued out during these episodes. Her coagulation profile and remaining labs are normal. What is the underlying pathology?

A. Artefactual purpura
B. Sneddon syndrome
C. Ppd
D. Gardner diamond syndrome
E. Purpura due to underlying infections.

Key: D

5. What would be the investigation of choice be in the above case

A. Serum ANA levels

B. D dimers
C. Serum fibronegen levels
D. Platelet with manual method
E. Intra dermal inj of rbcs

Key: E

6. An elderly woman presented to medical emergency with h/o headache and hypertension from last 2 months for which she was taking antihypertensive regularly. Now she was complaining of left sided body weakness since last night, on further inquiry she has significant h/o Raynaud phenomenona. O/E she has broad livedo pattern over trunk and proximal part of legs, what would be the most appropriate diagnosis in this patient

A. Degos disease
B. Sneddon syndrome
C. Malignant atrophic papupulosis
D. Polyarteritis nodosa
E. Livedo with summer ulceration

Key: B
Ref: Rook (101.21)

7. Which one of the following laboratory criteria is not included in the international consensus statement preliminary criteria for antiphospholipid antibody syndrome

A. Lupus anticoagulant
B. Prothrombin time
C. Beta 2 glycoprotein
D. IgM cardiolipin antibodies
E. IgG cardiolipin antibodies

Key: B
Ref: Rook (101.20)

8. Middle aged lady presented with h/o chronic lower legs lesion from last 4 years, she was police constable by profession but now she has quit her job due to difficulty in standing, O/E she has h/o persistent painful ulcer around the bilateral malleoli, keeping in mind diagnosis of above patient which statement is not true

A. Can also result due factor v Leiden mutation
B. Elevated homocysteine level can lead to livedo vasculopathic ulcer
C. Mainstay of treatment of above stated Condition is oral steroids
D. Healing results in porcelain white scar
E. Direct immunofluorescence positive in almost 90 percent cases

Key: C
Ref: Rook (101.22)

9. An elderly man with previous h/o hypertension and ischemic stroke on left side of body presented to derma opd with c/o Raynaud phenomena and acrocyanosis, O/E there is livedo racemose pattern over lower legs.

Regarding above condition prognosis, which statement is not true

A. Transient ischemic stroke are less common than complete stroke
B. Hypertension confers worse prognosis if untreated
C. Patients with apla have infacrts in distribution of main cerebral arteries
D. Mri and eeg helpful in confirmation of neurological event
E. There is generally no very effective treatment for this condition

Key: A
Ref: Rook (101.21)

10. Pregnant lady at 9 weeks of gestation presented to dermatology opd with diagnosed case of SLE from last 4 years, she has h/o 02 unexplained abortion in first trimester of pregnancy 2 year back, what would be the first treatment step in this patient

A. Heparin/warfarin
B. Heparin and low dose aspirin
C. Low dose aspirin
D. Low dose aspirin with hydroxycholoroquine
E. Oral steroids

Key: D
Ref: Rook (52.3)

Chapter 102

CUTANEOUS VASCULITITIS

1. A 45 year old man known case of rheumatoid arthritis on NSAIDs, presented with red-violaceous to red-brown papules, plaques or nodules in symmetrical fashion over the dorsa of the hands, knees, buttocks and Achilles tendons since last few months. Initially, the lesions are soft, but eventually they fibrose. True regarding this condition is:

A. It is common in prevalence
B. It is related to an Arthus-type reaction with immune complex deposition
C. The condition heals without scarring
D. No correlation with IgA antineutrophil cytoplasmic antibodies reported
E. Chronic lesions demonstrate angiocentric neutrophilic fibrosis

Key: B
Ref: Rook (102.8)

2. A 45 year old man known case of rheumatoid arthritis on NSAIDs, presented with red-violaceous to red-brown papules, plaques or nodules in symmetrical fashion over the dorsa of the hands, knees, buttocks and Achilles tendons since last few months. Initially, the lesions are soft, but eventually they fibrose and later leave atrophic scars. Which of the following features you expect in histopathology of this patient:

A. Neutrophils in upper and mid dermis
B. Leukocytoclastic vasculitis, with little fibrin deposition
C. Dermal nodules with lipid laiden macrophages present
D. Capillary atrophy is present
E. Chronic lesions demonstrate angiocentric neutrophilic fibrosis

Key: B
Ref: Rook (102.9 to 102.10)

3. A 38 year old man with type 2 diabetes mellitus, present to your opd with dusky palapable purpura on the both lower limbs sparing the intertriginous areas between the toes since last few weeks. There is associated itching and pain around the lesions. These lesions are macular in the early stages, later progresses to papules, nodules, plaques, with secondary findings of ulceration, necrosis and post inflammatory hyperpigmentation. Which of the following is responsible in development of his new crops of rash?

A. Glimipride
B. Insulin
C. Metformin
D. Acarbose
E. Glipizide

Key: B
Ref: Rook (102.4)

4. A 38 year old man present to your opd with dusky palapable purpura on the both lower limbs sparing the intertriginous areas between the toes since last few weeks. There is associated itching and pain around the lesions. These lesions are macular in the early stages, later progresses to papules, nodules, plaques, with secondary findings of ulceration, necrosis and post inflammatory hyperpigmentation. Following is one of the diagnostic criteria for classification as cutaneous small vessel vasculitis:

A. Age greater than 10 years at disease onset
B. History of taking a medication at onset that may have been a precipitating factor
C. Exclusion of palpable purpura
D. The absence of a maculopapular rash

E. A biopsy demonstrating histiocytes around an arteriole or venule

Key: B
Ref: Rook (102.5)

5. A 38 year old man present to your opd with dusky palapable purpura on the both lower limbs sparing the intertriginous areas between the toes since last few weeks. There is associated itching and pain around the lesions. These lesions are macular in the early stages, later progresses to papules, nodules, plaques, with secondary findings of ulceration, necrosis and post inflammatory hyperpigmentation. Following treatment options you may offer this patient except:

A. Colchicine
B. Oral prednisolone
C. Anakinra
D. Azathioprine
E. Methotrexate

Key: C
Ref: Rook (102.8)

6. A 40 years old male presented with history of recurrent episodes of palpable purpura on trunk in winter season. He also complained of frequent myalgia, headache, fever and weight loss over period of 1 year. He was diagnosed HCV positive from last 3 years. What is true regarding Cryoglobulinaemic vasculitis.

A. Low C3 and C4
B. Normal C3 and low C4
C. Low C3 and normal C4
D. Normal C3 and C4
E. Normal RA factor

Key: B
Ref: Rook (102.17)

7. Which of the following antibodies may not be found in IgA vasculitis

A. IgA rheumatoid factor
B. IgA anti cardiolipinantibodies
C. IgA anti endothelialcell antibodies (AECAs)
D. IgA ANCA
E. IgA beta-2 glycoprotein

Key: E
Ref: Rook (102.14)

8. A 10 years old boy presented with palpable purpura on extensor aspects of the limbs and buttocks in a symmetrical fashion. He also complained of abdominal pain and frank hematuria from last 5 days. Direct immunofluorescence showed perivascular IgA deposits. What could be the course of disease

A. About 5% of patients will relapse
B. It can become chronic in 25–30% of patients
C. Only 1–3% of these patients progress to end-stage renal disease
D. 10-15% will have end-stage renal disease.
E. Mortality is 10%

Key: C
Ref: Rook (102.16)

9. 50 years old male presented with history of recurrent asymptomatic brownish lesion on right cheek. On examination there were soft and red-brown nodules which were smooth, with prominent follicular orifices

and telangiectatic surface changes and scaling. Dermoscopy showed parallel, arborizing blood vessels, brown dots and globules and dilated follicular openings.
Histology showed mixed inflammatory infiltrate with predominance of

A. Mast cells
B. Neutrophils
C. Lymphocytes
D. Eosinophils
E. Giant cells

Key: D
Ref: Rook (102.12)

10. A 35 years old male came in derma opd with complain of pain.at lower limb. On cutaneous examination multiple palpable purpura were present with few haemorrhagic vesicles. For diagnosis skin biopsy should be taken

A. After 48 hours of fresh lesion
B. New fresh induced blister. less than 24 hours
C. Within 48 hours of fresh lesion
D. Older haemorrhagic blister
E. A n D

Key: C
Ref: Rook (102.4)

11. A 28 years old female came with complain of burning sensation at extremities since 2 weeks. On cutaneous examination there were multiple haemorrhagic blisters and painful palpable purpura around ankle and 2/3 of lower leg. Urine Dr showed RBCs and proteinuria .History of taking drugs, fever and weight loss were negative. Keeping diagnosis in mind all of the following will be associated with immune complex except

A. Henoch schonlein purpura
B. Cryoglobulinaemia
C. hypocomplementaemic urticarial vasculitis
D. Antiglomerular basement membrane vasculitis
E. Microscopic Polyangitis

Key: E
Ref: Rook (102.2)

12. A 28 years old female came with complain of malaise, dyspnea, multiple joint pain and low grade fever since 2 months. On cutaneous examination there were malar rash over face sparing nasolabial fold, oral ulcers and multiple haemorrhagic blisters and painful palpable purpura around ankle and 2/3 of lower leg and forearm. Urine DR showed RBCs and proteinuria. Raised ESR. Keeping diagnosis in mind all of the following will include in differentials except

A. Behcet vasculitis
B. lupus vasculitis
C. Sacroid vasculitis
D. Rhematoid vasculitis
E. Sweet syndrome with Vasculitis

Key: E
Ref: Rook (102.2)

13. All of the following are the presentations of vasculitis according to size of vessels except

A. Small size vessel presents with purpuric macules and papules
B. Medium sized vessels present with broken livedo, infarction

C. Small size vessels present with reticular pattern and deep nodules
D. Medium size vessels present with net like pattern ulceration, infarction and deep nodule
E. Small size vessels present with haemorrhagic blisters and urticarial plaques.

Key: C
Ref: Rook (102.3)

14. For the clinical diagnosis of vasculitis you will find all of the following examination points except
A. Hypertension, peripheral edema, protein and Rbc in urine dipstick, Non blanchable purpura
B. Wheezes , crepitations , pericardial rub
C. Painful blanchable palpable purpura, abnormal reflexes and peripheral edema
D. Abdominal tenderness, hepatosplenomegaly, edema
E. Psychiatric signs, edema , hypertension , Non blanchable purpura

Key: C
Ref: Rook (102.2)

15. A 36years old female presented with fever, malaise and arthritis for the last 01 month. She was being managed by local GP with no relief of symptoms. She then developed erythematous plaques on body which were itchy and lasted more than 24hrs.The plaques were erythematous, indurated with purpuric foci which used to resolve with areas of discoloration.There was livedo reticularis on legs.Considering the diagnosis, which of the following findings differentiate it from SLE.
A. Presence of anti C1q
B. Histopathology showing neutrophilic infiltrate rather than pleomorphic infiltrate.
C. He increased susceptibility to pyogenic infection.
D. Signs such as outer inflammation, Angioedema.
E. Arthritis, Glomerulonephritis is more common in this.

Key: D
Ref: Rook (102.19)

16. A 42 years old female, presented with the complaints of cough, and shortness of breath for the last 01 month. She is a non-smoker. On taking careful history, it was revealed that she had multiple episodes of hematuria in the last week. She had complaints of formation of itchy, erythematous, indurated plaques which persist for more than 24 hours. Which of the following is not a complication associated with this disease?
A. Myocarditis
B. Pleural and pleural effusion
C. Aseptic meningitis
D. Transverse myelitis
E. Emphysema

Key: A
Ref: Rook (102.19)

17. A 70years old male being investigated for fever, joint pains, weighloss and hematuria by medical team was referred to Dermatology opd for evaluation of skin lesions. On Examination reticulate erythema was present on legs. There were necrotic lesions on fingers and splinter haemorrhages were visible in nails Which of the following is not true about this disease?
A. 80% will have renal involvement.
B. Pulmonary haemorrhage can never be the presenting complaints.
C. Presentation may be explosive with Rapidly Progressive Glomerulonephritis.
D. Peripheral neuropathy is common.
E. MPO ANCA confers high risk of cardiovascular events.

Key: B

Ref: Rook (102.21)

18. A 70years old male referred to Dermatology opd with complaints of necrotic lesions on toes. He was having fever, malaise and joint pains for the last 3 months off and on. He also had persistent cough and dyspnea. His CT scan revealed pulmonary fibrosis. Which of the following is treatment for remission induction?

A. Azathioprine 2mg/kg/day.
B. Pulsed intravenous cyclophosphamide (15mg/kg every 2-3weeks.
C. Rituximab 375mg/m2 per week for 4weeks
D. Pulsed intravenous Methylprednisolone 1gm for 3 days
E. Oral prednisolone 1mg/kg/day.

Key: B
Ref: Rook (102.22)

19. Which of the following features differentiates MPA from EGPA?

A. Mastoidal or retro-orbital disease.
B. Nasal or paranasal sinus involvement.
C. Significant peripheral eosinophilia.
D. Non-fixed pulmonary infiltrates, cavutating nodules on CXR
E. Presence of blood, protein or red cell casts in urine

Key: E
Ref: Rook (102.22)

20. A 40 year old male patient with a colourful nature presents at your OPD with complain of palpable purpura and tender nodules on his distal lower extremities near the malleoli. On examination you also note necrotising livido reticularis. He is also tested as Hepatitis B positive. His biopsy is likely to reveal:

A. Giant cell arteritis
B. Takayasu arteritis
C. Polyarteritis nodosa
D. IgA Vasculitis
E. Cryoglobulinemic Vasculitis

Key: C
Ref: Rook (102.30)

21. What percentage of patients with the disease diagnosed in the above Question number1 are found to be affected by Hepatitis B:

A. 80-85%
B. 50-55%
C. 30-35%
D. 7-8%
E. 1-2%

Key: D

22. A 40 year old male patient with a colourful nature presents at your OPD with complain of palpable purpura and tender nodules on his distal lower extremities near the malleoli. On examination you also note necrotising livido reticularis. He is also tested as Hepatitis B negative. His biopsy reveals medium sized vasculitis. U suspect the following drug as the most closely related culprit:

A. Amoxicillin
B. Amlodipine
C. Minocycline
D. Prednisone
E. Statins

Key: C

Ref: Rook (102.30)

23. Hepatitis C infection is associated with all of the following EXCEPT:
    A. Necrolytic Acral Erythema
    B. Porphyria Cutanea Tarda
    C. Polyarteritis nodosa
    D. Mixed Cryoglobulinemia
    E. Oral Hairy Leukoplakia

Key: E

24. The mortality decreasing treatment in Kawasaki's disease is:
    A. Prednisone
    B. Paracetamol and IVIG
    C. Aspirin and IVIG
    D. Supportive care
    E. Antibiotic therapy

Key: C
Ref: Rook (102.33)

Chapter 103 DERMATOSES RESULTING FROM DISORDERS OF THE VEINS AND ARTRIES

1. A 38 years old man presented with 2 months history of multiple, bright red papule 1 to 3 mm on the trunk and abdomen. He complained of progressive extension of these lesions and mild pruritus at the affected areas. He had no family history of similar lesions, and an unremarkable medical history. Complete blood cell count and blood chemistry profile were within normal limit. What is your diagnosis?

A. Angiokeratomas
B. Blue rubber bleb nevus syndrome
C. Spider telangiectasia
D. Cherry angioma
E. Bacillary angiomatosis

Key: D
Ref: Rook (103)

2. A 70 years old male presented to skin OPD with single painless dark purple/blue papule on the lower lip, on Examination the papule is soft and compressible, he gave history of bleeding if traumatized. What is the diagnosis?

A. Pyogenic granuloma
B. Venous lakes
C. Cherry Angioma
D. Malignant melanoma
E. Angiokeratoma

Key: B
Ref: Rook (103)

3. Following is not cause of spider telangiectasia

A. Pregnancy
B. Liver disease
C. Oral contraceptives
D. Hereditary hemorrhagic telangiectases
E. Thyrotoxicosis

Key: D
Ref: Rook (103)

4. Which of the following is false regarding Angiokeratoma circumscriptum

A. Usually present on lower extremities
B. May coexist with klippel Trenaunay syndrome
C. It may b congenital
D. It may be acquired
E. May enlarge and has 15% risk of malignant potential

Key: E
Ref: Rook (103)

5. A 66 years old male presented to skin OPD with single dark purple, soft, comprehensible papule on face which often bleed if traumatized, Diagnosis of venous lake is made. Following are the treatment options except.

A. Topical antibiotic with corticosteroids
B. Surgical excision

C. Cryotherapy
D. Laser treatment (Argon, Carbon dioxide, Pulsed dye)
E. None of the above

Key: A
Ref: Rook (103)

6. 60 year old female presented with a 4 week hx of burning sensation of feet. Which was extremely painful. The pain partially relived by cold water soaks. Examination showed erythema of soles of feet which was very tender to touch. Clinical examination was normal. Pedal pulsations were normal. She had a hx of duodenal ulceration for which she took omeprazole.
Hematological investigations showed hb 12.5 g/dl, normal white cell and differential count and a platelet count of 550000. What's most likely dx?
A. Burning feet syndrome.
B. Erythromelalgia.
C. Omeprazole.
D. Peripheral neuritis.
E. Shamberg's disease

Key: B
Ref: Rook (103.6)

7. What can b cause of such complaints in above patient?
A. Idiopathic.
B. Multiple sclerosis.
C. Peripheral neuropathy.
D. Polycythemia rubra vera.
E. All of the above

Key: E

8. What could not be the treatment option for above pt?
A. Aspirin.
B. SSRIs.
C. TCAs.
D. Nifedipine.
E. All of the above

Key: D
Ref: Rook (84.10 & 103.8)

9. A 25 year old male, smoker presented with hx of pain in upper and lower limbs with intermittent claudication for past 6 months, cold extremities and gangrene at medial side of big toe. There is no h/o DM, HTN, IHD, and hyperlipidemia. What of the following are among treatment options?
A. Cessation of smoking.
B. Prostacyclin analogue.
C. Ca channel blockers.
D. Thrombolytics
E. All of the above

Key: E
Ref: Rook (103.6)

10. Which antibodies can be found in this pt?
A. Ana.
B. Anti-ds dna

C. Anti sm antibodies.
D. Anti-endothelial antibodies.
E. Anti endomysial antibodies

Key: D
Ref: Rook (103.5)

11. A 25 year old male presented with the capillary malformation of right side of his chest and right upper arm. On further examination there was a bony and soft tissue enlargement of his right upper limb. On auscultation of the involved area, no murmur was appreciated. There was no facial involvement. Most probable diagnosis is

A. Parker Weber syndrome
B. Proteus syndrome
C. Kippel- Trenaunay syndrome
D. Maffucci syndrome
E. Bannayan -Riley- Ruvalcaba syndrome

Key: C
Ref: Rook (103.25)

12. A 25 year old male presented with the capillary malformation of right side of his chest and right upper arm. On further examination there was a bony and soft tissue enlargement of his right upper limb. On auscultation of the involved area, no murmur was appreciated. There was no facial involvement. Additional features associated with this syndrome are all except

A. Syndactyly
B. Thrombosis
C. Gait abnormality
D. Heart failure
E. Midline crossing of port wine stain

Key: E
Ref: Rook (103.26)

13. A 62-year-old lady presented with swollen left lower limb since last 12 hours. Exam revealed tender erythematous swelling of her left lower limb with calf muscle tenderness. She recently had a surgery for which she was on bedrest. The treatment includes all except.

A. Low molecular weight heparin for 5 days or until INR >2 for 24 hours
B. Vitamin K analogue
C. Thrombolysis if symptoms less than 21 days duration
D. Compression hosiery with an ankle pressure
E. Above 23mm hg
F. Rivaroxaban

Key: C
Ref: Rook (103.30)

14. A 45-year-old woman presented with painful and restricted right shoulder movement from few months. On examination there were palpable painful cords bowstringing across her axilla creating a web of skin. She also had linear grooves on her right arm. She had undergone surgery for breast carcinoma eight months back. Most probable diagnosis is

A. Lymphangioma
B. Metastatic skin carcinoma
C. Mondor disease
D. Lymphangiectasia
E. cellulitis

Key: C
Ref: Rook (103.33)

15. A 55 year-old female came with history of hot and tender painful red subcutaneous lumps and streaks on her arms and abdominal walls. These lesion appears in crops. The overlying skin was normal. The underlying diseases associated with this are all us except

A. Behcet disease
B. Beurger disease
C. Systemic lupus erythematosus
D. Ca lung
E. Ca pancreas

Key: C
Ref: Rook (103.32)

16. A mother brought her 7 year old son, with complains of Telangiectasia on the child's face, neck, upper trunk, hands and feet.
They were not present at birth but he developed them during infancy.
There is no mucosal involvement and no history of bleeding. Following is true regarding his disease

A. Inherited as AD disease
B. Patient can have systemic involvement later in life
C. Inherited as AR disease
D. Presents usually in Blashkoid pattern
E. It has predilection for lower body

Key: A
Ref: Rook (103.18)

17. 45 years old female presents with complains of visible blood vessels on right lower limb. She has this condition for 4 months. They become more prominent on standing with ankle swelling.
Following is true about her disease

A. 20% of patients with this condition will develop leg ulcers in their lifetime
B. Patient can develop malignancy
C. It can complicate and cause dvt, thrombophlebitis
D. Genetic basis of disease occurs with mutations in foxc2, notch3 and tgf beta2 gene
E. Increasing age does not affect prognosis

Key: C
Ref: Rook (103.34 and 103.35)

18. 30 years old chef presents with dilated vessels on lower limb. He has this condition for 2 years. He complains of dull ache, often swelling and skin discoloration of limb and feet.
All the following is true regarding management of his disease except

A. Advice regarding weight control
B. Endothermal ablation, endovenous laser treatment of long sephanous vein
C. Ultrasound guided foam sclerotherapy
D. Surgery of the affected vessels
E. Exacerbations during pregnancy require surgical intervention immediately

Key: E
Ref: Rook (103.36)

19. A 40 year old male patient, obese, complains of swelling of legs for the last 4 years. He also has patchy hyperpigmentation of lower leg, erythema, and eczematous skin around ankles. He also complains of dull pain off and on.
All the following are true regarding pathogenesis of his condition except

A. Activated leucocytes shed L-selectin into the plasma and express members of the integrin family
B. Increased levels of activated leucocytes occur both locally and systemically

C. Proteolytic enzymes are released as inactive proenzymes
D. Vascular endothelial growth factor increases microvascular permeability
E. There is decrease level of ferritin and ferric oxide in affected skin

Key: E
Ref: Rook (103.37)

20. 50 years old female, known patient of Rheumatoid arthritis, complains of swelling of lower legs for 5 years. It becomes worse by the end of day and improves at night. She also has hyperpigmentation, itching and pain.
Following workup needs to be done except
A. Duplex ultrasonography
B. MRI venography
C. Venous plethysmography
D. Venous pressure measurement
E. RA factor

Key: E
Ref: Rook (103.40)

Chapter 104

ULCERATION RESULTING FROM DISORDERS OF THE VEINS AND ARTERIES

1. A 65 years old man presented in the opd with history of painful skin ulcer on the lateral aspect of left leg from last 3 months. On examination ulcer is 4x5cm located just above the lateral malleolus. The base of the ulcer is necrotic surrounded by black eschar. Which of the • following statement is tr
true?

A. Associated with obesity, DM, CAD
B. western lifestyle increases the risk for ulcer
C. PAD leads to tissue ischemia
D. Baloon angioplasty restores sufficient arterial inflow
E. All of the above

Key: E
Ref: Rook (104.9)

Chapter 105 DISORDERS OF THE LYMPHATIC VESSELS

1. Which of the following features indicate primarily a lymphatic cause.
   A. Persistent swelling which can be intermittent at first
   B. Oedema that does not resolve with overnight elevation
   C. A poor response to diuretic
   D. Recurrent cellulitis
   E. All of the above

Key: E
Ref: Rook (105. 6)

2. A 50 years old lady presented in the opd with history of bilateral swollen legs for last 8 months. On examination there is pigmented thickened skin. Kaposi Stemmer sign is positive. Which of the following is investigation of choice for the above mentioned patient?
   A. Lymphoscintigraphy
   B. MRI of root of limb
   C. Venous duplex USG
   D. Skin biopsy
   E. CT scan

Key: A
Ref: Rook (105.6)

3. A 50 years old man presented in the opd with history of bilateral swollen legs for last 5 months. On examination there is brown pigmentation on the lower third of leg. There is pitting edema of both legs above and below the pigmentation. There is no history of fever. CRP and LDH are in normal range. Which of the following is most likely complication?
   A. DVT
   B. Lymphorrhea
   C. Cardiac involvement
   D. Bone involvement
   E. None of the above

Key: B
Ref: Rook (105.9)

4. A 60 year old woman presented in the opd with history of bilateral swelling of lower one third of both legs for last 8 months. A diagnosis of lipodermatosclerosis was made. What is the only proven therapy for this disease?
   A. Compression therapy
   B. Antibiotics
   C. Endovenous therapy
   D. Traditional ligation and stripping of
   E. superficial veins
   F. All of the above

Key: A
Ref: Rook (105.10)

Chapter 106 FLUSHING AND BLUSHING

1. A 40 year old man presented with intermittent upper abdominal pain for 4 months, episodic hot flushes involving face and upper chest for 2 months, watery stools for 5-6 episodes per day for 1 month. His bp and cardiac evaluation was normal. Which investigation may help in reaching the diagnosis?
   A. 24 hr urine from 5-HIAA
   B. Serum tryptase
   C. 24h urinary metanephrines
   D. Bone marrow biopsy

Key: A
Ref: Rook (106.5)

2. Flush can be distinguished from blush by presence of?
   A. Localized involvement
   B. Absence of sweating
   C. More widespread involvement
   D. Circumoral pallor

Key: C
Ref: Rook (106.3)

3. Total skin blood flow during normothermic condition when body is at rest is 200-500 ml/min, this can be inc with full active vasodilation upto?
   A. 4L/min
   B. 5L/min
   C. 6L/min
   D. 8L/min

Key: D
Ref: Rook (106.1)

4. Regarding pathophysiology of flushing, which is false?
   A. External mediators include those found in food and drugs
   B. Internal mediators include substance-p, tachykinin, kalikrenin
   C. Neurally activated flushing may be aasociated with dry flushing
   D. Dry flushing is due to circulating vasoactive mediators

Ref: Rook (106.3)

Chapter 107 DERMATOSES OF THE SCALP

1. A 30 year old male presented with purulent discharge from scalp for last 3 weeks. She states that for past 3 months she developed pustules and nodules on scalp which improve with antibiotics but have worsened now. On examination scalp has multiple pustules and nodules with hair lost from summits and retained in valleys. What is the treatment of choice?

   A. Start a broad spectrum antibiotic
   B. Intralesional steroids
   C. Isotretinoin in combination with prednisolone
   D. Isotretinoin alone
   E. Acitretin

Key: C
Ref: Rook (107.8)

2. A 40 year old known diabetic patient came with thickening of skin over vertex and occipital scalp. on examination skin is thrown in anteroposterior folds. Which of the is not associated with disease?

   A. Down syndrome
   B. Acromegaly
   C. Turner syndrome
   D. Myxodema
   E. Eczema

Key: A

3. A 35 year old negro construction worker came to derma opd with complaint of boggy swelling of scalp. You perform skin biopsy which shows expansion of fatty layer with atrophy and fibrous replacement of hair follicle. How will you further plan management keeping in view course of disease?

   A. Advise CT abdomen /PET scan
   B. Advise endocrine profile
   C. Counsel patient that disease is not associated with any medical / physiological condition
   D. Advise MRI brain to look for the underlying extent of disease
   E. Measure Intraocular pressure

Key: C
Ref: Rook (107.9)

4. A 15 year old boy came to derma opd with complaint of a thick lesion growing on scalp since 2 years. On examination there is a nodule 9*6 cm, yellowish in colour with verrucous appearance. according to mother lesion was present as hairless patch since birth. You advise surgical removal of patch. All of the following can be present in aforementioned lesion except?

   A. Bcc
   B. Scc
   C. Trichoblastoma
   D. Syrningicystadenoma pappiliferum
   E. Eccrine poroma

Key: E
Ref: Rook (107.10)

5. A 36 year old male presented with painful lesions on scalp for past 4 weeks .he says that for past 6 months he is having thickening of scalp with hair loss .on examination there are superficial and deep abscesses, sinus tract formation with extensive scarring. Histopathology shows neutrophilic infiltrate around hair follicles. What is your dx?

A. Folliculitis decalvans
B. Erosive pustular dermatosis of scalp
C. Dissecting cellulitis of scalp
D. Cicatricial pemphigoid
E. Pyoderma gangrenosum

Key: 'C
Ref: Rook (107.8)

6. 25 years old male known case of epilepsy presented in derma opd with history of thick greasy yellow scales present on scalp and eyebrows for last 3 months.
On manual removal of scales perifollicular erythema is noted.
Which of the following statement is true regarding his condition?

A. Treatments is aimed to cure the condition
B. Systemic oral antifungals are first line of treatment
C. Infantile form is self-limiting improves in first year of life
D. Coal tar shampoos are cosmetically acceptable for this condition
E. Medicated shampoos containing zinc pyrithone selenium sulfhide need to be use on alternate basis for maintenances therapy.

Key: C
Ref: Rook (107.2)

7. 35 years old male presented in derma opd with history of well demarcated erythematous plaques with silvery scales present on scalp. His finger nails shows coarse pitting.
Which of the following is not the dermoscopic finding of this condition on scalp?

A. Red dots
B. Arborizing vessels
C. Globules
D. Twisted red loops

Key: B
Ref: Rook (107.1)

8. 20 years old male presented with recurrent history of yellowish greasy scales on scalp eyebrows and nasolabial folds for last 1 year. On manual removal of scale scalp is found to be moist and erythematous.
All of the following conditions are associated with increased prevalence of this skin condition except?

A. HIV
B. Parkinson disease
C. Epilespy
D. Syphilis
E. Spinal cord injury

Key: D
Ref: Rook (107.1)

9. 15 years old boy presented in derma opd with complain of localized patches of yellow coloured asbestos like scales which are binding the tufts of hair present on the scalp .when the scales are removed hairs come away and reveal moist erythematous scalp.
Which of the following is not the common cause of above condition?

A. Psoriasis

B. Tinea capitis
C. Lichen simplex
D. Eczema
E. Seborrheic dermatitis's

Key: B
Ref: Rook (107.3)

10. A 12 years sikh boy presented to OPD with history of gradual loss of scalp hair which stared initially from temporal regions & extending towards occipital regions. What is the cause of hair loss in this case
A. Alopecia aerata
B. Traction alopecia
C. Androgenetic alopecia
D. Dermatitis artefacta
E. Accidental alopecia

Key: B
Ref: Rook (107.5)

11. A 32 years female presented with symptoms of puffiness in fingers of hands & face and reduced hair growth as well as reduced sweating. On further inquiry she had long history of Raynauds phenomena.On examination, skin is taught, indirated & fix to underlying structures. She has mask like face & bird beak nose and difficulty in opening the mouth.consistent with diagnosis of disease which of following not included in differential diagnosis
A. Limited scleroderma
B. Pansclerotic morphea
C. Eiosinophilic fascitis
D. Scleromyxoedema
E. Porohyria cutanea tarda

12. A 14 years boy presented with history of frontal hair loss which progressively worsen. On examination, there are no inflammatory signs, lesional skin is thickened, indurated & slightly pallor from surrounding skin and there is marginal hyperpigmentation. What is most likely diagnosis?
A. Steriod induced atrophy
B. Lupus profundus
C. En coup de sabre
D. Actinic Lichen planus
E. Lipodystrophy

Key: C
Ref: Rook (107.6)

13. A 20 years female presented in OPD with frontal scalp hair loss. On examination, non- inflammatory, thickened, indurated & pallor plaque noted on frontal scalp extending upto tip of nose with marginal hyperpigmentation. Which of following treatment consider for this patient?
A. Potent topical/ Intralesional steroids
B. Systemic corticosteriods
C. Chloroquin
D. Surgical excision
E. All of above

Key: E
Ref: Rook (107.6)

14. A 60 year's male patient presented to OPD with history of erythematous, persistent, itchy follicular papules and boggy plaques which initially started on scalp and now on trunk & limbs. Hair loss also noted at site of skin eruption. Keeping in view the diagnosis which of following disease associated with it?

A. Mycosis fungoides
B. Discoid lupus erythematosus
C. Angiolymphoid hyperplasia
D. Verruca vulgaris
E. All of above

Key: E
Ref: Rook (107.7)

Chapter 108 DERMATOSES OF THE EXTERNAL EAR

1. A patient presented with painful nodule on helix with surrounding hyperemic skin and overlying crusting. The pain exacerbate by pressure and wind for last 2 months. What is your diagnosis?

A. Acitinic keratosis
B. Chondrodermatitis nodularis
C. Wheathring nodule of the ear
D. BCC
E. SCC

Key: B
Ref: Rook (108.9)

2. A female presented with painful ulcerated nodule on antihelix with erythema and overlying crusting for last 3months. The pain exacerbated by pressure and wind. What is first line treatment?

A. Surgical excision
B. Intralesional steroids
C. Pressure relief during sleep
D. Photodynamic therapy
E. Co2 laser

Key: C
Ref: Rook (108.9)

3. A 20 year old man presented with multiple pruritic papules and pustules on nape of neck just below the hairline. Some of them are coalescing to form plaques for last 6 months. What is the curative treatment?

A. Close shaving to nape of neck
B. Intralesional steroids
C. Topical Retinoids
D. Nd yag laser

Key: D
Ref: Rook (93.4)

4. A 45y/female presented to ENT department with c/o bluish-grey discoloration of her ears which is asymptomatic. Her past history includes backache and joint pain. She also noticed the Change in color of ear-wax to black

A. Raynaud's syndrome
B. Systemic sclerosis
C. Alkaptonuria
D. Sle

Key: C
Ref: Rook (108:10)

5. Distinctive Pendulous earlobes

A. Cutes laxa
B. Leprosy
C. Ehlers-Danlos
D. Bazex syndrome

Key: A
Ref: Rook (108-12)

6. Pseudocyst of the auricle
   - A. Lysosomal enzymes
   - B. Cytokines
   - C. LDH 4,5
   - D. Both c & d

Key: D
Ref: Rook (108.10)

7. Chondrodermatitis Nodularis chronic helius has association with
   - A. Vasculitis
   - B. Systemic sclerosis
   - C. Atopic eczema
   - D. None

Key: B
Ref: Rook (108.8)

8. A young female Presented to derma-OPD welk c/o Firm red - brown nodules at the enterance of external auditory canal. There is occasional itching as well. What could be possible diagnoses?
   - A. Gout
   - B. Angiolymphoid hyperplasia with eosiophilh
   - C. Porphyria
   - D. Dystrophic calcification

Key: B
Ref: Rook (108.12)

9. Commonest cause of Necrotizing otites externa is
   - A. Staph aureus.
   - B. Pseudomonas aeruginosa
   - C. Mycobacteria
   - D. Streptococci

Key: B
Ref: Rook (108.20)

10. Bazex- Dupré-christol syndrome.
   - A. X-linked
   - B. Basal cell carcinoma
   - C. Follicular atrophoderma
   - D. All of above

Key: D
Ref: Rook (108.12)

11. Necrotizing otites externa
   - A. Diabetes
   - B. Renal transplant
   - C. HIV
   - D. All of above

Key: D

Chapter 109 DERMATOSES OF THE EYE, EYELIDS AND EYEBROWS

1. A 60 years old man presented to opd with complaints of solid nodular lesion on lower eyelid from last 2 years. He is farmer by profession. On biopsy there are large polygonal cells with vesicular nuclei, prominent nucleoli, and overt evidence of keratinization. What is the likely diagnosis?

A. Bcc
B. Scc
C. Keratoacanthoma
D. Actinic keratosis

Key: B
Ref: Rook (109.50)

2. A 60 years old man presented to opd with complaints of solid nodular lesion on lower eyelid from last 2 years. He is farmer by profession. On biopsy there are large polygonal cells with vesicular nuclei, prominent nucleoli, and overt evidence of keratinization. Keeping in view the diagnosis what is the treatment of choice?

A. Cryotherapy
B. Cautery
C. Radiotherapy
D. Excison with addequate margins

Key: D
Ref: Rook (109.50)

3. A child presents with chronic itching, irritation and rubbing of the lids. The skin nearest to the base of the lashes shows small bluish spots .What is the causative agent?

A. Sarcoptes scabei
B. Borrelia burgdorferi
C. Syaphylococcus aureus
D. Phthirus pubis

Key: D
Ref: Rook (109.42)

4. A 3 year old boy presented to opd with one day history of rapidly spreading erythematous macules developing into flaccid vesicles and some yellow crusted lesions on right lower eyelid. He also gives history of fever. What is the likely treatment for this patient?

A. Topical antivirals
B. Topical and oral antibiotics
C. Topical steroids
D. Topical antifungals

Key: B
Ref: Rook (109.41)

5. 36 year old male presents to opd with 5 days history of painful erythematous swelling on the upper lid which subsequently points anteriorly and discharges close to the lash roots. Keeping in view the diagnosis what is the likely organism causing this disease?

A. Streptococcus
B. Syaphylococcus

C. Herpes simplex virus
D. Vzv

Key: B
Ref: Rook (109.41)

6. 36 year old male presents to opd with 5 days history of painful erythematous swelling on the upper lid which subsequently points anteriorly and discharges close to the lash roots.Keeping in view the diagnosis what is the likely organism causing this disease?
A. Streptococcus
B. Syaphylococcus
C. Herpes simplex virus
D. Vzv

Key: B

7. A 70-year-old male presented with a history of right eye redness, watering, irritation and mucoid discharge since 7 months. On slit lamp evaluation, both eyes showed localized upper lid trichiasis nasally, subepithelial fibrosis of inferior fornices. His right eye showed localized symblepharon. After investigations diagnosis of cicatricial pemphigoid was made based on clinical features, positive conjunctival biopsy and immunofluorescence.
What is the 1st line treatment of cicatricial conjunctivitis?
A. Low dose topical corticosteroids
B. Oral dapsone
C. Oral Methotrexate
D. Oral cyclophosphamide
E. IVIG

Key: A
Ref: Rook (109.33)

8. A 60 years old female patient presented in opd with the complaints of irritation, hyperamia and discharge from both eyes since 3 months. O/E of eyes, there was loss of plica, hyperaemia and shortening of the fornices.
There was no history of any chemical exposure although she was a known case of sjogren syndrome.
DIF shows linear deposition of IgG, IgA and C3 along the epithelial basement membrane zone.
What is the cause of her eye disease?
A. Pemphigus foliaceous
B. Pemphigus vulgaris
C. Mucous membrane pemphigoid
D. Paraneoplastic pemphigus
E. Pemphigus vegetans

Key: C
Ref: Rook (109.27)

9. 36 years old male patient presented with history of acute painful vesicular eruptions on the right side of his forehead. There was also involvement of the adjacent part of the face, extending up to the tip of the nose, of 2 weeks duration. There was redness, pain, and blurring of vision in his right eye. He was diagnosed as a case of HZO (right eye) and the following was added to his treatment, i.e., eye ointment acyclovir 3% five times daily as well as oral acyclovir 800 mg five times a day for 10 days.
What are the commonest ocular complications of herpes zooster?
A. Dendritiform keratopathy
B. Stromal keratitis
C. Uveitis
D. Polar bear rug cataract
E. A,B and C

Key: E
Ref: Rook (109.38)

10. 62 years old man presented to the ED with five days of increasingly blurry vision in his right eye. The blurring was associated with mild photophobia and a right-sided headache which he described as a burning pain over his forehead. The patient denied any trauma.
Ophthalmologic exam was significant for slight right-sided conjunctival irritation with no exudates or obvious corneal scarring.
Fluorescein staining yielded a 7mm branched dendritic corneal lesion. The remainder of his exam was unremarkable.
What is most likely diagnosis?
A. Herpes simplex
B. Herpes zooster
C. Behcet syndrome
D. Atopic eye disease
E. Ocular rosacea

Key: B
Ref: Rook (109.38)

11. 42 years old male patient was admitted with a chief problem of total vision loss in his left eye. The patient disclosed that he developed the gradual loss of vision in his left eye for the past 1.5 months; it was progressive and was associated with pain and redness but with no lacrimation.
MRI and brightness scan ultrasonography were performed on his eyes that suggested of endophthalmitis with dendritic involvement in the left eye. Viral DNA PCR was performed in aqueous humour sample that confirmed the presence of herpes simplex virus.
What is the most likely treatment?
A. Potent topical steroid drops
B. Oral acyclovir 400mg five times a day with topical acyclovir ointment.
C. Topical antibiotic eye drops
D. Topical lubricants
E. Oral methotrexate

Key: B
Ref: Rook (109.38)

12. The Onset of disease in Atopic Keratoconjunctivitis is:
A. 10 - 20 years
B. 5 - 15 years
C. 20 - 50 years
D. 10 - 40 years
E. None of the above

Key: C

13. The Corneal signs in Atopic Keratoconjunctivitis include ulich of the following?
A. Keratopathy
B. Pannus
C. Macroerosion
D. Herpes keratitis
E. All of the above.

Key: E

14. The onset of disease in vernal Keratoconjunctivitis is:
A. 10-20 years.
B. 5-15 years.

C. 20-50 year.
D. 10-40 years.
E. None of the above

Key: B

15. Which of the following is the associated disease in Atopic Keratoconjunctivitis?
A. Atopy and Atopic eczema
B. Herpes simplex keratitis
C. Staphylococcal lid disease.
D. Keratoconus
E. All of the above

Key: E

16. In Atopic Keratoconjunctivitis, the cytology report shows:
A. Eosinophils and mast cells
B. Eosinophils and basophils
C. Neutrophils and eosinophils
D. Neutrophils and mast cells
E. None of the above

Key: A

17. Which of the following is the associated disease in vernal Keratoconjunctivitis?
A. Keratoconus
B. Cataract
C. Atopy
D. All of the above
E. None of the above

Key: D

18. Mucous Membrane Pemphigoid is associated with ulichof the following disease?
A. Sjogren syndrome
B. Rheumatoid arthritis
C. Systemic lupus erythematosus
D. Polyacteritis nodosa
E. All of the above

Key: E

19. Which of the following are the predisposing factors in Mucous Membrane pemphigoid?
A. Drug induced pemphigoid (Pseudo Pemphigoid)
B. Steven-Johnson syndrome
C. Toxic Epidermal Necrolysis
D. Ectodermal Dysplasia
E. All of the above

Key: E

20. Differential Diagnosis of cicatrizing conjuetinits include which of the
A. Allergic Eye disease
B. Immmo Bullous disorders
C. Injection
D. Trauma
E. All of the above

Key: E

21. Which of the following is the ocular effect of Steven-Johnson syndrome and toxic epidermal Necrolysis?
    A. Corneal and conjunctival Keratinization
    B. Conjunctival scareing
    C. Retro placement of meibomian grand orifices
    D. Eutropion of upper and lower lids.
    E. All of the above

Key: E

22. Conjunctival Prophies for DIF in ocular mucous membrane pemphigoid shows the presence of:
    A. IgM, IgG, C3
    B. IgA, IgG, C3
    C. IgM, IgE, C3
    D. IgE, IgG, C3
    E. None of the above

Key: B

23. What are the principles of management of cicatrizing conjunctivitis and its ocular complicating?
    A. Treating any ocular surgace disease present
    B. Excluding and treating any secondary infection
    C. Identifying any treatment toxicity
    D. Preventing and treating fibrosis
    E. All of the above.

Key: E

Chapter 110

DERMATOSES OF THE ORAL CAVITY AND LIPS

1. A 30 yr old smoker presented to OPD anxious saying that his tongue has become increasingly red with thin white patches on it that appear on a new site every day. His mother also had the same problem. His oral hygiene appears satisfactory and he reports no drug intake or allergies. The underlying genetic association is

A. HLA B 27
B. HLA B 15
C. HLA B 11
D. HLA B 25
E. HLA DR 5

Key: B
Ref: Rook (110.14)

2. A16 yr old girl presented to the ER after developing sudden onset shortness of breath after a dental procedure. On examination swelling of the lips and face in general could be seen. Airway was secured and patient treated accordingly. The most important investigation to establish the diagnosis will be

A. Serum ige levels
B. Total eisonophil count
C. Plasma c3 levels
D. Plasma c4 levels
E. Plasma c1 levels

Key: E.
Ref: Rook (110.9)

3. A 4 yr old boy diagnosed as having atopic eczema, presents with a swelling in the oral cavity for past 3 months which is causing sleep apnea. on examination you notice a soft mass in the post 3rd of the tongue with a well demarcated mid line groove. The most likely diagnosis is

A. Lingual tonsil
B. Ingual thyroid
C. Accessory tonsil
D. Dermoid cyst
E. Lymphangioma

Key: A
Ref: Rook (110.10)

4. A 7 yr old boy presented with reticulate pigmentation, both hypo and hyper on the trunk for the past 4 months. You notice his nails show dystrophy and there is a whitish patch on the lateral surface of the tongue. The mode of inheritance in this case is

A. AD
B. AR
C. X linked recessive
D. X linked dominant
E. Sporadic

Key: C
Ref: Rook (110.12)

5. A 70 yr old diabetic presented with persistent white lesions in the mouth with foul smell and fissuring on the angles of the mouth for past 2 years. The most likely cause for her oral lesion is

A. Oral leukoleratosis
B. Hairy leukoplakia
C. Smoker's keratosis
D. Chronic mucocutaneous candiaisis
E. Underlying malignancy.

Key: D
Ref: Rook (110.17)

6. 16 years old girl, presented to derma opd with h/o white/ yellow spots over lower lip from last 2 years, these are asymptomatic but becoming more prominent with age, there is associated h/o similar genital lesion

Regarding this condition, which statement is not correct?

A. 80 percent population have them
B. Associated with rheumatic disorders
C. It's totally benign condition
D. No treatment is indicated other than reassurance
E. For extensive lesions, isotretinoin is the treatment of choice

Key: E
Ref: Rook (110.15)

7. 10 years old child brought by her mother to derma opd with c/o asymptomatic blue purple lesion on buccal mucosa, there is no associated h/o bleeding and pain

O/E it has lobulated surface, blanch on pressure and flucutant to palpate

Regarding this condition, which statement is not correct?

A. These are left alone unless causing symptoms
B. Can develop phlebolithiasis
C. Aspiration is better than biopsy
D. May be associated with posterior cranial fossa malformation
E. For small lesion, embolization is the best option of treatment

Key: E
Ref: Rook (110.15)

8. A 50-year-old male presented with history of recurrent upper lip swelling associated with fever, headache and lethargy from last 1 year. He laso had fissured tongue

Histopathology of lip showed perivascular dense pleomorphic infiltrate and small focal granulomas

Regarding treatment, which is least effective option

A. Intralesional steroid
B. Topical pimecrolimus
C. Metronidazole
D. Methotrexate
E. Azathioprine

Key: E
Ref: Rook (110.87)

9. Which of the following is not feature of Melkersson–Rosenthal syndrome

A. Scrotal tongue
B. Lymphadenopathy
C. Facial palsy of the upper motor neurone type
D. Loss of sense of taste and decreased salivary gland secretion

E. Hypoglossal nerve involvement

Key: C
Ref: Rook (110.86)

10. A 35 years old male came with complain of diffuse orofacial swelling. On examination he was unable to blow air from left cheek and dropping of corner of mouth of same side. Tongue was showing some abnormality. His HLA DR B1 was raised and HLA DRB1 03 was decreased considering diagnosis what will be his tongue finding

A. Geographic tongue
B. Ankyloglossia
C. Recurrent apthous ulcers
D. Plicated tongue
E. Hairy tongue

Key: D
Ref: Rook (110.20)

11. A 12 years old female came with backache. On examination she was short of her stature, with webbed neck, decrease sexual characteristics, high arched palate, cherubic jaw, oral keratoses, pectus excavatum. Her echo showed pulmonary stenosis. Genetic analysis showed Rasopathies. Her sister was having same features. What is your diagnosis?

A. Turner syndrome
B. Noonan syndrome
C. Jacob disease
D. Down syndrome
E. Leopard syndrome

Key: B
Ref: Rook (110.25)

12. A 38 years old female known case of sweet syndrome came with complain of pain in mouth during eating food. On examination she has multiple mucosal ulcers of 2-4mm in size located in buccal sulcus and ventrum of tongue with circumscribed margin erythematous halo and yellow floor. She has history of sane oral lesions 2-3 times in a year that usually heal within a week. No sign of scarring or fibrosis. What is your diagnosis?

A. Mikuliz ulcer
B. Sutton ulcer
C. Herpetiform Ulcer
D. Mucosal Pamphigus Vulgaris
E. Behcet syndrome

Key: A
Ref: Rook (110.29)

13. A 36 years old male known case of celiac disease came with difficulty in eating of food. On examination multiple oral ulcers with yellow base and erythematous halo located at dorsum of tongue about 15cm in size. He has frequent episodes in last 6 month. Healing take place within 20 days. Considering diagnosis all are true except

A. May heal with sacrring
B. Have increase ESR
C. Have associated with decrease plasma viscosity
D. Also known as Periadenitis mucosa necrotica recurrens
E. Healing take place in 10-40 days

Key: C
Ref: Rook (110.29)

14. A 28years old male came with difficulty in eating of food. On examination multiple oral ulcers with yellow base and erythematous halo located at dorsum of tongue about 15cm in size. He has frequent episodes in last 6 month. Healing take place within 20 days. Topical triamcinolone was applied but now not effective. Which of the following may be useful in induction of remission

A. Methotraxate
B. Nicorandil
C. Frequent smoking
D. NSAIDS
E. Thalidomide

Key: E
Ref: Rook (110.30)

15. A 30 years old male, known case of hypothyroidism, presented in emergency department with complaints of breathing difficult and swelling of face. He had similar episodes in the past for which he was given some injectable medicines but no definite diagnosis was established. This time this episode was severe. He gave history that he underwent dental extraction procedure a day before which went smooth. On examination, he had swelling of lips, mouth, face and neck region. There was no associated erythema, tenderness or any cutaneous eruption. Keeping in view the diagnosis which of the following is not a treatment option for this
Patient?

A. Tranexemic Acid
B. Danozol
C. Stanzolol
D. Ecallantide
E. ACE inhibitors.

Key: E
Ref: Rook (110.9)

16. 29 years old male referred to Dermatology opd with complaints of a lesion in mouth for the last 01 month. Its size was the same since then. On examination there was a solitary, done shaped translucent nodule. That was no bleeding or oozing from the lesion. Which of the following is true about this disease?

A. It should not be excuses as there is a risk of recurrence.
B. Superficial lesions are seen mainly in lichen planus.
C. These are common in upper labial mucosa.
D. Urgent treatment is indicated because of their malignant potential.
E. These are usually multiple, painful and do not respond to cryosurgery.

Key: B
Ref: Rook (110.61)

17. Which of the following is not a feature of Gorlin Goltz Syndrome?

A. Cleft lip and palate.
B. Taurodontia and enamel defects
C. Lingual tonsil
D. Hypodontia
E. Papillomas of oral mucosa and lips.

Key: C
Ref: Rook (110.10)

18. A 45 years old alcoholic presented in Dermatology opd with complaints of tickling sensation in mouth. He gave history of taking multiple courses of antibiotics over last few months. He was also taking a petition

pump inhibitor for acid periodic disease. On examination he had poor oral hygiene. The was blackish discoloration of posterior part of the Dorsum of the tongue. Which of the following drugs do not cause this condition?

A. EGFR inhibitors
B. Lansoprazole
C. Chlorhexidine
D. Ferrous sulphate
E. Clonazepam

Key: E
Ref: Rook (110.65)

19. A 38 year old male known case of Diabetes mellitus type 2 and inflammatory bowel disease presented with complaints of burning sensation of lips, gums and palate for the last 2 months. She feels this buying continuously throughout the day while sleeps peacefully at night whiten she is asymptomatic. This sensation relieved with intake of food. On examination of the oral cavity, there was no erythema or erosions. Sure, it's very anxious about this diagnosed as a case of burning moth syndrome. In this patient this is associated with which of these following?

A. Nutritional deficiency
B. Diabetes
C. Chronicles c Anxiety
D. Food allergy
E. Candidosis

Key: C
Ref: Rook (110.63)

20. A child presents with high grade fever for 5days, diffuse polymorphic exanthem, bilateral conjunctival injection without exudate, cracking of lips and edema of hands and feet. What additional finding / findings do u expect in this patient:

A. Lymphadenopathy usually bilateral
B. Strawberry tongue
C. Cardiac Aneurysms
D. Thrombocytosis
E. All of the above

Key: B

21. Which of the following is not a major diagnostic criterion for the disease mentioned in scenario#1?

A. Fever more than 5days
B. Cardiac Aneurysms
C. Strawberry tongue
D. Palmoplantar Erythema greater than desquamation
E. Cervical lymphadenopathy

Key: B

22. Strawberry tongue is seen in all of the following EXCEPT:

A. Scarlet Fever
B. Candidosis
C. Kawasaki Disease
D. Riley-Day Syndrome
E. Toxic Shock Syndrome

Key: B
Ref: Rook (110.72)

23. Strawberry tongue is seen in all of the following EXCEPT:
    A. Scarlet Fever
    B. Candidosis
    C. Kawasaki Disease
    D. Riley-Day Syndrome
    E. Toxic Shock Syndrome

Key: B
Ref: Rook (110.72)

24. A 39 year old patient presents with a white patch on the parakeratinized mucosa of the tongue bilaterally. On examination the lesions are corrugated with a hairy appearance. You suspect the following as possibilities EXCEPT:
    A. HIV
    B. Diabetes
    C. HAART
    D. EBV
    E. Candida

Key: B
Ref: Rook (110.74)

25. Predisposing factors to Leukoplakia include all of the following EXCEPT:
    A. Tobacco
    B. Vitamin B12 Deficiency
    C. Alcohol
    D. Beetle
    E. Syphils

Key: B
Ref: Rook (110.76)

26. A 30 years old male, known case of hypothyroidism, presented in emergency department with complaints of breathing difficult and swelling of face. He had similar episodes in the past for which he was given some injectable medicines but no definite diagnosis was established. This time this episode was severe. He gave history that he underwent dental extraction procedure a day before which went smooth. On examination, he had swelling of lips, mouth, face and neck region. There was no associated erythema, tenderness or any cutaneous eruption. Keeping in view the diagnosis which of the following is not a treatment option for this patient?
    A. Tranexemic Acid
    B. Danozol
    C. Stanzolol
    D. Ecallantide
    E. ACE inhibitors.

Key: E
Ref: Rook (110.9)

27. A 29 years old male refered to Dermatology opd with complaints of a lesion in mouth for the last 01 month. Its size was the same since then. On examination there was a solitary, done shaped translucent nodule. That was no bleeding or oozing from the lesion. Which of the following is true about this disease?
    A. It should not be excuses as there is a risk of recurrence.
    B. Superficial lesions are seen mainly in lichen planus.
    C. These are common in upper labial mucosa.
    D. Urgent treatment is indicated because of their malignant potential.
    E. These are usually multiple, painful and do not respond to cryosurgery.

Key: B

Ref: Rook (110.61)

28. Which of the following is not a feature of Gorlin Goltz Syndrome?
    A. Cleft lip and palate.
    B. Taurodontia and enamel defects
    C. Lingual tonsil
    D. Hypodontia
    E. Papillomas of oral mucosa and lips.

Key: C
Ref: Rook (110.10)

29. A 45 years old alcoholic presented in Dermatology opd with complaints of tickling sensation in mouth. He gave history of taking multiple courses of antibiotics over last few months. He was also taking a petition pump inhibitor for acid periodic disease. On examination he had poor oral hygiene. The was blackish discoloration of posterior part of the Dorsum of the tongue. Which of the following drugs do not cause this condition?
    A. EGFR inhibitors
    B. Lansoprazole
    C. Chlorhexidine
    D. Ferrous sulphate
    E. Clonazepam

Key: E
Ref: Rook (110.65)

Q30. A 38 year old male known case of Diabetes mellitus type 2 and inflammatory bowel disease presented with complaints of burning sensation of lips, gums and palate for the last 2 months. She feels this buying continuously throughout the day while sleeps peacefully at night whiten she is asymptomatic. This sensation relieved with intake of food. On examination of the oral cavity, there was no erythema or erosions. Sure it's very anxious about this diagnosed as a case of burning moth syndrome. In this patient this is associated with which of these following?
    A. Nutritional deficiency
    B. Diabetes
    C. Chronicles c Anxiety
    D. Food allergy
    E. Candidosis

Key: C
Ref: Rook (110.63)

Chapter 111 DERMATOSES OF THE MALE CENITALIA

1. A 39 years old asymptomatic male presented with staining of underclothes with blood. On examination well demarcated, glistening, moist, bright red/ brown patches involve glans and visceral prepuce with sparing of penile shaft and foreskin. What is your diagnosis?

A. Lichen sclerosus
B. zoon belanitis
C. Herpes genitalis
D. Erythroplasia of queyrat
E. Kaposi sarcoma

Key: B
Ref: Rook (111)

2. What is the pathology of above disease?

A. Epidermal attenuation with absent granular and horny layer
B. Dimond or lozenge- shaped basal cell keratinocytes e sparse dyskeratosis n spongiosis
C. Band of dermal in filtration with plasma cells
D. All of the above
E. None of the above

Key: D
Ref: Rook (111)

3. Lichen sclerosus is a common inflammatory dermatosis. Which of the following statement regarding lichen sclerosus is not correct?

A. In adults ano- genital LS is 10 times more common in men than in women
B. Autoimmune attack ECM-1 is responsible for LS.
C. HPV is present in 70% cases of childhood penile LS and 17.4% of adults.
D. Biopsy is rarely required for investigations
E. Respond well to topical corticosteroids

Key: A
Ref: Rook (111)

4. Palpable plaque with curved penis pointing to the side of the plaque is a feature of

A. Penile carcinoma
B. Condyloma acuminata
C. Hypospadias
D. Peyronie's disease
E. Lichen sclerosus

Key: D
Ref: Rook (111)

5. A 42 years old male presented to dermatology OPD for eryption on the fold of his penile prepuce, the lesion is indolent n asymptomatic., staining of the underclothes with blood has been noted by the patient. On examination well demarcated, glistening, moist, bright red/ autumn brown patches involve the glans n visceral prepuce, with soaring if the keratinized penile shaft and foreskin is observed. As his treating Dr your differential diagnosis includes all except

A. Lichen sclerosus, erosive lichen planus

B. Zoon belanitis, FDE, Contact dermatitis
C. Psoriasis, seborrheic dermatitis
D. Secondary syphilis, histoplasmosis
E. Elymphogranuloma venerum , Genital chlmydia infection

Key: E
Ref: Rook (111)

6. A 50 years old diabetic male patient presents with 1 week history of erythematous swelling of genital skin, there were black spots on scrotum. He also had high grade fever, mild to moderate pain.
He underwent surgery for repair of scrotal hernia 1 month back.
Regarding management of this patient which of the following is unlikely to be helpful
A. Surgical debridement of affected tissue
B. Broad spectrum systemic antibiotics
C. Unprocessed honey
D. High Dose systemic steroids
E. I/v immunoglobulin

Key: E
Ref: Rook (111.22)

7. 35 years old male noticed yellow sweat of his pubic area which also stained his clothes. He then noticed yellowish concretions on his pubic hair and some broken hair. He was asymptomatic.
Following is true regarding his condition
A. It is caused by different types of corynebacteria
B. It is caused by corynebacteria minutissimum
C. It is caused by superficial fungal infection
D. It is caused by group a streptococci
E. It is caused by propionibacteria

Key: A
Ref: Rook (111.22)

8. A 30 years old male patient presented in dermatology OPD with 3 years history of multiple nodules on scrotum. They were white in colour, hard in consistency, had smooth surface and there were no associated symptoms. They can arise from all the following except
A. Epidermoid cyst
B. verruciform xanthoma
C. Eccrine duct milia
D. Eccrine epithelial cyst
E. Dystrophy of dartos muscle

Key: B
Ref: Rook (111.26)

9. A 56 years old female presents with pruritis and discomfort in the vulvar region for over 6 months. On examination there were erythematous patches on labia minora. Biopsy showed epidermal thinning with absent horny and granular layers and distinctive lozenge shaped keratinocytes, dermis has plasma cell rich dence Inflammatory infiltrate,dilated blood vessels & hemosiderin. Which for the following is the first line of treatment of this patient
A. Emmolients and reassure that it is a benign condition
B. Lidocaine 5% topical
C. Emmolients and potent topical steroids
D. Topical Tacrolimus gives a very good response
E. Misoprostol and intralesional IFN alpha gives prompt response

Key: C
Ref: Rook (112.12)

10. A 40 years old male presents with 1wk history of fever, malaise, pain, erythema and swelling of genital skin especially scrotum. He has history of repeated urinary tract infections.
His plain X-ray shows soft tissue gas.
Regarding his condition, the risk factors can be all the following except

A. Diabetes Mellitus
B. Anogenital infections
C. HIV
D. Heroin addict
E. Warfarin therapy

Key: E.
Ref: Rook (111.22)

11. A 25-year-old sexually active, circumscribed male presented with multiple pigmented smooth topped warty lesions on his penis. Histopathology obtained on biopsy showed bowenoid histology with squamous intraepithelial lesion (SIL) . The HPV most commonly associated with this is

A. HPV 18
B. HPV39
C. HPV 51
A. HPV 21
B. HPV 16

Key: E
Ref: Rook (111.28)

12. A 64 year old male presented to clinic with complaint of shiny, red plaques on glance and purpeuce of his penis for one year. Histology on biopsy showed intraepithelial carcinoma. Following treatment modalities can be employed to treat the patient except

A. Topical 5 Fluorouracil 5 % cream
B. Cryosurgery
C. Topical imiquimod
D. Radiotherapy
E. MOHs micrographic surgery

Key: D
Ref: Rook (111.28)

13. A 60 year old male presented to clinic with complain of multiple urinary streams on micturition since one year. On examination he had thick scaly micaceous patches on his glands penis. Histology showed hyperkeratosis, parakeratosis, acanthosis and prolongation of rete ridges.
The following is most true about this disease

A. Variant of lichen sclerosus associated with HPV
B. Re-occurrence is uncommon
C. Metastatic spread negligible in presence of cutaneous horn
D. Variant of lichen sclerosus associated with verrucous carcinoma
E. Radiotherapy treatment of choice

Key: D
Ref: Rook (111.29)

14. A 50 year old male presented with itch , irritation, pain and bleeding with discharge from his penis from last three months. On examination an ulcerated lesion was found on his glans penis. He had preceding history of lichen sclerosus of his penis since many years.
The following is not true about this condition

A. Prognosis depends of extent of inguinal lymphadenopathy

B. It puts female sexual partners at risk of cervical cancer
C. Prognosis depends on involvement of corpus
D. Positive correlation with HPV status
E. Black men are at 18% higher risk of developing a second but I'm re-malignancy later on.

Key: D
Ref: Rook (111.31)

15. A 45 year old male presented with worsening of his chronic skin condition of 15 years. He has history of multiple discharging sinuses in his axilla, groin and intergluteal region for last 15 years. He was on Adalimumab for last few years with significant control of his disease, but he has now presented with a painful bleeding lesion on his scortum for last five months. On examination there is an ulcerated nodular lesion on his scortum with bleeding surface. The most probable diagnosis in this scenario is

A. Basal cell carcinoma
B. Kaposi's carcinoma
C. Pyoderma gangrenosum
D. Squamous cell carcinoma
E. Metastatic disease

Key: D
Ref: Rook (111.32)

Chapter 112 DERMATOSES OF THE FEMALE CENITALIA

1. A 48yrs old female presented to derma OPD with complaint of vulval itching for past 2yrs.she is diagnosed case of DM type 2 on oral hypoglycemic drugs. there was history of various treatments with creams and ointments without success. On physical examination Presence of whitish areas in left minora and majora labia, perineal and anterior perianal regions were seen. On H/P of lesions there is epidermal hyperplasia with infiltration of epidermis with cells having clear cytoplasm, large nuclei with pleomorphism and prominent nucleoli. On immunocytochemistry, CK7, CEA and PAS positive. Most likely diagnosis is

A. Bowen disease
B. Malignant melanoma
C. Lichen sclerosis
D. Extramammary Paget disease

Key: D
Ref: Rook (112.36)

2. A 50yr old female presented with complaint of itching and burning for last 3yrs.She took multiple treatments without success. On examination there are multiple moist erythematous plaques involving urethra and perianal areas. On biopsy lesion showed epidermal hyperplasia with infiltration of epidermis with clear cells which are PAS positive but diastase negative and stain with Alcian blue. Considering her diagnosis what is recurrence after Mohs micrographic surgery

A. 40%
B. 27%
C. 10%
D. 2%

Key: B
Ref: Rook (page no 112.37)

3. A 34yr old female presented with complaint of vulval itching and swelling for last 2years on and off for which she took multiple treatments buy symptoms recurred. On physical examination there is vulvovaginal erythema, excoriations are present. Thick white adherent discharge also seen. Erythema extended and also involved genitocrural folds and perianal areas. Considering her diagnosis, predisposing factors include all except

A. Pregnancy
B. DM
C. OCPs
D. High dose progesterone
E. Immunosuppression

Key: D
Ref: Rook (112.26)

4. A 59-year-old white woman presented with complaint of vulvovaginal itching and vulvar rash associated with a sensation of burning for 1½ years. On Physical examination revealed her entire vulva, perineal body, and perianal area were covered by a well-demarcated flat, atrophic and hypopigmented plaque with superficial erosions. Areas of fissuring and purpura were also present.On biopsy lesion showed epidermal thinning with flattened rete pegs. dermis is hyalinized and extravasated red cells are also present. Below

hyalinized area is a band of chronic inflammatory cells. Elastic fibers are absent in upper dermis. keeping her diagnosis in mind, commonest associated autoimmune disorder in these pts is,

A. Thyroid disease
B. Vitiligo
C. Alopecia Areata
D. Psoriasis

Key: A
Ref: Rook (112.6)

Q5. A 45yr old female with complaint of vulval itching for last 3yrs.pt also had history of discomfort and dyspareunia. On physical examination there is flat atrophic whitened plaque extended around vulval and perianal skin in figure of eight configuration. There was also erosions n fissuering were present. On H/P, thinned epidermis with flattened rete pegs n extravasation of rbcs and absence of elastic fibers in upper dermis. Considering her diagnosis, what is incidence rate of vulval SCC in Lichen sclerosis,

A. Less than 1%
B. less than 4%
C. less than 10%
D. less than 2.5%

Key: B
Ref: Rook (112.8)

Chapter 113 DERMATOSES OF PERINEAL AND PERIANAL SKIN

1. A 37 yrs old female presented with anal pain for 6 months. She described that the pain has started shortly after sitting for 40 min and was constricting in nature and moderately severe. There was no history of trauma. Aggravating factors included prolonged sitting and flatulence. She denied any hematochezia or hematuria associated with the onset of her pain. On digital rectal examination there was mild tenderness at the left side of rectal canal. Her aim is to eliminate pain during sitting. There was no observed swelling, discolouration, or deformity visualized over the gluteal or sacrococcygeal region. Lab shows mild anemia, with normal wbc and platelet count. The most likely diagnosis is

A. Anorectal abcess
B. Levator ani syndrome
C. Unspecified functional anorectal pain
D. Anal fistula

Key: B
Ref: Rook (113.32)

Chapter 114 CUTANEOUS COMPLICATIONS OF STOMAS AND FISTULAE

1. A 50 yr old man presented with a 4-month history of peristomal erythematous plaque. Because of rectal carcinoma, he had undergone rectal resection with permanent colostomy. An asymptomatic erythematous plaque appeared on peristomal skin. Examination revealed an asymptomatic well demarcated erythematous plaque with silvery white scales beneath and beyond the stoma bag. few similar lesions were also present over the extensor aspect of the limbs. Finger nails shows no abnormalities. The patient had no family history of similar lesions. Skin biopsy specimen showed moderate hyperkeratosis, parakeratosis with neutrophils, and elongated rete ridges. The granular layer was diminished. Under appliance, it will present like

A. Pustular psoriasis
B. Flexural psoriasis
C. Guttate psoriasis
D. Rupoid psoriasis

Key: B
Ref: Rook (114.4)

2. A 45 yr old male presented 6 months after he underwent an operation for tuberculosis peritonitis for which he had a small bowel resection with double end ileostomy. He was started anti tuberculous drugs. The antituberculous therapy ceased at the end of the sixth month. Now he is concerned with the appearance of stomatal prolapse that was irreducible since 6 h, with no transit disorder or other associated signs. To prevent complications, ideal spout length should be at least.

A. 5 cm
B. 10cm
C. 2 cm
A. D.8 cm

Key: C
Ref: Rook (114.2)

4. A 45 yr old women presented with painful, rapidly progressing ulcer surrounding her ileostoma site. The lesion initially appeared one week prior as a 'small papule'. Physical examination revealed an ulcer measuring 7 cm × 6 cm. It had violaceous and undermined borders. The patient had a resection of her sigmoid colonand end-ileostomy for segmental colitis. Laboratory tests were unremarkable. Tissue culture and stains were negative for infective microorganisms.
Keeping in mind the diagnosis, the next most appropriate step is,

A. Ulcer biopsy
B. Trial of topical treatment for 2 weeks before considering a skin biopsy
C. Skin biopsy with systemic treatment
D. Trial of topical treatment for 4 weeks before considering a skin biopsy

Key: B.
Ref: Rook (114.8)

5. A 55 yr old man presented with exophytic, peristomal skin lesion suspected to be peristomal dermatitis. Patient history was significant for prostate cancer. Cystoprostatectomy was done with ileal conduit urinary diversion and nephrectomy.
After 8 months, the patient presented with a 4 cm tender, flesh colored, exophytic papillomatous nodule around the ostomy site. The mass enlarged until the primary stoma site was completely occluded. Biopsy

revealed papillomatosis and massive parakeratosis with significant regular epidermal hyperplasia and vertical papillary dermal fibrosis with pallor of upper layer keratinocytes. Keeping in mind the diagnosis, appropriate treatment for this patient is

A. Systemic antibiotics
B. Surgery
C. 20 % vinegar soaks for 10 min each day
D. Systemic corticosteroids

Key: C
Ref: Rook (114.13)

Chapter 115 DERMATOSES OF PREGNANCY

1. A 30 years primigravida in her mid-second trimester developed intense pruritus. Physical examination showed multiple scratch marks and excoriated nodules on trunk, abdomen and limbs without skin dryness and erythema. No history of eczema and urticaria in childhood. Keeping in mind the diagnosis, select the most appropriate one

A. Maternal prognosis is dangerous
B. After delivery not improve
C. Condition never recurs
D. Risk of fetal distress and stillbirth
E. Obstetrics monitoring not required

Key: D
Ref: Rook (115.10)

2. A 38 years full term pregnant female presented in opd with rash associated with itching for few days. On cutaneous examination multiple papules were present over distended abdomen sparing mucosae and umbilicus while few erythematous and urticarial plaques on upper thighs. No any previous history of tense bulla. Liver function tests were normal except elevated ALP. Immunofluorescence studies were negative. What would be the most appropriate management in this case?

A. Early labor induction+topical steroids+emollients
B. Topical steroids with Azathioprine
C. Emollients with Calcineurin Inhibitors
D. Antihistamines alone
E. Plasma exchange

Key: A
Ref: Rook (115.13)

3. A 26 years pregnant female in her third trimester referred from gynecology department having pruritic eruption on neck, upper limb and lower limbs. On cutaneous examination there were multiple erythematous excoriated papules and few scaly patches associated with generalized skin dryness. Immunofluorescence studies were negative. Serum IgE levels were moderately elevated. LFTs were normal. What would be the second line treatment of this patient?

A. Emollients
B. Steroids
C. Antihistamine
D. Phototherapy
E. None of the above

Key: D
Ref: Rook (115.16)

4. A 23 year old primigravida at 37 weeks of gestation presented with a 1 week history of severely pruritic erythematous papules and plaques beginning on the abdomen with sparing of umbilicus and subsequently involving buttocks and thighs. Physical examination showed polymorphic,erythematous papules and confluent plaques with targetoid lesions on the abdomen, buttocks and thighs.
What is the disease course in this case?

A. It causes fetal distress and low birth weight
B. Its causes cutaneous involvement on newborn
C. Lesions are self-limiting and the disease tends not to recur; the exception being in a multiple pregnancy
D. Lesions are self-limiting and the disease tends to recur in next pregnancy with more severity
E. It causes preterm labor

Key: C
Ref: Rook (115.13)

5. A 30-year-old woman presented with a widespread, intensely pruritic eruption within abdominal striae, spreading to the inferior extremities and buttocks, with no periumbilical involvement. The eruption had appeared 1 week postpartum.
What is the fate of rash?
A. Rash resolves within 1 week
B. Rash appears at postpartum and resolves after 6 months
C. The rash usually resolves within 4–6 weeks independently of delivery.
D. This rash only disappears after treatment
E. The rash appear with more severity in subsequent pregnancy

Key: C
Ref: Rook (115.12)

6. A 22 year old primigravida presented with complaints of itching at 20 weeks which further progressed to hive like rashes over abdomen around umbilicus and later spreading on to arms and thighs within a week, not subsiding with antihistamines.
At 22 weeks patient started having intense itching along with tense fluid filled vesiculobullous lesions. Facial and mucosal membranes are spared.
What is the effect on fetus of this disease?
A. IUGR
B. Fetal death
C. Small for date babies
D. Fetal hypoxia
E. Polyhydramnios

Key: C
Ref: Rook (115.14)

7. A 25-year-old female presented with a 2 weeks history of skin lesions. Initially, she noticed erythema and highly-pruriginous bullous lesions in her abdomen. Extension to her back, upper and lower extremities was noted sequentially. The patient was 24 weeks pregnant.
Skin examination revealed multiple, disseminated, symmetrical and sharply defined 0.5-1.5 cm urticarial plaques, erythematous erosions and clear fluid-containing tense vesicles and bullae. They coalesced in plaques.
Direct immunofluorescence of perilesional skin shows linear C3 deposition along the dermo-epidermal junction. All of the following is treatment of this disease EXCEPT:
A. Topical steroids
B. Prednisolone
C. Ciclosporin
D. Intravenous immunoglobulin
E. Azathioprine

Key: C
Ref: Rook (115.15)

8. A 29 year old multiparous female, 17 weeks pregnant, reported a 2-month evolution of pruritic papules on her lower back. She had similar episodes in her previous pregnancies (G3 P2 A0) responding to treatment. Her first child is suffering from atopic eczema.
Physical examination revealed erythematous papules on trunk and limbs with severe dryness. All of the following is treatment of this disease EXCEPT:

A. Topical steroids
B. Prednisolone
C. Narrow band UVB therapy
D. Plasma exchange
E. Azathioprine

Key: D
Ref: Rook (2115.16)

9. Mouth & genital ulcers with inflamed coutilope syndrome include

A. Relapring polychondritis + Reiters
B. Relapring polychondritis + Behcet
C. RA + Bechcet
D. RA + Behcet + Reiters
E. None of the above

Key: B

10. Cord within the penis curative on erection, rosary beads denote which of the following disease?

A. Peyronie disease.
B. lichen sclerosis
C. Phimosis
D. syphilitic gumme
E. None of the above

Key: A

11. Trichamycosis pubis is caused by

A. Trichomonas
B. Shepkocown
C. Corynebacterium spp
D. Herpes gentalis.
E. None of the above.

Key: C
Ref: Rook (111.15 - 111.30)

12. A patient presents with multiple hand, smooth white papules and nodules on the scrotum. There is history
of secondary infections too. What is diagnosis?

A. Mucoid cysts
B. Scrotal calcinosis
C. Median raphe cysts
D. Genital work
E. None of the above

Key: C

13. A patient presents with itching, pain and ulceration on shaft of penis. There was long history of dysuria and whitish discoloration. What will be the most probable diagnosis?

A. Syphilis
B. Behcet disease
C. Lichen sclerosis
D. Lichen planus
E. Penile squamous cell carcinoma

Key: E

Chapter 116 DERMATOSES OF THE NEONATE

1. A father brought her 2 months old baby boy in opd with complaints of periorbital rash since birth. well defined annular erythematous rash was also present on other photoexposed sites. DIF was positive and showed igG, igM and complement deposition at DEJ and around blood vessels. keeping in mind the diagnosis, how will you treat???

   A. With frequent use of emollients
   B. With mild topical steroid
   C. No treatment
   D. With Pulse dye laser

Key: C
Ref: Rook (116.13)

2. A 29 year old pregnant female in her 2nd trimester referred by gynae dept to derma opd with an anomaly scan. Cutaneous examination is unremarkable but anti Ro antibodies were positive. she is worried about the condition of her baby. How will you counsel the mother???

   A. It is self-limiting
   B. Associated with structural cardiac defects
   C. High dose steroids will be required in case of heart failure
   D. All affected infants require pacemaker

Key: C
Ref: Rook (116.13)

3. New born baby presented in derma opd, with his father, having urticarial papules on the body. few blisters were also seen. Baby was also pre-mature. Mother also had history of urticated plaques and blisters in the peri umbilical region in her last trimester and was treated with oral steroids. Keeping in mind the diagnosis, which is appropriate:

   A. DIF remains abnormal for 3 months
   B. Risk in subsequent pregnancies
   C. Spontaneous resolution over 3 months
   D. No risk of adrenal insufficiency in a baby

Key: B
Ref: Rook (116.11)

4. A mother brought her 5 day old baby girl in opd and was concerned about skin condition of her new born. On examination, there was reddish brown atrophic lesion on side of neck with wrinkling of overlying skin. Histopathology showed atrophic epidermis and spindle cell proliferation in dermis. CD34 and factor XIII was also positive. What is the most likely diagnosis??

   A. Focal dermal hypoplasia of goltz
   B. Atrophic dermatofibrosarcoma protuberans
   C. Medallion like dermal dendrocyte hemartoma
   D. Anetoderma of prematurity

Key: C
Ref: Rook (116.11)

5. A 6 month pregnant female presented in derma opd with flat pigmented macule on arm. According to her, it's increasing in size and changing colour. You performed dermoscopy, which showed atypical network and structureless area at the periphery. How will the disease manifest in a new born?

A. Ulcerated plaque
B. Nodular skin lesion
C. Atypical naevi
D. No manifestation

Key: B
Ref: Rook (116.14)

6. A 9 months old male baby presented in opd with multiple pustules for few days. Physical examination showed few vesicles on scalp, trunk, palms, and wrists while multiple papules and pustules over fingers and ankles sparing flexures associated with intense pruritus. Similar lesions were also occurred at the age of 6 months which were resolved in 2 weeks. Tzanck smear showed no giant keratinocytes. Smear of a pustule showed eosinophils. Bacterial culture was negative. DIF negative. What would be the most likely diagnosis?
A. Eosinophilic pustulosis
B. Miliaria
C. Infantile acropustulosis
D. Transient pustular melanosis
E. Herpes simplex

Key: C
Ref: Rook (116.8)

7. A newborn baby developed lesions on face, neck and back. On cutaneous examination there were multiple pigmented macules and scattered flaccid pustules of 1-3mm size over forehead, neck and back without erosions, purpuric papules, urticarial plaques, hairs, nails and mucosae changes. Some were ruptured and crusted. Smear of a pustule contents revealed neutrophils while bacterial and viral cultures were negative. Keeping in mind diagnosis which would be the most appropriate management.
A. No treatment
B. Potent topical steroids under occlusion
C. Topical Calcineurin inhibitors
D. Oral dapsone
E. Sodium chromoglycate

Key: A
Ref: Rook (116.7)

8. 3 day old baby boy developed multiple erythematous papules with pustules on top of them within the last one day involving the trunk and proximal limbs. The patient has no fever, toxemia or abnormalities in laboratory investigations. You decide to perform a test to help to differentiate between its closest differential. Which of the following will be that test?
A. Eosinophilia
B. Neutrophilia
C. Smear of pustules showing neutrophils
D. Smear of pustules showing eosinophils
E. Smear of pustules showing gram positive cocci

Key: D
Ref: Rook (116.5)

9. 1 year baby boy presents with intensely itchy, 1–4 mm vesicopustules present on the soles and sides of the feet and palms for the last 1 month. Mucosa is spared and laboratory examination is within normal limits. The baby is irritable due to constant itching. Considering the prevalence of the disease in our country, what is the treatment that should be prescribed?
A. Topical mild steroids for 1 month
B. Potent topical steroid for 1 week

C. Topical permethrin 5%
D. Oral antihistamines
E. Only topical emollients

Key: C
Ref: Rook (116.8)

10. 6-month-old baby girl presents with 1–3 mm flaccid, superficial, fragile pustules, with no surrounding erythema. They resolve spontaneously leaving post inflammatory hyperpigmentation. The baby girl was otherwise well and her laboratory investigations are within normal range. You decide to proceed with a skin biopsy to confirm the diagnosis. Which of the following will be true regarding her management?

A. Lesions may persist for 3 months
B. Topical steroids is the treatment of choice
C. Skin biopsy would reveal subepidermal blistering
D. Smears of pustular content will show predominant eosinophils
E. Hyperpigmented macules persists for many years

Key: A
Ref: Rook (116.7)

11. Which of following is the most important differentiating feature between miliaria pustulosis and erythema toxicum neonatorum?

A. Age of onset
B. Level of intra epidermal collection of inflammatory infiltrates
C. Type of inflammatory infiltrate
D. Response to topical steroids
E. Recurring course

Key: C
Ref: Rook (116.6)

12. A 30 year old lady develops vescicular rash over her entire body along with fever a few days before her delivery, tzank smear shows acantholysis and giant cells. How will you manage newborn baby?

A. Oral aciclovir
B. I/v aciclovir and zoster immunoglobulin
C. Topical aciclovir
D. Live atenuated vacine

Key: B
Ref: Rook (25.26)

13. A 28 year pregnant lady in her last trimester presented with high grade fever, diarrhea, vomiting and delirium. On physical examination she had minute pustules arising on an acutely inflamed areas over flexures as well as trunk, extending centrifugally and forming plaques. Following are the fetal risk except?

A. Stillbirth
B. Neonatal death
C. Fetal abnormalities
D. Neonatal jaundice to

Key: D

14. Regarding skin tumors in pregnancy, what is true?

A. Pre-existing naevi my decrease in size
B. Transplacental metastasis spread of melanoma can occur
C. Ct scan is preferable over mri for melanoma diagnosis
D. Melanoma may have dec in breslow thickness in pregnancy

Key: B
Ref: Rook (115.7)

15. A 5 years old male child, known case of nephrotic syndrome presented to emergency room with fever, agitation and some rash on body. On examination, widespread eroded, erythematous plaques were present more commonly on face, axillae and genitalia but also on trunk, buttock and limbs. Some superficial bullae were also present along with impetiginized crusting around nose and mouth. Parents described this rash initially as very painful which started as macular erythema and edema on face and then became widespread. Labs were normal except deranged RFT's and raised ESR.
Regarding management of this patient, which among the following is not true?

A. Patient will be more comfortable, if lesions are dressed.
B. Penicillinase resistant penicillin analogues are used as first line treatment.
C. In severe cases, drugs can be used intravenously.
D. Systemic corticosteroids can be given, once initial infection settles down.
E. Appropriate compensation for heat and fluid losses should be made.

Key: D
Ref: Rook (116.24)

16. A 7 days old premature and low birth weight male neonate brought by his parents to skin opd with complaints of redness and discharge from umbilical stump. On examination there was periumbilical erythema, edema and purulent malodorous discharge from umbilical stump along with tenderness. He was febrile and tachypnic.
Total leukocytes count was also mildly raised. Rest of Examination and investigations were normal.
Regarding complications in this patient, which among the following is not true

A. Cellulitis
B. Tetanus
C. Diphtheria
D. Necrotizing fasciitis
E. Pneumonia

17. Level of blockage in Miliaria crystalline

A. At mid epidermal
B. At stratum corneum
C. Dermal-epidermal
D. All of above

Key: B

18. Miliaria may be associated with

A. Hyponatraemia
B. Hypernatraemia
C. Hyperglycemia
D. Hypoaldosteronism

Key: B

19. A 1 month old baby Presented with c/o erythematous papulovesicular rash on face upper trunk,1-4 mm in diameter on macular erythema background. On H/P, focal areas of spongiosis & spongiotic vesicles are seen which contain PAS +ve plug most likely Dx?

A. Miliaria Crystallina
B. Miliaria rubra
C. Miliaria profunda
D. Periporitis

Key: B

20. Miliaria Crystallina can be distinguishable from herpes simple by
   A. Lack of background erythema
   B. Absence of inflammatory cells
   C. Both a|& b
   D. None of above

Key: C

21. A 7 month old baby boy presented with c/o recurrent crops of intensely itchy vesicopustules, appear on soles & sides of feet and on plans. No Mucosal lesion seed-healed by macular post inflammatory hyperseguit T/m of choice in this in Disease
   A. Topical potent CS
   B. Dapsone
   C. a+b
   D. Antibiotics

Key: C

22. A premature male baby Presented in emergency with c/o multiple, extensive erosions along with scattered vesicles & bullae, affecting 75% body surface on trunk & limbs, Hands & feet are spand. On H/P, Spongiosis, epidermal necrosis, dermal haemorrhage & neutrophils deep dermlly. Scarred areas hang & dermal collagen & absence of eccrine sweat glands. Dx is
   A. Eb
   B. Bullous icthyosiform erythema
   C. Congenital erosive, & vesicular dermatosis healing with vesicular
   D. Infective blisters scarring

Key: C

23. Association of Congenital erosion and vesicular dermatosis healing with reticulated supple scarring include all except
   A. Preterm Birth
   B. Nail Dystrophies
   C. Neurological disorders
   D. Nose complications

Key: D

24. Anetoderma of prematurity seen in babies born between
   A. 24th & 29th wk of gestation
   B. 25th & 28th wk of gestation
   C. More than 27th wk.
   D. less than 20th wk

Key: A

25. Neonatal lupus Erythematosus is associated with maternal Autoantibodies include
   A. Ro. SSA
   B. La. SSB
   C. a+b
   D. U, RNP
   E. all of above

Key: E

26. Predisposing factors for Sub cutaneous fat necrosis of newborn include all accept.
   A. Birth asphyxia

B. Maternal Diabetes
C. Maternal pre eclampsia
D. Hyperthermia

Key: D

27. A preterm baby presented with c/o hardening of skin starts on buttocks, thighs and extends rapidly & become generalized during 1st wk of life. O/E skin hard, cold & Yellowish While in colour ē purplis mottling. On H/P radially arranged needle shaped clefts in adipocytes. Most likely Dx.
 A. Neonatal cold Injury
 B. Sclevema Neunaterum
 C. Subcutaneous fat necrosis
 D. Primary lymphoedema

Key: B

28. Best options for treatment of sclerema neonatorum include
 A. Repeated Exchange 2x
 B. IV Immunoglobulin
 C. Rituximab
 D. A+b
 E. All of above

Key: D

29. Lethal autosomal recessive Nev. Lasxora Syndrome characterized by following features except
 A. Collodion membrane
 B. IUGR
 C. CNS Disorders
 D. Smooth muscle Disorders
 E. All of above

Key: D

Chapter 117 DERMATOSIS AND HAEMANGIOMAS OF INFANCY

Q1. Which of the following virus is associated with exanthem subitum?
- A. HHV-6
- B. HHV-8
- C. EBV
- D. HSV-1
- E. HSV-2

Key: A
Ref: Rook (117.6)

Q2. A 2-year old male patient presented with history of high grade fever which lasted for 3 days. After which there was development of fine, lacy, macular erythema on the neck and trunk along with occipital lymphadenopathy. Keeping in mind the most likely diagnosis, how long does it take for the rash to disappear?
- A. 12 hours
- B. 24 hours
- C. 36 hours
- D. 48 hours
- E. 72 hours

Key: D
Ref: Rook (117.6)

Q3. Which of the following virus is associated with exanthem infantum?
- A. HHV-6
- B. HHV-7
- C. HHV-8
- D. Parvovirus B19
- E. Coxsackie B

Key: D
Ref: Rook (117.6)

Q4. An infant presented with history of hit, bright red cheeks. After few days, there was a reticulate rash over the limbs and trunk along with palmoplantar erythema. Keeping in mind the most likely diagnosis, how long does it take for the rash to disappear?
- A. 3 days
- B. 5 days
- C. 7 days
- D. 10 days
- E. 14 days

Key: C
Ref: Rook (117.6)

Q5. Which of the following is most commonly associated with hand, foot, mouth disease?
- A. Coxsackie A
- B. Coxsackie B
- C. Enteroviruse 71

D. Parvovirus B19
E. HHV-6

Key: A
Ref: Rook (117.7)

Q6. A 5 day old newborn baby presented in the opd with history of small pearly white bumps, predominantly on nose since birth. The lesions are multiple in number not associated with any erythema. Which of the following statement is true keeping in mind the above mentioned scenario.

A. The lesions are common and harmless
B. Epstein pearls and Bohn nodules can also be associated
C. Heals spontaneously within a few weeks after birth
D. Less frequent in children with low birth weight
E. All of the above

Key: E
Ref: Rook (117.13)

Q7. A 6 months old boy presented in the dermatology opd with history of papuleson his heels since birth. On examination the lesions were bilateral symmetrical, painless according to the parents, flesh colored. The lesions have not changed over the past few months. Which of the following statement is not true regarding the above scenario?

A. They may occur in 40% of infants
B. They are often named as plantar fibromatosis of heel
C. The papules are large and Asymptomatic
D. Pizogenic pedal papules have similar appearance
E. None of the above

Key: D
Ref: Rook (117.14)

Q8. A 12 months old boy presented in the opd with history of single cutaneous nodule on left heel for last 3 months. The mother of the child had twin pregnancy through C section and birth weight of the baby was less than normal due to prematurity. The child developed i jaundice on 2nd day of life for which he was pricked several times on heel to monitor bilirubin level. On examination, there is a single calcified nodule, approximately 2mm in diameter, non-tender. Serum calcium and phosphate level is normal. Which of the following statement is not true regarding the above-mentioned scenario?

A. Natural resolution may occur in a few days
B. In older children they may cause pain on pressure while walking
C. Arise from epidermal implantation through trauma
D. Less risk in healthy infants
E. All of the above

Key: A
Ref: Rook (117.14)

Q9. A 7 months old boy presented in the opd with history of red brown papules on face for last 3 months. According to the mother the lesions were first smooth pink bumps but later developed a yellowish-brown hue, non-tender and does not bleed on touching. Which of the following eye finding is not associated to the condition?

A. Spontaneous hyphema
B. Glaucoma
C. Pterygium
D. Cataract
E. Uveitis

Key: C

Ref: Rook (117.14)

Q10. A 7 months old infant presented with napkin rash for last 2 months. On examination of scalp there was redness and scaling. The greasy erythematous scales were also present on face axilla and diaper area. There were few yellow brown scaly papules and pustules present on trunk. Which of the following statement is not true?

A. Prognosis depends on age and organ involvement
B. Skin biopsy is needed to confirm the diagnosis
C. Children less than 2 years of age with LCH have mortality 40 to 50%
D. Disease limited to skin only may require aggressive treatment
E. When more than one organ is damaged chemotherapy is considered

Key: D
Ref: Rook (117.15)

Q11. A 12 month old boy presented with multiple ecchymotic and targetoid purpuric lesions on his face, ear and limbs which developed rapidly over last 48 hours. On examination he had odema of his limbs and face. Mother also gives history of mild fever which he developed after his routine vaccination of MMR two days back.

The following is true about this condition

A. Joint involvement is common.
B. Treatment comprises of IV immunoglobulins.
C. Resolution occurs within 1 week.
D. Reoccurrence is common feature
E. Perivascular IgA deposits on DIF.

Key: E
Ref: Rook (117.9)

Q12. A 5 month old infant was bought in by his mother with history of fever from 8 days which was not getting relieved by antipyretic. On examination he had erythematous swollen hands and feet, red cracked lips alongwith cervical lymphadenopathy.

The following factors predict poor response to treatment in this disease except

A. Age above one year
B. Low heamoglobin
C. High CRP
D. Peripheral blood eosinophilia > 4%
E. Low serum albumin level

Key: A
Ref: Rook (117.10 and 10.33)

Q13. A nine month old child was brought in by his mother due to profuse eruption of deep red itchy papules on on his buttocks, thighs, knees and cheeks for the last three days. On examination axillary and inguinal lymphadenopathy was appreciated. The child is fully vaccinated upto his age and he received his last recommended vaccination dose 4 days back.

The following is true for this condition

A. Associated with polio vaccination
B. Eruption fades in 2 to 8 weeks
C. Associated with high ESR
D. Treatment is with systemic steroids
E. Re-occurrence is frequent

Key: B
Ref: Rook (117.11 and 25.89)

Q14. A 10 month old boy presented with an itchy erythematous paulopustular rash on his scalp and limbs for the last five days. Mother gives history of similar rash 2 to 3 times in last two months which resolved by its self. The child on examination is otherwise healthy.
The following is true about histopathology of this disease except.

A. Perifollicular and periappendigeal infiltrate in lower dermis
B. Infiltrate is composed of eosinophils
C. Infiltrate is composed of neutrophils and mononuclear cells
D. Eosinophillic flame figures between collagen Bundles may be seen
E. Pustular lesions show intra follicular accumulation of Eosinophils

Key: A
Ref: Rook (117.11 and 116.5)

Q15. A mother of a 2 months old infant born with a history of a red colour birth mark over face, scalp n neck, now brought him with the complains of increasing size of that red plaque, dandy-walker cysts and some eye abnormalities on the corresponding eye. Mother z worried after the cardiac workup of child, which shows coarctation of aorta.
In regards with above findings, what could be the probable diagnosis of this child?

A. portwine stain
B. PHACES Syn
C. sturge weber syn
D. spitz naevus
E. bean syn

Key: B
Ref: Rook (117.20)

Q16. A 2 n half month old child presented to u with hepatomegally and high output cardiac failure.u/s shows a single hepatic haemangioma. There are no cutaneous features and the patient z asymptomatic.
Which of the following is correct regarding this condition?

A. this z a low flow lesion
B. GLUT- 1 positive
C. GLUT- 1 negative
D. VEGFR has no role in it

Key: C
Ref: Rook (117.21)

Q17. Haemangiomas usually have an excellent prognosis, but if it z periocular infantile haemangioma, then all of the following complications can occur except?

A. Cataract
B. Astigmatism
C. Amblyolia
D. Permanent visual loss

Key: A
Ref: Rook (117.22)

Q18. A 1 month old infant presented to you with a faint telangiectatic patch over the forehead and cheek,which rapidly becomes red and raised in few weeks, u perform biopsy and immunohistochemistry of this lesion to distinguish from other vascular anomalies.the child's immunohistochemistry z positive for ?

A. Factor Vlll, CD31 and von wilbrand
B. Factor X, CD33, and von wilbrand
C. Plasminogen, CD 56 and von wilbrand
D. Factor Vlll, CD 36, vonwillbrand

Key: A

Ref: Rook (117.18)

Q19. The mother brought a 2 month old infant to you with a red coloured, raised plaque overhead n neck area and upper chest. The plaque z rapidly growing in size and causing disfigurement and distortion of the structures. multiple medical treatments tried, but failed. now pt has also developed congestive cardiac failure which one of the following z best treatment options for this child?

A. i/L steroids
B. Propranolol
C. Timolol maleate gel
D. Surgery and embolization
E. PDL

Key: D
Ref: Rook (117.22 & 117.23)

Q20. A 10 month old male infant presented with tachycardia and fever from last eight days. On examination he had red cracked lips, conjunctival injection and acral odema with widespread rash.
Which statement is true regarding treatment of this condition?

A. IV Immunoglobulin 4g/ kg over 12 hours in a single dose.
B. IV immunoglobulin 2g/ kg over 10 hours
C. IV immunoglobulin 2g/ kg over 10 hours with Aspirin 100 mg /kg/day till fever settles than reduced.
D. IV immunoglobulin 2g/ kg over 12 hours with Aspirin 100 mg /kg/day till fever settles than reduced.
E. Aspirin 100 mg/kg/ day for 6-8 weeks.

Key: D
Ref: Rook (117.10 and 102.33)

Q21. 12 months old female infant was brought by her mother with 4 days history of fever, malaise and irritability. She also developed erythematous eruption which was widespread but more so in her axillae and groin which rapidly progressed to blisters. Nikolsky was positive. Her most of the body surface was tender as she became irritable when touched.
Which of the following is incorrect regarding disease course and Prognosis?

A. It usually settles within few wks when treated with appropriate systemic antibiotics
B. Localised form of disease may be prolonged with episodes of relapse over several months
C. In adults mortality rate is higher up to 60 percent
D. Generalized form of disease is considered to be more severe
E. When treated with appropriate antibiotics, it tends to improve after 8 to 10 wks of treatment

Key: E
Ref: Rook (117.7 and 26.28)

Q22. A mother brought her 7 month old male infant to dermatology OPD. Baby had 10 days history of developing erythematous rash over groin region. There were erythematous macules and papules on groin extending upto thighs but skin folds were not involved. Mother was using cloth diaper for the baby.
Regarding treatment which of the following should not be used in treatment of this patient

A. Frequent use of Emmolients
B. Mild topical corticosteroids
C. topical antifungal
D. potent topical corticosteroids
E. Zinc oxide containing ointment

Key: D
Ref: Rook (117.3)

Q23. A 6 month old female infant was brought to dermatology OPD with rash in peri anal area for 1 month. On examination, she had shallow punched out ulcers in the peri anal area and surrounding erythema and erythematous rash in groin. Rash started in the groin area and later developed peri anal ulcers. Mother was using cloth diapers for the baby.
What is the diagnosis?

A. Napkin dermatitis
B. Jacquet Dermatitis
C. Infantile gluteal Granuloma
D. Infantile Psoriasis
E. Seborrhoeic dermatititis

Q24. A mother bought her 13 months old female baby with 3 days history of fever, malaise being irritable, along with widespread erythematous skin. Skin was peeling off in sheets. There were blisters in axillae and nikolsky was positive. Skin was tender to touch and she became irritable and started crying on touching.
Which of the following in not correct regarding management of the disease

A. Parenteral penicillinase resistant antibiotics should be used as first line therapy
B. Clindamycin may be used in combination with rifampicin or tetracycline
C. Parenteral vancomycin if MRSA suspected
D. Parenteral tobramycin if MRSA suspected
E. Administration of Corticosteroids will help in quick and early recovery.

Key: E
Ref: Rook (117.7)

Q25. A 3 month old female was brought to dermatology OPD with 4 weeks history of non-healing rash in groin area. Mother was using cloth diaper. The rash initially started in groin area and after few days she developed punched out ulcers in the peri anal area.
Regarding management of this patient, which of the following is not correct?

A. use of emmolients
B. Mild topical corticosteroids
C. Topical antifungal
D. frequent diaper change
E. Use of wet wipes for cleaning diaper area

Key: E
Ref: Rook (117.4)

Chapter 118 BENIGN CUTANEOUS ADVERSE REACTIONS TO DRUGS

1. A 15 yr opd boy presented with an erythematous papular rash on the body for the past 12 hours. On examination you notice sharply demarcated erythema over the gluteal region involving the inguinal area and a papulopustular eruption over both the axillae with intense erythema. He is hemodynamically stable and only reports using antibiotic for an upset stomach few days back. The most likely diagnosis is

A. AGEP
B. SCPD
C. SDRIFE
D. D Acrodermatitis enteropathica
E. Flexural psoriasis

Key: C
Ref: Rook (118.6)

2. A 33 yr old complained of periorbital swelling and a maculopapular facial rash with oral ulceration accompanied by fatigue and arthalgias after initiation of hydrazaline by his gap to control his blood pressure. The culprit gene defect in his case is

A. HLA-DR4
B. HLA DQB3
C. HLA B27
D. HLA B4
E. HLA DQB1.

Key: A
Ref: Rook (118.10)

3. In a suspected case of lichenoid drug eruption, the most distinguishing feature between lichenoid drug eruption and lichen planus is

A. abundance of lymphocytic infiltrate
B. higher freq of necrotic keratinocytes
C. basal vacoular changes
D. pigmentary incontinece
E. compact hyperkeratosis

Key: B
Ref: Rook (118.10)

4. A 56 year old newly diagnosed hypertensive patient presents to skin opd with intensely itchy lesions on the dorsum of hands and lower legs for 1 week. On examination small polygonal papules and plaques are seen. Oral mucosa, genitals and nails are normal. The most likely drug responsible for her rash is

A. ACE inhibitor
B. Beta blocker
C. ARB
D. Methyldopa
E. Thiazide diuretic

Key: E.
Ref: Rook (118.10)

5. A 13 year old boy presented with an extensive rash distributed symmetrically over the arms and legs. On examination, multiple shiny papules were seen also exhibiting koebners phenomenon. The oral mucosa showed a white lacy network inside the buccal mucosa. Nails were normal. He denied any systemic symptoms at present but gave history of sore throat for which he took a macrolide prescribed by his GP. The most likely cause of his rash is

A. lichen nitidus
B. lichen anylodosis
C. lichen simplex chronicus
D. lichen planus
E. lichenoid drug eruption

Key: D
Ref: Rook (118.10)

6. A 40 yr old man came to our opd with sharply defined oval dusky violaceous plaques. Sone of these plaques evolve to become bullae involving the trunk and few lesions were present on limbs. Mucosae, palms and soles were spared. On probing history, he told that he had toothache for which he was taking some NSAID. Keeping the diagnosis in mind what is the time frame for developing such lesions after taking drug?

A. 1 to 2 days
B. 1 to 2 weeks
C. 1 to 2 months
D. 30 min to 8 hrs
E. 5 to 30 min

Key: D
Ref: Rook (118.12)

7. A 35 yrs old lady taking tetracyclines for acne treatment came to u with violaceous coloured well defined eruption mainly involving genitals. Some of these lesion progress to form bulla. She told that she had taken first dose of her drug in the morning. Regarding the pathogenesis of disease which cells of immune system are culprit in development of such lesions?

A. CD 4 T cells
B. CD 8 T cells
C. B cells
D. Regulatory T cells
E. Eosinophils

Key: B
Ref: Rook (118.2)

8. A 50 yrs old male came to our opd with sudden eruption of monomorphic papules and pustules involving the face, neck, chest and back. He told u that he had pulmonary tb for which he was taking ATT from 3 months. Which one of the ATT Drugs least responsible for such eruption?

A. Isoniazid
B. Rifampicin
C. Ethionamide
D. Pyrazinamide
E. None of the above

Key: D
Ref: Rook (118.12)

Chapter 119 SEVERE CUTANEOUS ADVERSE REACTIONS TO DRUGS

1. A 30 yrs. old pregnant lady came to u with history of eruption of erythematous plaques studded with pustules involving the major flexures, inframammary and inguinal folds. Mucosa were spared. On further history she told that she was epileptic since childhood and his doctor has shifted her to new drug due to pregnancy. She is febrile and labs showed raised CRP. Best treatment option after stopping culprit drug for this patient should be

A. Let it resolve on its own
B. Potent topical steroids
C. Start oral steroids with monitoring
D. Plasma excahnge
E. Both c and d

Key: C
Ref: Rook (119.4)

2. You have to review a patient presented with one day history of fever and rash, 3 days back patient came to u with tinea corpora's and was given terbinafine. Cutaneous examination revealed widespread erythema along with multiple no follicular sterile pustules. What is most likely diagnosis?

A. Acute generalized exanthematous pustulosis
B. Acute generalized pustular psoriasis
C. Dress syndrome
D. Generalized candidal folliculitis
E. Sneddon wilkinson disease

Key: A
Ref: Rook (119.2)

3. 50 years old female newly diagnosed case of rheumatoid arthritis, was on DMARDS presented to dermatology opd with h/o malaise, fever and dyspnoea, she has h/o itchy scattered distribution of vesicles and purpuric macules formation over upper limb and trunk, O/E Nikolsby sign positive and she was unable to open the mouth due to severe oral involvement

What would be the possible diagnosis of this patient?

A. Pemphigus vulgaris
B. Bullous mastocytosis
C. Steven johnson syndrom
D. Felty syndrome
E. Rheumatoid neutrophilic dermatoses

Key: C
Ref: Rook (119.13)

4. 40 years old male, known case of non-Hodgkin lymphoma, presented to oncology depth with h/o wide spread bulla formation and haemorrhagic microsites from 2 days

He has associated h/o polyuria

O/E pulse rate 130/min

BSR 320mg/dl

Keeping in mind disease parameter of this patient, what would be the predicted mortality of this patient?

A. 4 %
B. 13 %

C. 32 %
D. 85 %
E. 62%

Key: C
Ref: Rook (119.16)

5. 8 years old boy presented with h /o high grade fever and upper rasp tract infection ,he took some antibiotics from local GP ,after which he developed large area of confluent erythema and detached skin with severe oral involvement along with conjunctivitis
Keeping in mind diagnosis of this child, which one is least likely to be present in healing phase of this disease

A. telogen effluvium
B. eruptive melanocytic naevi
C. heterotopic ossification
D. splinter hemorrhages
E. onychomadesis

Key: D
Ref: Rook (119.18)

6. Keeping in view the diagnosis of above patient, which statement is not correct about treatment of this child?

A. Catheterize the patient immediately
B. Take bacterial and fungal swabs from multiple sites
C. Non opiates based analgesia is the best choice for pain control
D. Dressing of the lesion will reduce fluid and protein loss
E. Replace fluid with crystalloids 2ml/kg body weight /% bsa

Key: C
Ref: Rook (119.19)

7. 50 years old lady known case of gout, was on treatment presented to derma opd with h /o widespread blisters and skin detachment from last 1 day along with severe haemorrhagic microsites and purulent conjunctivitis. Regarding etiopathogeneses of this condition which one is false statement?

A. Mhc class ll cd8 + cytoxic t cells proliferation
B. Proapoptotic molecules including no synthase induce keratinocyte damage
C. Necroptosis mediated by annexin a1
D. Presence of high concentration of granulysin in blister fluid
E. Soluble fas ligand involving epidermal cells damage

Key: A
Ref: Rook (119.13)

8. A 36-year-old asthmatic, and epileptic since childhood presented to the emergency department with 5-day history of sore throat, high-grade fever and difficulty swallowing with worsening facial swelling. The patient was on divalproex sodium for many years. He was switched to phenytoin about 6–8 weeks back because of repeat seizures. About 7 days prior to presentation, he was not feeling well and reported throat pain that made it difficult to swallow. Over the next 2 days, he developed facial and neck swelling along with eruption of an erythematous pruritic skin rash. In the emergency department, his review of symptoms was positive for fever, chills, arthralgias, sore throat, decreased per oral intake and facial and neck swelling. His oral cavity examination was essentially negative except erythematous areas on hard palate. Cervical and submandibular lymph nodes were enlarged. An erythematous, confluent, slightly warm to morbilliform rash covered the upper chest, upper back and both forearms, extending to the dorsal hands but sparing the palms and soles.

Considering the diagnosis what is the most frequent long term sequelae of this presentation?

A. Burkits lymphoma
B. Exfoliative dermatitis
C. Red cell aplasia
D. Hypothyroidism
E. Liver failure

Key: D
Rooks reference 119.9

9. A 55-years-old patient presented with erythematous skin eruption associated with fever, lethargy, neck swelling, and peripheral edema. On physical examination, he was erythroderma, tachycardia, and febrile. There was an exfoliate facial dermatitis and a diffuse maculopapular eruption over the arms, trunk, and lower limbs additionally he also noted to be having facial and accrual swelling and prominent no tender left cervical lymphadenopathy. His Laboratory results showed hb (111 g/L), white cell count, 13.6 x 109/L, eosinophils (4.6 x 109/L). His history was significant for gout for which he was started on medication 1 month back.

Considering the diagnosis which one of the following is not a feature of this disease?

A. Lymphadenopathy
B. Mucosal ulceration
C. Atypical lymphocytes
D. Hla dr3
E. Oedema of face

Key: B
Ref: Rook (119.4)

10. A 43-years-old man presented to the emergency department with a 1-week history of fever, sore throat, and a diffuse pruritic macular rash that started on the face and trunk before spreading to all extremities. One month before this presentation, the patient had been treated with naproxen 500 mg twice a day for 3 days by a local health center for back pain. On admission he had a low-grade fever, with otherwise stable vitals. Physical examination showed a diffuse maculopapular rash with centrifugal distribution on the head, nape of the neck, and extremities, including palms and soles. The lips were involved, but the oral cavity, conjunctiva, and mucous membranes were spared. There was mild facial edema but no peripheral edema. Nonblanching purpura was noted on the lower limbs with negative Nikolsky sign. Initial laboratory studies revealed a white blood cell count of 12.4 ×103/μL, with 60% neutrophils, 30% lymphocytes, and 4% eosinophils. A blood smear showed many pleomorphic atypical lymphocytes.

Considering the diagnosis which of the following is consider to be associated with severe outcome?

A. Oral mucosa involvement
B. Atypical lymphocytes
C. Erythema multiforme like lesions
D. Hhv 6 infection
E. Ebv infection

Key: C
Ref: Rook (119.10)

11. A 63-year-old woman diagnosed 1week back with TB on ATT reported to dermatology department, for complaints of acute onset erythema along with severe itching all over the body. Dermatological examination revealed generalized involvement of the body with extensive no uniform dusky erythematous scaly plaques involving the scalp, face, nape of the neck, trunk, arms, legs, palms, and soles. Erythema and scaling were more pronounced over trunk and legs. Furthermore, the pruritic plaques were first noted on trunk and legs which increased in size and coalesced to involve the entire body in a few days. Scalp lesions

formed red-yellow scales with hair loss. On palms and soles, the exfoliate eruption led to severe sloughing of the epidermis. No significant lymphadenopathy or hepatosplenomegaly was observed.
Considering the diagnosis which of the following is not the complication of this presentation?

A. Hypothermia
B. Cardiac failure
C. Hyponatremia
D. Sepsis
E. Acute necrotizing eosinophilic myocarditis

Key: E
Ref: Rook (119.11)

12. A 35 years old HIV positive patient presented with erythmatous and scaly plaques over the face, neck, trunk and back and involving almost whole of his body there was No mucosal and genetalia involvement. Hair and nails are normal. His history was only significant for starting HAART treatment 1 month back.
Which of the following can aid in diagnosing the cause?

A. CBC with eosinophilia
B. Biopsy
C. Patch testing
D. ANCA
E. None of the above

Key: C
Ref: Rook (119.11)

Chapter 120 CUTANEOUS SIDE EFFECTS OF CHEMOTHERAPY AND RADIOTHERAPY

1. A middle aged patient presented to you in opd, she is an old patient of Psoriasis, was on topical treatment and her disease was well controlled. Now she has presented after a few years, during which her Psoriatic lesions were relapsing and remitting, and she has CA breast for which she took treatment form a cancer hospital, and is now on follow-up. Now, she complains of joint pains and morning stiffness, you examine and diagnose Ps. arthritis and prescribe methotrexate.
She came back the very next day after taking metho, with a painful rash in her breast area, which comprise of itchy painful oozing lesions, redness and swelling in her breast area.
What is the pathophysiology of this?

A. Idiosyncratic drug hypersensitivity reaction
B. Continued low level secretion of inflammation mediating cytokines induced by radiation
C. Radiotherapy induced mutation in skin, yield cells that are vulnerable to cytotoxic therapies
D. Same as fixed drug eruption
E. All above hypothesis are considered true

Key: E
Ref: Rook (120.11)

2. An old age patient presented to you with conplaint of a non-healing ulcer in her right thoracic area, where she had mastectomy and radiotherapy about 10 years back for CA breast. Your biopsy the lesion to rule out any secondary malignancy, but report came back negative. You start treatment of ulcer, but it is not responding very well to treatment and the underlying skin is very hard and fixed.
What could be the cause of this type of skin changes?

A. Skin mets
B. Post irradiation morphea
C. Lsc
D. Senile skin changes
E. Post irradiation systemic sclerosis

Key: B
Ref: Rook (120.12)

3. A patient presented to you with severe rash in his cervical area, there is erythema of skin with few areas of ulceration and deaquamation, and there is intense redness inside the oral cavity as well. On inquiring history, you came to know that, he was diagnosed with SCC of tongue last year,and is on treatment. he is done with surgery and chemo, and now started with radiotherapy last week.
What statement is NOT true about his condition??

A. Radiation induces DNA injury repair via activation of p53
B. Inflammatory cytokines are released as a consequence of generation of free radicals
C. Main cytokines involved are TNF alpha, Il 1 and 6
D. Obesity and poor nutrition are risk factors that increase the chance of radiation dermatitis
E. These side effects are not dose dependant

Key: E
Ref: Rook (120.12)

Chapter 122 DERMATOLOGICAL MANIFESTATIONS OF METAL POISONING

1. 35 years old man presented with 2 weeks H/O lethargy, malaise, headache, nausea and cramping abdominal pain. He also noticed intermittent paresthesia and weakness of the hands. He has been employed at a construction site for renovation of an old building and his work involves removal of old paint. On /e he has mild abdominal tenderness. His labs show Hb 9.2, wbc and platelets are normal. What is the diagnosis

A. Arsenic poisoning
B. Hydrargyria
C. Argyria
D. Plumbism

Key: D
Ref: Rook (122.4)

2. 17 year old girl presented to ER with complaints of severe abdominal pain and vomiting. 2 months ago she was diagnosed with acute appendicitis and underwent appendicectomy, however the pain persisted. On/E you notice a bluish line on her gingival margin. Rest of skin examination is normal. The girl has family pottery business and she thoroughly enjoys helping her father.
She was diagnosed with lead poisoning and treated with Succimer with gradual improvement in her symptoms. Which of the following is not seen in plumbism?

A. Contipation and lead colic
B. Burtons lead lines
C. Arthralgia and gout
D. Infertility
E. Hyperthyroidism and hyperpitrutism

Key: E
Ref: Rook (122.4)

3. 46 years old male from bangladash is referred to your clinic for evaluation with C/O numbness and tingling in his toes and fingertips since past 3 months. The symptoms have progressed slowly and now Involve feet and hand in symmetric stocking glove fashion. Examination reveals diminished proprioception in hand and feet. Muscle bulk, tone and power is normal. Patient also gives history of hyperkeratotic lesions over palm and soles since 2 years. On/ E of skin you also notice brown patches of hyperpigmentation with scattered overlying pale spots. Keeping diagnosis in mind which of the following is not seen in chronic exposure

A. Black foot
B. Peripheral Neuropathy
C. Liver Lung and Bladder malignancy
D. Intraepidermal SCC
E. Oral herpetiform ulcers

Key: E
Ref: Rook (122.2)

4. 65 years old man presented with complaint of progressive greyish discolouration of hands and soles for last 10 years. He gives H/O using local ayuverdic medication containing colloidal silver protein for cough and flu since 15 years in order to avoid use of medicines. On /E uniform bluish grey pigmentation is noticed over face/ neck/ back/ Dorsum of hands. Biopsy of the skin shows brown pigment deposited in dermal elastic fibre, blood vessels and basement membrane. Keeping diagnosis in view what treatment options can be suggested to him

A. Sunscreen use
B. EDTA
C. ND YAG 1064nm
D. Both A and C

Key: D
Ref: Rook (122.7)

5. 13 year old girl presented to you with complain of abdominal pain since past 2.5 months. Now for the last 20 days she is experiencing increased pain in the legs. On/e you notice she has erythematous skin lesions involving her gluteal region and is accompanied with itching and sensation of burning and pain. Her brother has similar complaint of abdominal pain. Skin biopsy was performed and shows spherical, opaque globules with zone of necrosis around them along with brown black granules in the dermis. The mother gives history that both siblings like to play with batteries at home. In view of the diagnosis which of the following can be used in management

A. D-Penicillamine
B. Peritoneal dialysis
C. Dimercaprol
D. All of the above

Key: D
Ref: Rook (122.5)

Chapter 123 MECHANICAL INJURY TO THE SKIN

1. A patient presented to the GP in opd, he is worried because he wanted to donate blood to someone, but prior tests show he is HIV positive, which he never knew before.
He is unmarried, and denies any sexual relationship, hadn't received any blood transfusion in recent times.
You examine him for any genital ulcer/ discharge or lymphadenopathy...but there is nothing if significance, no rash, no ulcer except that you notice a tattoo on his back.
Which of the following is the least important disease according to case reports which will you consider with tattooing?

A. Hep C
B. MRSA positive infection
C. viral warts
D. syphilis
E. MCs

Key: D
Ref: Rook (123.21)

2. A medical student presented in ER with sudden excruciating pain in his right hand followed by swelling and discolouration of the fingers, this whole development was rapid, occurring within minutes. There is no history of cold intolerance or sequential color changes. On examination the hand was swollen, especially volar aspect of fingers, and there is bluish discoloration of medial 3 fingers.
He is a student and does nothing of note except that he was busy in shifting his hostel room these days.
What next would you suggest?

A. Doppler of hand
B. X-ray of hands
C. No treatment is needed, it will settle on its own
D. Autoimmunity profile
E. Rest the hand cool the area and avoid triggers

Key: E
Ref: Rook (123.13)

3. A 45 years old obese male known case of Diabetes came with complain of skin lesions at the site of vaccination. On cutaneous examination he has salmon-colored silver scaly plaques at left arm. On enquiry he told he has similar skin problem for last 5 years but it was controlled. Regarding diagnosis all conditions can present with this response except

A. Lupus erythematosus
B. Scleromyxoedema
C. Multicentric reticulohistiocytosis
D. Necrobiosis lipoidica
E. Calciphylasix

Key: E
Ref: Rook (123.2)

Chapter 125 CUTANEOUS REACTIONS TO COLD AND HEAT

Q1. A 36 years old soldier came to you with complain of pain at extremities. He has history of posting at Siachein glacier in last month. On cutaneous examination his fingers and toes were erythematous tender and edematous with few blisters. Regarding diagnosis which is not true.

A. Fast freezing tends to produce intracellular ice
B. Ice crystals not only injure cellular architecture but also disturb the flux of electrolytes and water across cell membranes
C. Reflex vasoconstriction in the extremities results in decreased capillary perfusion
D. Slow rewarming by immersion in water at 37–39°C is recommended
E. Rapid rewarming has been shown to be more effective than slow rewarming

Key D
Ref: Rook (125.2)

2. A 25 years old female without any comorbids came with complain of cold intolerance since childhood. On inquiry she told that most of her fingers of both hands become blue whenever she exposed to cold and then red when she used warm water. On examination fingers and nail were unremarkable. Considering diagnosis which of the following is not true for its pathogenesis

A. Aberrant expression of nitric oxide, endothelin, angiotensin II
B. Disturbance in vascular homeostasis
C. Down-regulation of nitric oxide
D. Increased contractile response to cold
E. Role of α2 -adrenergic antgonists is associated with increased activity of protein tyrosine kinase and tyrosine phosphorylation in vascular smooth muscle

Key: E
Ref: Rook (125.9)

3. A 48 years old female referred to you from oncology department with complain of burning of hand and feet.On cutaneous examination you found her fingers and toes were swell and bluish in colored with some red-purple colored papules and small nodules at fingers and toes, nose and both ears.No other cutaneous finding were positive . She told that it get subside spontaneously. skin biopsy showed large atypical mononuclear cell perivascular and peri-ecrine distribution with dermal edema.ANA was negative.Cbc showed pancytopenia while Bone marrow biopsy showed hypercellulrity with dysplastic cell. What is your diagnosis

A. Hutchinson lupus
B. Perniosis
C. Acrocynosis
D. Sweet syndrom
E. Papular sarcoidosis

Key: B
Ref: Rook (125.4)

4. A 15 years old anxious girl came in opd with diarrhea and skin problem. On examination she was underweight as per age. She used to take some medicine without any prescription. Her fingers and toes showed mottled bluish red mottled discoloration which was not subside on rewarming and remain persistent for 6 months. Pulses were palpable. All labs were unremarkable. Duplex ultrasound showed no thrombosis. what is your diagnosis

A. Raynaud phenomenon
B. Acrocynosis
C. Cryglobulinemic vasculitis
D. Frosbite
E. Erythrocynosis

Key B
Ref: Rook (125.5)

Chapter 127

CUTANEOUS PHOTOSENSITIVITY DISEASES

1. A 10-year-old boy with no significant family history presented with an itchy rash on his ears. This occurred one to two hours after he had been playing outside at school in early springtime. He had developed the same rash several times in the past in similar circumstances. What is 1st line of treatment?
   A. Topical steroids
   B. Sunlight avoidance
   C. Oral antihistamine
   D. Emolients

Key: B
Ref: Rook (127.9)

2. A 9-year-old girl presented with intensely pruritic crops of papules and vesicles often arising on a background of erythema and oedema,occur on exposed sites within 12–24 h. Associated with burning sensation, pain and fever.
Physical examination found dry crusted vesicles on the face, lips, and ears and facial edema mostly in the periorbital and perioral areas. vesicle resolves with pock like scarring. Management option are, except?
   A. Photoprotection
   B. Topical corticosteroids
   C. Springtime desensitization with narrow-band UVB phototherapy.
   D. Topical retinoids

Key: D
Ref: Rook (127.26)

3. A 54-year-old male presented with a long-standing severe photodistributed eczematous eruption on his face, neck, chest, back, and extremities. His past medical history was significant for atopic dermatitis (AD), hypertension, and dyslipidemia. His medications include amlodipine, and atorvastatin. On Examination prominent involvement of photo-exposed sites of the head, neck and limbs, with sparing of areas covered with clothes, hats, watches and spectacles. What is association of this condition?
   A. HIV
   B. Leprosy
   C. Hepatitis b
   D. Hepatitis c

Key: A
Ref: Rook (127.13)

4. A 10-year-old boy presented with an itchy rash on his ears. This occurred one to two hours after he had been playing outside at school in early springtime. He had developed the same rash several times in the past in similar circumstances. What could be association of the disease?
   A. Polymorphic light eruption
   B. Atopic dermatitis
   C. Hand eczema
   D. Solar urticaria

Key: A
Ref: Rook (127.8)

5. A 12-year-old boy presented with varioliform scars on cheeks, nose and back of hands. He has past history of intensely pruritic crops of papules and vesicles following 15 min to a few hours of direct or window glass-transmitted light. What is the prognosis of the condition?

A. Relapsing and chronic coarse
B. The condition improves and resolves in later teenage years.
C. Agravate in later teenage years
D. Agravate in older age

Key: B
Ref: Rook (127.25)

6. A 25 year old male farmer presented to our clinic with a 8 month history of pruritic and erythematous rash showing sun-exposed distribution. The skin eruptions began in early summer and were mainly on the sun-exposed areas. He felt worse after sun exposure, and facial sunscreen did not result in any improvement. He was healthy and was not using any medicines. He denied a personal history and family history of photosensitivity. Dermatologic examination revealed erythema and erosions on the face including dorsum of nose, scalp, and ears. Additionally, erythematous papules and nodules were present on the extensor forearms, dorsal hands, and feet.
On investigations only positive finding is presence of the DRB1*0407 subtype.
All of the following are treatment options EXCEPT:

A. Potent corticosteroids
B. Narrow band UVB phototherapy
C. Psoralen UVA phototherapy
D. Methotrexate
E. Chloroquine

Key: D
Ref: Rook (127.12)

7. A 55-year-old woman presented to her local hospital with a 2 month history of purpura on her bilateral lower extremities that rapidly progressed to extensive gangrenous necrosis with black eschars involving both legs. On examination, the patient was in no acute distress with normal vital signs. Her skin examination was notable for a palpable purpuric rash with extensive gangrenous necrosis with large black eschars on the bilateral lower extremities.
Laboratory testing low complement C4, and borderline elevated rheumatoid factor. Renal function, liver function, and complete blood counts were normal other than mild anaemia of chronic disease thought to be related to her presenting illness.
All of the following cutaneous signs are present EXCEPT:

A. livedo reticularis
B. Raynaud phenomenon
C. Atypical ulceration of the legs
D. Cold urticaria
E. Perniosis

8. A 10-year-old boy with no significant family history presented with an itchy rash on his ears. This occurred one to two hours after he had been playing outside at school in early springtime. He had developed the same rash several times in the past in similar circumstances. What is 1st line of treatment?

A. Topical steroids
B. Sunlight avoidance
C. Oral antihistamine
D. Emollients

Key: B
Ref: Rook (127.9)

9. A 9-year-old girl presented with intensely pruritic crops of papules and vesicles often arising on a background of erythema and oedema, occur on exposed sites within 12–24 h. Associated with burning sensation, pain and fever. Physical examination found dry crusted vesicles on the face, lips, and ears and facial edema mostly in the periorbital and perioral areas. Vesicle resolves with pock like scarring. Management option are, except?

A. Photo protection
B. Topical corticosteroids
C. Springtime desensitization with narrow-band UVB phototherapy.
D. Topical retinoid

Key: D
Ref: Rook (127.26)

10. A 54-year-old male presented with a long-standing severe photo distributed eczematous eruption on his face, neck, chest, back, and extremities. His past medical history was significant for atopic dermatitis (AD), hypertension, and dyslipidaemia. His medications include amlodipine, and atorvastatin. On Examination prominent involvement of photo-exposed sites of the head, neck and limbs, with sparing of areas covered with clothes, hats, watches and spectacles. What is association of this condition?

A. HIV
B. Leprosy
C. Hepatitis B
D. Hepatitis C

Key: A
Ref: Rook (127.13)

11. A 10 year-old boy presented with an itchy rash on his ears. This occurred one to two hours after he had been playing outside at school in early springtime. He had developed the same rash several times in the past in similar circumstances. What could be association of the disease?

A. Polymorphic light eruption
B. Atopic dermatitis
C. Hand eczema
D. Solar urticarial

Key: A
Ref: Rook (127.8)

12. A 12 year old boy presented with varioliform scars on cheeks, nose and back of hands. He has past history of intensely pruritic crops of papules and vesicles following 15 min to a few hours of direct or window glass-transmitted light. What is the prognosis of the condition?

A. Relapsing and chronic course
B. The condition improves and resolves in later teenage years.
C. Aggravate in later teenage years
D. Aggravate in older age

Key: B
Ref: Rook (127.25)

13. A 13 years old girl from gilgit presented with a long-standing itchy rash resistant to topical and systemic steroids more in summer. Physical examination revealed a Centro-facial rash consisting of erythematous papules, excoriations and crusts on an erythematous basis also involving dorsum of nose and excoriated papules on her upper extremities and chest. Chelates and conjunctivitis are present Standard laboratory investigations, complement factors and autoantibodies were all within normal range. Porphyrin screening was negative. Monochromatic photo testing showing severe abnormal photosensitivity. What is the fate of this disease?

A. Continue during whole summer season
B. Can be controlled but doesn't completely resolve
C. Spontaneously improves and may resolve by teenage years or early adulthood
D. Remissions and recurrences are common whole life
E. Self-limiting

Key: C
Ref: Rook (127.11)

14. A 25 year old male farmer presented to our clinic with a 8 month history of pruritic and erythematous rash showing sun-exposed distribution. The skin eruptions began in early summer and were mainly on the sun-exposed areas. He felt worse after sun exposure, and facial sunscreen did not result in any improvement. He was healthy and was not using any medicines. He denied a personal history and family history of photosensitivity. Dermatologic examination revealed erythema and erosions on the face including dorsum of nose, scalp, and ears. Additionally, erythematous papules and nodules were present on the extensor forearms, dorsal hands, and feet. On investigations only positive finding is presence of the DRB1*0407 subtype. All of the following are treatment options EXCEPT:
A. Potent corticosteroids
B. Narrow band UVB phototherapy
C. Psoralen UVA phototherapy
D. Methotrexate
E. Chloroquine

Key: D
Ref: Rook (127.12)

15. A 55 year old woman presented to her local hospital with a 2 month history of purpura on her bilateral lower extremities that rapidly progressed to extensive gangrenous necrosis with black eschars involving both legs. On examination, the patient was in no acute distress with normal vital signs. Her skin examination was notable for a palpable purpuric rash with extensive gangrenous necrosis with large black eschars on the bilateral lower extremities. Laboratory testing low complement C4, and borderline elevated rheumatoid factor. Renal function, liver function, and complete blood counts were normal other than mild anaemia of chronic disease thought to be related to her presenting illness. All of the following cutaneous signs are present EXCEPT:
A. Live do reticular is
B. Raynaud phenomenon
C. Atypical ulceration of the legs
D. Urticarial
E. Peronists

Chapter 128 ALLERGIC CONTACT DERMATITIS

1. A 25 year old lady developed erythematous rash around the eyes for last 2 weeks. Systemic examination is unremarkable. What can be the possible diagnosis?
   A. Atopic eczema
   B. Allergic contact dermatitis due to nail varnish
   C. Dermatomyositis
   D. Irritant contact dermatitis

Key: B
Ref: Rook (128.3)

2. A 35yr old male developed well defined erythematous rash on hands after using disinfectant (Dettol). What is the active allergen?
   A. Chloroxylenol
   B. Chlorocresol
   C. Isothiazolinones
   D. Quaternium 15

Key: A
Ref: Rook (128.38)

3. A 40yr old male developed erythematous rash on scalp, ears and eyes. He gives history of using semi-permanent hair dye 2 weeks ago. What is the active allergen?
   A. Onppd
   B. Ethylenediamine
   C. Ppd
   D. Ptd

Key: A
Ref: Rook (128.41)

4. A 30yr old lady developed erythema on face after applying BB cream. What is formaldehyde releasing active ingredient in cosmetic products?
   A. Quaternium 15
   B. Paraben
   C. Lanolin
   D. Fragrance

Key: A
Ref: Rook (128.34)

5. A patient developed well defined erythematous rash on both legs 2 weeks after applying wax.what is the cause of her rash?
   A. Colophony in the wax
   B. Paraben in the wax
   C. Irritant contact dermatitis
   D. Thermal burn

Key: A
Ref: Rook (128.31)

6. A jewellery maker presented with itchy scaly erythematous plaques over face upper chest fingers and ear lobes. Scalp showed few hyperkeratotic areas with scarring alopecia. Oral examination revealed plaques with white streaks. cbc showed eosinophila. the following patch test should be done to confirm dx?

A. Potassium dichromate 0.5% in petrolatum
B. Mercurochrome 2%in petrolatum
C. Gold sodium thiosulphate 0.5% in petrolatum
D. Nickel sulphate 5%in petrolatum
E. Palladium chloride1% in petrolatum

Key: C.
Ref: Rook (122.3 n 128.23)

7. 5yrs old boy presented with scarlet cheeks, ears n nose with erythema n scaling of extremeties with palmoplantar hyperkeratosis. Mother c/o irritability photophobia and loss of few nails.
Considering dx the culprit is

A. Cinnabar
B. Mercurous chloride
C. Methyl mercury
D. Mercurial bromide
E. Ammoniated mercury

Key: B
Ref: Rook (122.5 n 128.24)

8. A much concerned nurse brings her 3 yrs old child with c/o persistent pruiritic s/c nodules over left arm for last 1 year. Rest hx is insignificant. Biopsy revealed granulomatous reaction.
The best patch test would be:

A. 10%aluminium acetate in finn chamber
B. 2%aluminium chloride in plastic chamber
C. 0.5%sodium thiosulphate in petrolatum
D. 5%aluminium acetate in plastic chamber
E. 0.5%mercurochrome in petrolatum.

Key: B
Ref: Rook (128.24)

9. 30 years old european male, fisher man by profession presented in dermatology opd with complain of rash on bilateral hands and feet associated with itching and no constitutional symptoms of 2 days duration. There was no history of skin disease previously. On examination there is diffuse erythema swelling and multiple papules and vesicles present on bilateral hands and feet extending upto mid forarms and legs with no sharp demarcation of rash. what could be the cause of this rash?

A. Dimethyl sulfoxonium ion
B. Quaternium 15
C. Chlorocresol
D. Lanolin
E. Paraphenylendiamine

Key: A
Ref: Rook (128.10)

10. 45 years old male construction worker presented in dermatology opd with complains of dryness and itching of his both palms since 2 years.
Itching gets better on weekends but recurs on weekdays. On examination there is diffuse thickening of both palms with mild scaling and fissuring noted.
Rest of the examination is normal. There is no family history of similar disease.
Patch test performed was positive.
Regarding the pathophysiology of the disease All of the following statement are true except?

A. It is a type 4 hypersensitivity reaction

B. T reg cells influence sensitization and elicitation process
C. Sensitization is posible only if connection to regional lymph nodes is intact
D. IL-5 IL-4 IL-14 are all required for activation maturation and migration of langerhan cells
E. T reg cells control and terminate inflammatory response

Key: D
Ref: Rook (128.7)

11. 32 years old male cement worker presented in dermatology opd with complains of recurrent episodes of palmar itching redness and scaling for last 2 years. Symptoms improve on weekends but recur on weekdays. There is no history of asthma or family history of similar complains. Regarding the pathophysiology of this condition which cells are resopnsible for initial sensitiization with T cells?
A. Langerhan cells
B. Macrophages
C. Keratinocytes
D. Histiocytes
E. Plasma cells

Key: A
Ref: Rook (128.6)

12. 50 years old female known case of 1st degree haemmorhoids for which she is taking over the counter medicines presented in dermatology opd for complains of rash on perianal region associated with itching for last 3 days. On examination diffuse erythema with multiple scattered papules and vesicles was noted in perianal region with no clear demarcation. Patch test was performed and came out to be positive. ALL of the following drugs decrease skin reactivity in patch testing except?
A. Topical steroids
B. Antihistamines
C. Ciclosporin
D. Puva therapy
E. Systemic steroids

Key: B
Ref: Rook (128.6)

13. 32 years old female married mother of 5 years old boy presented in dermatalogy opd with complains of pruritis and rash on both earlobes. she has previous history of similar episodes whenever she use to wear ear rings for last 10 years which setlles with some topical medicines.
On examination both earlobes are erythematous swollen with small excoriated papules and slight scaling was noted.
How much is the chance of having this condition in her child?
A. 10%
B. 60%
C. 2%
D. 90%
E. 30%

Key: B
Ref: Rook (128.10)

14. A 70yrs old lady presented with itchy erythematous utricated papules n few plaques in the perianal region. she has c/o blood-stained stools n chronic constipation n had recently applied something topically. the most likely contact allergen is
A. Balsum of peru
B. Corticosteroids

C. Lanolin
D. Neomycin
E. Parabens

Key: A
Ref: Rook (128.26)

15. An actress presented with severely itchy erythematous papules n plaques of variable sizes over face neck n axillae for past 2 days. Considering dx the commonest sensitizer now a days is
A. Balsum of peru
B. Lyral
C. Farnesol
D. Both b n c
E. Sandalwood

Key: D
Ref: Rook (128.27)

16. A 32 yr old female doctor developed itchy erythematous rash on dorsum of hands especially on knuckles and wrist with a sharp proximal margin. Following is true regarding latex dermatitis except
A. Black rubber most frequently causes problems
B. Most type of rubber contains 5%of potential allergic additives
C. Sensitivity to mercapto compounds suggest rubber gloves
D. Sensitivity to carbamates and thiurams suggest rubber gloves

Key: C
Ref: Rook (128.43)

17. A 15 yr old boy presented with erythematous itchy scaly rash over dorsum of both feet and toes with sparing of interdigital spaces and instep. Following is true regarding shoe dermatitis except
A. Mostly sweating causes allergens to leach out .
B. In sport shoes dermatitis only involves the heels
C. Nikle allergy from buckles causes localized dermatitis
D. Rubber chemical allergy has increased tendency to affect soles

Key: B
Ref: Rook (128.47)

18. A paint factory worker presented with erythematous weeping itchy rash over hands and arms. Face and periorbital area was also involved. Following is true except
A. Worker is allergic to acrylate resin
B. Worker is most probably suffering from epoxy resin contact dermatitis
C. Worker is suffering from dermatitis due to plants surrounding his work place
D. Rubber dermatitis can cause such eruption

Key: B
Ref: Rook (128.48)

19. A beauty therapist presented with erythematous scaly rash involving her hands especially fingertips. The allergen mostly commonly responsible for such eruption is
A. Epoxy resins
B. Acrylate resins
C. Chromate and rubber
D. Nickel

Key: B
Ref: Rook (128.5)

20. Common sensitizers in rubber shoes dermatitis includes
A. Mercapto mix
B. Thiuram mix

C. Black rubber mix
D. Carba mix
E. All of above

Key: E
Ref: Rook (128.43)

21. A 40 years male presented to OpD with history of erythematous rash over hand and forearm associated with itching after visiting his village. He gave history of this rash every time he visited there. On examination there is streaky dermatitis over dorsum of hands and forearms.
What is most likely causative agent?
A. Spurge
B. Dieffenbachia
C. Primula obonic
D. Poison ivy
E. Both c & d

Key: E
Ref: Rook (128.14)

22. A 30 years female housewife presented to OPD with history of dry, scaly skin rash over dorsum of his hands associated with intense itching. This rash started initially as papules and some of papulovesicles. on examination there is dry scaly , thickened skin with some areas of fissuring. What is most likely diagnosis?
A. Acute contact dermatitis
B. Chronic contact dermatitis
C. Pomphlyx
D. Photocontact dermatitis
E. Medicament contact dermatitis

Key: B
Ref: Rook (128.13)

23. A 42 years anxious male painter by profession presented with history of recurrent stomatitis which mostly started at start of week. He uses multivitamins for past 5 years without any prescription. What is causautive agent in this case?
A. Cobalt
B. Chromium
C. Aluminium
D. Gold
E. None of above

Key: A
Ref: Rook (128.21)

24. A 47 years mason presented to OPD with history of dry scaly eruption over hands and feet for many years which was insidious in onset. On examination there is fissuring and latensification with flexural accentuation. He also gave history of on & off palmar vesicular eruption. What is most likely allergen in this case?
A. Cobalt
B. Leather
C. Nickle
D. Chromium
E. Aluminium

Key: D
Ref: Rook (128.22)

25. A 23 year old male presented with pruritic lichenified dermatitis on his lower abdomen and eczematous dermatitis on his extremities, flanks and face that had lasted several weeks. We suspected his belt buckle had led to allergic contact dermatitis with subsequent autoeczematization.
Patch testing disclosed an edematous and papulovesicular reaction to nickel at 72 hours.
Regarding patch testing, All of the following can cause false positive reaction EXCEPT;

A. Excessive concentration
B. Even dispersion
C. Irritant vehicle
D. Adhesive tape reactions
E. Current dermatitis at patch test site

Key: B
Ref: Rook (128.68 table 128.7)

26. A 50 year old man with lifelong history of Allergic Dermatitis presented with a 2-month history of acute hand and foot dermatitis. Previously, his Allergic Dermatitis was reasonably controlled with emollients and intermittent topical corticosteroids. He was a guitar player and repairman, with frequent exposure to glues, varnishes, epoxies, and metals. Examination found hyperkeratotic eczematous plaques and distal onycholysis affecting the dorsal and volar fingers and toes.
The most preferable site to apply patch test in this patient is;

A. Lateral aspect of upper arm
B. Medial aspect of upper arm
C. Upper back
D. Abdomen
E. Thighs

Key: C
Ref: Rook (128.66)

27. A 42 year old man worker of metal industry (since 1 month) presented in dermatology opd with the complaints of itching and burning on hands and arms since 15 days. On examination there were discrete discoid excoriated plagues of various sizes distributed asymmetrically on both upper limbs.
History revealed previous sensitization to nickel in childhood.
All of the following are causes of relapse EXCEPT;

A. overzealous use of antiseptics and cleansers
B. Re-exposure to allergens
C. Ingestion of allergens
D. Stress
E. Barrier function of skin is intact for months after dermatitis attack.

Key: E
Ref: Rook (128.63)

28. A 28 years old girl presented in dermatology opd with the complaints of multiple vesicular itchy eruptions on palms of hands since 2 months. she has started working in hair salon since 6 months
She has used topical steroids plus oral antihistamines but the condition has not resolved.
Suspecting allergic contact dermatitis, patch test was done, which came out positive for which allergen?

A. P-phenylenediamine(ppd)
B. Epoxy resin
C. Formaldehyde
D. Potassium dichromate
E. Neomycin sulphate

Key: A

Ref: Rook (128.70(Topic patch testing Table 128.9)

29. A 31 year old male presented in opd with the complaints of multiple scaly pruritic papules on face since 1 month, he used mild topical steroid plus antihistamine but the condition worsoned and the rash spread to the abdomen and upper limbs since 10 days. On history taking he told that he has not used any cosmetic product nor has used any hair product. He has recently started using metal frame spectacles. Microscopy of Scrappings was negative for superficial fungal infection. On the basis of above,what is the likely diagnosis?

A. 'id'reaction due to nickle allergy
B. pemphigus foilaceous
C. Pityriasis Alba
D. pityriasis versicolor
E. None of the above

Key: A
Ref: Rook (128.63)

30. A middle aged lady with history of itchy rash in wrist n fingers after wearing jewellery. She has stopped the use of jewellery a few yrs ago, but she continued to have vesicular lesions on hands n wrist with treatment only mild improvement. But again vesicular lesions on hands. Regarfing diagnosis in this pt. She got avrecent flare when iv line passed for some treatment. What can be reasons of this rash except

A. Stainless steel utensils used for cooking
B. Drinking water contaminated
C. Peripheral iv lines
D. Cosmetics
E. Orthodontic appliances

Key: D
Ref: Rook (128.59)

31. A young male who is a diagnosed case of vitiligo that is static for last few years. He developed dermatitis at arm after foing cleaning in his garden in summers. Dermatitis settled with time bt he developed extension of vitiligo patches on his arm. What can be allergy in third case.

A. Insect bite
B. Poison ivy
C. Primula obconica
D. Compositae family
E. Alliaceae family

Key: C
Ref: Rook (128.61 or 128.27)

32. A middle aged lady on her visit to a garden in a vacation trip of north America developed streaky rash with erythema, papules n vesicobullous rash on arms while she touched some plant sap. A few days later on her return she developed urticarial eruption on different areas of body. N developed decreased urine output. on labs. All normal except deranged renal function tests. While going through history she told about her visit to garden n rash in arms which left black spots on skin. What can be diagnosis in this case

A. Phytophotodermatitis
B. Allergy to primula
C. Tulip n lily allergy
D. Poison ivy
E. Compositae plants

Key: D
Ref: Rook (128.52)

33. An old age farmer had history of rash on exposed parts of body for two decades. He developed dermatitis multiple times now has developed marked thickening of facial skin. He has exacerbations in summers while removing weeds from his fields. Regarding diagnosis of this pt. Which patch testing is helpful in this pt.

A. 0.01%primin i. Petrolatum
B. Sesquitrepene lactone mix0.033%
C. 1% diallyl disulphide in petrolatum
D. 0.1% lichen acid mix in petrolatum
E. 0.01% tulipalin A in petrolatum

Key: B
Ref: Rook (128.52)

34. A young lady with history of rashes to adhesive tapes n footwear developed facial n eye eczema after using mascara. Patch testing was done. With a standard allergen which had 2 to 6% prevelance of allergy in patch tested population. Regarding diagnosis of this pt. Which of the following can be cause of dermatitis except?

A. Chewing gum
B. Herbal medicines
C. Shoe polish
D. Garlic n onion
E. Varnishes n coatings

Key: D
Ref: Rook (128.55)

35. 25 years old female known case of sle well controlled on hydroxycloroquine presented with new onset itchy rash on face and hands for last 1 week.
On examination diffuse erythema of face with some scaling present with sparing of area below chin and behind the earlobes. similar rash was also noted on dorsum of both hands.
Her drug history includes hydroxychloroquine 200 mg bd and she uses sunscreen regularly while going outdoor. Your senior asked to perform photo patch test on this patient. What will be the ideal dose of UVA for performing this test?

A. 10 J/cm2
B. 2 J/cm2
C. 5 J/cm2
D. 15 J/cm2
E. 20 J/cm2

Key: C
Ref: Rook (128.80)

36. 26 years old male resident of Sweden presented with complain of itchy rash on face and neck for last 1 week on examination diffuse erythema and mild scaling of face and v of neck present sparing the area below chin and behind earlobes. On further inquiry he told that he developed an annular itchy rash with central clearing on trunk 3 weeks ago for which he applied topical fentichlor and rash was resolved.
What is your diagnosis of current rash?

A. Tinea facei
B. Photoallergic contact dermatitis
C. Solar urticaria
D. Allergic contact dermatitis
E. Irritant contact dermatitis

Key: B
Ref: Rook (128.78)

37. 32 years old male cement worker presented in dermatology opd with complains of recurrent episodes of palmar itching redness and scaling for last 2 years. symptoms improve on weekends but recurs on weekdays. there is no history of asthma or family history of similar complains.
patch test was performed for suspected allergic contact dermatitis but came out to be negative. What could be the cause of false negative reaction?

A. Inappropriate vehicle
B. Uneven dispersion of allergen
C. Adhesive tape reactions
D. Impure substance
E. Excess allergen applied

Key: A
Ref: Rook (128.7 and 128.8)

38. 50 years old female known case of 1st degree haemorrhoids for which she is taking over the counter medicines presented in dermatology opd for complains of rash on perianal region associated with itching for last 3 days. On examination diffuse erythema with multiple scattered papules and vesicles was noted in perianal region with no clear demarcation. Patch test was performed and came out to be positive but you are not sure whether it is true positive allergic reaction or false positive non allergic irritant reaction. All of the following points will favour false positive non allergic irritant reaction except?

A. Infiltration
B. Lack of itching
C. Deep redness
D. Sharp delineating corresponding to margins of patch test

Key A
Ref: Rook (128.67)

39. 32 years old female presented in dermatology opd with complains of pruritis and rash on both earlobes. she has previous history of similar episodes whenever she uses to wear ear rings for last 10 years which settles with some topical medicines.
On examination both earlobes are erythematous swollen with small excoriated papules and slight scaling was noted.
Regarding the management of this condition which of the following statement is true?

A. Clioquinol most effective therapy
B. Trientine gives very good result
C. Disulfiram chleates nickel and free of side effects
D. Barrier creams are not helpful
E. Clioquinol steroid combination is contraindicated

40. Which allergen should be tested in addition when clothing allergy is suspected?

A. Nickel
B. chromate
C. Rubber
D. Formaldehyde based resins
E. Cellulose derivatives

Key: D

41. Regarding patch test with Paraphenylene derivatives (PPD), testing should be done at which concentration?

A. 0.25%
B. 0.1%
C. 0.5%

D. 2%
E. Both a & b

Key: E

42. Regarding shoe dermatitis, which statement is incorrect?
A. Interdigital spaces are normally spared.
B. Rubber Chemical allergy has tendency to effect soles
C. Hyperhidrosis is common in shoe dermatitis
D. All cases are bilateral
E. All are true.

Key: D

43. Pseudophotodermatitis
A. Exposed sites are involved
B. Airborne pattern of dermatitis
C. Leonine facies is feature in chronic cases-
D. True photo allergy to compositae is not a feature
E. All are true.

Key: E

44. Linear papulovesicles, oedema and hemorrhagic blisters on palms, dorsa of hands is classic appearance of allergy to plant?
A. Compositae
B. Primula
C. Alliaceae
D. Lilaceae
E. Alstroemeriaceae

Key: B

45. Pattern of dermatitis with compositae plant
A. Erythrodermatous exfoliativa
B. Hand eczema
C. Pseudophotodermatitis
D. Atopic eczema like
E. All of the above.

Key: E

46. Regarding distribution of contact dermatitis, which statement is incorrect,
A. Areas of sweating and friction.
B. Start in axilla sparing hairy vault.
C. Long sleeves cause eruption in elbow extensors
D. Allergy to dyes in soaks & Stockings on dorsa of feet.
E. Lesions are popular on shoulder and chest.

Key: C

47. Which allergen should be tested in addition when clothing allergy is suspected?
A. Nickel
B. Chromate
C. Rubber
D. Formaldehyde based resins
E. Cellulose derivatives

Key: D

48. Regarding patch test with Paraphenylene derivatives (PPD), testing should be done at which concentration?
    A. 0.25%
    B. 0.1%
    C. 0.5%
    D. 2%
    E. Both a & b.

Key: E

49. Regarding shoe dermatitis, which statement is incorrect?
    A. Interdigital spaces are normally spared.
    B. Rubber chemical allergy has tendency to affect soles
    C. Hyperhidrosis is common in shoe dermatitis
    D. All cases are bilateral
    E. All are true.

Key: D

50. Pseudophotodermatitis
    A. exposed sites are involved
    B. Airborne pattern of dermatitis
    C. Leonine facies is feature in Chronic cases.
    D. True photo allergy to compositae is not a feature.
    E. All are true.

Key: E

51. Linear papulovesicles, oedema and hemorrhagic blisters on palms, dorsa of hands is classic appearance of allergy to plant?
    A. Compositae
    B. Primula
    C. Alliaceae
    D. Lilaceae
    E. Alstroemeriaceae

Key: B

52. Pattern of dermatitis with compositae plant
    A. Erythro dermatous exfoliative
    B. Hand eczema
    C. Pseudo photo dermatitis
    D. Atopic eczema like
    E. All of the above.

Key: E

53. Regarding distribution of contact dermatitis which statement is incorrect?
    A. Areas of sweating and friction.
    B. Start in axilla sparing hairy vault
    C. Long sleeves cause eruption in elbow extensors.
    D. Allergy to dyes in soaks & Stockings start on dorsa of feet.
    E. lesions are papular on shoulder and chest

Key: C

Chapter 129 IRRITANT CONTRACT DERMATITIS

1. A newly appointed helper for laboratory assistant who was handling with formaldehyde presented with localized eruption erythema and weal on his hands ..he has no history of previous such eruptions neither he had ever come in contact with chemicals. You notice that while sitting his flare starts to fade away and disappear within an hour. Based on history and presentation what is your diagnosis?

A. Non allergic contact urticaria
B. Allergic contact dermatitis
C. Immunological contact urticaria
D. Chronic ordinary urticaria

Key: A
Ref: Rook (129.8)

2. A 35 year old labourer presents in derma OPD with erythema of face. on examination there is sparing of shaded areas. he gives history of taking doxycycline for his urinary symptoms by a local GP for past 3 days. What is your diagnosis? what is your diagnosis?

A. Photoallergic dermatitis
B. Phototoxic contact dermatitis
C. Irritant contact dermatitis
D. Allergic contact dermatitis
E. Solar urticaria

Key: B
Ref: Rook (129.9)

3. A 18 year old female comes to derma opd with complaint of stinging and burning sensation of face for past few years. She has been to multiple dermatologists but states that her condition is not improving. she is adamant that her skin is very sensitive and her condition becomes worse in summers. You asses her condition by applying 5% lactic acid to her i folds which causes stinging within minutes if applying chemical. which of the following factor is not associated with the condition?

A. Sweating
B. Cold weather
C. Atopic eczema
D. Flushing and blushing
E. Dry skin

Key: B
Ref: Rook (129.10)

4. A Gardner presents in derma OPD with linear erythematosus streaks on his trunk and arms after he had worked in a garden and remained in sun for most of the day. You make a diagnosis of phytophotodermatitis in basis of clinical picture. which if the following will the most critical step in management of the disease?

A. Potent topical steroids
B. Primary prevention of phototoxin
C. Changing occupation
D. Sun avoidance
E. Wearing fully covered clothes

Key: B
Ref: Rook (129.10)

5. A girl trying a new recipe for cooking fish came to skin opd with complain of erythema and burning sensation in hands. In examination there are weals on her birth hands. She states that she was marinating fish in some local sauce. based on history you make a provisional Dx of non-immune contact urticaria. Which of the following is the underlying mechanism?

A. Ige mediated
B. Stimulation of sensory endings of hands
C. Direct release of inflammatory mediators
D. Previous sensitization to chemicals
E. Decrease in thickness of stratum corneum

Key: C
Ref: Rook (129.9)

Chapter 130 OCCUPATIONAL DERMATOLOGY

1. A 36 year old refinery worker presented in opd with multiple comedowns predominantly on his malar and retro auricular area. Keeping the diagnosis in mind which of the following statement is true about the condition?

A. in chlorine, most common site is buttocks and proximal extremities
B. associated systemic findings are berry rare in halogen acne
C. temporal comedowns are diagnostic
D. oral isotretitoin is treatment of choice
E. Chemicals can induce acne at any site, usually within 5-7 days of exposure

Key: C
Ref: Rook (130:12-13)

2. A 56 year old tar distilling worker presented with small pigmented papules on face predominantly around eyes and on back of hands from last 8 months. He was diagnosed with Tar Warts. All of the following statements are true regarding this condition except

A. Polycyclic hydrocarbons are now most important carcinogen in occupational skin cancers
B. Primary prevention is the mainstay of management
C. Ionizing radiations are causative agents in uranium mining
D. Shale oil can cause occupation related skin cancer
E. Soot formed by burning wood has lower levels of polycyclic hydrocarbons and benzopyerene compared with coal soot

Key: A
Ref: Rook (130: 13-14)

3. 18 year old female presented in emergency department after exposure to certain chemical which she cannot recall by name. There was erythema and blister formation on ler left wrist within minutes after exposure to chemical with severe pain. All of the following statements are true regarding chemical burns except

A. Milk/egg whites can be used as antidote for oxidising agents
B. Antidote for hydrofluoric acid is 2, 5% calcium gluconate gel
C. Nitric oxide can be neutralised with magnesium hydroxides
D. Early debridement can be done in chromic acid toxicity to reduce blood levels
E. Hydrofluoric acid carries a risk of systemic toxicity when there is more than 20 % cutaneous involvement

Key: E
Ref: Rook (129- 12, 13)

4. In textile workers, contact urticarial can be caused by?

A. Glutaraldehyde's
B. Formaldehyde
C. Nickel
D. Mordents
E. E-all of the above

Key: B
Ref: Rook (130:10)

5. 35 year old male presented with asymptomatic hypo pigmented macules on bilateral dorsa of hands. He had prolonged exposure with certain chemicals at his work place. All of the following statements are true regarding this condition except? Phenols can cause permanent pigmentation of the skin?

A. Physostigmine can cause occupational leukoderma
B. Apoptosis of melanocytes may be caused by chemical agents associated with occupational leukoderma
C. Topical corticosteroids are first line treatment
D. Motor oils can cause depigmentation at work

Key: D
Ref: Rook (130.12)

Chapter 132

BENIGN MELANOCYTIC PROLIFERATIONS AND MELANOCYTIC NAEVI

1. A 12 year male presented to you with hyper pigmented macules that do not fade away in absence of UV exposure since young age. On examination there are pigmented macules in oral mucosa, lips and GI symptoms are also present. On colonoscopy there are GI polyps also present. True regarding this condition is:

A. Autosomal recessive
B. Autosomal dominant
C. X linked recessive
D. X linked dominant
E. Sporadic disorder

Key: B
Ref: Rook (132.2)

2. A 22 years old African female came with complaint of vaginal discharge. On examination, there was incidental finding of multiple blue black pigmented macules with irregular borders in the vulva. Histopathology of the lesions showed mild acanthosis of the epidermis, hyperpigmentation of basal layer keratinocytes, melanin incontinence and a slight increase in the number of melanocytes without nesting. What could be the best treatment option?

A. Surgical excision
B. Topical imiquimod
C. Topical retinoid
D. No treatment
E. Topical imiquimod followed by surgical excision

Key: D
Ref: Rook (132.11)

3. A mother brought her 1 month old child with multiple uniform round to oval faint bluish grey patches on lower back and buttocks since birth. These lesions are increasing in size over time. Which of the following is not an association

A. Down syndrome
B. Congenital hemangioma
C. Nevus of ota
D. Congenial melanocytic Naevi
E. Cafe au lait macules

Key: D
Ref: Rook (132.13)

4. A 16 years old girl presented with history of asymptomatic bluish grey macular discoloration over right shoulder since 1 year of age. Histology showed elongated dendritic melanocytes scattered among collagen bundles of superficial dermis. Area innervated by which of the following nerves is affected in this condition

A. Anterior supraclavicular and superficial cutaneous brachial nerve
B. Posterior supraclavicular and lateral cutaneous brachial nerve
C. Posterior supraclavicular and anterior cutaneous brachial nerve
D. Anterior supraclavicular and lateral cutaneous brachial nerve
E. Posterior supraclavicular and posterior cutaneous brachial nerve

Key: B
Ref: Rook (132.15)

5. Which of the following histopathological feature of Mongolian spot differentiate it from Blue Nevus

A. Presence of fibrosis and melanophages
B. Elongated dendritic melanocytes in middle and lower dermis
C. Absent dermal melanopages
D. Spindle-shaped dendritic melanocytes located in the dermis in an inverted wedge shape
E. Dumb bell shaped extension of lesion to deep reticular dermis and subcutaneous fat

Key: C
Ref: Rook (132.12 and 132.38)

6. A 12 years old female presented with history of asymptomatic discoloration of left side of upper half of face for 1 year. On Examination there is speckled brown pigmentation in reticular pattern involving bulbar and palpebral conjunctiva, temple and forehead. Which of the following is not a complication of this condition

A. Meningeal melanocytoma
B. Retinal melanomas
C. Choroidal melanoma
D. Iris melanoma
E. Cutaneous melanoma

Key: B
Ref: Rook (132.14)

7. A young female presents to you in opd with concerns regarding pigmentation in her complexion. On examination she had light to dark brown macules which do not fade away once it appears present on her dorsal hands and cheeks. You sent a skin biopsy sample for histopathology. What will you expect in the histopathology of this lesion?

A. Increase number of melanocytes along dermo-epidermal junction
B. Melanocytes in increased number in form of nests
C. Epidermal atrophy with inflamatory infiltrate and melanosomes
D. Elongated dendritic melanocytes among collagen bundles
E. Hyperpigmentation of basal layer with elongation of rete ridges and acanthosis

Key: A
Ref: Rook (132.4)

8. A young female presents to you in opd with concerns regarding pigmentation in her complexion. On examination she had light to dark brown macules which do not fade away once it appears present on her dorsal hands and cheeks. You sent a skin biopsy sample for histopathology. Treatment modalities will include all of following except:

A. Photo protection
B. Chemical peels
C. Photodynamic therapy
D. PDL lasers
E. Depigmenting topical peels

Key: D
Ref: Rook (132.6)

9. A 37 year male returned from a vacation in South Africa 01 month back and presents to you in opd for appearance of brown macules on his upper arms and face. He gives history of sunbathing on the beaches at Cape Town. He is cosmetically concerned for these lesions and seeks medical help. What is the crucial step and foremost effective treatment in managing this patient?

A. Rigourous Photoprotection with High sun protection factor sunscreen
B. Pulsed dye laser

C. Selective Electrocautery of the lesions
D. Topical Tacrolimus
E. Oral Hydroxychloroquine

Key: A
Ref: Rook (132.7)

10. A 37 year male returned from a vacation in South Africa 01 month back and presents to you in opd for appearance of brown macules on his upper arms and face. He gives history of sunbathing on the beaches at Cape Town. A few weeks later he developed densely pigmented black macules with markedly irregular outline with few patches of sun burnt skin and erythema intervening. He is concerned for malignant transformation of these new lesions therefore you advise a skin biopsy for histopathology. What histological changes will you expect in this patient?

A. Atypical mononuclear cells in dermis with epidermotropism
B. Basaloid hyperpigmented cells in groups or nests in papillary dermis with alternating areas of achromatic skip areas
C. Squamous metaplastic cells
D. Pleomorphic keratinocytes, with premature keratinised cells, increased intracytoplasmic PAS positive glycogen containing cells
E. Solar elastosis and disordered epidermal keratinocyte proliferation, cytological atypia

Key: B
Ref: Rook (132.8)

11. A 13 yr. old girl presented in opd with single light brown patch on trunk since childhood now recent changes in that path. On examination there is light brown patch on upper trunk about 4*4 cm studded with foci of dark brown macules n few papules up to 4 mm size. There is risk of developing melanoma so monitoring is advised to pt. What can be diagnosis in above case?

A. Segmental lentigenosis
B. Beckers naevus
C. Speckled lentigenous naevus
D. Cafe au lait spots
E. Agminated naevomelanocytic naevus

Key: C
Ref: Rook (132.15)

12. An 18 yr. old male presented in opd. He had few dark brown macular lesions on trunk. He observed change in appearance of these lesions for last one yr. while he came back from a holiday trip where he had took sunbath on beach multiple times.. He observed that there us rim of depigmented areas around these lesions. He consulted doctor who did Demoscopy only advised him reassurance n advised sun protection only. Regarding above scenario. Which one is not true?

A. It can be associated with vitiligo, atopic eczema n alopecia aerate
B. Stress n puberty can be triggring factors
C. White halo is more visible in summer months.
D. It is basically a disease of old age
E. Melanoma should be excluded if lesion is single n in old age

Key: D
Ref: Rook (132.28)

13. A 23 old male had few dark brown macules n patches on trunk. He presented in opd with itching n redness over these dark brown macules. On examination there are multiple naive with erythematous halo n overlying scale. He is labourer n working in hot summers in outdoor. He also gave history of atopic eczema in one of his siblings. There is no other important in history n examinations. Doctor advised topical

steroids. N asked him to follow-up after 2 wks. For re-evaluation n Demoscopy. What can be diagnosis in this case?

A. Multiple halo naevi
B. Pitryasis rosea
C. Roseola of secondary syphilis
D. Mayerson naevi

Key: D
Ref: Rook (132.29)

14. A 24year old male patient presented in dermatology opd with multiple papules on his limbs, which had appeared four years previously. On physical examination, many pink and skin-coloured papules were seen, which under Demoscopy were observed to be homogeneous, pink vascular lesions. Histopathologic study revealed melanocytic epithelioid cells arranged in groups or singly in the dermis and dermo-epidermal junction. They were HMB-45 positive in the superficial dermis, and Ki-67 < 1% and s100A6 positive.
Given these findings, and diagnosis;
What is the most likely association?

A. Diabetes
B. B.LAMB syndrome
C. Addisons disease
D. chrons disease
E. Sweet syndrome

Key: C
Ref: Rook (132.33)

15. A 3 years old female child was presented in dermatology opd with a pigmented lesion on her right cheek since birth, recently began to enlarge. She had no family history of melanoma. On examination, there was 1cm heavily pigmented lesion with irregular borders located at junction on the lower eyelid. Histopathology revealed, asymmetrical poorly demarcated infiltrating irregular spacing and disorderly arranged nests of epithelioid melanocytic cells reaching up to dermis. Immunohistochemistry shows, strong expression of ki-67 and weaker expression of S100-A6 On the basis of above findings, what is the diagnosis?

A. Classic spitz naevus
B. Atypical spitz naevus
C. halo nevus
D. blue nevus
E. neavus of reed

Key: B
Ref: Rook (132.36, Table 132.4)

16. A 14 old female patient presented to us with a pigmented lesion on the lateral aspect of the left arm for 1 year, slowly enlarging and itchy over the past 2 months. O/E a brown-blue irregular, well defined macule, with approximately 8 mm, with black-brown dots on the periphery. On dermoscopy, there was a black-brown lesion, in a homogenous pattern, composed of structure less areas and with streaks in the periphery and satellite gray-blue lesions. Histopathology revealed spindle-shaped and dendritic, strongly pigmented melanocytes, amid dense fibrous stroma and melanophages, predominantly occupying upper and mid dermis. On the basis of above findings and diagnosis, what is the most likely association?

A. LAMB syndrome
B. Addisons disease
C. Pyoderma gangrenosum
D. Inflamatory bowl disease
E. Pemphigus vulgaris

Key: A.

Ref: Rook (132.38)

17. A 39year old man was referred to the dermatology clinic for evaluation of multiple irregular moles since he was 14 years. He denied a family history of multiple moles or melanoma. O/E, the patient had more than 100 melanocytic nevi, and a few of these nevi appeared clinically atypical. The largest nevus, on the right side of his chest, measured 1 cm in greatest diameter
Dermoscopy showed black dots, globules, and structure less areas. The histopathologic findings revealed intraepidermal, irregular placement of melanocytic nests of variable size and shape, fusion of nests, and asymmetric extension of the junctional component beyond the confines of the intradermal nevus component. Melanocytes contains large nuclei with irregular contours, papillary dermal fibroplasia with a sparse lymph histiocytic infiltrate was present. In the light of above findings, what is the major histological criteria?

A. The basilar proliferation of atypical naevomelanocytes (extending in at least 3 rete ridges beyond any dermal endovascular component.
B. The presence of lamellar fibrosis
C. Neovascularization
D. Inflammatory response
E. Fusion of rete ridges

Key: A
Ref: Rook (132.43)

18. A 54 year-old man with no family history or personal history of melanoma was presented with 15cm congenital blue nevus of the upper back. Examination revealed a 15 × 13cm blue patch of the didapper back, within which were multiple discrete and confluent blue papules and a 6cm palpable nodule in the importation of the lesion. A full mucocutaneous examination revealed more than 50 nevi, of which four were atypical. No hepatosplenomegaly or lymphadenopathy was detected. An incisional biopsy was performed and a diagnosis of malignant blue nevus was made.
All are true regarding malignant blue naves EXCEPT;

A. It occurs in old ages
B. More common in men
C. Most common site is upper chest
D. It can arrise on previously excised blue naevus site.
E. Both A and D

Key: C.
Ref: Rook (132.41)

19.A 31 yr. old fair coloured male undergone renal transplantation 1 yr. back. He noticed an increase in no of brown macules on limbs n trunk. He got anxious n visited derma opd. On examination few dark brown pigmented macules were present on his arm legs. Two oval papules brown in colour present on trunk.. Dermoscopy done n doctor reassured the patient. Regarding diagnosis of above patient. Which one cannot be predisposing factor of above condition?

A. Chemotherapy in childhood usualy for leukemia
B. Renal transplant
C. Local trauma
D. Atopic eczema
E. Turner syndrome

Key: D
Ref: Rook (132.18)

20. A 16 yr. old girl had chemotherapy of leukaemia 1 yrs. back... She noticed that there is increase in no of dark brown macules on his body. Then she had painful swelling n redness after trauma in a flesh coloured dome shaped papule on his scalp after itching in his scalp few days back.. She visited a doctor. He did

dermoscopy of brown lesions. Bt he did biopsy n histopathology of scalp lesion fuel to risk of malignant transformation. After that he ruled out malignancy. What can be histopathological findings of that lesion?

A. Round to cuboidal sinhle naevus cells in basal layer. N nests in rete ridges
B. Nests of naevoid cells in rete ridges n in upper dermis
C. Nests of naevi cells n isolatef naevi cells in dermis. DEJ is normal n epidermis is hyperkerstotic only.
D. Nests of atypical melanocytic naevi cells in dermis n epidermis

Key: C
Ref: Rook (132.20, 132.21)

Chapter 133

BENGN KERATINOCYTIC ACANTHOMAS AND PROLIFERATIONS

1. A 50 year old female patient with Fitzpatrick skin type 1V presented to dermatology opd with complaints of pruritic verrucous plaques that vary from dirty yellow to black in colour and had a loosely adherent greasy keratin on the surface. Keeping in view the diagnosis what are the possible associations of this disease?

A. Spitz naevi
B. Thyrotoxicosis
C. Gastric and colon carcinoma
D. malignant melanoma

Key: C
Ref: Rook (133.1)

2. A 65 year old male with Fitzpatrick skin type 1V presents with complain of hyper pigmented patch on his face. On examination, its surface had numerous plugged follicular orifices. When dermoscopy was done it revealed cerebriform pattern, milia like cysts, come do like openings and fingerprint structure. Skin biopsy was done and Histopathology report was awaited. What are the histopathological variants of the disease patient the patient is suffering from?

A. Solid, Hyperkeratotic, Reticular
B. pleomorphic, angioamtoid, myxoid
C. infiltrative, morpheoform, micronodular
D. Reticular, superficial spreading, solid

Key: A
Ref: Rook (133.2)

3. 35 year old female presents to dermatology clinic with complaints of pigmented papular eruption on her cheeks and forehead. On skin biopsy there was irregular acanthosis and hyperkeratosis. Keeping in view the diagnosis what are the mutations seen in these patients?

A. P53
B. NRAS
C. FOXP3
D. FGFR3

Key: D
Ref: Rook (133.4)

4. An elderly male presented to dermatology opd with red to brown dome shaped papule on his right leg. There was a thin collarette of scale and a vascular puncture was visible. His skin biopsy revealed psoriasiform acanthosis with pale periodic acid Schiff positive glycogen rich keratinocytes. Papillary dermis was oedematous. What is the likely diagnosis?

A. Cutaneous horn
B. Dermatosis papulosa nigra
C. lichenoid keratosis
D. clear cell acanthoma

Key: D
Ref: Rook (133.6)

5. A 45 year old Male patient presents with chronic non healing ulcer on his right forearm. On examination, the ulcer has irregular surface with heaped up margins giving the appearance of rolled border. The edges

are not indurated. DNA microscopy studies reveals higher expression of KRT9 and lower expression of Gene C15orf48.what is the likely diagnosis?

A. Squamous cell carcinoma
B. Basal cell carcinoma
C. Keratoacanthoma
D. Pesudoepitheliomatous hyperplasia

Key: D
Ref: Rook (133.8)

Chapter 134 CUTANEOUS CYTS

1. A 25 year old boy is referred to you by a gastroentologist for multiple small skin colored nodular swellings on the extremeties and face for past 10 years. These swellings were asymtomatic and hence he did not report them earlier. However, his new onset hematochezia caused him to seek medical advice. Considering the underlying diagnosis the most likely cause of his cutaneous manifestation is

A. Vellous hair cyst
B. Trichellemal cysts
C. Syringomas
D. Epidermoid inclusion cysts
E. Steocystomas

Key: D
Ref: Rook (134.2)

2. A 40 yr old female presented to you with nodular swelling on the scalp. You excise the lesion and send it for histopathology. The report shows homogenous and eosinophilic cystic contents lined by stratified sqamous epithelium. A distince palisaded border at the periphery is seen. The cholestrol clefts in this case will show positivity to following on immunohistochemistry

A. K10
B. K9
C. CK7
D. CK8
E. CK19

Key: A
Ref: Rook (134.3)

3. A 60 yr old female presented with a well-defined solid cystic nodule on the scalp for past 4 yrs. On H/P cysts are filled with keratin with calcification. Peripheral palisading of basaloid cells and bulky squamous cells large eosinophilic cytoplasm and abrupt keratinization with mild atypia are seen. The most likely cause of her cystic swelling is

A. Trichelemmal cyst
B. Proliferating benign trichelemmal cyst
C. Malignant trichelemmal cyst
D. Scc
E. Poro ca

Key: B
Ref: Rook (134.3)

4. A 25 yr old boy presented with multiple, smooth skin colored compressible dermal papules and nodules on the face and trunk for 3 months. No punctum was seen however, comedones were evident. There was considerably high sebum secretion on the face. What will the 1st line of management be in this patient?

A. Excision of cystic lesions
B. CO2 laser theraphy
C. Doxycyline
D. Topical benzoic acid
E. Isotretinion

Key: E
Ref: Rook (134.4)

5. A 30 yr olr male presented with multiple small white to yellow papules on the infra orbital area. The lesions were asymtomatic but cosmetically disfiguring. He reports a similar papulo pustular eruption behind the ear few years back for which he took minocylcine. The underlying pathology in this patient is

A. Pilar cyst
B. Vellous hair cyst
C. Subepidermal keratin cyst
D. Inclusion cyst
E. Infundubalar cyst

Key: C
Ref: Rook (134.5)

Chapter 135 LYMPHOCYTIC INFILTRATES

1. A 28yrs old female presented with asymptomatic plum coloured nodules and plaques involving face, ear lobules and trunk. She also gives history of photosensitivity. Histology shows dense full thickness dermal nodular lymphocytic infiltrate separated from normal looking epidermis by acellular grenz zone. What is most likely diagnosis?

A. cutaneous sarcoidosis
B. Granulomatous rosacea
C. Granuloma Facial
D. Jessen lymphocytic infiltrate
E. Lymphocytoma cutis

Key: E
Ref: Rook (135.9)

2. A 26 yrs. old female presented with recurrent episodes of skin rash which resolves spontaneously within few weeks. Skin examination revealed multiple erythematous to purple crusty papules, pustules, vesicles along with some varioliform scarring at few areas. Biopsy showed interface dermatitis with CD 8 positive lymphocytes and some necrotic keratinocytes. Most likely diagnosis is?

A. Lymohomatoid papulosis
B. pseudoporphyrias
C. pityriasis lichenised chronical
D. PLEVA
E. small plaque Para psoriasis

Key: D
Ref: Rook (135.3)

3. A 40yrs old male came to OPD with eruption of asymptomatic nodules and plaques on body involving neck, limbs, axilla and trunk. On probing history he told u to have nocturnal itch from last 5 months for which he took multiple treatments but didn't resolved completely took biopsy and see conspicuous tagging of lymphocytes along basal epidermis in a band like manner. No atypia or epidermotropism was found. What is most likely diagnosis?

A. T cell pseudo lymphoma
B. Lymphocytoma cupid
C. Jessner lymphocytic infiltrate
D. Granuloma Faciale
E. CD 4+ve Cut.T cell lymphoma

Key: A
Ref: Rook (135.2)

4. A 30 yrs. old female u was known case of Hep. C came to ur OPD with asymptomatic lichenoid papules reddish brown in colour with mica like scale which when detached reveal shiny brown surface. A diagnosis of pityriasis lichenised chronical was made. Most important step in management is?

A. Vigorous application of Topical emollients
B. Topical steroids
C. start INF alpha and ribavarin therapy
D. Hydroxychloroquine
E. PUVA therapy

Key: C
Ref: Rook (135.4)

5. A 10 yrs. old boy came to u with history of asymptomatic popular and plaques with Mica like scales for 5 months. He was diagnosed as case of pityriasis lichenised chronical and was given topical steroids but his condition didn't resolved. What is the best second line treatment option for him?

A. Tetracyclines
B. Erythromycin
C. Acitretin
D. Dapsone
E. Methotrexate

Key: B
Ref: Rook (135.6)

6. Pregnant lady at 20 weeks of gestation ,presented to dermatology opd with h/o pinkish oedematous papule with central vesication and necrosis over trunk, thighs and upper arm with sparing of face and scalp , these lesion heal with scarring that resemble small pox scar
There is associated h/o headache and malaise
Keeping in mind the diagnosis of this patient, which statement is not true about the pathogensis of this disease?

A. It is immune complex mediated disease
B. Associated with chemotherapy agents
C. Linked with viral trigger
D. Its type 4 hypersensitivity reaction
E. Associated with vaccination

Key: D
Ref: Rook (135.4)

7. 11 years old child brought by his mother to opd with h/o lichenoid papules with adherent detachable scale over trunk and thighs from last 2 months, few of them healed spontaneously with post inflammatory hypopigmentation, he was treated with initially topical steroids but got no relief
What would be the next possible treatment option in this patient?

A. Phototherapy
B. Hydroxycholoroquine
C. Methotrexate
D. Acetretin
E. Erythromycin

Key E
Ref: Rook (135.6)

8. A 40 year old female presented with erythematous papules and plaques on face and neck for few months...these are asymptomatic and non-scaly and there is no history of prior sun exposure. She states that she had similar lesions few years back, but those resolved spontaneously in few weeks.
Considering the diagnosis, what is the most likely picture of Histopathology?

A. Normal epidermis, grenz zone, nodular dense infiltrate in dermis
B. Normal epidermis, superficial and deep perivascular infiltrate, upper dermal edema and some basal liquefaction necrosis
C. Oedematous epidermis with interface dermatitis and deep dense wedge shaped infiltrate
D. Normal epidermis with no atrophy or follicular plugging, superficial and deep perivascular lymphocytic infiltrate. No copious dermal mucin
E. Epidermal atrophy, follicular plugging, sparse dermal infiltrate, focal liquefaction degeneration of basal epidermis, colloid bodies and mucin are present

Key: D
Ref: Rook (135.10)

9. A 50 year old male presented with a rash on his trunk...he says that the rash is asymptomatic, but since it is present for quite a long time now, so it is bothering him. On examination, you see monomorphic round erythematous patches ranging 3-5 cm in dia, with mild scaling. There is involvement of trunk and limbs but sparing of pelvic girdle. He says that these are present for good 3, 4 years and become more obvious in winters. He has a prior Histopathology report but it is nonspecific.
Which of the following treatment is NOT correct regarding your diagnosis?

A. As the condition is benign, just symptomatic treatment is needed
B. Topical nitrogen mustard give response in few pts
C. Early stage cutaneous lymphoma can b considered
D. Can go for TCR gene analysis if in doubt
E. It progresses to MF in majority of the long standing cases

Key: E
Ref: Rook (135.6)

10. A 45 year old male presented with atrophic yellow orange patches and plaques on trunk and limbs, according to the patient, these are persistent, and increasing gradually for a few months you go for Histopathology, and report says epidermal atrophy and band like lymph infiltrate in papillary dermis and few free red cells are present Immunophenotyping reveals a normal T cell phenotype. Regarding management, which of the following should be least considered?

A. Topical emollients
B. Topical steroids
C. Phototherapy
D. Nitrogen mustard
E. Intermittent derma review

Key: B
Ref: Rook (135.7)

11. 25 years old male presented with h /o pinkish brown papules distributed over trunk, thighs and upper arm with relative sparing of face and scalp, there is also involvement of oral mucosa. These lesions heal with varioliform scarring. Which finding is not true about the histopathology report of this patient?

A. Parakeratosis
B. Interface dermatitis mainly of cd4 lymphocytes
C. Exocytosis of lymphocytes
D. Pseudomunro microbes
E. Deep dense dermal wedge shape infiltrate

Key: B
Ref: Rook (135.5)

12. A 37 year old female presented with asymptomatic persistent erythematous plaques and papules on face and neck for few months, there is no significant history of relation of these lesions with sun exposure, these are asymptomatic and she wants treatment because they look unsightly. You have a list of differentials and you want to proceed with diagnosis....which of the following is LEAST correct in this regard?

A. Go for ANA and anti RO anti LA
B. Histopathology should be done
C. DIF is done along with Histopathology
D. Photo testing to rule out PLE
E. CBC and urinalysis

Key: D
Ref: Rook (135.10)

13. 30 years old HIV positive male presented with h/o high grade fever and large ulceronectoic lesions over trunk. There is associated h/o cognitive impairment O/E there is occipital lymphadenopathy. On histopathology of skin lesions, there is fibrinous necrosis of deep vessels and partial necrosis of follicles and complete necrosis of eccrine glands. What would be the possible diagnosis in this patient?

A. Steven Johnson syndrome
B. Pyoderma gangrenous
C. Dermatitis artefact
D. Sclerosing panniculitis
E. Mocha Huberman disease

Diagnosis Mocha Huberman disease

Key: E
Ref: Rook (135.4)

14. 8 years old child presented with h /o crops of lichenoid papules over trunk, arms and legs with adherent scale, on gentle scraping it reveals shiny brown surface. Which statement is not correct about the prognosis of this patient?

A. Acute phase of this disease resolve within 6 months
B. It has longer course
C. In healing phase more pigmentation can occur
D. Accrual variant has poor prognosis
E. Excellent response to conventional treatment

Key: E
Ref: Rook (135.4)

Chapter 136 CUTANEOUS HISTIOCYTOSES

1. A 23 years old female presented with history of asymptomatic yellow coloured flat plaques on eyelids, neck, buttocks and cubital fossae from last 3 years. Histology showed accumulation of foamy macrophages infiltrate in the dermis, with a distinct perivascular accentuation and mixed inflammatory cell reaction. Which of the following is not associated disorder

A. Paraproteinaemia
B. Dyslipidaemia
C. Lymphoma
D. CML
E. Salary syndrome

Key: B
Ref: Rook (136.18)

2. A 3 year old male presented with history of asymptomatic erythematous, yellow brown papules and nodules, which are symmetrically distributed on proximal extremities for last 1 year. He had history of 2 episodes of seizures in last 6 months. Otherwise patient has achieved milestones normally and has no other systemic illness. Histology of the lesion showed infiltration of the dermis with spindle-shaped mononuclear cells, foamy histiocytic, giant cells, lymphocytes, polymorphs and eosinophils. Trouton giant cells were also observed. Which of the following is best treatment option

A. CO2 laser
B. Cautery of the lesions
C. Surgical excision
D. Corticosteroids
E. ND YAG laser

Key: D
Ref: Rook (136.18)

3. A 30 years old lady presented with history of multiple asymptomatic reddish-orange deep nodules on right shoulder for last 2 months. Some lesions have overlying telangiectasias. Histology of the lesion showed accumulation scalloped histiocytic with some infiltrating lymphocytes. Stains for S100 and CD1a were negative. Which is true regarding this condition

A. Mucosae can be involved
B. Flexures are mostly involved
C. Chemotherapy is effective in late lesions
D. Associated with systemic involvement
E. Can involute spontaneously

Key: A
Ref: Rook (136.16)

4. A 20 years old male presented with history of asymptomatic plaques in axillae for 2 years. On examination, there were erythematous, yellow brown verrucous plaques, symmetrically distributed in both axillae. Patient also had stridor. Histology showed infiltration of the dermis with spindle-shaped mononuclear cells, foamy histiocytic, giant cells, lymphocytes, polymorphs and eosinophils. Trouton giant cells were also observed. Cells label strongly with factor XIIIa, CD68 and Ki-M1p and are negative for S100 and CD1a. Which of the following is not best treatment option

A. Corticosteroid
B. Carabine

C. HCQ
D. Azathioprine
E. Acipimox

Key: C
Ref: Rook (136.18)

5. A 30 years old lady presented with history of multiple asymptomatic reddish-orange deep nodules on right shoulder for last 2 months. Some lesions have overlying telangiectasia. Histology of the lesion showed accumulation scalloped histiocytic with some infiltrating lymphocytes. Stains for S100 and CD1a were negative. Which is true regarding this condition

A. Mucosae can be involved
B. Flexures are mostly involved
C. Chemotherapy is effective in late lesions
D. Associated with systemic involvement
E. Can involute spontaneously

Key: A
Ref: Rook (136.16)

6. 30 years old male presented with symmetrical, small, red-brown papules on the trunk and arms, sparing the flexures. Histology showed proliferation of monomorphic histiocytic cells in the upper and mid dermis. No giant cells or foam cells were seen. Cells were positive for CD68, Mac-387, lysozyme and factor XIIIa and negative for S100 and CD1a. Which of the following is least effective treatment option

A. PUVA
B. Wait and watch
C. Oral steroid
D. Tacrolimus
E. Thalidomide

Key: D
Ref: Rook (136.15)

7. A 18months old girl bought to you by her parents with complain of some skin lesions. On examination you found erythematous scaly greasy papules and plaques at inguinal and gluteal folds with surrounding petechial. Her parents told it's started from age of two months, and resistant to multiple topical medications. Skeletal survey showed lytic lesions in left femur. Complete blood count showed low platelets. Regarding diagnosis which one of the following is true?

A. Patient is not at risk of developing disseminated disease
B. Skin manifestation is present in about 20%
C. Above condition is associated with risk of developing renal failure
D. Systemic therapy is not required
E. It is associated with worst prognosis.

Key: E
Ref: Rook (136.5)

8. A 5 years old boy bought to you by parents with complain of increase urination and skin lesions. He used to drink water frequently .On skin examination multiple yellowish brown discrete nodules scattered on his body. Oral examination showed gingival ulceration and haemorrhage. Electron microscopy showed collection of abnormal cells with tennis racket shaped organelles. What is your diagnosis?

A. Hashimoto-Pritzker disease
B. Letterer Siwe Disease
C. Hand Schuller Christian disease
D. Congenital self-healing Histocytosis

E. Histiocytoma

Key: C
Ref: Rook (136.5)

9. A 18months old girl bought to you by her parents with complain of some skin lesions. On examination you found erythematous scaly greasy papules and plaques at inguinal and gluteal folds with surrounding petechial. Her parents told its started from age of two months, and resistant to multiple topical medications Complete blood count showed low platelets. Skeletal survey showed lytic lesions in femur. After skin biopsy you started her treatment with vinblastine and prednisolone. After 2 months of treatment patient came back with exacerbation of her disease.
What will be your next step in management?

A. Observe the child until there is ulceration
B. Start UVB therapy
C. Continue same salvage protocol
D. Consider reduced intensity conditioning haemopoietin stem cell transplant RIC-HSCT
E. Localised electron beam therapy

Key: D
Ref: Rook (136.7)

10. A 15 years old girl bought to you by parents with complain of increase urination and skin lesions .On skin examination multiple yellowish brown greasy papules and plaques at present at scalp and t inguinal area. Oral examination showed gingival ulceration. Electron microscopy showed collection of abnormal cells with tennis racket shaped organelles. Considering diagnosis all of the following are true except

A. Premature tooth eruption is the first manifestation of this variant
B. X-ray of bones may showed lytic lesions
C. Immunophenotype showed CD1a positive staining
D. Reduced expression of CD207
E. Nucleus of cells are of coffee bean shaped

Key: D
Ref: Rook (136.2)

11. A 25 years old girl came with complain of burning at axilla and groin. On examination you found hyperpigemented and hypo pigmented patches at same site with few talengactasias. She told that she has some skin problem since many years. Systemic examination was unremarkable. Histopathology showed collection of abnormal cells with boat shaped nucleus and positive CD1a.
Regarding diagnosis how u will treat her

A. No need of treatment just observe the fate
B. Start UVB therapy
C. Start systemic therapy with Vinblastine / prednisolone
D. Treat her with topical medication like high potent topical steroid or topical tacrolimus
E. Localised radiation therapy

Key: D
Ref: Rook (136.8)

12. A mother is referred from medical department to you with her 8 month old child with generalised exanthema, high grade fever, hepatosplenomegaly and pancytopenia's. Pallor, anorexia, vomiting, irritability, hepatosplenomegaly and lymphadenopathy are present at presentation. Which of the following investigation is crucial to establish diagnosis:

A. Serum ferritin < 500 ug/L
B. Bone marrow picture showing hem phagocytosis
C. Peripheral picture showing increased retic count

D. Soluble CD25 - IL 2 < 2500 units
E. Hyperfibroginemia > 1.5 g/dl

Key: B
Ref: Rook (136.2)

13. A mother is referred from medical department to you with her 8 month old child with generalised exanthema, high grade fever, hepatosplenomegaly and pancytopenia's. Pallor, anorexia, vomiting, irritability, hepatosplenomegaly and lymphadenopathy are present at presentation. Management will include all except:

A. Low-dose continuous dexamethasone for life
B. Etoposide and cyclosporine
C. Combination of corticosteroids, cyclosporine A and antithymocyte globulin
D. High-dose pulse corticosteroids
E. Addition of rituximab in association with EBV associated ethology

Key: A
Ref: Rook (136.11)

14. A mother is referred from medical department to you with her 8 month old child with generalised exanthema, high grade fever, hepatosplenomegaly and pancytopenia's. Pallor, anorexia, vomiting, irritability, hepatosplenomegaly and lymphadenopathy are present at presentation. The underlying pathology includes all except:

A. Autosomal recessive entity
B. X-linked lymphoproliferative syndrome (XLP)
C. Associated with HIV infection commonly
D. Diffuse infi ltrate with lymphocytes and mature histiocytes
E. Associated with lymphomas

Key: C
Ref: Rook (136.9 to 136.10)

15. A 8 months male baby is brought to you by his mother with complaints of single to multiple papules or nodules with a predilection for the face, head and neck, followed by the upper torso and upper and lower extremities. They usually start as reddish yellow macules/papules, which may enlarge and evolve into yellow brown patches/ plaques with surface telangiectasia. The consistency is generally fi rm and rubbery. How will you proceed with this case to establish your diagnosis?

A. Skin biopsy for histopathology showing racket shaped cells
B. Immunohistochemistry showing CD68-positive immunopositivity
C. Blood complete examination showing pancytopenias
D. Liver biopsy showing infiltration with dendritic cells
E. Gene studies showing neuroleptic gene defects

Key: B
Ref: Rook (136.12 - 136.13)

16. A 8 months male baby is brought to you by his mother with complaints of single to multiple papules or nodules with a predilection for the face, head and neck, followed by the upper torso and upper and lower extremities. They usually start as reddish yellow macules/papules, which may enlarge and evolve into yellow brown patches/ plaques with surface telangiectasia. The consistency is generally firm and rubbery. Management will include all except:

A. Resolves spontaneously
B. Surgical excision or cautery
C. Ocular therapy includes topical, intraregional and sub conjunctival corticosteroids
D. Oral hydroxycholoroquine for life-threatening disease

E. Low-dose 'non-cataract genic' radiation therapy (300–400 cGy)

Key: D
Ref: Rook (136.13 - 136.14)

17. 27 year's male presents in opd with large yellowish plaques on eyelids from 2 years. On examination of whole body few are also present on buttocks. On h/p large foamy cells are infiltrating dermis. Serum lipids are normal. How will you manage it?

A. Excision
B. Er yag laser
C. Treat underlying cause
D. All of above

Key: D
Ref: Rook (136.18)

18. 11 years male presents to skin opd with recurrent multiple draining abscesses, sinuses on arms, legs from 3-4 years On Histopath large cells with abundant cytoplasm with fine eosinophilic granules involving epidermis and dermis. And round basophilic inclusion bodies.
What is the diagnosis?

A. Nxg
B. Malakoplakia
C. Dorfman disease
D. Malignant histiocytosis

Key: B
Ref: Rook (136.21)

19. 22 years male presents with periorbital red yellow plaques with necrosis. On eye examination conjunctivitis is present. On histo granulomatous masses present as nodules in dermis. Hyaline areas of necrobiosis separating nodules.
What is the association of this disease?

A. Hematologic n lymphoproliferative malignancies
B. Leukaemia
C. Git malignancies
D. Cns disorders

Key: A
Ref: Rook (136.22)

20. Regarding NXG treatment which is correct?

A. Alkylating agents -melphalan results in permanent clearing
B. Chlorambucil is always first line treatmnt
C. Co2 laser successfully treats it
D. Thalidomide is regarded as first line according to guidelines

Key: C
Ref: Rook (136.22)

21. Regarding malakoplakia what is correct?

A. It means hard plaque
B. Chronic infection plays role
C. Michael is guttmann bodies if present results in good prognosis
D. Most commonly affects skin.

Key: B
Ref: Rook (136.21)

22. A 40 year old female, presented with firm scaly papule of 3 cm over right arm showing dimple sign. Histopathological spindle shaped cells with pink cytoplasm ans focal stipiform pattern. This lesion can be differentiated from malignant dermto fibro sarcoma protuberans by?

A. Focal CD 34 positivity and positive staining for factor 13 a
B. Toluidine blue stain.
C. CD 20.
D. S100

Key: A.
Ref: Rook (137.20)

23. A 50 year old male with alcoholic liver cirrhosis presented with ill-defined area of thickening over left palm for last 1 month. Keeping dx in mind which is not variant of this disease?

A. Knuckle pad.
B. Plantar fibromatosis.
C. Peronei disease.
D. Claw hand

Key: D
Ref: Rook (137.13)

Chapter 137 SOFT – TISSUE TUMOURS AND TUMOUR-LIKE CONDITIONS

Q.1 A 10 years old male presented with a lesion localized in the left labial commissure of two months of duration. The lesion was asymptomatic and has rapidly grown in size. O/E firm, red to purple nodule with a sessile base, measuring approx. 1cm in diameter. The lesion was diagnosed clinically as pyogenic granuloma due to its appearance & patient reported trauma in the region before appearance of the lesion. Based on clinical diagnosis of pyogenic granuloma an excisional biopsy was performed. The microscopic exam revealed an endothelial cell proliferation in nodular arrangements with a "cannon ball" pattern cover by oral mucosa. Based on the histological features of the lesion what is your diagnosis now?

A. Pyogenic granuloma
B. Haemangioma
C. Tufted anima
D. Kaposi sarcoma
E. Traumatic ulcer

Key: C
Ref: Rooks (137.25)

Q.2 A 30 years old female presented in skin opd with sudden onset of multiple erythematous/ haemorrhagic macules, papules and plaques located on the trunk, forearms & low limbs, some of which are ulcerated. Hx of frequent headache, fatigue and malaise present n patient had previous history of miscarriages in last 3 years. What is the prognosis of this disease?

A. Worse in females
B. Resolve spontaneously
C. progress to organ damage
D. Mortality rate is more than 35%
E. All of the above

Key: B
Ref: Rooks (137.24)

Q3 A 41 years old diabetic male presented with multiple nodules on dorsal surface of penile shaft. He also complains of penile pain and curvature during erection. Keeping the diagnosis in mind all of the following are treatment options except.

A. Surgery
B. I/L interferon alpha 2a
C. I/ L interferon alpha 2b
D. I/L collagenase clostridium histolytic

Key: B
Ref: Rooks (137.13)

Q4 A 48 years old female known case of system sclerosis presented with sudden onset of multiple haemorrhagic tender lesions involving her face, upper chest and dorsa feet. She also gave history of fever, malaise and weight loss. Biopsy revealed dilated blood vessels lined by several rows of endothelial cells contain fibrin thrombus no extraction of RBC's. What is your diagnosis?

A. FDE
B. Angiolymphoid hyperplasia
C. Reactive angioendotheliomatosis
D. vasculitis

E. Degos disease

Key: C
Ref: Rooks (137.24)

Q5. A 33 years old male admitted in medicine department n treated there for some polyneuropathy and monoclonal gammopathy disorder. Presented to you with multiple erythematous and haemorrhagic papules and plaques present over trunk and thighs, along with some hyperpigmentation and hypertrichosis. On general examination he had hepatosplenomegaly, as cities and finger clubbing. Following are true regarding the cutaneous disorder except.

A. Lesion spontaneously regress
B. Lesion do not regress spontaneously
C. Histopathology show clusters of dilated capillaries in dermis
D. Histologically similar to cherry angiomas
E. Reactive vascular proliferation to POEMS

Key: A
Ref: Rooks (137.25)

Q6. A 70 year old, CVA patient for last 5 years, presented to derma opd his attendants are concerned with a subcutaneous swelling over right iliac crest. What are the histological features of this disease?

A. Poorly circumscribed mass with areas of fibrosis, vascular proliferation, necrosis and focal amyloid change.
B. Endothelial damage, spongiosis, acanthosis
C. Basal cell vacillation,
D. Irregular elastic and collagen fibers.
E. Fibrosis

Key: A.
Ref: Rooks (137.6)

Q7. An adult male presents with a solitary dome shaped lesion on his index finger. It has a collarets of slightly raised skin at its base. Histopathology shows thick collagen, thin elastin, increased fibroblasts and vascularity. He is likely suffering from:

A. Supernumery digit
B. Acquired digital fibrokeratoma
C. Verruca
D. Infantile digital fibroma
E. Acrochordon

Key: B
Ref: Rooks (137.4)

Q8. An adult female presents with a fibro epithelial poly like peri-anal lesion. You excise the lesion and request a histopathological examination. The report reads as mildly acanthosis epidermis surrounding a collagenous and vascular stroma containing scattered bizarre mono or multinucleated cells with hyperchromatic and pleomorphic nuclei. A few mitotic figures are also seen. You diagnose her excised lesion as:

A. Fibrous papule
B. Stipiform collagenoma
C. Fibrokeratoma
D. Pleomorphic Fibroma
E. Pseudo tumour

Key: D
(Ref: Rooks (137.4)

Q9. An adult male presents with a rapidly enlarging tumour on his forearm which is present only for 2weeks. You excise and send it for histopathological evaluation. The report reads as benign subcutaneous neoplasm with a focally circumscribed mass composed of bundles of fairly uniform fibroblasts and my fibroblasts with pink cytoplasm present at the periphery and probing facial planes and fat and muscle with a high mitotic rate. Multinucleated giant cells are also seen. Tumour cells are negative for smooth muscle markers like Desman and h-caldesmon and variably positive for SMA and Calponin. You diagnose your patient as:

A. Fibrous papule
B. Stipiform collagenoma
C. Fibrokeratoma
D. Pleomorphic Fibroma
E. Nodular Fasciitis

Key: E
Ref: Rooks (137.5)

Q10. A 80 year old male patient underwent hip replacement surgery and is bedbound for last 6 months presented with subcutaneous swelling over sacral area, dx as ischaemic fasciitis, what is the main pathophysiological feature of this patient?

A. Deposition of calcium
B. H/O contact dermatitis due to topical applied
C. Osteosarcoma/malignancy
D. Reactive pseudosarcomatous proliferation as a result of sustained pressure.

Key: D
Ref: Rooks (137.6)

Q11. An adult female presents with multiple small, asymptomatic skin coloured papules and nodules scattered on her head, neck, upper arms and trunk. Oral cavity is also involved. Other siblings are also suffering from similar lesions. Histology shows well circumscribed dome shaped papule with an overlying attenuated epidermis. Dermis is composed of thickened homogenous collagen that is arranged in whorls with a thumbprint or grains of wood appearance. Overall the lesion exhibits low cellularity and the elastic fibres are absent. The tumour stains positively with valentine, Factor XIIIA and focally for CD34. You decide to investigate her further for:

A. Birth hog due syndrome
B. Brook Spengler Syndrome
C. Torre Muir Syndrome
D. Cowden Disease
E. Bannayan Riley Ruval Caba Syndrome

Q12. The mode of inheritance of all the syndromes mentioned in the above scenario is:

A. XR
B. XD
C. AR
D. AD
E. Polygenic

Key: D

Q13. A male baby boy of 2 years presented with a 5 cm nodule over right axilla which wasn't visible at birth but has grown rapidly since then, histopathological biopsy was done and dx as fibrous hamartoma of infancy, which statement is incorrect regarding histopathology of this disease?

A. Bundles of interlacing, elongated, bland, wavy spindle shaped cells in a variable collagenous background.

B. Mesenchymal cells, arborizing shwann cells, in collagenous interstitial tissue
C. Nests of more immature cells with focal amyloid change.
D. Manure adipose tissue

Key: B
Ref: Rooks (137.7)

Q14. Which of the following is NOT a feature of Syndrome diagnosed in scenario number 4?
A. Carcinoma of breast
B. Carcinoma of Thyroid
C. Trichoepitheliomas
D. Cylindromas
E. Stipiform collagenases

Key: D
Ref: Rooks (80.14)

Q15. A 50 year old patient presented in dermatology department with ongoing shoulder and arm pain for 3 years. He had noticed a painless tumour with feeling of pressure in his upper right arm for some months. There was no history of recent trauma or injuries. There is no systemic signs of infection, weight loss, or fever and no prior medical history. Clinical examination showed a painless subcutaneous mass on the right upper arm, starting lateral to the axillary fold expanding about 8 cm distally. On palpation, the tumour was elastic and firm. There was no sensory or motor dysfunction. The overlying skin showed no signs of infection. Skin biopsy showed adipocytes with eosinophilic granular multivacuolated cytoplasm and centrally located nucleolus. By immunohistochemistry, adipocytes are positive for S100 protein. Keeping in mind the diagnosis, the prognosis of disease is
A. Malignant with recurrence
B. Benign with local recurrence
C. Benign with no local recurrence
D. Malignant with short duration

Key: C
Ref: Rooks (137.59)

Q16. A 40 year old man presented with large painful mass on his left arm. The mass had been present for 8 years and had been enlarging progressively during this period. The patient complained of discomfort, disfiguration and difficulty in dressing. He did not have sensory or motor defects. On examination, the mass was found to be above the deltoid muscle, and was soft, well-circumscribed and mobile. Histopathology showed encapsulated, mature adipose tissue with prominent vascular component. Some of the blood vessels contain fibrin thrombi. The most probable diagnosis is
A. Hibernia
B. Angiolipoma
C. leiomyosarcoma
D. Smooth muscle hamartoma

Key: B
. Ref: Rooks (137.58)

Q17. A 35 yr. old man presented with soft painless subcutaneous mass on the volar aspect of the proximal and middle phalanx of the right index digit. The mass appeared three years prior to the medical consultation. And was asymptomatic until 12 months ago, when the patient first complained of limitation in flexion and pain during manual manoeuvres. On clinical examination he had a soft, mobile, elastic mass at the volar aspect of the 2nd digit with no disturbance of sensibility. He had no ulceration
Or pigmentation on the overlying skin, neither any other inflammatory changes such as redness, heat or pain on palpation. Plain x-ray of the digit showed no bone invasion. Histopathology showed encapsulated

tumour with lobules of manure adipose tissue divided by delicate fibrous septa. There is no nuclear atypia and no mitotic activity seen. Keeping in mind the diagnosis, the most correct statement is

A. More common in males
B. Can progress to lip sarcoma.
C. Benign but rapidly grow
D. Malignant in nature

Key: B
Ref: Rooks (137.59)

Q18. A 53 year old man presented with painless nodule on chest region, which had been progressively increasing in size for 7 years. Physical examination revealed an irregular, firm, tender exophytic swelling, measuring 5cm diameter at the anterior trunk. There were no signs of infection and the overlying skin was normal. The remainder of the clinical examination was normal. Lymph nodes were not palpable. His past history was significant of a local trauma. Histopathological examination revealed fascicles of eosinophilic spindle shaped cells with cigar shaped nuclei. Mitotic figures are common. Immunohistochemically positive for actin, desmin and keratin. The most probable diagnosis is

A. Lipoblastomatosis
B. Granular cell tumour
C. Leiomyosarcoma
D. Superficial angiomyxoma

Key: C
. Ref: Rooks (137.57)

Q19. A 33 year old man with multiple skin lesions, presenting as papules that were erythematous-brownish with a firm consistency, clustered in the upper left chest region. The lesions increased gradually during the past 2 years, becoming painful in the last year. On clinical examination, he reported severe pain only with a gentle palpation of the site. Histopathology showed bundles of spindle shaped cells which are strongly eosinophilic with elongated nuclei and blunt edges. Tumour cells are positive for actin and desmin. Keeping in mind the diagnosis, the medical treatment that will relieve pain include

A. Topical Corticosteroids
B. Systemic Antibiotics
C. Calcium channel blockers
D. Systemic corticosteroids

Key: C
Ref: Rooks (137.56)

Q20. A 66yr old female who underwent radical mastectomy for breast CA ten years earlier and also developed swelling of left arm for last 5yrs which was diagnosed as lymphedema of left arm now presented with complaint of multiple, red nodules on left arm. On examination multiple red colour nodules along with some ulcerated lesions were present. On biopsy, collagen is lined by tumour cells in dissection of collagen pattern. Considering dx of pt., immunohistochemically markers positive for this condition are

A. CD34
B. CD31
C. FLI-1protein
D. ERG
E. All of above

Key: E
Ref: Rooks (137.37)

Q21. A 35-year-old woman presented with a cluster of small translucent nodules on her ears and her hairline. On biopsy histopathology showed proliferating capillaries and thick blood vessels lined by plump endothelial cells with little cytological atypia and rare mitotic figures. There was a perivascular inflammatory infiltrate composed of lymphocytes and large number of Eosinophils. What are specific vascular markers for this disease?

A. CD 30, CD 31, actin
B. CD34, CD31, actin
C. CD34, CD31, ERG
D. CD39, CD 31, ERG
E. CD34, CD30, keratin

Key: C
Ref: Rooks (137.29)

Q22. A 26 year old male presented with a cluster of small translucent nodules on his neck and ears. Histopathology of these lesions Showed clusters of proliferating capillaries and thick blood vessels lined by plump epithelioid endothelial cells with little cytological atypia. There was perivascular inflammatory infiltrate composed of lymphocytes and large number of eosinophils.
Following is not true for this condition

A. Peripheral eosinophilia present in less than 10% of patients.
B. May involve oral mucosa
C. Associated with lymphadenopathy
D. Endothelial cells stain positive for CD34, CD31
E. Local recurrence is common

Key: C
Ref: Rooks (137.28)

Q23. A 25-year-old male presents with an asymptomatic solitary reddish targeted lesion on his left lower limb. On histopathology there are dilated vascular channels in the papillary and high reticular dermis, with single layer of endothelial cells lining intraluminal papillary projections. Perl stain is positive for hemosiderin deposition.
What is the most likely diagnosis?

A. Microvenular hemangioma
B. Sinusoidal hemangioma
C. Hobnail hemangioma
D. Pyogenic granuloma
E. Epitheloid hemangioma

Key: C
Ref: Rooks (137.31)

Q24. A 12-year-old child presented with lymphedema and multiple reddish blue nodules on his lower limbs. On examination he had early onset varicose veins of bilateral lower limbs .Histopathology of one of the lesions showed dilated thin walled congested , cavernous like vascular spaces intermixed with more cellular areas composed of bland short Spindle shaped cells with the formation of slit like spaces. The spindle cells are a mixture of endothelial cells, pericytes and fibroblasts.
What is not true regarding this disease?

A. Associated with MAFFUCI Syndrome
B. It's a benign condition
C. Associated with Klippel Trenaunay syndrome
D. High tendency of local recurrence
E. Immunohistochemistry positive for CD34, CD31 and actin

Key: D
Ref: Rooks (137.32)

Q25. A one year old infant was brought in by his parents for bruising on his body and swollen right knee joint. On further examination he had tumour like growth on his left elbow. On investigation his PT, PTT are raised and investigations for knee joint swelling revealed haematosis. Histopathology of lesion on left elbow showed lobular and infiltrative growth pattern. Multiple nodules with haemorrhage and surrounding fibrosis were seen. Tumour lobules were composed of bland spindle-shaped cells with poorly defined pink cytoplasm. Cleft like spaces in between spindle shaped cells were also appreciated. Staining for HHV8 was negative.

Following are the treatment options except

A. Simple excision as local recurrence is uncommon
B. Chemotherapy with vincristine
C. Embolization
D. Low dose radiotherapy
E. Interferon alpha

Key: A
Ref: Rooks (137.33)

Q26. A 25 years old female patient presents in dermatology OPD with 5 years history of a single papule on her right arm. It is brown in colour, firm in consistency, slightly scaly, with no complains of itching or discharge. There has not been any change in size or colour.

On examination, on squeezing the skin, dimple sign was seen.

Which of the following is true regarding Histopathology of this condition

A. Epidermis shows hyperplasia, dermis has histiocyte and fibroblast like cells with focal storiform pattern
B. Epidermis is normal and dermis shows uniform storiform pattern of spindle shaped Tumer cells
C. Epidermis is normal and dermis shows histiocyte like pleomorphic cells which are multinucleated
D. There are multifocal dermal proliferation of clusters of closely packed dilated capillaries with similarly to renal glomeruli
E. There are spindle shaped cells arranged in short fascicles and surrounded by collagenous stroma and mitotic figures are seen

Key: A
Ref: Rooks (137.19 to 137.21)

Q27. A 40 years old male presents with a 2 years history of papule on left lower limb. It was single, yellow brown in colour and firm in consistency. There was no complain of pain, itch or discharge and its size has been consistent. Its histopathology shows epidermal hyperplasia, bundles of spindle shaped cells, pink cytoplasm and focal stipiform pattern. Staining for FXIIIa is positive.

Regarding the condition of patient, it can present with multiple lesions in association with all the following except

A. HIV
B. Lupus erythematous
C. Haematological malignancies
D. HAART
E. Vaccination

Key: E
Ref: Rooks (137.19 to 137.2)

Q28. A 19 years old male patient presents with 2 wks. history of a nodule on left index finger. It was a fleshy nodule, reddish in colour and patient did not complain of pain. The patient gave history of few episodes of bleeding from the nodule on touching it. There is no significant past history except that he had a minor trauma on fingers 1 month back.

All the following factors can cause the development of this condition in a patient except

A. Oral retinoid

B. Pregnancy
C. Protease Inhibitors
D. Lupus erythematous
E. Immunosuppressive drugs

Key: D
Ref: Rooks (137.26 to 137. 27)

Q29. 26 year's old female presents, presents during pregnancy in the second trimester with a nodule on the tongue. It was a small nodule, fleshy, red coloured, developed 3 wks. Back. Patient gave history that it developed and had rapid growth in initial few days.it was painless .It frequently caused minor bleeding. Which of the following shows the histopathology of the condition

A. Multifocal dermal proliferation of clusters of closely packed dilated capillaries
B. Multiple circumscribed vascular lobules in a cannonball distribution in dermis
C. Lobular proliferation of small blood vessels which erupt through a breach in epidermis to produce globular pedunculated tumor
D. Poorly circumscribed lobular lesion composed of clusters of proliferating capillaries and thick blood vessels lined by plump epithelioid endothelial cells
E. There are dilated vascular channels in papillary and reticular dermis with single layer of endothelial cells lining intraluminal papillary projections

Key: C
Ref: Rooks (137.26)

Q30. A 34 years old female patient presented in dermatology clinic with a papule on her left forearm for 3 years. It was a single papule, brown in colour, firm, smooth and slightly scaly. It was painless. Dimple sign was positive. Histopathology showed epidermal hyperplasia and dermal localised proliferation of histiocytic like and fibroblast like cells, focal stipiform pattern. Tumour blends with surrounding dermis. Which of the following is true regarding disease course and Prognosis

A. Ordinary and Epithelioid Fibrous Histiocytoma rarely recur locally, cellular FH recur in 25 % cases
B. Ordinary and epithelioid FH recur locally in 25 % cases and cellular FH rarely recur
C. Metastasis is common after excision of the lesion
D. Atypical variant commonly shows distant and local metastasis after excision
E. Cellular and Epithelioid variant hardly recur locally and Aneurysmal variant recur in 29 % cases

Key: A
Ref: Rooks (137.21)

Q31. 26 years old female presents, presents during pregnancy in the second trimester with a nodule on the tongue. It was a small nodule, fleshy, red coloured, developed 3 wks back. Patient gave history that it developed and had rapid growth in initial few days.it was painless. It frequently caused minor bleeding. Which of the following shows the histopathology of the condition?

A. Multifocal dermal proliferation of clusters of closely packed dilated capillaries
B. Multiple circumscribed vascular lobules in a cannonball distribution in dermis
C. Lobular proliferation of small blood vessels which erupt through a breach in epidermis to produce globular pedunculated tumor
D. poorly circumscribed lobular lesion composed of clusters of proliferating capillaries and thick blood vessels lined by plump epithelioid endothelial cells
E. There are dilated vascular channels in papillary and reticular dermis with single layer of endothelial cells lining intraluminal papillary projections

Key: C
Ref: Rooks (137.26)

Q32. A 34 years old female patient presented in dermatology clinic with a papule on her left forearm for 3 years. It was a single papule, brown in colour, firm, smooth and slightly scaly. It was painless. Dimple sign was positive.

Histopathology showed epidermal hyperplasia and dermal localised proliferation of histiocyte like and fibroblast like cells, focal storiform pattern. Tumor blends with surrounding dermis.

Which of the following is true regarding disease course and Prognosis?

A. Ordinary and Epithelioid Fibrous Histiocytoma rarely recur locally, cellular FH recur in 25 % cases
B. ordinary and epithelioid FH recur locally in 25 % cases and cellular FH rarely recur
C. Metastasis is common after excision of the lesion
D. Atypical variant commonly shows distant and local metastasis after excision
E. Cellular and Epithelioid variant hardly recur locally and Aneurysmal variant recur in 29 % cases

Key: A
Ref: Rooks (137.21)

Q33. A 45 years old lady presented in the opd with history of solitary painful purplish nodule approximately 20mm in size on the dorsum of right index finger from last 3 months. Which of the following statement is true according to the above mentioned scenario?
Surgical excision is curative

A. Local recurrence is very common
B. Subungual glomus tumors are associated with Neurofibromatosis type 2
C. Glomus tumors do not involve Internal organs
D. They are more common in females

Key: A
Ref: Rooks (137.43)

Q34. A 50 years old lady presented in the opd with history of painful rounded well circumscribed nodule approx. 3x2cm in diameter. It was firm in consistency and the color of the lesion was pink-grey. The lesion was slowly growing. The nodule was present on the flexor aspect near the elbow along the course of nerve. Which of the following statement is not true?

A. Most nerve sheath tumors are benign
B. Verocay body are seen on histology
C. Malignant transformation can occur commonly
D. Arises most frequently from acoustic nerve
E. All of the above

Key: C
Ref: Rooks (137.46)

Q35. A 30 years old man presented in the opd with history of multiple skin coloured soft papules present all over the body most predominant on trunk and back from last 20 years. These papules have now increased in number. Which of the following statement is true?

A. Arise from the endoneurium
B. More common in adults
C. Associated with Neurofibromatosis type 1
D. Simple excision is treatment of choice
E. All of the above

Key: E
Ref: Rooks (137.48)

Q36. A 25 years old man presented in the opd with history of multiple hanging folds on the right side of face from last 20 years. The overlying skin is hyperpigmented. On examination bag of worms like feeling was felt. Which of the following statement is true

A. Tumor is parhognomic of Neurofibromatosis type 1
B. Surgical removal is difficult
C. Present in children and young adults of both sex
D. Tumors are located in dermis and subcutis and even in deeper soft tissues
E. All of the above

Key: E
Ref: Rooks (137.48)

Q37. A 60 years old lady presented with a solitary, firm, sessile lesion with indefinite margins on the left lateral aspect of tongue from last one year. The lesion was flesh colored with warty appearance. Which of the following statement is not true?

A. Abrikossoff tumor mimic squamous cell carcinoma on histology due to prominant pseudoepitheliomatous hyperplasia
B. These tumors are very common
C. Multiple lesions arw reported in Noonan syndrome
D. Malignant transformation is rare
E. Simple excision is treatment of choice

Key: B
Ref: Rooks (137.51)

Q38. A 34yr old female presented to dermatology Old with complaint of single erythematous painful swelling on right forearm for last 6months.she also had hx of abdominal pain on and off. On physical examination a single erythematous, soft but painful nodule involving right forearm. On histopathology, lesion is composed of strands and nests of endothelial cells having epitheloid morphology, pink cytoplasm, vesicular nuclei and inconspicuous nucleoli.ERG, CD31and D2-40markers were positive. Considering dx of pt what will the mortality rate in deeper tumors

A. 15%
B. 20%
C. 25%
D. 10%

Key: B
Ref: Rooks (137.39)

Q39. A 21yr old male pt with history of stage 2 synovial sarcoma in left thigh 4yrs back. for which he was treated with surgical resection followed by radiotherapy. Now he presented with complaint of painless grouped lesions in left popletial area with rapid growth for last 5months.on excisional biopsy, irregular lymphatic like vascular channels, lined by single layer of endothelial cells having hobnail appearance's. my gene amplification by immunohistochemistry was negative. Most likely diagnosis is

A. post irradiation angiosarcoma
B. Stewart treves syndrome
C. Atypical vascular proliferation after radiotherapy
D. Acquired progressive lymphangioma

Key: C
Ref: Rooks (137.40)

Q40. A 59 yrs old male presented with complaint of cough and shortness of breath for last 2months.on investigations he is diagnosed as case of pulmonary diffuse lymphangiomatosis.in management of this pt, all options cab be use except

A. supportive treatment
B. Sirolimus
C. Bevacizumab
D. taxanes

Key: D
Ref: Rooks (137.41)

Q41. A 79-year-old woman visited outpatient clinic with a 1-month history of a red, easy to bleed, nodule on the right thigh. She had undergone resection of a cervical cancer 24 years before and developed prominent lymph edema in the lower extremities. During her initial visit, physical examination revealed a dark-red nodule with extended purpura on the right thigh together with prominent lymph edema. Histologically, these were irregularly anastomosing vascular channels lined by single layers of enlarged, atypical endothelial cells that existed between the collagen bundles. Immunohistochemical staining revealed that these atypical endothelial cells were positive for vimentin, CD31, CD34, and Factor VIII. myc gene amplification and over expression is positive. Most likely DX is

A. Acquired progressive lymphangioma
B. Atypical vascular proliferation after radiotherapy
C. Stewart treves syndrome
D. Epitheloid hemangioendothelioma

Key: C
Ref: Rooks (137.37)

Q42. A 50 year old patient presented in dermatology department with ongoing shoulder and arm pain for 3 years. He had noticed a painless tumor with feeling of pressure in his upper right arm for some months. There was no history of recent trauma or injuries. There is no systemic signs of infection, weight loss, or fever and no prior medical history.

Clinical examination showed a painless subcutaneous mass on the right upper arm, starting lateral to the axillary fold expanding about 8 cm distally. On palpation, the tumor was elastic and firm. There was no sensory or motor dysfunction. The overlying skin showed no signs of infection. skin biopsy showed adipocytes with eosinophilic granular multivacuolated cytoplasm and centrally located nucleolus. By immunohistochemistry, adipocytes are positive for S100 protein. Keeping in mind the diagnosis, the prognosis of disease is

A. Malignant with recurrence
B. Benign with local recurrence
C. Benign with no local recurrence
D. Malignant with short duration

Key: C
Ref: Rooks (137.59)

Q43. A 40 year old man presented with large painful mass on his left arm. The mass had been present for 8 years and had been enlarging progressively during this period. The patient complained of discomfort, disfiguration and difficulty in dressing. He did not have sensory or motor defects. On examination, the mass was found to be above the deltoid muscle, and was soft, well-circumscribed and mobile. Histopathology showed encapsulated, mature adipose tissue with prominent vascular component. Some of the blood vessels contain fibrin thrombi. The most probable diagnosis is

A. Hibernoma
B. Angiolipoma
C. leiomyosarcoma
D. Smooth muscle hamartoma

Key: B.
Ref: Rooks (137.58)

Q44. A 35 yr old man presented with soft painless subcutaneous mass on the volar aspect of the proximaland middle phalanx of the right index digit. The mass appeared three years prior to the medical consultation. and was asymptomatic until 12 months ago, when the patient first complained of limitation in flexion and pain during manual maneuvers. On clinical examination he had a soft, mobile, elastic mass at the volar aspect of the 2nd digit with no disturbance of sensibility. He had no ulceration or pigmentation on the overlying skin, neither any other inflammatory changes such as redness, heat or pain on palpation. Plain xray of the digit showed no bone invasion. Histopathology showed encapsulated tumor with lobules of mature adipose tissue divided by delicate fibrous septa. There is no nuclear atypia and no mitotic activity seen. Keeping in mind the diagnosis, the most correct statement is

A. More common in males
B. Can progress to liposarcoma.
C. Benign but rapidly grow
D. Malignant in nature

Key: B.
Ref: Rooks (137.59)

Q45. A 53 year old man presented with painless nodule on chest region, which had been progressively increasing in size for 7 years. Physical examination revealed an irregular, firm, tender exophytic swelling, measuring 5cm diameter at the anterior trunk. There were no signs of infection and the overlying skin was normal. The remainder of the clinical examination was normal. Lymph nodes were not palpable. His past history was significant of a local trauma. Histopathological examination revealed fascicles of eosinophilic spindle shaped cells with cigar shaped nuclei. Mitotic figures are common. Immunohistochemically positive for actin, desmin and keratin. The most probable diagnosis is

A. Lipoblastomatosis
B. Granular cell tumor
C. Leiomyosarcoma
D. Superficial angiomyxoma

Key: C.
Ref: Rooks (137.57)

Q46. A 33 year old man with multiple skin lesions, presenting as papules that were erythematous-brownish with a firm consistency, clustered in the upper left chest region. The lesions increased gradually during the past 2 years, becoming painful in the last year.On clinical examination, he reported severe pain only with a gentle palpation of the site.
Histopathology showed bundles of spindle shaped cells which are strongly eosinophilic with elongated nuclei and blunt edges. Tumor cells are positive for actin and desmin. Keeping in mind the diagnosis, the medical treatment that will relieve pain include

A. Topical Corticosteroids
B. Systemic Antibiotics
C. Calcium channel blockers
D. Systemic corticosteroids

Key: C
Ref: Rooks (137.56)

Q47. A 66yr old female who underwent radical mastectomy for breast CA ten years earlier and also developed swelling of left arm for last 5yrs which was diagnosed as lymphedema of left arm now presented with complaint of multiple, red nodules on left arm. On examination multiple red colour nodules along with some ulcerated lesions were present. On biopsy, collagen is lined by tumor cells in dissection of collagen pattern. Considering dx of pt, immunohistochemical markers positive for this condition are

A. CD34
B. CD31

C. FLI-1protein
D. ERG
E. All of above

Key: E
Ref: Rooks (137.37)

Q48. A 35-year-old woman presented with a cluster of small translucent nodules on her ears and her hairline. On biopsy histopathology showed proliferating capillaries and thick blood vessels lined by plump endothelial cells with little cytological atypia and rare mitotic figures. There was a perivascular inflammatory infiltrate composed of lymphocytes and large number of Eosinophils.
What are specific vascular markers for this disease.

A. CD 30, CD 31, actin
B. CD34, CD31, actin
C. CD34, CD31, ERG
D. CD39, CD 31, ERG
E. CD34, CD30, keratin

Key: C
Ref: Rooks (137.29)

Q49. A 26 year old male presented with a cluster of small translucent nodules on his neck and ears. Histopathology of these lesions Showed clusters of proliferating capillaries and thick blood vessels lined by plump epithelioid endothelial cells with little cytological atypia. There was perivascular inflammatory infiltrate composed of lymphocytes and large number of eosinophils.
Following is not true for this condition

A. Peripheral eosinophilia present in less than 10% of patients.
B. May involve oral mucosa
C. Associated with lymphadenopathy
D. Endothelial cells stain positive for CD34, CD31
E. Local recurrence is common

Key: C
Ref: Rooks (137.28)

Q50. A 25-year-old male presents with an asymptomatic solitary reddish targetoid lesion on his left lower limb. On histopathology there are dilated vascular channels in the papillary and high reticular dermis, with single layer of endothelial cells lining intraluminal papillary projections. Perl stain is positive for haemosiderin deposition.
What is the most likely diagnosis?

A. Microvenular hemangioma
B. Sinusoidal hemangioma
C. Hobnail hemangioma
D. Pyogenic granuloma
E. Epitheloid hemangioma

Key: C
Ref: Rooks (137.31)

Q51. A 12-year-old child presented with lymphedema and multiple reddish blue nodules on his lower limbs. On examination he had early onset varicose veins of bilateral lower limbs. Histopathology of one of the lesions showed dilated thin walled congested, cavernous like vascular spaces intermixed with more cellular areas composed of bland short Spindle shaped cells with the formation of slit like spaces. The spindle cells are a mixture of endothelial cells, pericytes and fibroblasts.
What is not true regarding this disease

A. Associated with MAFFUCI Syndrome

B. It's a benign condition
C. Associated with Klippel Trenaunay syndrome
D. High tendency of local recurrence
E. Immunohistochemistry positive for CD34, CD31 and actin

Key: D
Ref: Rooks (137.32)

Q52. A one year old infant was brought in by his parents for bruising on his body and swollen right knee joint. On further examination he had tumour like growth on his left elbow. On investigation his PT, PTT are raised and investigations for knee joint swelling revealed heamarthosis. Histopathology of lesion on left elbow showed lobular and infiltrative growth pattern. Multiple nodules with haemorrhage and surrounding fibrosis were seen. Tumour lobules were composed of bland spindle-shaped cells with poorly defined pink cytoplasm. Cleft like spaces in between spindle shaped cells were also appreciated. Staining for HHV8 was negative.
Following are the treatment options except
A. Simple excision as local recurrence is uncommon
B. Chemotherapy with vincristine
C. Embolization
D. Low dose radiotherapy
E. Interferon alpha

Key: A
Ref: Rooks (137.33)

Q53. 26 years old female presents, presents during pregnancy in the second trimester with a nodule on the tongue. It was a small nodule, fleshy, red coloured, developed 3 wks back. Patient gave history that it developed and had rapid growth in initial few days.it was painless. It frequently caused minor bleeding.
Which of the following shows the histopathology of the condition?
A. Multifocal dermal proliferation of clusters of closely packed dilated capillaries
B. Multiple circumscribed vascular lobules in a cannonball distribution in dermis
C. Lobular proliferation of small blood vessels which erupt through a breach in epidermis to produce globular pedunculated tumor
D. poorly circumscribed lobular lesion composed of clusters of proliferating capillaries and thick blood vessels lined by plump epithelioid endothelial cells
E. There are dilated vascular channels in papillary and reticular dermis with single layer of endothelial cells lining intraluminal papillary projections

Key: C
Ref: Rooks (137.26)

Q54. A 34 years old female patient presented in dermatology clinic with a papule on her left forearm for 3 years. It was a single papule, brown in colour, firm, smooth and slightly scaly. It was painless. Dimple sign was positive.
Histopathology showed epidermal hyperplasia and dermal localised proliferation of histiocyte like and fibroblast like cells, focal storiform pattern. Tumor blends with surrounding dermis.
Which of the following is true regarding disease course and Prognosis?
A. Ordinary and Epithelioid Fibrous Histiocytoma rarely recur locally, cellular FH recur in 25 % cases
B. ordinary and epithelioid FH recur locally in 25 % cases and cellular FH rarely recur
C. Metastasis is common after excision of the lesion
D. Atypical variant commonly shows distant and local metastasis after excision
E. Cellular and Epithelioid variant hardly recur locally and Aneurysmal variant recur in 29 % cases

Key: A

Ref: Rooks (137.21)

Q55. A 30 years old man presented in the opd with history of multiple skin coloured soft papules present all over the body most predominant on trunk and back from last 20 years. These papules have now increased in number. Which of the following statement is true?

A. Arise from the endoneurium
B. More common in adults
C. Associated with Neurofibromatosis type 1
D. Simple excision is treatment of choice
E. All of the above

Key: E
Ref: Rooks (137.48)

Q56. A 60 years old lady presented with a solitary, firm, sessile lesion with indefinite margins on the left lateral aspect of tongue from last one year. The lesion was flesh colored with warty appearance. Which of the following statement is not true?

A. Abrikossoff tumor mimic squamous cell carcinoma on histology due to prominent pseudoepitheliomatous hyperplasia
B. These tumors are very common
C. Multiple lesions are reported in Noonan syndrome
D. Malignant transformation is rare
E. Simple excision is treatment of choice

Key: B
Ref: Rooks (137.51)

Q57. A 59 yrs old male presented with complaint of cough and shortness of breath for last 2months.on investigations he is diagnosed as case of pulmonary diffuse lymphangiomatosis.in management of this pt ,all options cab be use except

A. Supportive treatment
B. Sirolimus
C. Bevacizumab
D. Taxanes

Key: D
Ref: Rooks (137.41)

Chapter 138 TUMOURS OF SKIN APPENDAGES

1. A young female presented with multiple scattered skin colored, flat topped 2mm sized papules over face sparing nasolabial folds, more pronounced on bilateral cheeks, neck and upper chest. No history of photosensitivity, oral ulcers, joint pain and weight loss. She was treated with CO2 laser few months back but lesions recurred. Similar lesions also seen in her 5 years old brother's face, chest and abdomen who is known case of Downs's syndrome. Keeping diagnosis in mind. What would be the most appropriate pathological findings related to this familial condition.

A. Cystic ducts collection in upper dermis lined by double layer of cells.
B. Cystic structures filled with keratin in epidermis
C. Lobular structure having peripheral palisading
D. Foamy histiocytes laden with fat deposits in upper dermis
E. None of the above

Key: A
Ref: Rook (138.28)

2. An elderly female presented in opd with two nodules over her scalp for 4 years. No history of prior trauma, infection, fever and weight loss. On cutaneous examination there were two nodules seen, one above left ear of 3 cm size and one over temporal side of forehead skin having 5cm size. Both were mildly tender, erythematous, smooth, hairless surface and firm in consistency. Rest of the hairs, nails and mucosae examinations were unremarkable. Select the correct statement regarding this condition.

A. Autosomal recessive
B. Not a familial condition
C. Can be associated with Brooke-Spiegler Syndrome
D. Malignant transformation very frequent
E. All of the above

Key: C
Ref: Rook (138.31)

3. A 26 years male patient came with a solitary lesion on front of his trunk for 1 year, not associated with any prior naevus in same location, insect bite and drug abuse. He developed on and off pain in it for few months. On cutaneous examination there was tender, firm, dome shaped, bluish dermal nodule of 5mm size. Dimple sign was not appreciated. HIV test was negative. Skin biopsy done which showed lobular structures comprising large pale and small dark cells surrounded by condensed connective tissue encroaching on the islands as hyaline droplets. Few areas of haemorrhage and ischemic necrosis also seen. What would be the most suitable treatment option for this lesion?

A. Topical steroids for 4 weeks
B. Topical Imiquimod for 6 months
C. Topical Salicylic acid for 2 weeks
D. Diathermy
E. Complete excision and follow up

Key: E
Ref: Rook (138.32)

4. A 72 years female patient presented in opd with solitary lesion having on and off bleeding on lateral side of her left foot for 2 years. No history of pain, injury, infection and weight loss. She took multiple sessions of cryotherapy but condition persists. On cutaneous examination there was a single ulcerated flesh colored shiny nodule of 3cm size. Biopsy report revealed tumor lobules comprising of small cells, infiltrate the

dermis and subcutaneous tissue with ductal squamous differentiation. Immunohistochemistry showed CEA and EMA. Keeping in mind diagnosis, What would be the most appropriate statement representing this condition.

A. Pigmented variant mimic melanoma
B. Risk of regional lymphnodes and systemic metastasis
C. Wide local excision and follow up
D. Mortality more with lymphnode metastasis
E. All of the above

Key: E
Ref: Rook (138.34)

5. A 58 years male patient, no known comorbids, came in dermatology department with increasing size of few of the multiple lesions on his scalp for 3 years. On cutaneous examination there were multiple dermal nodules having pink colored smooth hairless surface over parietal region of scalp. Largest one measuring about 6cm size associated with pain occasionally. History of similar lesions in his elder sister which was treated with wide local excision. Histopathology showed irregular sized deeply basophilic small cells infiltrate the dermis having marked nuclear atypia and abnormal mitotic figures. What would be the prognosis of this disease?

A. Lesion is benign
B. Locally aggressive
C. Never metastasize
D. No follow up is required
E. All of the above

Key: B
Ref: Rook (138.36)

6. A 66 years male patient came with complaints of swelling around eye lateral to outer canthus since 2 years, insidious, gradually progressive with bluish hue, without altered sensation overlying the affected area. On examination there was 2.5 × 3 cm cystic swelling around eye lateral to outer canthus, non-tender, non-compressible.
If multiple lesions are present in this case what is the treatment??

A. Electrocautery
B. Cryotherapy
C. 5 flourouracil
D. Trichloroacetic acid
E. Salicylic acid

Key: D
Ref: Rook (138.20)

7. A 25 year old woman presented with multiple nontender and nonpruritic verrucous papules and nodules on the scalp. She had these lesions since birth and they had gradually increased in number and size over the years. Currently, she presented with a 6-month history of progressive enlargement of the eruption. She admitted to have applied traditional topical treatment to the lesions.
On examination, multiple erythematous papules and nodules were observed on the scalp arranged in a linear fashion. These papules and nodules measured up to 1.5 cm in diameter with the largest measuring 5 cm in diameter. Erosion was seen on the surface of some of the lesions.
Which one of the following carcinomas is NOT associated with it?

A. Basal cell carcinoma
B. Squamous cell carcinoma
C. Malignant melanoma
D. Ductal carcinoma
E. Invasive apocrine carcinoma

Key: C
Ref: Rook (138.21)

8. A 46-year-old female, chef by profession, presented with multiple, tiny, skin-colored discrete lesions on her cheeks and eyelids. The lesions were present for the last three years, increasing in summer and subsiding in winter. On examination, there were numerous blue-colored cystic present on the malar area of the face and eyelids.
Which one of the following is NOT the treatment?

A. Salicylic acid
B. CO2 laser
C. Electrodesiccation
D. Pulse dye laser
E. Excision

Key: A
Ref: Rook (138.24)

9. A 45 year old man presented with a swelling over the sole of left foot. The lesion was present for 6 years and had been rapidly growing over the prior 2 months. The patient had a 3 x 3-cm exophytic red nodular growth that was mobile and not fixed to underlying structures.
The histopathology showed clear margin between adjacent epidermal keratinocytes and smaller cuboidal cells with darker nuclei.
All of the following are associations of this condition EXCEPT:

A. Pregnancy
B. Graves disease
C. Naevus sebaceous
D. Radiotherapy
E. Hidrotic ectrodermal dysplasia

Key: B.
Ref: Rook (138.26)

10. A 13 year old girl presented with multiple asymptomatic papules over right lower leg present since the age of 2 months. The lesions were gradually progressive with a rapid enlargement in the last 1 year. On examination there were multiple erythematous warty papules with superficial erosions in a linear pattern over the right lower leg. What is treatment of this condition??

A. Electrocautery
B. Cryotherapy
C. Trichloroacetic acid
D. Surgical excision
E. Salicylic acid

Key: D
Ref: Rook (138.21)

Chapter 140 CUTANEOUS LYYMPHOMAS

1. A 59 year old female pottery worker presented with polymorphic lesions consists of patches on buttocks and lower back along with mild pruritis. Examination shows fine scaly erythematous patch with wrinkled surface. Biopsy showed lymphoid cells lined up at DEJ. Lymph nodes are not involved. Which of the following is the independent prognostic factor of disease??

A. Female gender
B. Age less than 60 years
C. Folliculotropic lesions
D. Poikiloderma

Key: C
Ref: Rook (140.14)

2. A 55 years old male presented with multiple plaques on the buttocks which are polymorphic and persistent associated with pruritus. Now he is experiencing pain in lesions due to ulceration. Examination shows psoriasiform scaling and involvement of draining lymph node. Biospy showed epidermotropism. What is the stage of the disease??

A. IB
B. B.IIA
C. IIB
D. D.IIIA

Key: B
Ref: Rook (140.3)

3. A 24 year old male presented with hypopigmented scaly patches on lower back. No history of pruritus, no loss of sensation, no history of any skin lesion prior to this. History of atopy is there. Peripheral blood smear shows large cells with large nucleus and little cytoplasm. About disease:

A. Thin plaques are prognostically important
B. Large cell transformation can't occur
C. CD8+ cases are more common in childhood variant
D. Fine needle aspiration is useful for lymph node assesment

Key: C
Ref: Rook (140.6)

4. A 50 year old worker in glass industry presented with erythroderma and scaling. There is no history of drug intake or any skin disease. Examination showed scalp alopecia, ectropion and subungal hyperkeratosis, peripheral lymphadenopathy. Peripheral smear shows atypical cells more than 1000/microlitre of peripheral lymphocytes.
About treatment:

A. PUVA is the first line of treatment
B. Relapse rate is lower with radiotherapy
C. These tumours are chemoresistant and response is short lived
D. Retinoids can't be combined with PUVA in early stage.

Key: C
Ref: Rook (140.25)

5. A 40 years old female presented with itchy lesions on breast. Examination shows altered pigmentation, atrophy and telengiectasia. No history of photosensitivity. Histology showed epidermal atrophy and

collection of atyical cells in epidermis. She was started on retinoids but her condition didnot improve. You plan to start a latest modality of fusion protein. Which of the following is the appropriate choice?

A. Pralatrexate
B. Onzar
C. Romidespin
D. Lenalidomide

Key: B
Ref: Rook (140.26)

6. 62 year old male presented with prolonged history of generalized exfoliative dermatitis involving almost 95 percent of BSA and took multiple topical treatments but no improvement observed. Examination showed peripheral lymphadenopathy and ectropion. skin biopsy was done. Keeping in mind the diagnosis which of the following statement is true?

A. Always positive for CD 7, Cd 26
B. Atypical, mononuclear cells more than 20 % of total lymphocyte count are part of triad for diagnosis
C. Prognosis is excellent
D. Variant with cells size more than 16 micrometers is commonest
E. Always presents as a progression from classic MF

Key: B
Ref: Rook (140-18, 19)

7. A male patient diagnosed with sezary syndrome from 1 year and was on phottherapy treatment presented in opd for follow up. Which of the complication cannot be the seen in these patients?

A. chronic Renal Failure
B. high output cardiac failure
C. subungual hyperkeratosis
D. scalp alopecia
E. palmolanter hyperkeratosis

Key: A
Ref: Rook (140.19)

8. a 52 year old male presented with erythematous scaly rash on whole body. His examination showed peripheral lymphadenopathy. Histopathology was done which showed superficial and perivascular lymphocytic infiltrate. Some of them are atypical with cerebriform nucleus. What is the most likely diagnosis?

A. Psoriasis
B. Atopic dermatitis
C. Sezary syndrome
D. Graft Vs Host disease
E. Severe Drug reaction

Key: C
Ref: Rook (140.18 -19)

9. You diagnosed an old male patient with sezary syndrome. While counceling him for treatment options. He asked you about prognosis and course of his disease. Which of the following statement is true?

A. The degree of peripheral blood involvement is an independent prognostic factor
B. Most patients die of complications as high output cardiac failure
C. Median survival is of 32 months from diagnosis
D. Prognosis is poor with 30% 5-year survival
E. Presence of lymph node and gender are not key prognostic factors

Key: C

Ref: Rook (140.20)

10. All of the statements regarding sezary syndrome are correct except?
   A. CD 26+, CD7+ and CD 8+ variants have also been reported
   B. Sezary syndrome is derived from skin resident, peripheral, memory T cells
   C. Sezary cells can be seen in peripheral blood of normal healthy individuals
   D. Diagnostic critieria for sezary syndrome should include clinical triad plus presence of a peripheral blood T cell clone detection by TCR gene analysis
   E. Sezary syndrome can present rarely ad pregression from classic MF

Key: B
Ref: Rook (140. 18, 19)

11. A 50 yr female with history of atopic eczema, complain of polymorphic scaly plaques on buttock with mild itching now pain too. O/e psoriasiform scaleing seen on plaques n enlarged draining lymph nodes. Biopsy was advised. Suspecting the diagnosis following investigation should be done except.
   A. Elliptical skin biopsy
   B. Lymph node excision n its biopsy
   C. TCR gend analysis
   D. PET / CT scan.
   E. Immunological markers

Key: D
Ref: Rook (140.2)

12. A 61 yr male working in ceramic industry presented in opd with mildly itchy scaly lesions on buttock. O/e scaly erythematpus patches on buttock n lower legs with wrinkled surface. Lymph nodes not enlarged. Biopsy of skin showed moderate lymphocytic infiltrate at DEJ n epidermotropism. Next appropriate step in making diagnosis is
   A. Flow cytometry
   B. Complete blood count
   C. TCR gene analysis
   D. Immunohistochemistry
   E. Chest x ray

Key: C
Ref: Rook (140.2)

13. A 14years old girl presented with multiple pruritic skin papules of 11 months duration. Examination with dermatoscope revealed multiple small papular lesions on an erythematous base measuring approximately 0.5mm.
Histopathology showed mucinous degeneration of the hair follicles and perifollicular chronic inflammation with no atypical cytological features.
The upper dermis showed slight edema with minimal lymphocytic infiltrates. The overlying epidermis showed no significant abnormalities with no obvious spongiosis.
Regarding the above diagnosis, all are true EXCEPT?
   A. It is also called alopecia mucinosa
   B. It is usually CD3+ve, CD4+ve and CD8 -ve
   C. It has worse prognosis
   D. Dapsone is not a treatment option
   E. It is treated with skin directed therapy.

Key: D
Ref: Rook (140.16)

14. A 58yearold woman presented with a verrucoid pink plaque on the right heel, measuring 3 cm in diameter.

It had been present for approximately 1 year. There were no cutaneous lesions elsewhere, and the remaining physical examination also showed no abnormalities. The results of biochemical blood survey was normal.
Histological analysis showed a well demarcated, discrete area of hyperkeratosis and parakeratosis with epidermal acanthosis. The surface epithelium was permeated by an infiltrate of atypical mononuclear cells with pale eosinophilic cytoplasm, large nuclei, and prominent nucleoli. They were dispersed randomly throughout the epidermis, singly and in small nests, with the greatest density being in its basal aspect. Immunostaining showed that the lesional cells were reactive for CD2, CD3, CD7, CD43, and CD45R0. CD8+ lymphocytes were sparse, and CD7 labeling was less intense than that of the other lymphoid markers. CD30 was absent.
Regarding above findings,what is the likely diagnosis?

A. Epidermodysplasia verruciformis
B. Pagetoid reticulosis
C. Pityriasis rubra pilaris
D. Discoid lupus erythematosis
E. Necrolytic acral erythema

Key: B
Ref: Rook (140.16)

15. A 35yearold man presented to the dermatology opd for evaluation of longstanding widespread erythematous patches for 16 years.
The patient 1ST noticed involvement in the left popliteal fossa of skin-colored nodules with diameters 1-3cm. The lesions then slowly grew in size and number over the next decade. New plaques and papules appeared on the neck, extremities, and trunk.
Lesional skin became pendulous and atrophied. The patient reported no obvious accompanying symptoms other than occasional pruritus.
On examination, well demarcated erythematous and purplish papules and plaques were observed on the left chest, lower back, buttocks, and all extremities Lax skin was found in intertriginous areas.
On the basis of above findings, most likely histopathological features would be?

A. Dense granulomatous dermal infilterate with cytological atypia and destruction of elastic tissue
B. Epidermal necrosis with dermal mucin deposition
C. Band like lymphocytic infilterate at DEJ
D. Naked granulomas in dermis
E. Caseation necrosis in granulomas

Key: A
Ref: Rook (140.17)

16. A 10year old girl with no medical history of interest presented with a lesion on the dorsum of the nose that had appeared 2 months previously. She had been treated unsuccessfully with 1% hydrocortisone cream prescribed by her primary care physician.
The lesion was a well delimited, slow growing, prominent, pruritic, and slightly infiltrated erythematous plaque (0.7×1cm) with follicular hyperkeratosis. The patient reported no history of injury, local infection, or insect bite and had no other lesions or palpable regional lymph nodes.
Histopathology revealed several hair follicles with abundant intraepithelial mucin in the dermis, although there was no evidence of an inflammatory infiltrate or other signs of malignancy.
What is the most likely diagnosis?

A. Follicular mucinosis
B. Phrynoderma
C. Discoid lupus erythematosis
D. Lichen nitidus
E. Keratosis pilaris

Key: A
Ref: Rook (140.15)

17. A 46 yearold man developed a 1cm pearly white tan lesion on the chest, which had evolved over approximately 3 years. In the previous 3-4 months, it had increased in size and began to burn and itch. Histological examination of an excisional biopsy specimen showed epidermal acanthosis with marked exocytosis. The intraepithelial lymphoid cells were atypical cytologically, and they contained occasional mitotic figures.
A mixed, superficial, perivascular dermal inflammatory infiltrate was also present. Immunohistochemical studies showed diffuse lesional reactivity for CD3, but labeling for CD7 was significantly diminished. Intraepidermal lymphoid cells were nearly all reactive for CD4 and CD8.
What is FALSE regarding the disease?
A. It is also known as woringer-kolop disease
B. It has excellent prognosis
C. Localized variant is called ketron-Goodman variant.
D. Treated with surgical excision and superficial radiotherapy
E. Histologically shows intense epidermotropism

Key: C
Ref: Rook (140.17)

18. 45 year old female presented to the dermatology opd with recurrent crops of papular or papulonecrotic or nodular lesions predominantly affecting the trunk and also lower limbs. These lesions grew rapidly over a few days and developed ulcerated necrotic centres. There were also few areas of varioliform scarring. Her skin biopsy for histopathology was done that showed relative lack of epidermotropism and Pautrier microabscesses. The histological subgrouping was done after skin biopsy. Which of the following indicated Subgroup D on histopathology?
A. Scattered large, strikingly atypical CD30+ cells similar to those seen in Hodgkin disease
B. Smaller atypical T lymphocytes with convoluted nuclei similar to those seen in MF predominate and are CD3+ and CD4+ but CD30–
C. Atypical CD30+ lymphoid cells expressing CD8 with a cytotoxic phenotype
D. have large clusters of CD30+ cells

Key: C
Ref: Rook (140.28)

19. 55 year old male presents to the dermatology department with subcutaneous nodules on his lower limbs. There is no ulceration. Patient gives history of fever. On examinations there is hepatospleenomegaly and CBC shows pancytopenia. His skin biopsy was done that showed diffuse infiltrate restricted to and extending throughout the subcutis without epidermotropism. Rimming of the tumour cells around fat cells was seen.
What is the ist line treatment for the above patient?
A. Nitrigen mustard
B. CHOP (cyclophosphamide, doxorubicin, vincristine, prednisolone)
C. surgical excision
D. prednisolone

Key: D
Ref: Rook (140.32)

20. 45 year old female presented to the dermatology opd with recurrent crops of papular or papulonecrotic or nodular lesions predominantly affecting the trunk and also lower limbs. These lesions grew rapidly over a few days and developed ulcerated necrotic centres. There were also few areas of varioliform scarring. Her skin biopsy for histopathology was done that showed relative lack of epidermotropism and Pautrier

microabscesses, but the dermis showed a mixed infiltrate composed of atypical lymphocytes with large nuclei and frequent abnormal mitoses, eosinophils, neutrophils, extravasated red cells and large histiocytic cells What is the likely diagnosis?

A. Papulonecrotid tuberculid
B. Lymphomatoid papulosis
C. Lipoid proteinosis
D. Prurigo nodularis

Key: B
Ref: Rook (140.29)

21. A young male patient presents to dermatology opd with large multiple and ulcerated nodules, most often on the trunk. There are no patches or plaques elsewhere on his body. His skin biopsy was done and it revealed a dense lymphocytic infiltrate consisting of sheets of large atypical cells with an anaplastic morphology and mitoses and there is no epidermotropism. On immunophenotyping tumour cells are CD4+ and CD30+ with expression of cytotoxic proteins such as perforin, granzyme B and T-cell intracellular antigen I (TIA-I). What is the likely diagnosis?

A. Lymphomatoid papulosis
B. Sezary syndrome
C. Subcutaneous panniculitis-like t-cell lymphoma
D. primary cutaneous anaplastic (CD30+) large-cell lymphoma

Key: D
Ref: Rook (140.29)

22. 55 year old male presents to the dermatology department with subcutaneous nodules on his lower limbs. There is no ulceration.Patient gives history of fever. On examinations there is hepatospleenomegaly and CBC shows pancytopenia. His skin biopsy was done that showed diffuse infiltrate restricted to and extending throughout the subcutis without epidermotropism. Rimming of the tumour cells around fat cells was seen. Immunophenotyping was done. Which of the following shows the results of the given patient keeping in view the diagnosis??

A. CD3+, CD8+, CD4–, CD30- and CD56-
B. CD 3-, CD8+, CD4+, CD30+ and CD56+!
C. CD3+, CD4+, CD56+
D. CD30+, CD56+, CD 3-, CD8-, CD 4-

Key: A
Ref: Rook (140.32)

23. A 40 year old patient presented in OPD with complaints of few persistent plaques on his abdomen and trunk area. these are persistent, gradually increasing and resistant to treatment. On examination you see there are patches and plaques which are pleomorphic with mild scales. regional lymph nodes are also palpable. you opt for investigations. Histopathology is done that shows epidermotropism and cellular atypia. No internal organs are involved and there is absence of significant blood involvement.
According to staging of disease, what do you think is the first line treatment?

A. Ontak
B. MTX
C. PUVA +Bex
D. ECP
E. Radiotherapy

Key: C
Ref: Rook (140.9)

24. A 40 year old female presented with few eczematous patches on breast and trunk area that are pleomorphic and non-responsive to treatment. you investigate the disease and establish diagnosis of early CTCL and opt for SDT.
Which of the following is NOT true regarding topical chemotherapy?

A. mechlorethamine is contraindicated in pregnancy
B. hypersensitivity reactions are more common with mechlorethamine than carmustine
C. with carmustine maintenance therapy should be given so that to avoid recurrence of disease
D. regularly monitor cbc and give treatment foe only 2-4 weeks with carmustine
E. there are reports of NMSC with topical mechlorethamine

Key: C
Ref: Rook (140.23)

Chapter 141

BASAL CELL CARCINOMA

1 A 21 years old patient came to Derma opd with complaints of multiple nodules on face and trunk for last 1 year. On examination there were 'ice-pick marks' on both cheeks and multiple small pigmented pearly nodules with telengiectatic edges on cheeks and back. There were enlarged follicular ostia on the dorsa of the hands, elbows and feet. On further inquiry she complained of anhidrosis of the face and head. Which of the following is best treatment option in this case?

A. Radiotherapy
B. Retinoid 2mg/kg
C. Excision
D. Cryotherapy
E. Vismedogib

Key: E.
Ref: Rook (141.20)

2. A 55 years old white male came with history of small nodule at left lower eye lid since 5 years. But for last two months he noticed some bleeding and oozing from it. On examination there were an ulcerated plaque of 5*6cm at left lower eye lid with indurated margins and depressed floor. If it remains untreated what will be the major complication patient at risk

A. Lymphadenopathy
B. Hepatic Mets
C. Pulmonary Mets
D. Ulcer terebrans
E. Pulmoary Mets

Key: D
Ref: Rook (141.10)

3. A 58 years old male farmer by occupation came with complain of skin problem at nose since 5 years. On examination there was 2*3cm skin colored pearly hairless nodule with surrounding talengactasias. No lymphnode was palpable. Diascopy was inconclusive. Considering clinical diagnosis demoscopsy will show all of the feature except

A. Spoke wheel areas
B. Arborizing vessels
C. Maple leaf like areas
D. Blue grey ovoid nest
E. Hairpin vessels

Key: E
Ref: Rook (141.11)

4. A 10 years old girl bought by her parents with complain of change of color of hands and feet since few months. On examination of skin hands and feet showing bluish discoloration, while her bilateral cheek showed pinpoint scarring. She told that she noticed loss of her eye lashes and eye brows as well. Family history was also positive. Considering diagnosis which one the following is not true

A. This is Autosomal Dominant
B. This is X linked Dominant
C. Patient is at risk of developing Basal cell carcinoma in adult life
D. No extracutaneous feature was noticed
E. Trichoepithiloma may also be present

Key: B
Ref: Rook (141.4)

5. A 59 years old white female came with bleeding and discharge from skin lesion at face. On examination there were an ulcerated plaque of 5*6cm at left nasolabialfold with indurated margins and depressed floor. She told u that there was some rounded raised lesion since 6 years at same site. Left cervical lymphnode was also palpable. Considering daignosis which one of the following gene is highly associated with it

A. P53
B. PTCH1
A. C.TYR
B. D.B CATENIN
F. ASIP

Key: D
Ref: Rook (141.3)

6. A 65 years old female came with complain of skin lesion at right outer canthus of eye since 5 years. On examination there were 2*2cm skin colored shiny nodule with talengactasia. Skin biopsy showed cords and strand of basloid cells with pallisading arrangement infiltrated in dermis with surrounding retraction artefact. Considering diagnosis which of the following will not be helpful in immunohistochemistry to differentiate it with other diagnosis

A. CD10
B. BCL -2
C. CK 20
D. CK 15
E. Citrulline

Key: E
Ref: Rook (141.6)

7. A 17 year male presented to you with smooth surfaced rounded elevated papules, flesh coloured or pigmented, varying in size from 1 to 15 mm in diameter mostly present on face, back and chest. The lesions increased in size and number previously. There are fine telangiectasia and milium-like bodies just below the surface. Tumours of the axillae neck and eyelids tend to be pedunculated. True regarding the pathogenesis of these lesions EXCEPT:

A. Deeper penetration, ulceration and invasion can occur, with lymphocytic infiltration
B. There may be pigmentation in and around the masses
C. Occurrence of Merkel cells is believed to be an indication that the tumour is more closely related to trichoblastoma than to BCC
D. The presence of calcification and the general architecture can resemble trichoepithelioma
E. Palmoplantar pits show focal absence of the stratum corneum with vacuolization of the spinous layer

Key: C
Ref: Rook (141.18 - 141.19)

8. A 17 year male presented to you with smooth surfaced rounded elevated papules, flesh coloured or pigmented, varying in size from 1 to 15 mm in diameter mostly present on face, neck and upper chest. The lesions increased in size and number previously. There are fine telangiectasia and milium-like bodies just below the surface. Tumours of the axillae neck and eyelids tend to be pedunculated. The assessment criteria include all the following except:

A. Dental examination
B. PTCH (Patched), HSMO(Smoothened), SHH (Sonic H hedgehog)
C. Bronchoscopy
D. Head circimference
E. CT scan of facial bones

Key: C
Ref: Rook (141.2 page 141.20)

9. A 65 year female presented to your opd with slowly growing, pink or red, fleshy nodule on the trunk, especially the lower back and extremities. Regarding pathogenesis of this condition which of the following is true:

A. Squamous tumour embedded in a loose fibrovascular stroma and displaying a connection with the epidermis
B. Codeletion of PATCHED (PTCH1) gene
C. Merkel cells in lesion is an indication that the tumour is related to trichoblastoma
D. Presence of calcification and the general architecture can resemble trichoepithelioma
E. Premature desquamation with a reduction in desmosomes and tonofibrils resulting from delay in maturation of the epidermal basal cell

Key: C
Ref: Rook (141.17)

10. A 65 year female presented to your opd with slowly growing, pink or red, fleshy nodule on the trunk, especially the lower back and extremities. All of the following treatment options you will offer except:

A. Surgical Removal
B. Curettage
C. Cryotherapy
D. Electrodessication
E. Radiotherapy

Key: C
Ref: Rook (141.17)

11. A 65 year female presented to your opd with slowly growing, pink or red, fleshy nodule on the trunk, especially the lower back and extremities. Which of the following is least likely to be kept in your differential diagnosis?

A. Fibroma
B. Papillomatous nevus
C. Seborrhoeic Keratosis
D. Fibroepithelial polyp
E. Amelanotic melanoma

Key: C
Ref: Rook (141.17)

Chapter 142 SQUAMOUS CELL CARCINOMA AND ITS PRECURSORS

1. A 60 years old male presented with history of scaly papule on left side of neck. On examination there was 2cm papule with overlying thick scale on it. Histology of the lesion showed hyperkeratosis, parakeratosis, hypogranulosis and Dyskeratotic cells with increase mitotic activity. Which of the following is not predisposing factor?

A. HPV
B. Thiazide
C. Coal exposure
D. Red hair and blue eyes
E. Captopril

Key: E
Ref: Rook (142.2)

2. A 65 years old lady came with history of thick scaly macules on cheeks for last 3 years. On examination there were multiple discrete scaly lesions along with atrophy, hyperpigmentation, telengiectasia. On removing the scale there was hyperaemic base with bleeding points. Histology showed parakeratosis, hypogranulosis and dyskeratotic cells with increase mitotic activity and funnel shaped orthokeratosis. Considering diagnosis of the patient which of the following is not considered high risk feature of the disease

A. Multiple thick lesions
B. Extensive actinic damage
C. Immunosuppression
D. Tender enlarging lesion
E. Full thickness epithelial dysplasia

Key: E
Ref: Rook (142.6)

3. A 50 years old truck driver came with history of thick scaly hyperkeratotic papule on forehead for last 2 years. On examination there was solitary discrete hyperkeratotic papule with brown c olored adherent scale on forehead. On removing the scale there was hyperaemic base with bleeding points. Histology showed parakeratosis, hypogranulosis and dyskeratotic cells with increase mitotic activity and funnel shaped orthokeratosis. Which of the following is least effective treatment option

A. topical retinoid
B. cryotherapy
C. 5% fluorouracil
D. imiquimod
E. Diclofenac gel

Key: A
Ref: Rook (142.11)

4. A 70 years old male presented with history of multiple scaly macules and papule on face. On examination there was thick adherent brown scale. Surrounding skin showed telengiactasia and hyperpigmentation, wrinkles and skin atrophy. Histology of the lesion showed hyperkeratosis, parakeratosis, hypogranulosis and Dyskeratotic cells with increase mitotic activity. There was dense lymphoid infiltrate in dermis. Which of the following medical treatment can cause long term prophylaxis?

A. sunscreen

B. topical retinoid
C. Vitamin C cream
D. dermabrasion and TCA peel
E. photodynamic therapy

Key: D
Ref: Rook (142. 11)

5. A 65 year old man presented with an asymmetric plaque over pinna of righr ear which is firm in consistency, irregular margins and bleeds easily, slow growing over past 10 years. Provisional dx or scc was made what is true regarding investigation.
A. MRI detects 95% peri neural invasion in head and neck tumor
B. CT scan is superior in detectinh PNI.
C. Sentinel lymph node biopsy is indicated.
D. High resolution micro coil MRI is recommended as part of routine investigation.
E. PET scan is recommended as part of routine investigation

Key: A.
Ref: Rook (142.30)

6. A 50 year old man dx case of hidradenitis suppurativa presented with slow growing verrucous plaque on lower lip which crusted n then became ulcerated. Which of the following is not a high-risk feature of such plaque?
A. Diameter more than 20 mm
B. Immunosuppression.
C. Sites as feet, nose, forearms.
D. Arising in scars, burn Bowen disease, inflammatory conditions.
E. Lesion arising in non-sun exposed skin

Key: C.
Ref: Rook (142.29)

7. A 40 year old pt of renal transplant presented with 4cm scc on right forearm, what should be the tumor margins for surgical excision in this pt?
A. 1mm.
B. 2mm
C. 4mm.
D. 5mm.
E. 6mm

Key: E.
Ref: Rook (142.32)

8. in an old man of 64 years with multiple solar keratosis on head and neck area, regarding scc which is the most favoured site to develop?
A. Helix of ear.
B. Pinna of ear.
C. Tragus of ear.
D. Anti helix.
E. None of the above.

Key: A

9. Regarding scc which of tje following is not a high-risk subtype?
A. Desmoplastic.
B. Spindle cell.
C. Acantholytic.
D. Pseudoangiosarcomatous.
E. All of the above

Key: E
Ref: Rook (142.31)

10. A 18 years old boy had motor vehicle accident 4 months back. He presented with a firm keratotic rapidly enlarging ulcerated nodule on the lateral aspect of left elbow. He states that his nodule is 8 weeks old. On histopathology crateriform nodule with focal papillomatosis, invaginations n broad proliferative epidermal mass composed of squamous cells with variable glassy cytoplasm n keratinization is seen. Which of the following is most appropriate for this?

A. Surgical removal
B. Self-limiting
C. Benign
D. Reassurance
E. Malignant always

Key: D
Ref: Rook (142.33)

11. A 25 years old man with skin type 1 presented with crenellated scar on nose which was red and crusted n 2-3cm in diameter 3 months back. Keeping the diagnosis in mind all of the following are true except.

A. AR_ TGFBR1 gene
B. AD_TGFBR1 gene
C. Chronic condition patient develops multiple tumors in their life time
D. The lesion develops mostly on light exposed skin
E. Develop self-healing Scc

Key: B
Ref: Rooks (142.36)

12. A 55 years old farmer presented in skin outdoor with a lesion on his under the angle of the mandible that grows rapidly and then regresses. Following factors are responsible for initiating of its formation except.

A. Sun exposure
B. dust exposure
C. tar exposure
D. trauma, Injury,
E. infection, burn

Key: B
Ref: Rooks (142.33)

13. A 38 years old male presented in skin Opd with yellow papules and nodules on face for 8 months. Recently he has developed a shiny skin coloured nodule with telangiectases and a central plug. His uncle has died due to colorectal cancer at the age of 50. Which of the following is not true about this disease?

A. Autosomal dominant
B. it is caused by germline mutations in the DNA mismatch repair genes
C. MSH2 gene mutation
D. it is characterized by the presence of cutaneous tumors (sebaceous carcinoma, keratoacanthoma, & visceral neoplasms)
E. It is considered a phenotypic variant of familial adenomatous polyposis.

Key: E
Ref: Rooks (142.38)

14. A 60 years old male farmer presented in dermatology clinic with multiple, itchy nodules on photo exposed sites. O/E they are red/flesh in colour and dome shaped, filled with keratin. He has mask like face n has ectropion & hoarseness. What is your diagnosis?

A. Fergusin smith disease
B. Muir Torre syndrome

C. Grzybowski syndrom
D. Viral warts
E. Scc

Key: C
Ref: Rook (142.37)

15. A 60 year-old female of European descent presents at ur OPD with a well-demarcated, scaly, erythematous plaque on her right shin. Her biopsy report shows full thickness epidermal atypia with scattered mitotic figures and overlying parakeratosis. The
Basement membrane is also found breached by atypical keratinocytes. Her immunohistochemical profile is positive for EMA, P63 and P40. Your likely diagnosis is:
A. BCC
B. SCC
C. Bowen's disease
D. Angiosarcoma
E. CTCL

Key: B
Ref: Rook (142.27, 142.17 and 142.19)

16. With regards to your diagnosis in scenario number 1, which of the following factors may NOT contribute towards a increase in its incidence:
A. Sun exposure
B. Immunosuppression
C. Increasing age
D. Proximity to the equator
E. None of the above

Key: E
Ref: Rook (142.26, 142.27, 142.28).

17. Which substance is normally inactivated to allow advancement of Actinic Keratosis to SCC?
A. P21
B. P19
C. P17
D. P16
E. None of the above

Key: D
Ref: Rook (142.26)

18. Which of the following is true regarding HPV-associated squamous cell cancers?
A. The rate of metastasis approaches 15%.
B. HPV18 is the most common associated subtype.
C. Mohs micrographic surgery yields a 50% recurrence rate.
D. Women outnumber men 2:1.
E. These lesions only occur in association with immunosuppression.

Key: B
Ref: Rook (142.26, 142.27, 142.30, 142.31 and 25.58)

19. Prominent histopathological evidence of epidermotropism is characteristically typical for which of the following conditions:
A. Merkel cell carcinoma
B. SCC

C. BCC
D. CTCL
E. All of the above

Key: D
Ref: Rook (142.27 & 140.5)

20. High risk features of primary SCC include all of the following EXCEPT:
A. Tumour diameter greater than 20mm
B. Tumour thickness greater than 4mm
C. Immunosuppression
D. Perineural invasion
E. SCC on Finger

Key: E
Ref: Rook (142.29, Table 142.6)

21. 52 years male presents to skin opd with asymptotic rash on dorsa of hands-off n on from last 1 year.
O/e there were macules with rough scaly surface.2 mm in size.
Scale can't be picked off easily. He also has telangictasias and hyperpigmentation on face.
He is Gardner by profession
On biopsy hyperkeratosis, parakratosis, hypogranulosis, keratinocytes have cytological atypia Basant membrane is intact.
What should be the management?
A. no treatment only sun avoidance and sunblock
B. cryotherapy
C. 5% fluorouracil
D. excision with 1 mm border

Key: A
Ref: Rook (142.7)

22. 60 yrs male doing duty at checkpost. came with complaint of hard brown outgrowth on right hand. With circumferential ridges.
On histo dyplastic epidermal changes and loss of granular layer. No loss of polarity
When is chance of malignancy increased in this pt?
A. decreased inflammation
B. loss of pain in that area
C. low height to base ratio
D. decrease in size

Key: C
Ref: Rook (142.12)

23. A 40 years old farmer presented with a solitary raised red plaques with adherent scales. The scales are irregular and fissured. Histopathology of lesions shows atypical keratinocytes at all levels within epidermis. The atypical cells don't breach the dermo epidermal junction. What could be the probable diagnosis?
A. Extramammary pagets disease
B. Actinic keratosis
C. Amelanotic melanoma
D. Superficial BCC
E. Bowen's Disease

Key: E
Ref: Rook (142.18)

24. A 52 years old man has developed solitary indurated lesion on the dorsum of right hand which is slowly enlarging. It started as a slightly raised red plaque with adherent dry scaling. On close examination, the surface has irregular fissured and adherent scales. Borders are slightly elevated but not rolled. The most likely diagnosis is?
   A. Psoriasis
   B. Bowenoid keratosis
   C. Seborrheic Keratosis
   D. Superficial BCC
   E. Localized chronic eczematous dermatitis

Key: B
Ref: Rook (142.18)

25. All are the variants of Bowens disease except?
   A. Atrophic
   B. Annular
   C. Verrucous
   D. Psoriasiform
   E. Irregular

Key B
Ref: Rook (142.18)

26. Regarding bowens disease, following statement is incorrect except?
   A. Bowen disease on perianal skin carries a higher risk of invasion, recurrence and an association with cervical vulval dysplasia.
   B. Pigmented Bowen disease is very common variety, on extensors and subungual sites.
   C. Verrucous Bowens disease is common and carries a risk for invasive carcinoma
   D. Complications are more and prognosis is poor.
   E. For multiple and larger lesions, destructive method is the treatment of choice

Key: A
Ref: Rook (142.19)

27. Cutaneous diseases resulting from arsenic exposure include all of the following except?
   A. Keratotic papules on soles
   B. Hypopigmented macules
   C. Bowens disease
   D. D)Bowenoid papulosis
   E. Multiple BCC

Key: D
Ref: Rook (142.17)

28. 53 years male came with hyperkeratotic lesions of palms. On examination multiple hyperpigmented and hypo pigmented lesions are present.
Which other organ is to be assessed?
   A. Liver
   B. prostate
   C. bladder
   D. kidneys

Key: C
Ref: Rook (142.13)

29. 42years male gardener came with brown red follicular papules initially. It was treated as folliculitis but it expanded and became slightly atrophic with raised margin. Sweating is absent inside lesion
On histo narrow altered keratin column is seen
Whats the prognosis?

A. malignant change is common
B. scc is most common in these
C. no increase in malignancy
D. malignant change is low

Key: D
Ref: Rook (142.16)

Chapter 145

MERKEL CELL CARCINOMA

1. A 76 yr old post renal transplant recipient presented to your opd with a fleshy red and smooth nodule of size 5cm with an overlying telengectasia on the forearm for the past 3 months.2 satellite lesions were also observed. H/P shows cells with small multiple nucleoli with atypical vesicular like chromatin giving an appearance of salt and pepper. The most likely pathology is

A. Bcc
B. Scc
C. Mcc
D. Amelonotic melanoma
E. Cutaneous mets of B cell lymphoma

Key: C
Ref: Rook (145.3, 145.4)

2. Merkel cell carcinoma on histology can show the following patterns except

A. Intermediate
B. Small cell
C. Trabecular
D. Infiltrative
E. All of the above

Key: D
Ref: Rook (145.2, 145.3)

3 .A 80 yr female with fitzpatrick type II presented with a rapidly growing,violaceous, soft,firm nodular swelling on the right lateral side of the neck for past 4 months.The histology shows the tumor arises from the basal layer of epidermis along hair follicle anf nerve sheath.The immunohistochemistry in this case will be positive for

A. Vimentin
B. CK20
C. Melan-A
D. Leukocyte common antigen
E. NK2 homeobox 1

Key: B
Ref: Rook (145.3)

4. In a case of Merkel Cell Carcinoma the factors which show a good prognosis include all except

A. Tumour size 2cm
B. Solitary lesion
C. Upper limb involvement
D. Age <50
E. Male gender.

Key: E
Ref: Rook (145.6)

5. A 70 yr old male patient presented to you with a right sided red firm lesion of size 2cm on the forearm and few cutaneous satellite lesions on the contralateral arm with rt sided axillary lymph nodes involvement. No visceral involvement was seen on organ imaging. monoclonal integration of non-enveloped double stranded DNA virus into host genome was evident. The TNM staging in this case shows disease is of

A. Stage IV A
B. Stage IV B
C. Stage III A
D. Stage III B
E. Stage II A

Key: A
Ref: Rook (145.7)

Chapter 146

SKIN CANCER IN THE IMMUNOCOMPROMISED PATIENT

1. A 12 yrs. old boy came to OPD with reticulate pigmentation of skin in head and neck. On examination, u found whitish coating of tongue along with nail dystrophy. His peripheral blood smear showed decreased cell counts. A diagnosis of dyskeratosis congenital was made. These patients are more prone to develop which cancer?
   A. BCC
   B. Mucocutaneous SCC
   C. Hodgkin lymphoma
   D. CLL
   E. Merkel cell carcinoma

Key: B
Ref: Rook (146.2)

2. A 50 year old patient presented in medical emergency with fever and extensive skin rash...You examine the patient and finds out that his almost all body is covered with erythematous plaques and patches. No lymphadenopathy is appreciated on palpation. He says that he had these plaques for a few months now, they were very few initially, they increased gradually, and his condition deteriorated over a few days. He has a skin biopsy report that was done 2 months back and it says there is epidermotropism and dermis shows few large cells with cellular atypia. Considering the diagnosis in mind, what should be the first line treatment of this disease after initial resuscitation and management of patient?
   A. PUVA
   B. PUVA +interferon alpha
   C. MTX
   D. Alemtuzumab
   E. TSEB

Key: C
Ref: Rook (140.9)

3. A 40 year old patient presented with pruritic plaques and patches on skin that cover less than 10 percent of his BSA.No lymph nodes were palpable...his Histopathology shows mild spongiosis,moderate lymphocytic infiltrate in papillary dermis and atypical large lymphoid cells in epidermis.Immunophenotyping was done and diagnosis of MF established with stage 2A.. You want to start his treatment with PUVA and adarotene. How will you proceed with adarotene?
   A. Start with a dose of 150mg/m2 weekly and titrate the dose after 2-4 weeks
   B. Start fibrate and levothyroxine and then start bexarotene at dose of 300mg/m2
   C. Start with a dose of 150 mg/m2 daily and increase the dose to 300 after 2-4 weeks
   D. Evaluate the response at 6 months after start of treatment to check if the disease is still active or progressive
   E. Monitor blood tests fortnightly until stable

Key: C
Ref: Rook (140.25 page Fig 140.26)

4. You have a patient in your ward....he presented with eczematous plaques on skin for many months that respond to conventional therapies only temporarily but then reappear. You suspect CTCL while his report is awaited you want to teach the residents in ward about the treatment options and their MOA.... Which one of the following is NOT true regarding MOA of respective treatments?
   A. Interferons...promote generation of cytotoxic T and Th 1 cytokine response
   B. HDAC.....affect gene expression by promoting acetylation of histone proteins which cause chromatin structure adopt an open configuration....thus allowing gene transcription
   C. Bexarotene...selectively binds and activates retinoid X receptor and promote apoptosis and inhibit cell proliferation

D. ECP.......UVA exposed lymphocytes including tumour lymph's undergo apoptosis and dendritic cells are activated during ex vivo circulation with induction of a host antitumor immune response
E. Ongar...inhibit protein synthesis in tumour cells expressing high levels of IL.2 receptor resulting in cell death

.Key: B
Ref: Rook (140.27)

5. A 20 yrs. old male came to u with disseminated plan topped skin coloured lesions all over body. Few hypo pigmented lesions with fine scales were also found in all over body. On investigations EVER 1 gene mutation was found. What percentage of such patients are more prone to develop cutaneous SCC?
A. 20 percent
B. 40 percent
C. 60 percent
D. 80 percent
E. 10 percent

Key: C
Ref: Rook (146.1)

6. A patient was diagnosed with HIV 10 yrs. back was taking treatments for that noticed a verrucous ulcerated growth on his nose. These patients are more prone to develop SCC when Cd 4 count falls below?
A. 500 cells/ul
B. 200 cells/ ul
C. 100cells/ul
D. 400 cells/ ul
E. E.300 cells/ ul

Key: B

7. A patient who was diagnosed as case of aspergillus's and was taking treatment for that from about 6 months. Now he presented with a warty growth on left cheek which was increasing in size and occasionally accompanied by blood discharge. A suspicion of SCC was made. Which antifungal is more prone to develop SCC?
A. Viriconazole
B. Itraconazole
C. Amphotericin B
D. Griseofulvin
E. Ketoconazole

Key: A
Ref: Rook (146.6, 146.2)

8. A 60 yrs. old male with skin type 2 developed ulcerated nodule on right cheek with rolled over edges. A diagnosis of BCC was made which was excised and grafting was done. What surveillance protocol will u advice to advice to the patient to prevent further carcinoma
A. 4 , 8, 12 months then annually
B. 6, 12 months ten annually
C. 3, 6, 9, 12 months then annually
D. No need to do follow up

Key: B
Ref: Rook (146.17)

Chapter 147

CUTAMENOUS MARKERS OF INTERNAL MALIGNANCY

1. A middle age male patient, smoker, refferd to dermatology department with gradual increase in thickness of palmar skin having velvety pattern for last 7 months. On further inquiry he told that he had frequent visits to chest physician due to persistent bloody cough associated with localised chest pain on and off for the last 8 months. Along with this he also noted significant weight loss and bulbous enlargement of all finger nails and some toe nails. No any history of night sweats and lymphadenopathy. Rest of the cutaneous and systemic examination was unremarkable. Which of the following statement is true regarding his above condition?

A. If nail clubbing is present then bronchial carcinoma is very likely.
B. If acanthosis nigricans is present then underlying malignancy will be pheochromocytoma
C. Onset of palmar condition never precede or occurred concurrently with unsuspected malignancy.
D. More common in females if underlying tumour is a lung cancer.
E. All of the above

Key: A
Ref: Rook (147.16)

2. A 14 years male patient came in dermatology department with the presenting complaint of short stature, learning difficulty, excessive lacrimation and hyperhidrosis for last few years. On further inquiry his mother told that he also got some nail problem when he was 6 years old. On cutaneous examination reticulate hyperpigmented atrophic patches along with some telengiectasia visible over face, neck, upper back and thighs. Nails were short having longitudinal ridges and pterygium formation. Dorsal hands were atrophic and shiny. Oral mucosa showed few erosions and solitary white patch of 1×0.7cm size over lateral border of tongue. Teeth were defective and gums were swollen and tender to touch. No history of photosensitivity, lymphadenopathy and previous malignancy. Investigation showed Hb 6gm/dl, WBC 4.8 × 10^9/L and platelets 77,000. Above findings are consistent with which of the following features of this syndrome.

A. Aplastic anaemia in early teenage is the main cause of mortality.
B. Oropharyngeal carcinoma is the most common malignancy
C. Condition can be x-linked, autosomal dominant and recessive
D. Mostly genes in this condition are involved in telomere maintenance.
E. All of the above

Key: E
Ref: Rook (147.13-14)

3. An elderly male patient came in dermatology department with sudden onset multiple hyperpigmented patches and verrucous plaques of variable shapes and sizes developed over trunk without pain, bleeding and discharge but associated with pruritus on and off. No history of HIV, erythroderma and radiochemotherapy in the past. Rest of the skin, nail and mucosae examinations were normal. Keeping in mind diagnosis, which of the following malignancies can be associated with this disease.

A. Adenocarcinoma, osteosarcoma and nephroblastoma
B. Adenocarcinoma, renal carcinoma and bladder carcinoma
C. Fibrosarcoma, astrocytoma and melanoma
D. Keratoacanthoma and sebaceous carcinoma
E. Pheochromocytoma and neuromas

Key: B
Ref: Rook (147.16)

4. A 7 years female child presented with fever, jaundice and sloughing of oral mucosa for last 3 days. She also had on and off epileptic attacks and recurrent pyogenic infections in the past. On cutaneous examination child is having generalised depigmented skin and scalp hairs along with moderate intensity photophobia and nystagmus. Systemic examination showed abnormal gait, hepatosplenomegaly and cervical lymphadenopathy. Investigations revealed decrease white cell counts and giant inclusions inside polymorphonuclear neutrophils in peripheral blood smear. Keeping in mind diagnosis, which among the following virus will be responsible for accelerated lymphomatous phase of this disease.

A. HIV
B. HSV
C. CMV
D. EBV
E. HPV

Key: D
Ref: Rook (147.13)

5. A middle age male patient refferd for skin lesions to dermatology department by gastroenterologist after endoscopy. On cutaneous examination there were symmetrical hyperpigmented plaques having velvety pattern over nape of neck, bilateral axilla, palms and soles for last few years. Rest of the hairs, nails and mucosae examinations were normal. On further inquiry he told that for last 8 months he had progressive pain in his abdomen and black stools associated with fatigue and weight loss. No history of night sweats and lymphadenopathy. Rest of the systemic examination was unremarkable. HIV test negative. Bone scan normal. Keeping in mind diagnosis, which of the following is not true regarding this disease.

A. Skin changes improve with eradication of the cancer
B. Benign type mostly occur in obese children
C. Commonest site of malignancy is lung
D. Acanthosis palmaris and sign of leser-Trélat may coexist
E. Denovo development can occur in adults

Key C
Ref: Rook (147.14)

6. A 70-year old man who is a chronic smoker gives history of cough, hemoptysis, dyspnea and weight loss presented to dermatology OPD with symmetrical erythematous hyperkeratotic lesions on the hands, feet, ears and nose along with palmoplantar keratoderma and dystrophic nails. There is also cervical lymphadenopathy. On histopathalogy, there is hyperkeratosis, parakeratosis, focal spongiosis and a mixed inflammatory cell infiltrate. What is the most likely diagnosis?

A. Acrokeratosis paraneoplastica
B. Bazex-Dupré-Christol syndrome
C. Allergic contact dermatitis
D. Chronic plaque psoriasis
E. Reiter syndrome

Key: A
Ref: Rook (147.19)

7. A 50-year old woman presented with the history of insidious onset and gradually progressive pain and weakness of the proximal muscles of both upper and lower limbs for the past four years. She also complained of dusky red rash with swelling, itching, and photosensitivity over the face and extremities since the past three years. On cutaneous examination, there are confluent violaceous, edematous macules around eyelids, forehead, cheek, and chin along with erythematous firm papules of size 0.5 X 0.5 cm over metacarpophalangeal, proximal interphalangeal, and distal interphalangeal joints. The nails were dystrophic

and had ragged cuticles. The clinical diagnosis of dermatomyositis was made. Which of the following statement about the related malignancy is false?

A. Malignancy can precede the development of dermatomyositis
B. Malignancy can be found during follow-up (usually in the first 6 months after diagnosis of dermatomyositis)
C. AntiNXP-2 is frequently cancer-associated dermatomyositis antibodies
D. Anti-TIF-1 γ is common cancer-associated dermatomyositis antibodies
E. Among men, renal cell carcinoma is most prevalent

Key: E
Ref: Rook (147.20)

8. A 40-year old woman presented with multiple well-demarcated erythematous annular plaques with slight scale over the neck, shoulders and upper back. She also has fatigue, photosensitivity, and arthralgia of bilateral wrists and small hand joints. Serology examination was remarkable for positivity of ANA, anti-Ro and anti-La. Considering the most likely diagnosis, which of the following malignancy is most frequently associated with this disease?

A. Renal cell carcinoma
B. Colorectal carcinoma
C. Breast cancer
D. Non-hodgkin lymphoma
E. Chronic lymphocytic leukemia

Key: D
Ref: Rook (147.21)

9. A 60-year man with a history of hypertension and a thymoma, presents to the dermatology OPD with extensive painful oral and conjunctival erosions and haemorrhagic bullae on his hands and feet. A perilesional biopsy for DIF shows deposition of C3 and IgG intercellularly and along the basement membrane zone. What is the most likely diagnosis?

A. Cicatricial pemphigoid
B. Epidermolysis bullosa
C. Toxic epidermal necrolysis
D. Paraneoplastic pemphigus
E. Bullous pemphighoid

Key: D
Ref: Rook (147.21)

10. Which of the following immunobullous disorder is associated with hepatocellular carcinoma?

A. Pemphigus vulgaris
B. Pemphigus foliaceus
C. Paraneoplastic pemphigus
D. Bullous pemphighoid
E. Cicatricial pemphigoid

Key: B
Ref: Rook (147.22)

11. A 51 year old female presented with numerous raised solid lesions over neck, axillae, groins and forehead since 5 years. She had undergone subtotal thyroidectomy for multinodular goitre 2 years ago. Physical examination revealed pallor, macrocephaly, adenoid facies Dermatological examination revealed multiple, forehead papules skin tags over neck axillae and groin, one verrucous nodule each over dorsa of left middle and right ring fingers and cobblestone tongue.
Which carcinoma is most associated with this condition?

A. Lung carcinoma
B. Gastric adenocarcinoma
C. Breast Carcinoma
D. Colorectal carcinoma
E. Pancreas carcinoma

Key: C
Ref: Rook (147.11)

12. A 18 year old boy was admitted because of excessive weight gain over 3 years and purple striae for 1 year. Physical examination revealed Cushingoid features and spotty skin pigmentation on his face, lip, and sclera and multiple blue naevi.
Which one the following tumour is NOT associated with it??

A. wilms tumor
B. Sertoli cell tumor
C. Ovarian tumor
D. Pituitary tumor
E. Adrenal tumor

Key: A
Ref: Rook (147.11)

13. A 52 year old woman presented to the out-patient clinic with a 3 cm diameter lump near the left arm, which was excised. The histopathologist reported this as a sebaceous adenoma and also raised the possibility of the association of these lesions with visceral neoplasms. The patient had undergone hysterectomy for endometrial cancer at the age of 32 years. She also had an actinic keratosis and a basal cell carcinoma previously.
What internal malignancy is associated with it?

A. Gastric adenocarcinoma
B. Esophageal carcinoma
C. Colonic adenocarcinoma
D. lung carcinoma
E. Pancreas carcinoma

Key: C
Ref: Rook (147.12)

14. A 20 year old male suffers from rash over the sun exposed areas and photosensitivity started during the first months of his life.
Skin examination demonstrated poikilodermatous rash on the face, neck, V zone and extensor surface of the arms and legs. Histopathology of the affected skin was consistent with poikiloderma. Eyelashes, eyebrows and scalp hair were normal. Punctate keratoderma was presented on both palms.
There is small stature and premature ageing present.
Which one of the following malignancies is most common associated with it??

A. Retinoblastoma
B. Osteocarcoma
C. Ewing sarcoma
D. Basal cell carcinoma
E. Wilms tumor

Key: B
Ref: Rook (147.12)

15. A 77 year old man was referred for pruritic verrucous lesions on the face abdomen and legs that had appeared more than 3 months earlier. A dermatological examination revealed several small warty papules on the face abdomen and legs.

There is also acanthosis nigricans in axillary
There is recent history of weight loss.
This condition is associated with which carcinoma??

A. Lung carcinoma
B. Breast Carcinoma
C. Gastric adenocarcinoma
D. Oesophageal carcinoma
E. Transitional cell carcinoma of bladder

Key: C
Ref: Rook (147.16)

16. A 38 year old female presented with occasional complaints of GERD symptoms approximately 3 times a week, sometimes related to diet which worsened during evening and nighttime.
There is also palmoplantar keratoderma.
There is also history of oral leukoplakia.
Which one of the carcinomas is associated with it???

A. Gastric adenocarcinoma
B. Oesophageal carcinoma
C. Colorectal carcinoma
D. Thyroid carcinoma
E. Nasophargeal carinoma

Key: B.
Ref: Rook (147.7)

Chapter 148 THE SKIN AND DISORDERS OF HAEMATOPOIETIC AND IMMUNE SYSTEMS

1. A 46 year old male presented with history of intermittent fever, arthralgias and non-itchy erythematous raised patches on skin which lasted about 72 hours and then disappeared. Examination showed lymphadenopathy and hepatosplenomegaly labs show increased WBC count with neutrophilia, raised igM and igG. Inflammatory markers were also raised. Skin biopsy shows neutrophilic infiltrate without vasculitis. keeping in mind diagnosis what could be the complication if the disease left untreated:
   A. Endocrinopathies
   B. Glomerulonephritis
   C. Dermatomyositis
   D. Amyloidosis

Key: D
Ref: Rook (148.11)

2. A 20 year old boy presented with diffuse pigmentation of extensor surfaces, neck, axillae and back. He also complaints of weakness in legs and arms. Examination shows gynaecomastia and mild hepatomegaly. Oral cavity examination is unremarkable. Lab shows increased glucose level. He was advised bone marrow examination which showed plasma cell infiltrate. What should be the first line treatment option in this patient?
   A. Radiotherapy
   B. Lenalidomide
   C. Hematopoetic stem cell transplantation
   D. Reduced conditioning chemotherapy

Key: C
Ref: Rook (148.11)

3. A 27 years old female presented with erythematous EM like lesions on photoexposed areas predominantly on face. There was also history of fever, sore throat, night sweats and weight loss for which she took antibiotics. Oral cavity, nails and scalp is normal. Examination shows tender lymphadenopathy involving cervical lymph node. Lymph node biopsy was done which showed complete loss of architecture and necrosis of cortical and paracortical areas. Extensive infiltrate of small lymphocytes, immunoblasts and plasmacytoid T cells was seen with no neutrophils. Regarding diagnosis which is inappropriate:
   A. Work up for SLE should be advised
   B. High dose steroids and immunoglobulins should be started
   C. Spontaneous resolution over few months
   D. Can also be accompanied by macrophage activating syndrome

Key: B
Ref: Rook (148.13, 51.31)

4. A 30 year old male presented with bilateral neck swelling associated with fever. Examination showed subcutaneous mass around neck with normal overlying skin. No other findings were noted. labs showed eosinophilia and increased igE levels. Histopathology showed follicular hyperplasia, inflammatory infiltrate of eosinophils, arborizing vascular proliferation of post capillary venules. About disease, which of the following systemic involvement has prognostic value:
   A. Hepatobiliary
   B. Neurological
   C. Renal
   D. Cardiac

Key: C
Ref: Rook (148.13)

5. A mother brought his 6 year old child with history of erythematous rash since birth. There was also history of recurrent skin infections. He was hospitalised twice for some respiratory problem. Examination showed white patches on tongue, hyperkeratotic lesions on scalp and nail problems. Facial features were also abnormal with double layer of teeth's. labs showed eosinophilia and increased igE levels. which of the following gene is mutated in this disease?

A. WAS
B. STAT3
C. Haploinsufficiency of Tbx1
D. RAG1

Key: B
Ref: Rook (148.17)

6. A 60 years old man presented in the opd with history of multiple, monomorphic violaceous, haemorrhagic skin nodules present on both legs and arms for last 10 months. He was a known case of CLL and was on chemotherapy. Which of the following statement is true regarding the above-mentioned scenario?

A. The appearance of skin lesions is not specific for particular subtype of leukemia
B. Leukemia cutis does not affect the prognosis of CLL except for Richter syndrome where prognosis is grave
C. Treatment is supportive and radiotherapy can be given
D. The most sensitive markers are CD43, CD68 and lysozyme
E. All of the above

Key: E
Ref: Rook (148.2)

7. A 50 years old patient presented in the opd with history of skin thickening, woody induration and non-pitting edema of face and neck for last 1 year. There was no involvement of hands and feet. He was a known case of Monoclonal gammopathy of undetermined significance. Which of the following statement is not true

A. 5 clinical variants are recognized
B. There is dermal and subcutaneous thickening due to an increase in glycosaminoglcans separating collagen fibers
C. It is associated with POEMS syndrome
D. Internal organs may be involved
E. All of the above

Key: A
Ref: Rook (148.9)

8. A 56 years old man Known case of Multiple Myeloma presented in the opd with history of widespread papular eruption on face ears neck from last 6 months. The papules are firm slightly translucent and waxy in appearance. Patient also complains of dysphagia and hoarseness of voice. Which of the following statement is true?

A. Scleromyxedema is a common generalized cutaneous mucinosis
B. 70% of patients have IgA paraproteinemia
C. The main cause of death is progression of heamatological disease and CNS involvement
D. IVIG is the second line treatment option
E. All of the above

Key: C
Ref: Rook (148.8)

9. A 45 years old lady Known case of AML presented in the opd with history of multiple infiltrated erythematous papules and plaques predominantly on the face, upper trunk, arms and Palmoplantar surface from last 6 months. She was having chemotherapy whi h included cytarabine and vincristine. Which of the following statement is not true?

A. The disease is characterized by eosinophilic infiltrates around eccrine glands
B. The disease has an association with HIV and other infections like staph aureus, Serratia marcescens, Enterobacter species
C. Disease can resolve spontaneously
D. It is rarest disease
E. None of the above

Key: A
Ref: Rook (148.7)

10. 5 years old boy presented in the opd with history of fever and soar throat for last 5 days. 3 days after the development of fever he developed erythmatous to violaeceous papules and nodules arranged in vesicle like plaques that were painful and itchy present on the sternum, back and proximal part of upper limbs. which of the following statement is true.

A. 20 perecent of the cases are associated with hematological neoplasm.
B. Hyoersensitivity reaction to tumor antigens or autoinflamatory IL 1 mediated process exists in paraneoplastic disease form.
C. Optic neuritis and chorioretinitis are common complications.
D. Isomorphic variant develops at the site of trauma.
E. All of the a above

Key: E
Ref: Rook (148.6)

Chapter 149 THE SKIN AND ENDOCRINE DISORDERS

1. A 35 year old male presented to medical specialist complaining of episodic headaches, sweating, palpitations, and a tremor. The symptoms started a few years ago but now have worsened.
The episodes often occur when the patient has work stress at office. His life quality is disturbed because nothing he does changes the severity of his symptoms.
He does not have a history of serious illnesses, hospitalizations, or trauma. He is not on any medication except Panadol which he takes for headache family history of hypertension is positive. He has not had fevers, chills, chest pain, and shortness of breath, nausea, vomiting, or diarrhoea. he has history of change in colour of limbs from white to red after exposure to cold.
On examination, a male of average built sweating profusely with facial pallor with elevated blood pressure of 189/90mm Hg, heart rate 120 beats per minute, a respiratory rate of 20 breaths per minute, and a temperature of 98°F.
There are small nodular outgrowths scattered his limbs and trunk for which he is referred to dermatology OPD too?
What will be the diagnosis?
A. Hyperthyroidism
B. Carcinoid syndrome
C. Glucaganoma
D. Pheochromocytoma
E. Paraganglioma

Key: D
Ref: Rook (149.19)

2. A 35-year-old male patient who is known case of chronic kidney disease and is on peritoneal dialysis since 2 years. he regularly comes to skin opd for complains of dry skin with severe pruritis. now presented with ecymotic necrotic plaques on his lower abdomen and thighs which are very painful and developed acutely.which of the following hormonal assay you will advise in this patient?
A. Thyroid hormone levels
B. Parathyroid hormone levels
C. Hba1c
D. A and B
E. B and C

Key: E
Ref: Rook (61.6 and 149.21)

3. A 50 year of female with 8 months history of weight loss, progressive pallor, diarrhea and abdominal pain. on examination red annual rash on lower abdomen having blisters and vesicles at margin. the rash is waxing and waning in nature. Which of the following is the first line management??
A. distal pancreatectomy
B. somatostatin analogue: octeriotide
C. chemotherapy for pancreatic tumor
D. embolization if hepatic Mets
E. resection of segment of liver

Key: A
Ref: Rook (149.20)

4. A 28-year-old anxious air hostess presented in derma OPD with complaint of hair and nail problems. she says that she is observing that hair are dry rough and brittle and nails break easily with roughened surface for past 1 year. She has been to multiple dermatologists in past and is using high end multivitamins and dietary changes but no improvement seen yet.
She says that she has spent a lot of money in previous years on cosmetics and medicines to improve her hairs and nails and is now very frustrated. you examine the patient and find that she has dryness of skin all over body with coarse hairs on legs with excoriation marks on abdomen and limbs. the nails of the fingers are splitted distally, the cuticles are normal. she is talkative and looking directly into eyes while talking. what will be your diagnosis?

A. Hypothyroidism
B. Hypoparathyroidism
C. Body dysmorphic disorder
D. Hyperthyroidism
E. Social phobia

Key: B
Ref: Rook (149.21)

5. A 69-year-old man with medical history of Parkinson disease is admitted in gastroenterology ward with history of diarrhea, abdominal pain, irregular bowel movements dyspepsia and weight loss, asthenia and anorexia, associated with occasional flushing episodes for 10 months.
A dermatology opinion was seeked for red facial flush and facial spider-like veins.
What is not true regarding the condition??

A. It's a neuroendocrine tumor arising from chromaffin cells
B. The tumor cells secrete serotonin
C. Substance p and bradaykinin are involved in flushing
D. Flushing is the predominant skin presentation occuring in 80 % cases of disease
E. 5 year survival in patients is only 30%

6. A 24 years female presented with history of weight gain, fatigue, and infrequent menstruation and decreased pubic hair growth after the birth of her baby. During labour she suffered post-partum haemorrhage. On further inquiry she unable to breast feed her baby and has decreased sweating. On examination, B.P 90/50mmHg and reduced skin capacitance & sebum contents. What is most likely diagnosis?

A. traumatic brain injury
B. Growth hormone deficiency
C. Sheehan syndrome
D. Craniopharyngioma
E. Congenital POMC deficiency

Key: C
Ref: Rook (149.16)

7. A 18 years boy presented with history of enlargement of earlobes and fingers and said that his ring is tightened. on examination, he has coarse facial features, large frontal skin fold & cutis verticis gyrata. keeping diagnosis in mind which of following not used in treatment of this patient

A. Pegvisomant
B. Phenothiazines
C. Octreotide
D. Bromocriptine
E. Cabergoline

Key: B
Ref: Rook (149.174)

8. You are called to see a Middle Ages patient on medical floor admitted with history of profound fatigue, weight loss, vomiting & diarrhea.1 year back he was treated for pulmonary tuberculosis. On examination, B.P 80/40mmHg, hyperpigmentation of palmar creases, nail bed and oral mucosa. Labs show BSR=45g/dl, Na=116meq/l, K=6 meq/L.
Keeping diagnosis in mind what is the etiological factor?

A. Tubeculosis
B. Autoimmune adrenilitis
C. Systamic fungal infection
D. Obesity
E. All of above

Key: E
Ref: Rook (149.18)

9. A 46 years female diagnosed case of type 2 diabetes mellitus with poor compliance to medication presented with acne, skin darkeninig of axilla, groin & back of neck and menstrual irregularities. On examination she has hirsutic hair, male pattern baldness and velvety skin thickening. Hai is most likely diagnosis?

A. Congenital adrenal hyperplasia
B. polycystic ovarian syndrome
C. hyoerprolactinaemia
D. HAIR-AN syndrome
E. Cushing disease

Key: D
Ref: Rook (149.18)

Chapter 150

THE SKIN AND DISORDERS OF THE HEART

1. A 40 yr old male presented with few months history of red brown plaques on his right cheek. Diascopy revealed apple jelly nodules. Baseline Labs showed increased ESR n increased serum calcium. Skin biopsy showed aggregates of epithelioid cells with sparse lymphocytic mantle. Chest X ray showed hilar lymphadenopthy. Regarding diagnosis. Upto 25% of these pt develop heart involvmnt. Most imp complication is sudden death due to

A. Conduction defects n ventricular arrythmia
B. Cardiomyopathy
C. Pericarditis
D. Valvular heart disease
E. Respiratory failure

Key: A
Ref: Rook (150.4)

2. A 28 yr old lady with history of abortion n DVT presented in opd with painful ulcers on legs for few months. Skin biopsy revealed inflammatory thrombosis of dermal blood vessels. Regarding diagnosis 50% pt develop valvular heart disease. Most frequently affected valve is

A. Tricuspid
B. Mitral
C. Aortic
D. Bicuspid

Key: B
Ref: Rook (150.5)

3. A 1.5 yr old boy with history of high-grade fever for 5 days then developed erythema of limbs n trunk. Conjunctival congestion. Dry fisdured lips n red swollen tongue. Dema of limbs also noted. Cervical lymoh nodes also enlareged. but pt condition deteriorted taken to emergency. Cardiac involvmnt seen. Pt had pericardial effusion, cardiomegaly. Myocarditis n coronary artery aneurysm was diagnosed. Regarding above pt. This myicarditis n coronary artery aneurysm develops in which %age of pt

A. 10%
B. 50%
C. 25%
A. D.70%
D. 5%

Key: C
Ref: Rook (150.5)

Chapter 151 THE SKIN AND DISORDERS OF THE RESPIRATORY SYSTEM

1. A 62 yr old known treated case of hodgkins lymphoma presented in derma opd with oral ulcers n blisters, n tense blisters on trunk. Biopsy done. DIF aldi done which showed igG n C3 depodits. Pt have progressive dyspnea. Regardinv diagnosis of this pt. Which can be cause of death.

A. Cardiac failure
B. Metastasis
C. Respiratory failure
D. Secondary infection

Key: C
Ref: Rook (151.6)

2. Diffuse alveolar hemorrhage due to extensive pulmonary capillaritis is life threatening complication. Which occurs in all except

A. Granulamatosis with polyangitis
B. Microscopic polyangitis
C. SLE n APLA
D. Bechets disease
E. Iga vasculitis
F. Drugs like D penicillamin

Key: E
Ref: Rook (151.4)

Chapter 152

THE SKIN AND DISORDERS OF THE DIGESTIVE SYSTEM

1. A 43yearold female referred to dermatology opd for diffuse hyperpigmentation mainly on sun exposed areas.
She had a history of a 6month hypochromic microcytic anemia. She had 6months abdominal pain and liquid stools, in addition, she had an 8month small and medium joint pain, without edema or erythema. Endoscopy showed red spots in the duodenum and ulcerations in the jejunum and proximal ileum covered by fibrin
Histological report showed macrophages with positive periodic acid-schiff reaction staining (PAS staining).
What is the most likely diagnosis?

A. Bronze diabetes
B. Whipple disease
C. Inflammatory bowel disease
D. Primary biliary cirrhosis
E. BADAS

Key: B
Ref: Rook (152.4)

2. A 38yearold male known case of ulcerative colitis presented to hospital with large painful ulcerating lesions under his right axilla and on his back. He had first noticed a few boils in his axilla which grew bigger, coalesced and formed large sloughy ulcers.
On examination, there were multiple pustular lesions with a white surface across his back and several deeper ulcers with purple undermined edges and yellow discharge in his axilla, which developed a cribriform appearance on healing.
Initial blood tests revealed a microcytic anaemia and raised CRP. His renal and liver function tests were normal. Wound swabs did not grow any pathogen and a skin biopsy revealed a deep suppurative folliculitis with a dense neutrophilic infiltrate.
Regarding the above diagnosis, all are true EXCEPT?

A. It is a reactive lesion of IBD
B. It is more common in chrons disease than in ulcerative colitis
C. It is more common in females
D. It is associated with haematological disorders
E. Immune cross reactivity between the skin and gut seems to play important role in its development.

Key: B
Ref: Rook (152.2)

3. A 14yr old boy from the presented with obstructive jaundice from early infancy. He had deep set eyes, a prominent, wide forehead, a straight nose, and a pointed, small chin. He also had recurrent fractures of his upper limb bones, intermittent bleeding from his nose, productive cough, decreased night vision, progressive enlargement of his abdomen, retardation of growth. Histological examination of a liver biopsy specimen revealed a paucity of bile ducts and changes suggestive of chronic liver disease.
Regarding the diagnosis, what are other skin signs present in these patients apart from jaundice?

A. Severe pruritis
B. Widespread xanthomas
C. Polyarteritis nodosa
D. pyoderma gangrenosum
E. A and B

Key: E

Ref: Rook (152.5)

4. A 31yr old female presented in emergency with spontaneous pneumothorax which was treated successfully with drainage. She also gave family history of same condition.
O/E she had multiple solitary skin-coloured papules and nodules on face around nose and skin tags in both axillas. HRCT scan showed multiple cysts in the basal parts of the lungs. Regarding diagnosis, which is the most common association of this condition?

A. Lung Cancer
B. Renal Tumour
C. Breast Tumour
D. D.BADAS
E. Bladder cancer

Key: B
Ref: Rook (153.2)

Chapter **154**

THE SKIN AND DISORDER OF THE MUSCULOSKELETAL SYSTEM

1. Your rheumatologist friend wants your opinion about a non-healing ulcer in a patient who is admitted in her ward with severe arthritis and carpal tunnel syndrome.
His x-rays are done and they show symmetrical irregular periosteal ossification, predominantly at distal end of long bones.
On examination, you notice thickened forehead skin, folliculitis and nail clubbing.
Keeping the diagnosis in mind, which of the following statement is correct about this disease.

A. Inheritance is mostly autosomal recessive
B. There is decreased synthesis of collagen and procollagen in this disorder
C. Advice your friend to look for any underlying malignancies or chronic diseases
D. Primary form of disease is inherited and pts generally don't survive beyond childhood
E. Gene involved is STK11

Key: C
Ref: Rook (154.13)

2. A patient presented to you with fever and skin rash that involves his face, trunk and arms. there are blisters on his skin, few of them are intact and others are not leaving the raw skin visible. On examination, there is bleeding from his nose, his oral cavity is also involved, and there is a thick discharge from his eyes. He says that he was alright 2 days back, and suddenly developed all this.
He is not diabetic or hypertensive, but has chronic joint pains for which his doctor started him a medication few days back.
What could be the medicine?

A. Febuxostat
B. Allopurinol
C. Probenecid
D. Sulfinpyrazone
E. Colchicine

Key: B
Ref: Rook (154.14)

3. A 37 year old female patient is referred from rheumatologist for opinion, she is admitted there for workup of her chronic arthritis. Now she has developed urticaria like papules on trunk and limbs that do not fade away in 24 hours. You opt for Histopathology, and the report shows heavy dermal infiltrate of neutrophils...but no frank vasculitis.
Apart from this, all of the following findings can be expected in this patient EXCEPT?

A. Non segmental vitiligo
B. Livedo reticularis
C. Fibroblastic rheumatism
D. Peiungal infarcts
E. Delayed wound healing1

Key: C
Ref: Rook (154.7 and box 154.1)

4. A 30-year-old patient presented in your clinic with rash and burning sensation in oral cavity and his genital area... On examination you see serpiginous ring shaped small lesions on glans penis...and oral erosions with geographic tongue. There was also keratoderma and few pustular lesions on his soles.

On taking history you came to know that is a healthy young male, with no co-morbid, except that he has off and on pain is his right knee joint since last week. He is a businessman by profession and keeps on travelling, recently he came back from Bangkok where he lived for few months without his family.
Keeping his diagnosis in mind. Which of the following is False??

A. It can progress to chronic arthritis in around 20 percent of cases
B. Strongly linked with HLAB27
C. Co-infection with HIV and other stds should be considered
D. Common causes are yersenia, chlamydia, Neisseria, salmonella
E. Ocular inflammation in form of posterior uveitis is common

Key: E
Ref: Rook (154.2)

5. A 40 year old patient presented with red swollen painful ear for which he is taking antibiotics prescribed by a local GP for 5 days, without any improvement. He says that he also had same attacks two times in the past, but improved without taking medication within a couple of days.
On examination, you see his ear is red, swollen and tender, but ear lobe is spared.
Keeping your provisional diagnosis in mind...which of the following statement is NOT true?

A. It is a TH1 mediated disease
B. There is increased urinary excretion of acid mucopolysacchrides in relapses
C. Cartilage thinning leads to blue ear sign
D. Ra and ana factor are negative
E. Immune deposits of IgG, lgA, lgM are seen at fibrochondral junction

Key: D
Ref: Rook (154.11, 154.12)

Chapter 157 SOFT TISSUE AUGMENTATION (FILLERS)

1. A middle-aged lady was concerned about her wrinkles on forehead and along nasolabial folds. U tell her the details of fillers and methods of injecting via injection or cannula. Which of the following statement is least correct about injecting fillers with cannula technique?
   A. less chances if haemorrhage and hematoma
   B. PLLA cannot be injected by this method
   C. It is used for both coarse and fine wrinkles
   D. It can be used for volume restoration
   E. Both B and C

Key: E
Ref: Rook (157.3)

2. A patient was planned with HA Filler to treat wrinkle around nasolabial fold. During procedure the area became pale with white vascular reaction and immediate pain started in that area .You suspected arterial occlusion and decided to inject hyalorunidase. upto how many hours after procedure u can inject hyalurinidase?
   A. 1 hr
   B. 2 hrs
   C. 4 hrs
   D. 8 hrs
   E. upto 2 days

Key: C
Ref: Rook (157.10)

3. Nodule formation is common complication if fillers injection. First line treatment of nodule formation with injectable filler other than hyaluronic acid is?
   A. Oral antibiotics
   B. Injectable antibiotic
   C. Injectable steroids/ 5 fu
   D. Excision
   E. Co2 laser

Key: C
Ref: Rook (157.10)

4. PLLA is the only injectable filker with significant collagen stimulating potential. The results of initial treatment may last upto how much duration?
   A. 2 yrs
   B. 4 yrs
   C. 6months
   D. 1 yr
   E. Upto few weeks

Key: A
Ref: Rook (157.4)

5. A person sees you in ur office for cosmetic consultation for submental fullnes. when unjecting Deoxycholic anid (kybella) you inform her that there is risk of marginal mandibular nerve injury.it will menifest as?

A. Difficulty swallowing on affected side
B. Frequent salivation on affected side
C. Inability to elevate and retract lip
D. Inability to chew properly
E. Inability to depress and retract lip on affected side

Key: E

Chapter 158

AESTHETIC USES OF BOTULINUM TOXINS

1. A 46 years old female came to you with facial asymmetry. On examination you found there is forehead facial asymmetry with left brow ptosis. On enquiry she told that she had few procedures few days back. Considering diagnosis which of the following intervention need to be taken

A. No need further intervention
B. Resolve by facial exercises
C. Botox injection at Procerus and corrugator of left side
D. botox injections at process and corrugator at right side
E. 5.Botox injection at frontalis

Key: C
Ref: Rook (158.4)

2. You retreated the patient in scenario no 1 with injection Botox, few days later patient came to you with complain of dryness of mouth, dry eye and bluish discoloration forehead. All of the following points need to asked in history from patient before procedure except

A. History of taking Aspirin, Alcohol
B. History of taking Naproxen, Warfarrin
C. History of taking ciproflaxacin
D. History of takin erythromycin and zinc
E. History of taking oily fish in meal

Key: C
Ref: Rook (158.8)

3. Botolium toxins are indicated for correction facial wrinkling and hyperhidrosis. All of the following anatomical lines can be corrected by inecting toxins in respective muscles except

A. Gummy lines: Levator labi superior Alaque Nasi
B. Crow's feet: Orbicularis Oculi
C. Bunny lines: Nasalis
D. Smoker lines: Orbularis Oris
E. Anger line: Frontalis

Key: E
Ref: Rook (158.4-158.7)

4. A famous middle age anxious looking film actress came to you with her skin problem. On examination her bilateral eye brows are excessivley arched medially. She told about some facial injection few weeks ago at same site. You decided to correct her forehead asymmetry. All of the following are approved for it except

A. Botox
B. Dysport
C. Xeomin
D. Neurobloc
E. Both A and C

Key: D
Ref: Rook (158.3)

5. A 24 years old Air hostess came to you with complain of sweating during working hours. She told her cloths become wet during working hours for which she feels embarrassed. She used topical medications but not improved. You decided to treat her by botolium toxins. Which of the following statement is not correct?

A. BTX A used for muscular relaxation
B. Synaptobrevin prevent ACh transportation
C. BTX A prevents exocytosis of Ach
D. Ona BTX A 1U = Inco BTX 1-1.25
E. Ona BTX A 1 U = Abo BTX 1-1.25

Key: E
Ref: Rook (158.2-158.3)

Chapter 159

CHEMICALS PEELS

1. A 25 year old boy comes to you with papules and pustules with post inflamatory hyperpigmentation as a result of acne. You decide to use a superficial chemical peel of a metabolic nature. All the following fall in this category except
   A. Glycolic acid peel
   B. Azeleic acid
   C. Retinoid acid
   D. Trichloroacetic acid
   E. Oxalic acid

Key: D
Ref: Rook (159.1, 159.2)

2. A 30 year old female comes to you for her mask like pigmentation on the face for past 5 years. She has used topical lightening agents with little relief. You decide to use a trichloracetic acid peel with a medium depth. The concentration needed to reach the papillary dermis will be
   A. A.70%
   B. 35%
   C. 10%
   D. 20%
   E. 25%

Key: B
Ref: Rook (159.2)

3. A young female comes to you for a peeling session with 35% TCA for her acne. Immediate erythema and frosting is seen. Next, you inform the patient of the possible side effects or complications to look out for in the coming week except
   A. numbness and tingling
   B. facial edema
   C. acneform eruption
   D. milia
   E. scarring

Key: A.
Ref: Rook (159.10 (bix 159.1)

4. Indications for salicylic acid peel include all the following except
   A. rosacea
   B. post inf hyperpigmentation
   C. acne vulgaris
   D. oily skin
   E. dermal melasma

Key: E
Ref: Rook (159.3)

5. A 30 year old man comes to your office for treatment of acne scarring. You notice ice-pick and rolling scars. The patient is anxious and you decide to use chemical peeling along with other modalities. The concentration of the chemical acid used to achieve a medium depth peel in this patient will be.
   A. Glycolic acid 30%
   B. Glycolic acid 40%
   C. jessner solution 1-3 coats
   D. TCA 10%
   E. TCA 50%

Key: A.
Ref: Rook (159.3 (table 159.1)

Chapter 160

LASERS AND ENERGY BASED DEVICES

1. 25 years old man, famer by profession presented to derma opd with h /o erythema and sunburn over face. O/E he has telengiectasias for which he is concerned
Which laser therapy will be most useful for this patient?
   A. KTP laser
   B. Pulsed dye laser
   C. ND : yah laser
   D. Alexandrite
   E. CO2 laser

Ref: Rook (160.2)

2. Middle aged lady, with skin type 4 to 5, presented with h/o hirsutism, what will be the best treatment option for this patient
   A. long pulse diode
   B. QS alexandrite
   C. QS ruby
   D. Erbium yag
   E. ND yag 1064nm

Key: E
Ref: Rook (160.6)

3. Which laser therapy is the best treatment option for red tattoo removal?
   A. QS ruby
   B. QS alexandrite
   C. ND: yag
   D. PDL
   E. KTP laser

Key: E
Ref: Rook (160.4)

4. Middle aged lady, presented in derma opd, she was concerned about fat deposition in abdomen and flanks.
And she was offered high intensity focused ultrasound.
At which temperature this device work for adipocytes necrosis.
   A. 30 degree
   B. 44 degree
   C. 56 degree
   D. 64 degree

Key: C
Ref: Rook (160.12)

5. Tell-tale sign which is permanent line of demarcation between treated and untreated area is side effect observed which laser treatment
   A. Ablative devices
   B. Radio frequency devices
   C. Cryolipolysis
   D. Hifu
   E. Alexandrite laser

Key: A
Ref: Rook (160.7)